IQ
challenge

Compiled by Joe Cameron

Main Street
A division of Sterling Publishing Co., Inc.
New York

Library of Congress Cataloging-in-Publication Data Available

10 9 8 7 6 5 4 3 2 1

Published in 2005 by Sterling Publishing Co., Inc.
387 Park Avenue South, New York, NY 10016

Sterling ISBN 1-4027-3285-6

Printed in China

Are you ready for the **IQ Challenge**? Over 500 logic puzzles, mind-benders and mathematical teasers to exercise, occupy and defy your mental abilities.

The book has been carefully compiled into twenty levels of ascending difficulty, with the first chapters being easier than the last. The best place to start is at the beginning, with level one, and if you work methodically through the earlier chapters, you should be able to spot the patterns and flow of logic to help with some of the later chapters.

If you become stuck on a particular puzzle, it might be best to move on and come back to it later - always resisting the temptation to flick through to the answer page to put you out of your misery. Often, if you look at the puzzle from a different perspective, then the solution becomes apparent – it's all a question of logic.

IQ Challenge is not just about getting the right answer – it's about sharpening your wits and training your mind to think logically. If you get an answer wrong, then look back over the puzzle to see how the solution was arrived at. Armed with the tools and techniques learned in the first nineteen chapters, you should have a fighting chance of solving chapter twenty – the most twisted and devious puzzles we could devise!

On the next page are several tables, which you may find useful. All the puzzles can be solved using standard mathematical or alphabetical calculations, so no other general knowledge is required.

Good luck and enjoy the IQ Challenge!

Multiplication Table

	1	2	3	4	5	6	7	8	9	10	11	12
1	1	2	3	4	5	6	7	8	9	10	11	12
2	2	4	6	8	10	12	14	16	18	20	22	24
3	3	6	9	12	15	18	21	24	27	30	33	36
4	4	8	12	16	20	24	28	32	36	40	44	48
5	5	10	15	20	25	30	35	40	45	50	55	60
6	6	12	18	24	30	36	42	48	54	60	66	72
7	7	14	21	28	35	42	49	56	63	70	77	84
8	8	16	24	32	40	48	56	64	72	80	88	96
9	9	18	27	36	45	54	63	72	81	90	99	108
10	10	20	30	40	50	60	70	80	90	100	110	120
11	11	22	33	44	55	66	77	88	99	110	121	132
12	12	24	36	48	60	72	84	96	108	120	132	144

	Cube Numbers	Square Numbers
1	1	1
2	8	4
3	27	9
4	64	16
5	125	25
6	216	36
7	343	49
8	512	64
9	729	81
10	1000	100
11	1331	121
12	1728	144
13	2197	169
14	2744	196
15	3375	225
16	4096	256
17	4913	289
18	5832	324
19	6859	361
20	8000	400

Numerical Values

1	A	26
2	B	25
3	C	24
4	D	23
5	E	22
6	F	21
7	G	20
8	H	19
9	I	18
10	J	17
11	K	16
12	L	15
13	M	14
14	N	13
15	O	12
16	P	11
17	Q	10
18	R	9
19	S	8
20	T	7
21	U	6
22	V	5
23	W	4
24	X	3
25	Y	2
26	Z	1

Prime Numbers

2
3
5
7
11
13
17
19
23
29

1 PUZZLE

What number is missing?

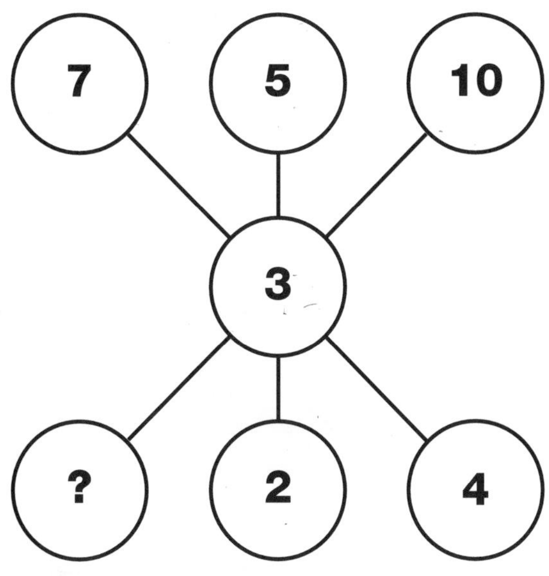

Which number completes the puzzle?

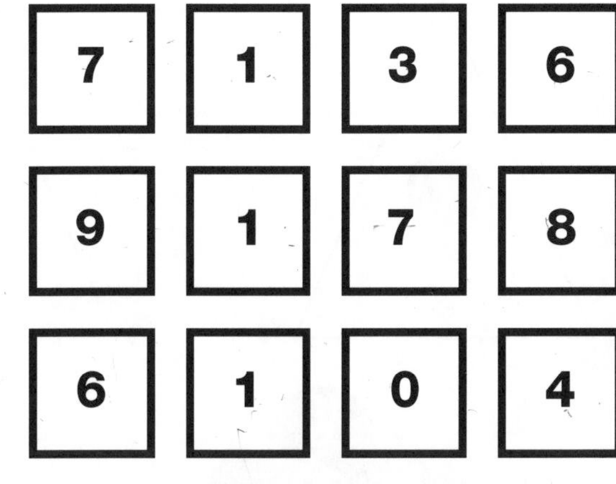

Which number completes this sequence?

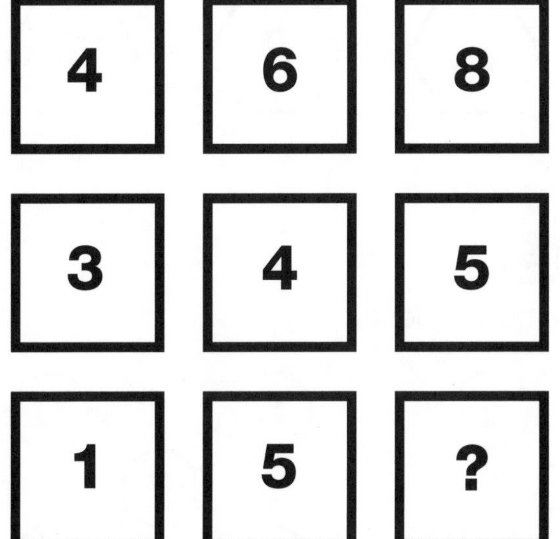

Following a logical sequence, can you complete this puzzle?

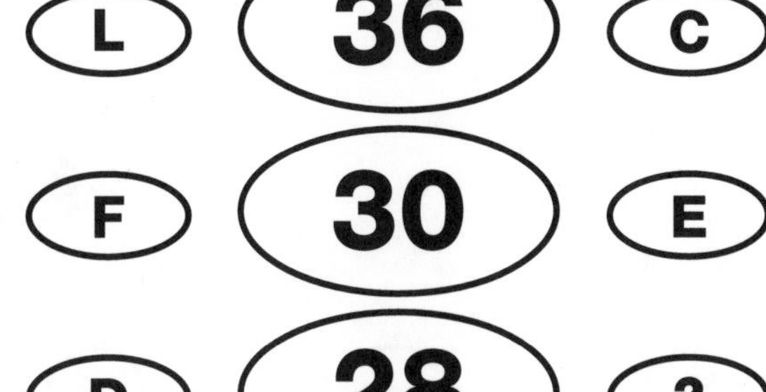

PUZZLE 5

Following a logical sequence, which number needs to be added to complete the puzzle?

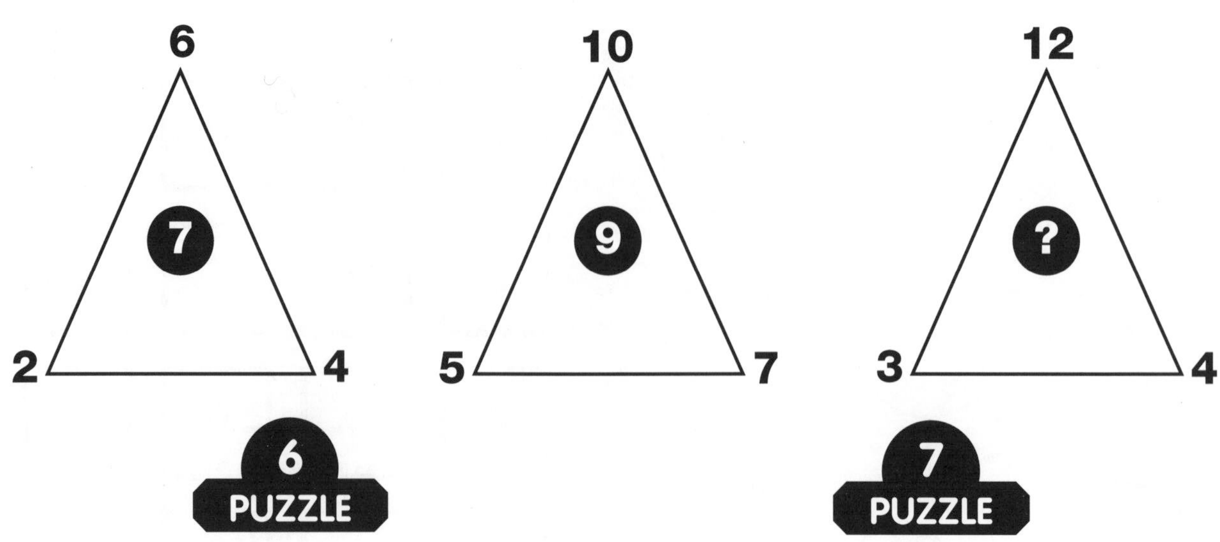

PUZZLE 6

What number is missing?

PUZZLE 7

Which number completes the puzzle?

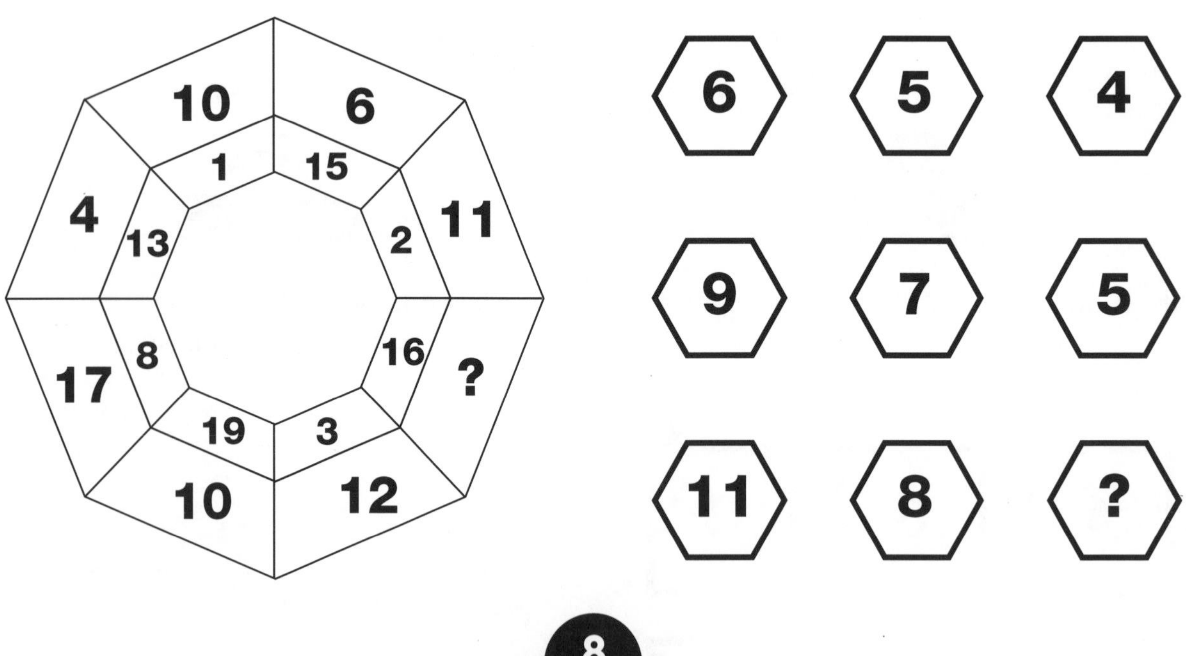

PUZZLE 8

Which letter completes this sequence?

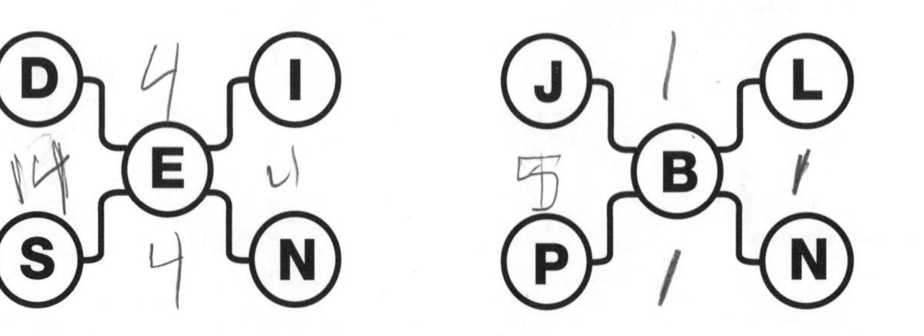

9
PUZZLE

What number is missing?

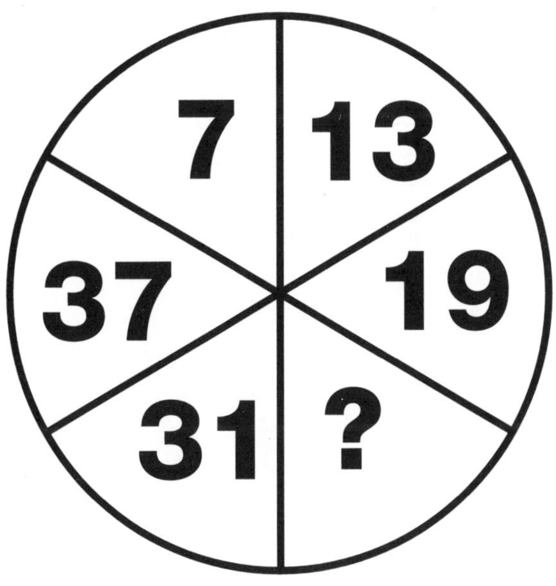

Which letter completes the puzzle?

11
PUZZLE

Which number completes this sequence?

Following a logical sequence, can you complete this puzzle?

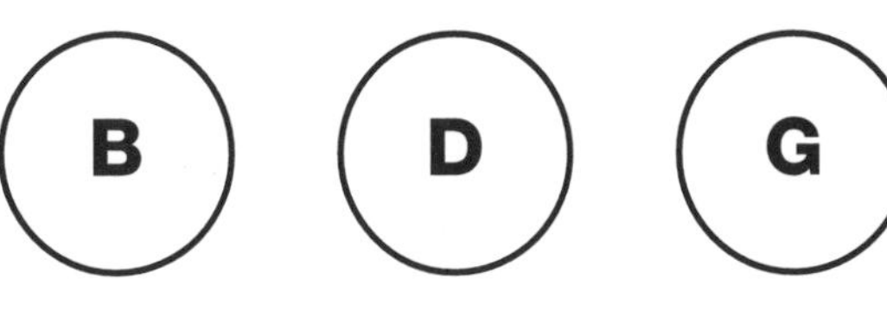

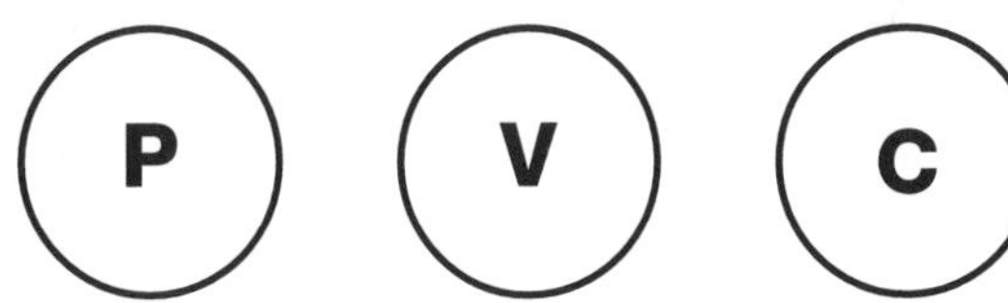

Which watch completes the sequence?

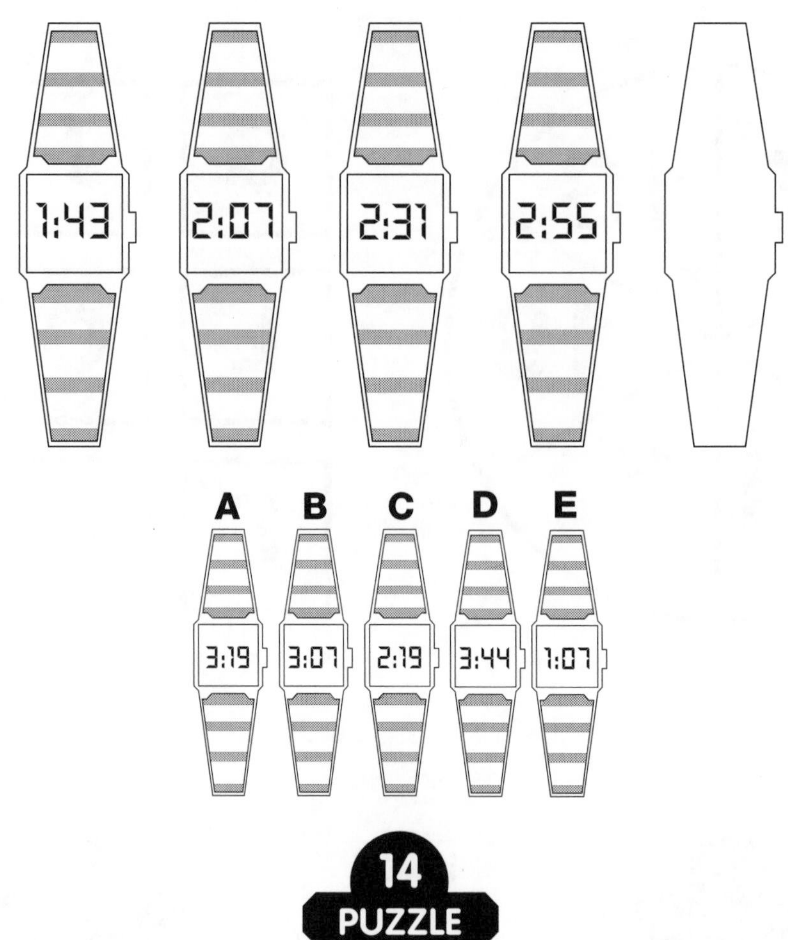

14 PUZZLE

Which letter is missing from the last star to make this puzzle complete?

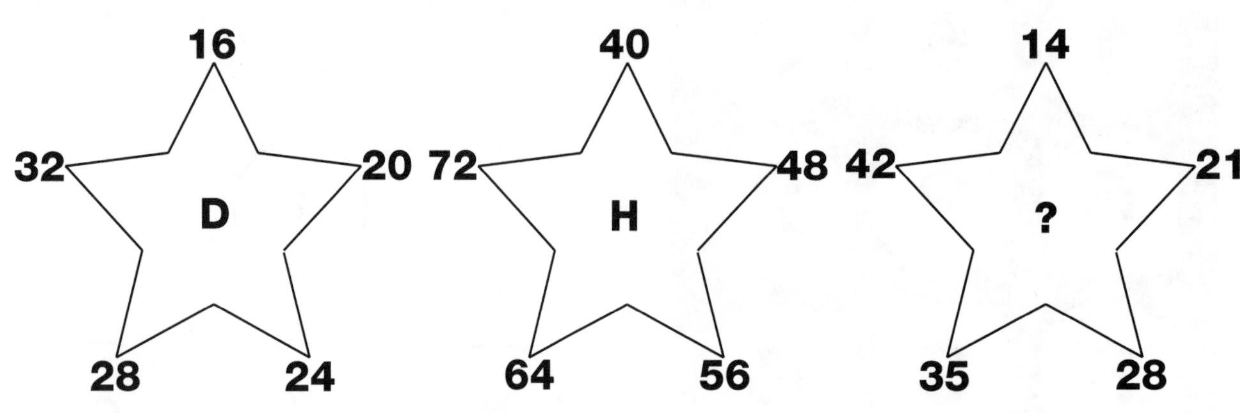

15 PUZZLE

Which number completes this sequence?

4	6	3
7	11	5
13	21	?

16 PUZZLE

Which number completes this sequence?

5 | 8 | 14 | 26 | ?

17 PUZZLE

Which letter needs to be added to continue the sequence?

E | H | L | Q | ?

18 PUZZLE

What number needs to be added to the last triangle to complete the puzzle?

3

6

10

15

21

?

19 PUZZLE

Which number should be added to complete the sequence?

25

36

49

64

?

LEVEL 1

Which pattern completes the line?

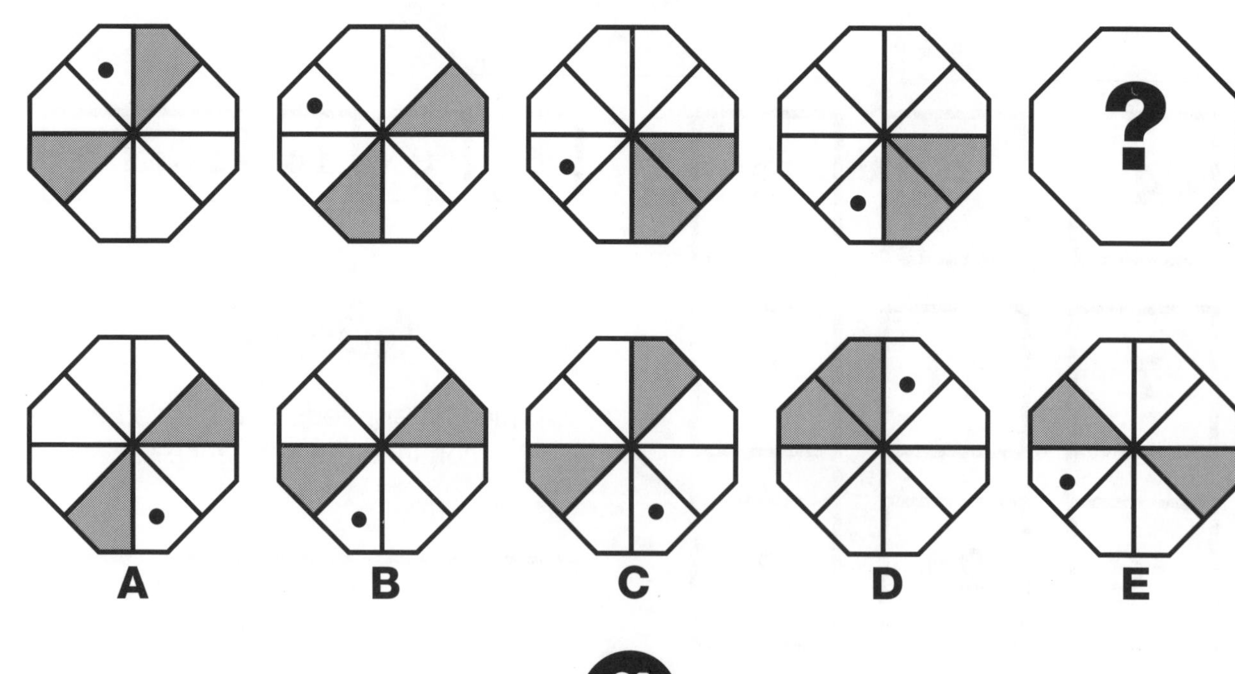

21 PUZZLE

Which of the lower six patterns completes the puzzle?

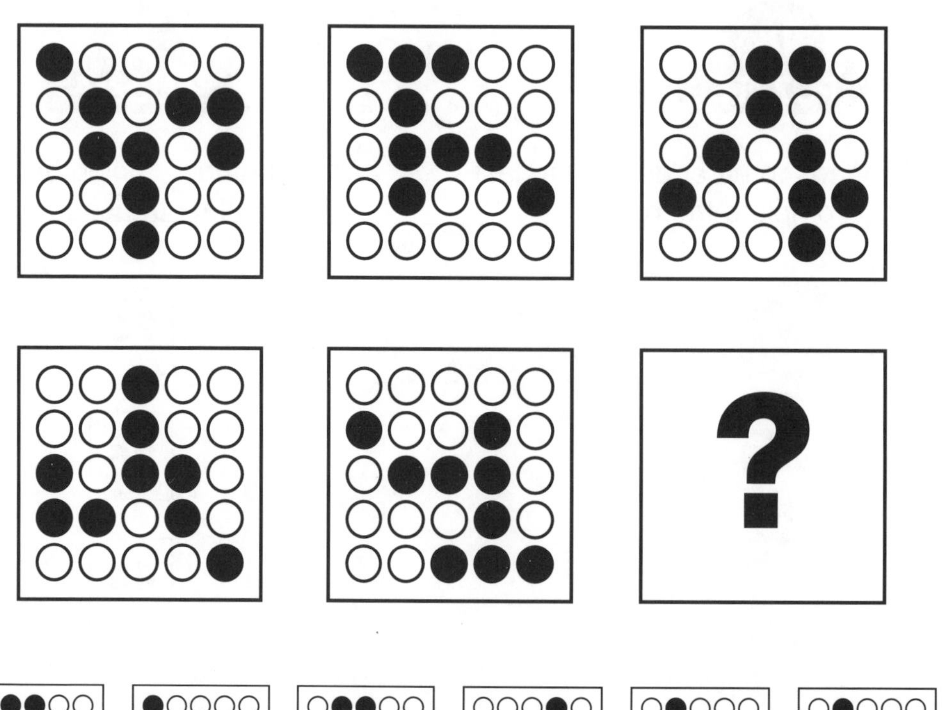

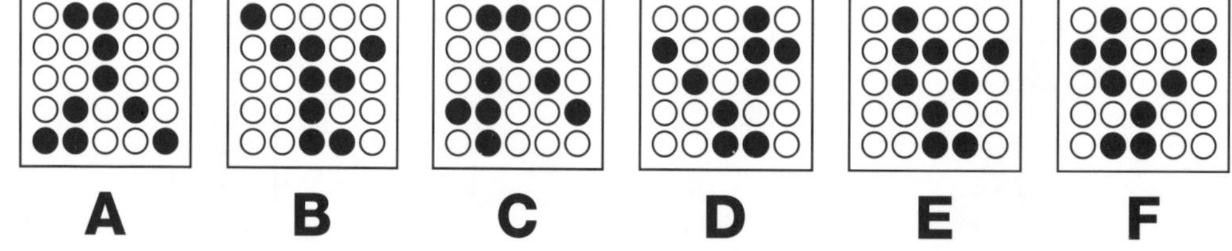

A B C D E F

22 PUZZLE

Which playing card goes in the empty space?

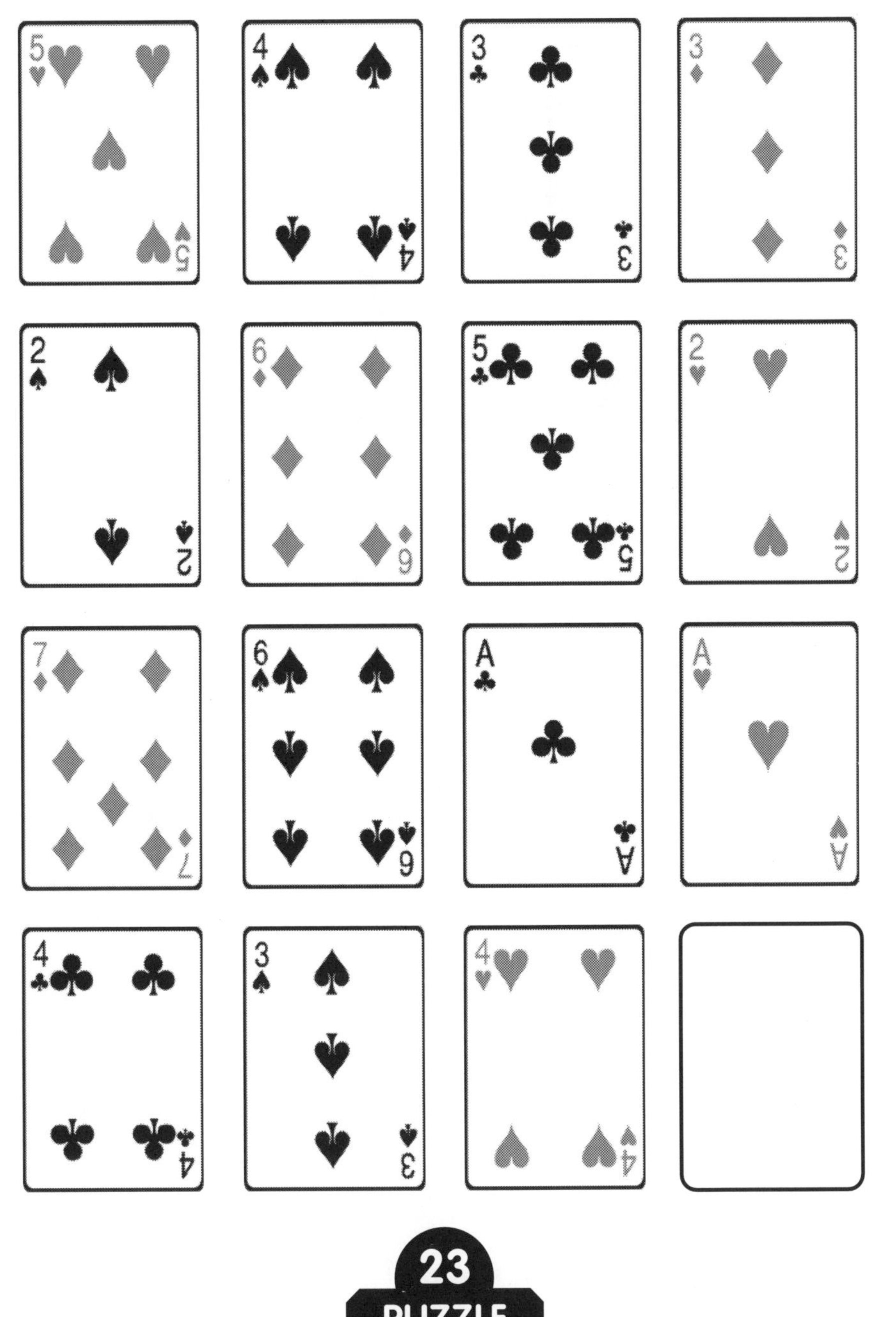

23 PUZZLE

Which number completes the puzzle?

5 6 8

7 8 9 7 9 10

2 3 1 ?

LEVEL 1

LEVEL 1

24 PUZZLE

What is missing from the last circle?

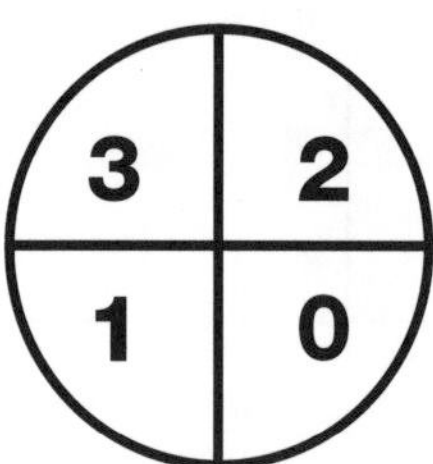

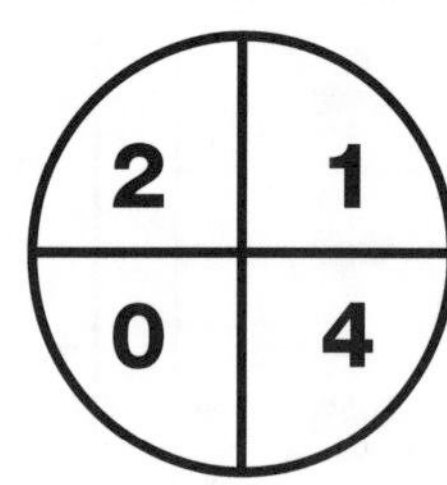

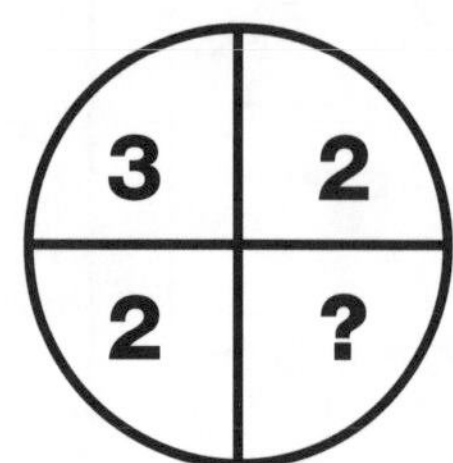

25 PUZZLE

Which letter completes the puzzle?

26 PUZZLE

This arrangement of 8 coins produces a square, with 3 coins per side, can you move 4 of the coins to give a square with 4 coins per side?

27 PUZZLE

Which number replaces the question mark and completes the puzzle?

What is the missing arrangement?

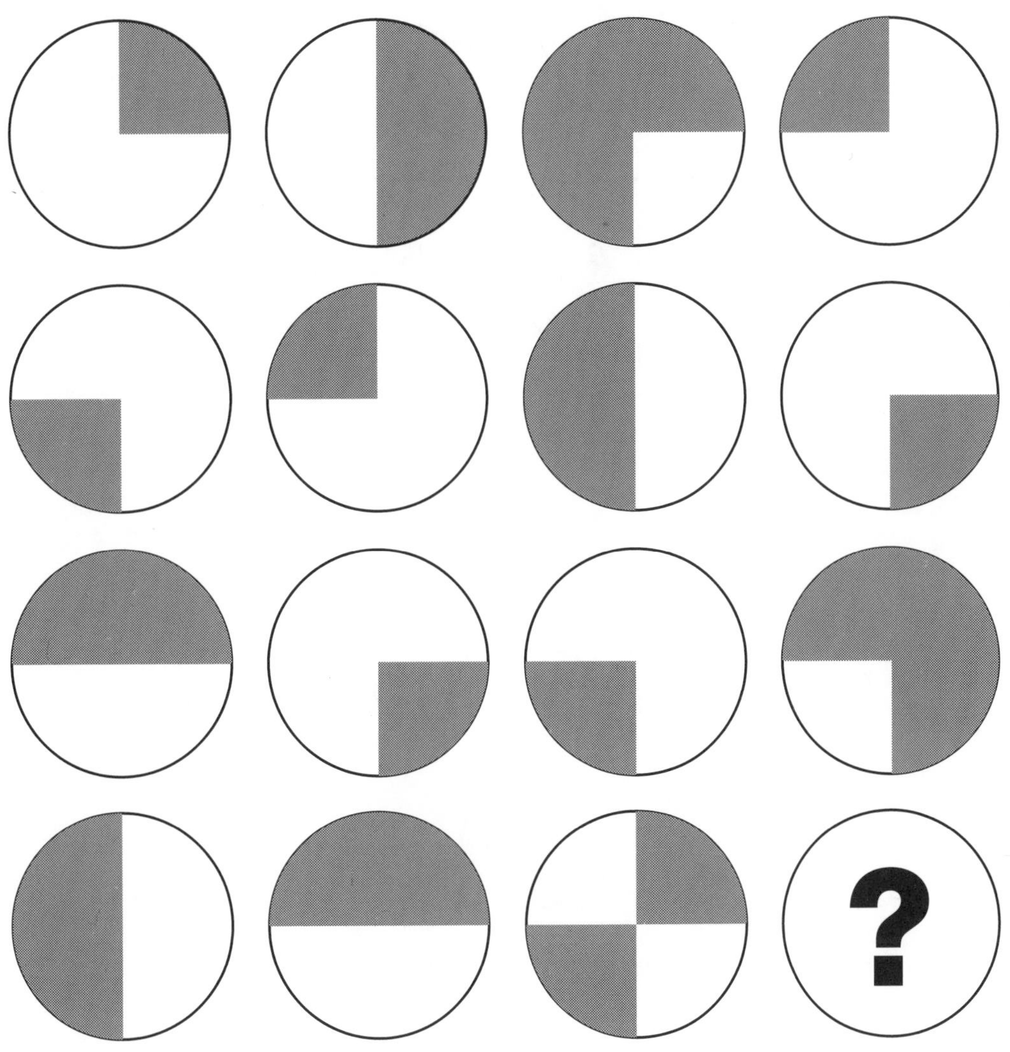

29 PUZZLE

Which domino completes the puzzle?

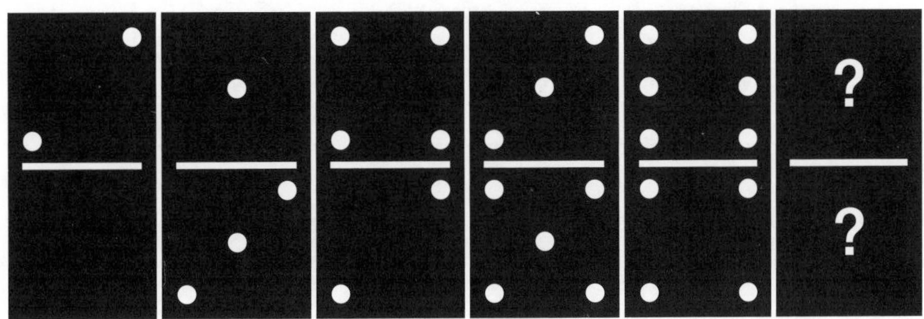

LEVEL 1

LEVEL

2

Which number goes in the empty circle?

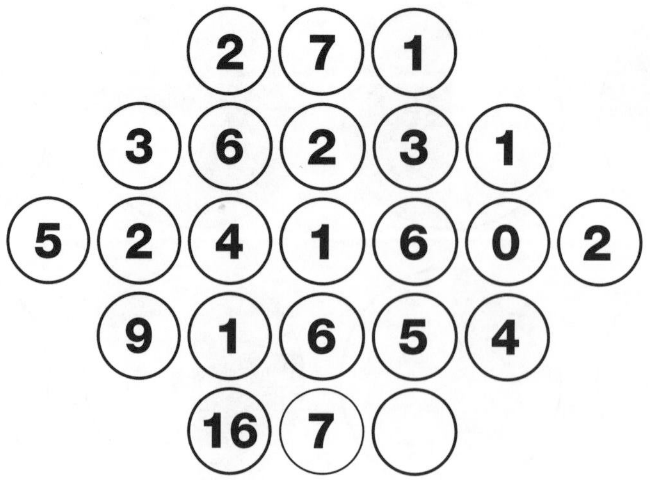

2 PUZZLE

Which of the smaller boxes follows the same rule as these six?

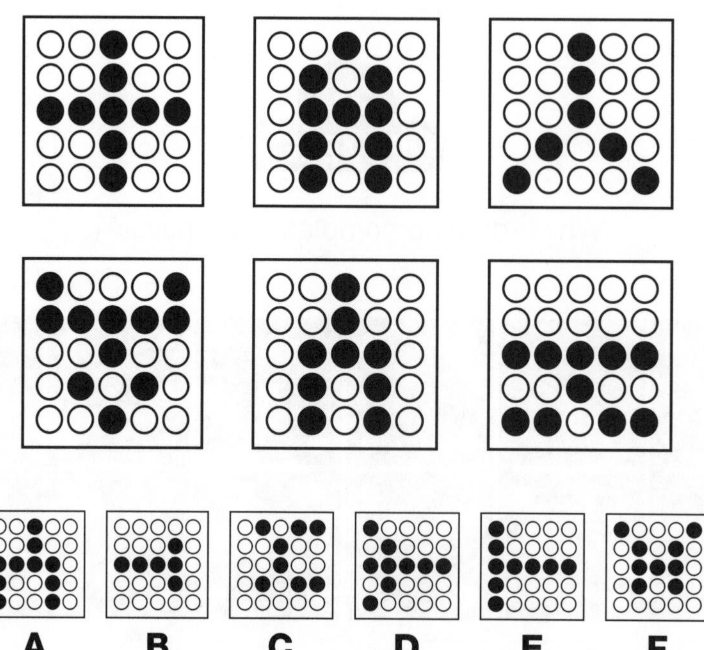

3 PUZZLE

Where does the missing hand go?

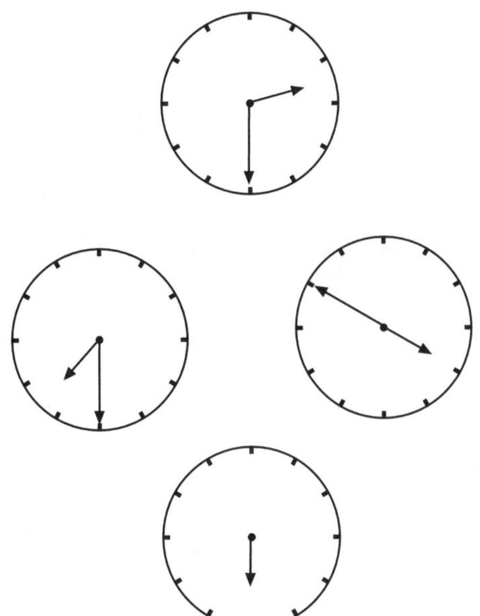

What is missing from the last circle?

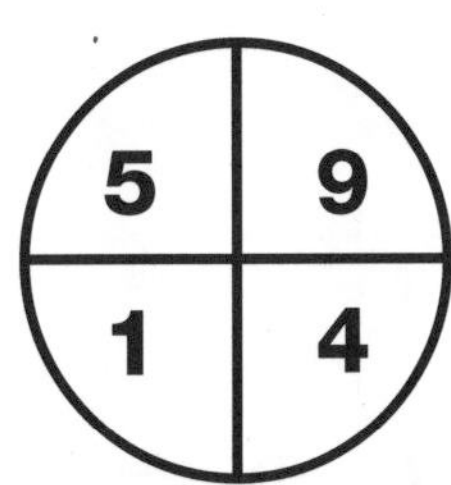

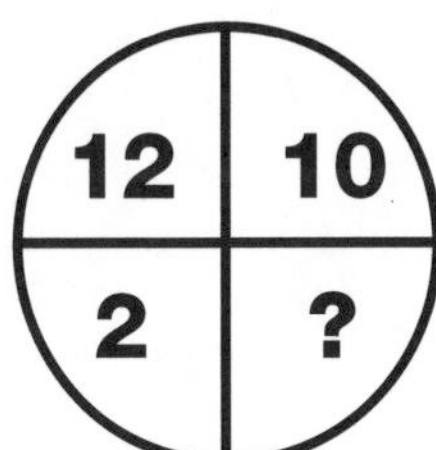

5 PUZZLE

Which letter completes the puzzle?

L

6 PUZZLE

Which number completes the puzzle?

2

4

6

What is missing from the last star?

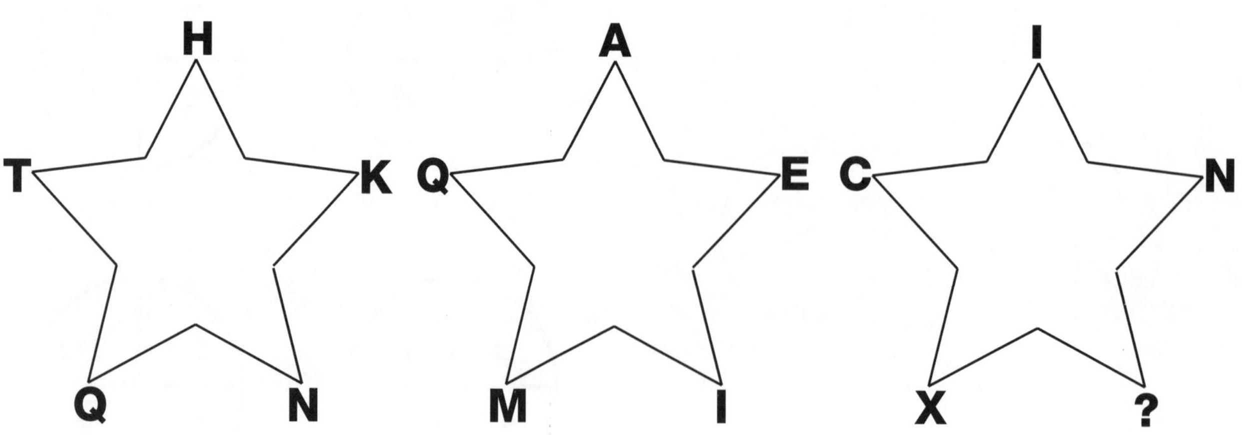

What completes the last triangle?

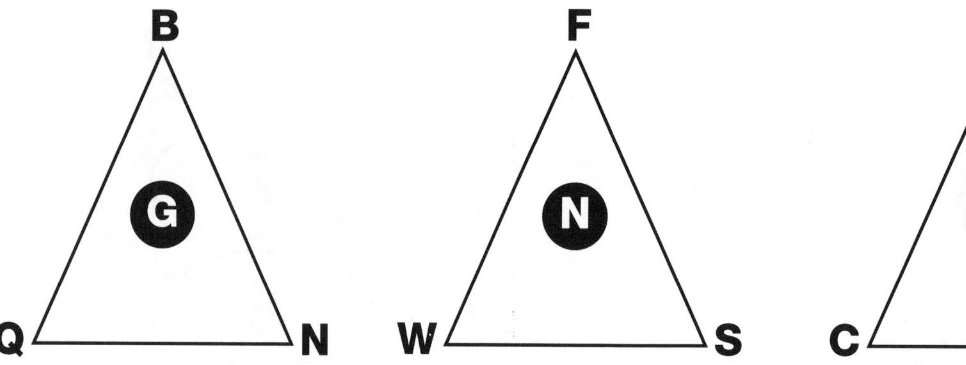

PUZZLE 9

Which letter goes in the lower right hand square to complete the puzzle?

B	K	E
G	M	E
I	X	?

PUZZLE 10

Which number completes the puzzle?

5	11	6
	3	
8	14	?

PUZZLE 11

In this circle which letter goes in the empty segment?

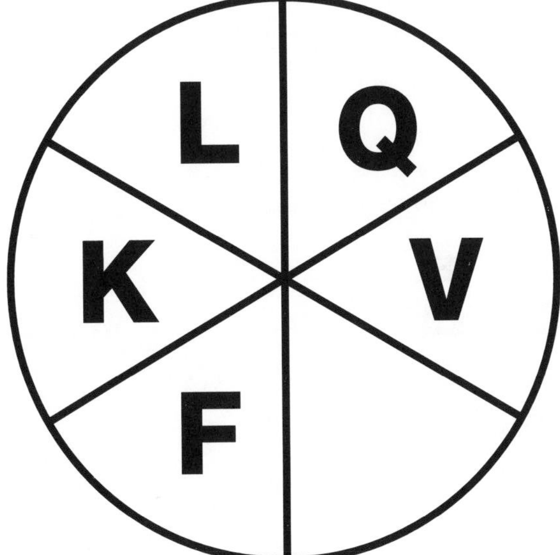

PUZZLE 12

What number fits in this triangle to complete the puzzle?

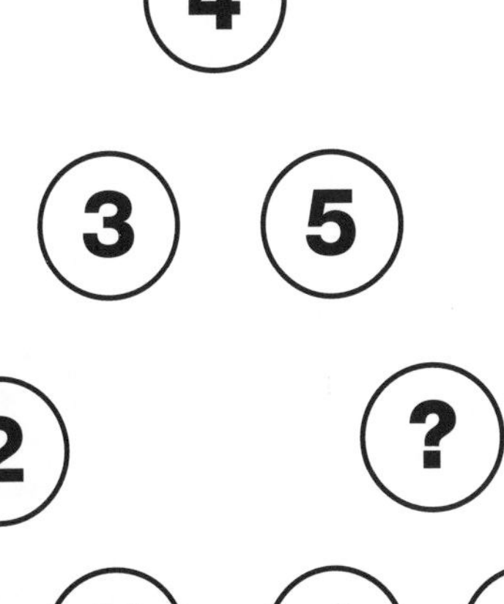

LEVEL 2

LEVEL

2

13 PUZZLE

Which number goes in the bottom square to complete the sequence?

2
6
14
30
?

14 PUZZLE

Which number replaces the question mark and completes the puzzle?

7	9	11
6	3	4
4	5	?

15 PUZZLE

Which watch will complete the sequence?

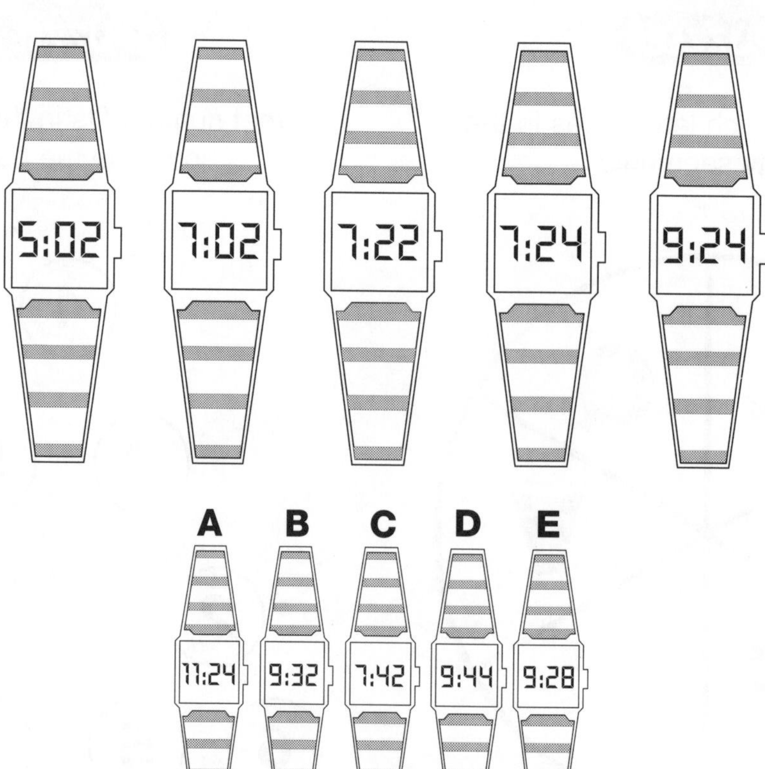

Which pattern completes the puzzle?

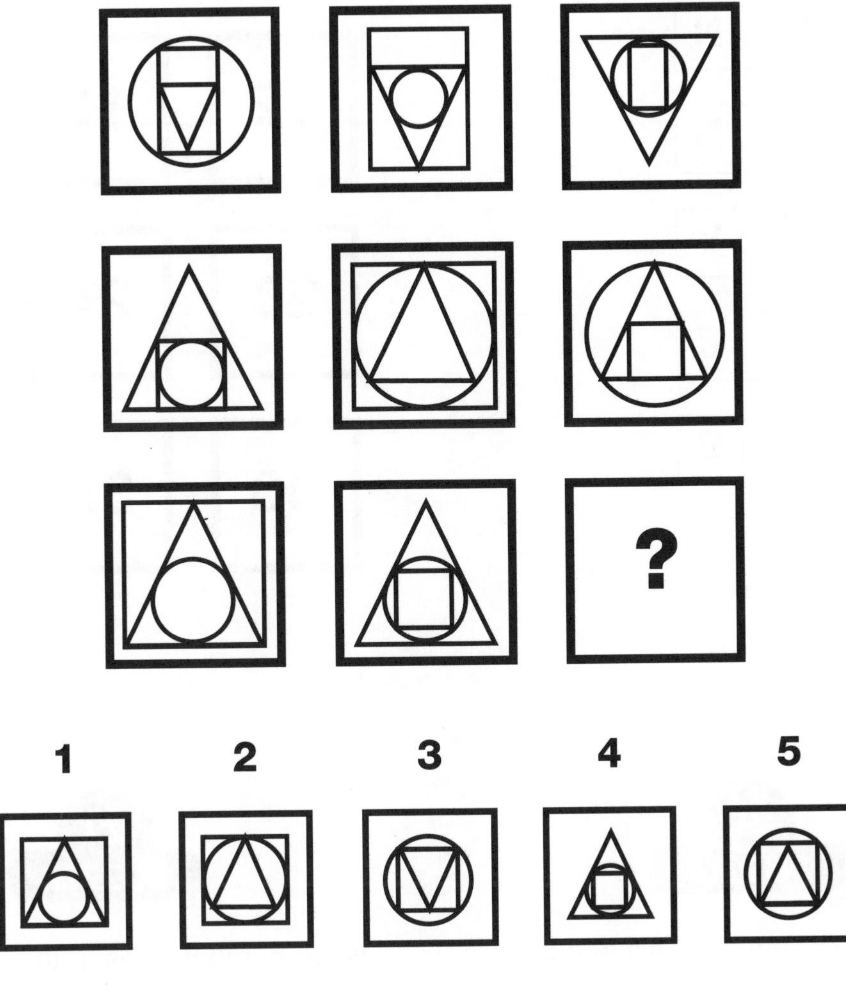

17 PUZZLE

What is missing from the last grid?

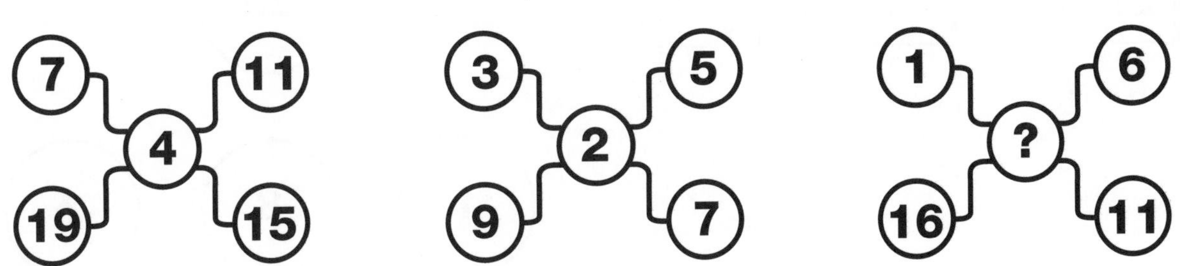

LEVEL 2

18 PUZZLE

In this sequence of letters what needs to be added to make the puzzle correct?

P	N
T	R
X	V
B	Z
F	D
J	?

19 PUZZLE

Which number replaces the question mark and completes the puzzle?

12	15	18
20	24	28
30	35	?

20 PUZZLE

Which number completes this sequence?

21	28	35	42	?

21 PUZZLE

What number goes in the bottom right circle?

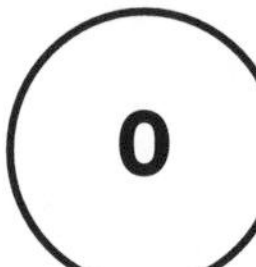

0

23

8

What is missing from the last triangle?

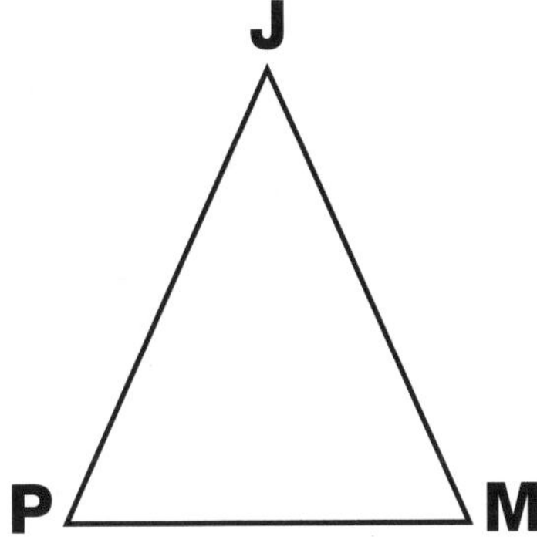

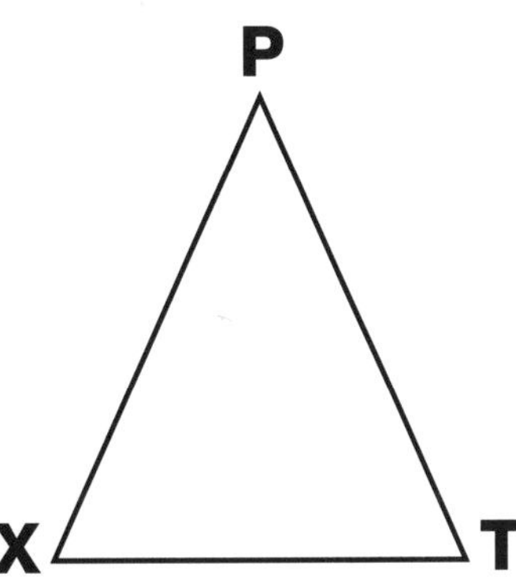

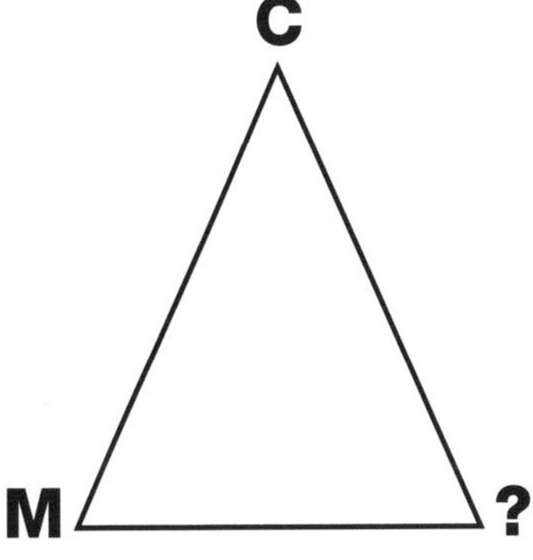

23
PUZZLE

Where does the missing hand go?

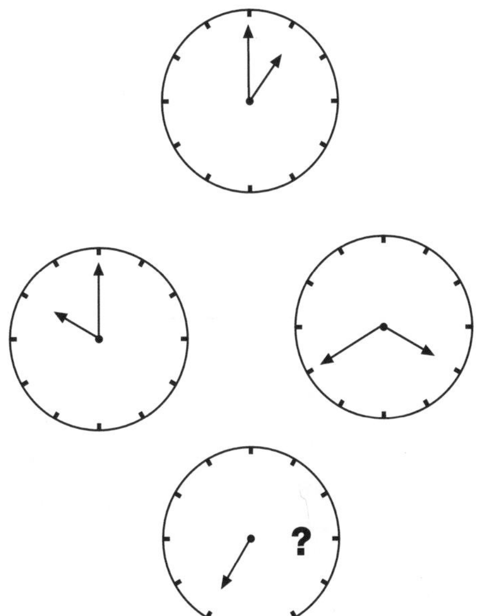

Which letter replaces the question mark and completes the puzzle?

LEVEL 2

LEVEL 2

25 PUZZLE

Which number completes this sequence?

26 PUZZLE

What is missing from this circle?

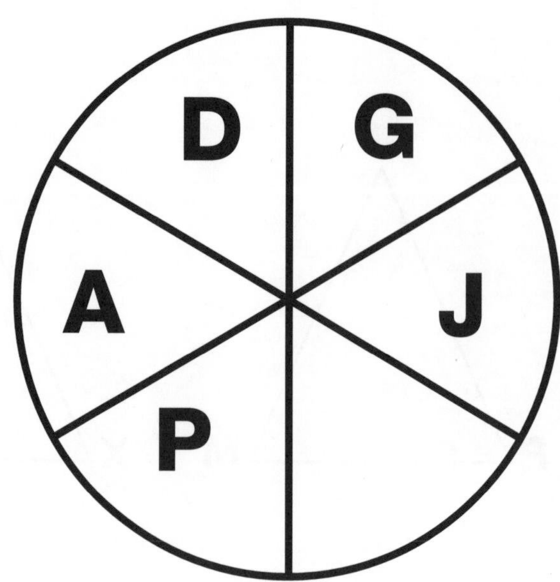

27 PUZZLE

Can you move just 2 matches to create 7 squares?

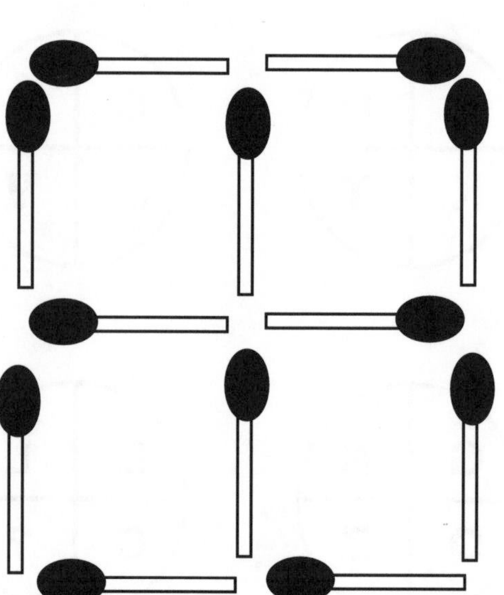

28 PUZZLE

What is missing from this pyramid of numbers?

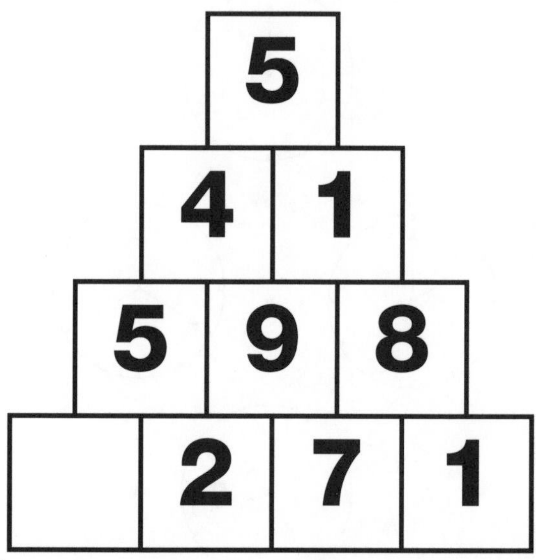

What time should be displayed on the bottom clockface?

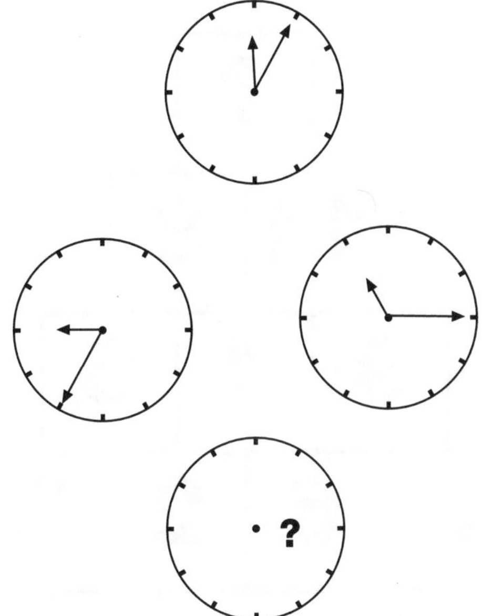

2 PUZZLE

Which four letters complete this puzzle?

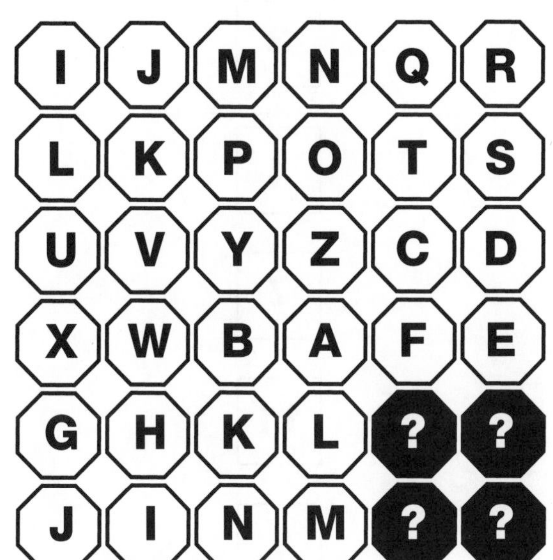

3 PUZZLE

What should be added to the bottom right circle to complete the puzzle?

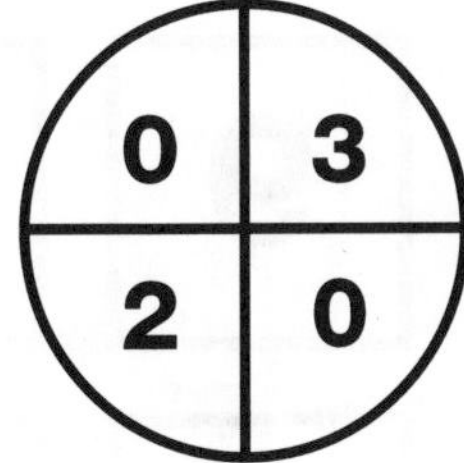

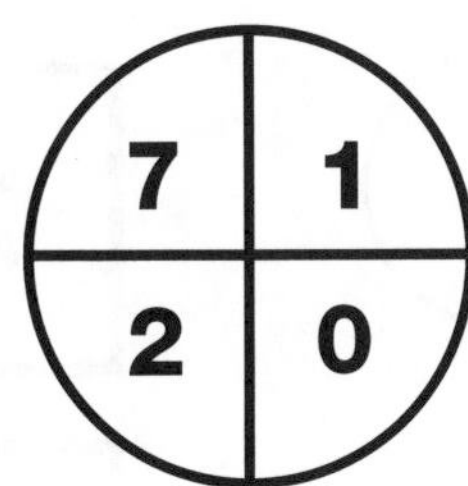

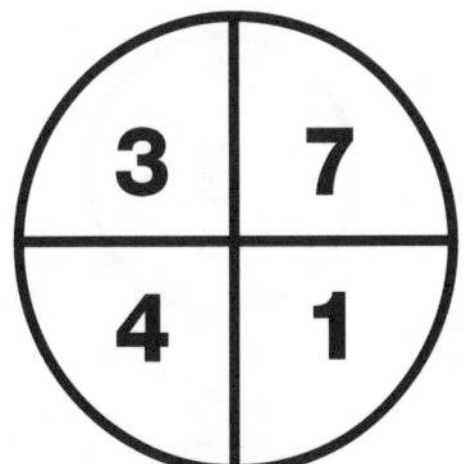

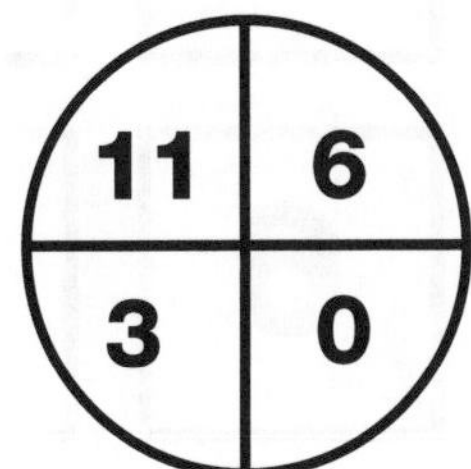

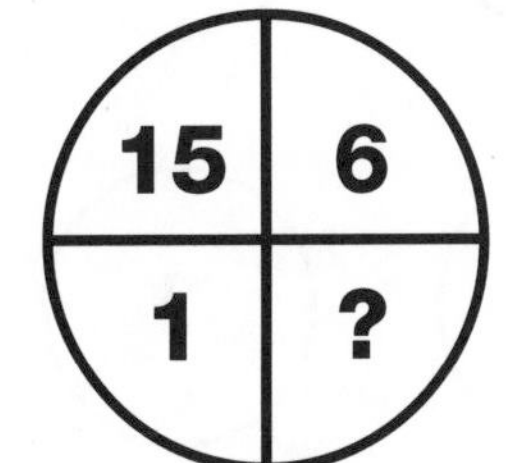

LEVEL 3

PUZZLE 4

What completes this sequence?

4

7

11

?

PUZZLE 5

Which number completes this pyramid?

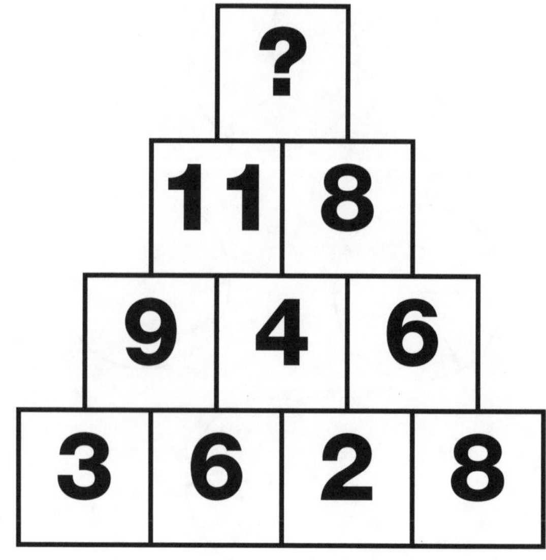

		?		
	11	8		
9	4	6		
3	6	2	8	

PUZZLE 6

What number is missing from the bottom right circle?

4	8	9
9	2	1
5	6	?

PUZZLE 7

Which number replaces the question mark and completes the puzzle?

2	9	7
5	7	2
6	7	?

Which of the bottom six grids completes this pattern?

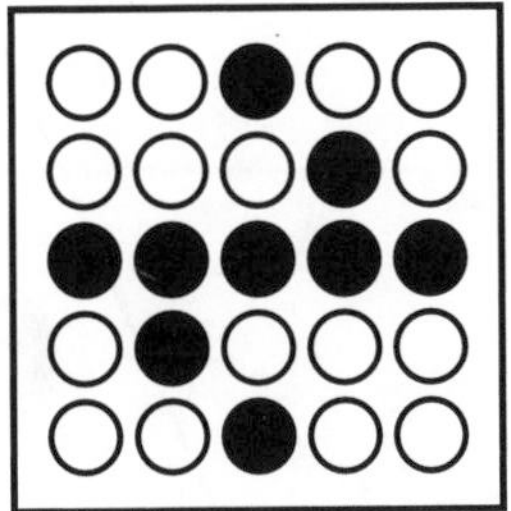
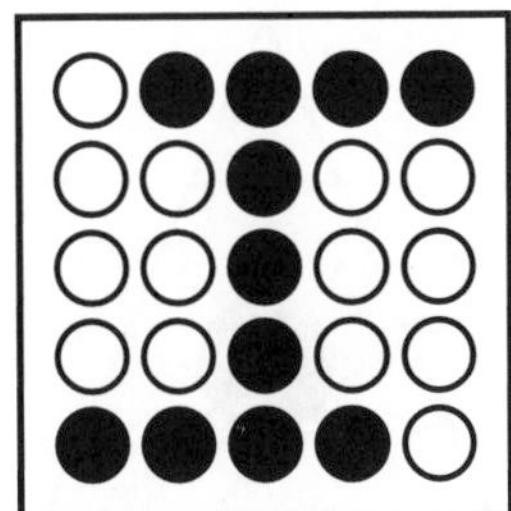
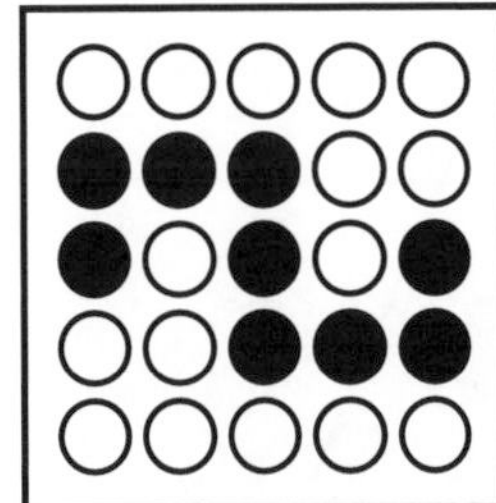
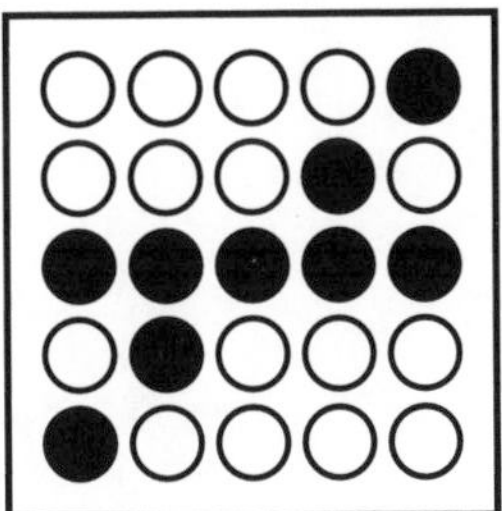
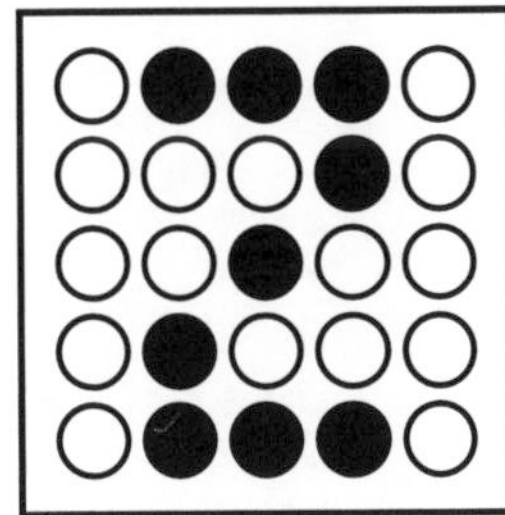

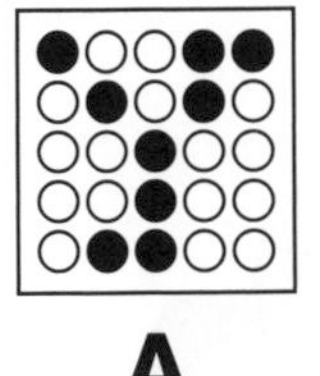
A

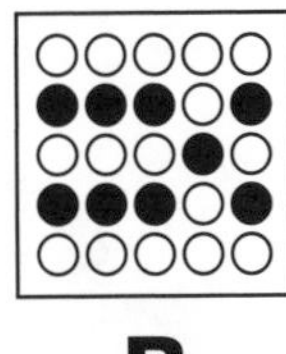
B

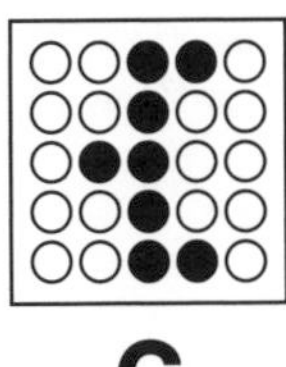
C

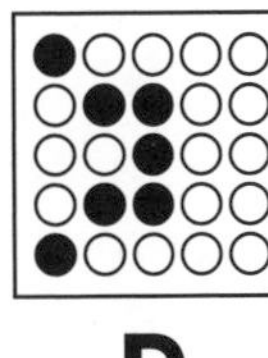
D

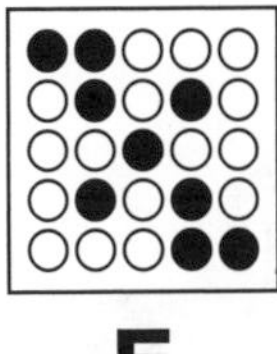
E

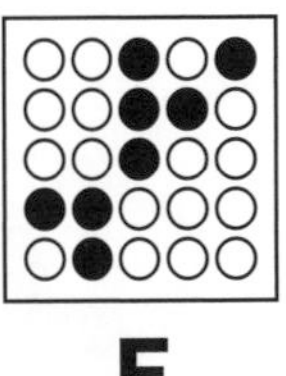
F

9 PUZZLE

What is missing from the last shape?

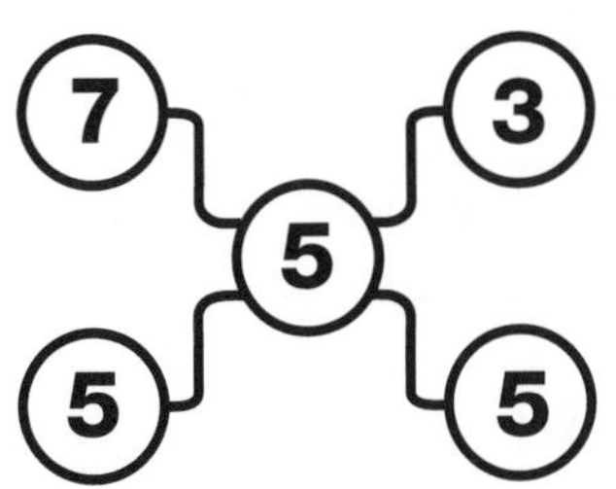

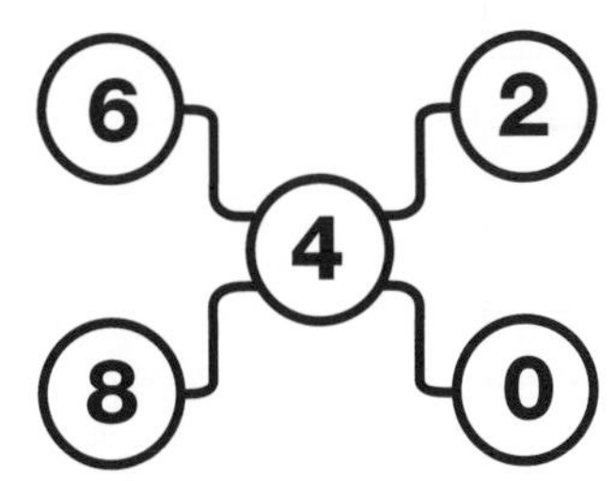

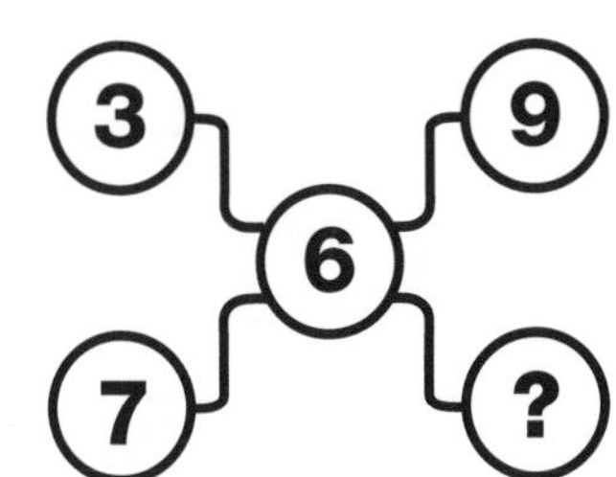

Which number completes the last triangle?

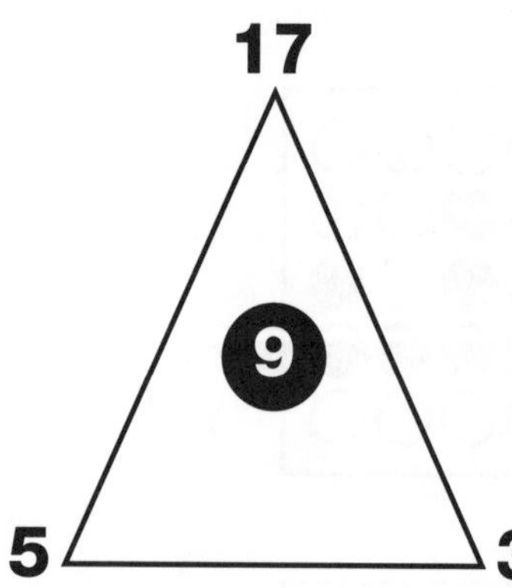

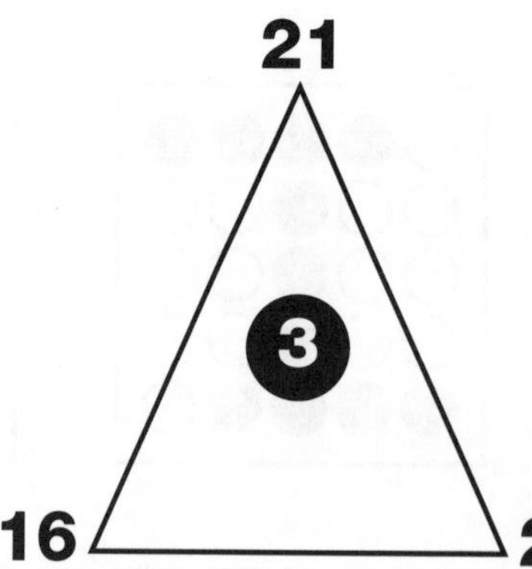

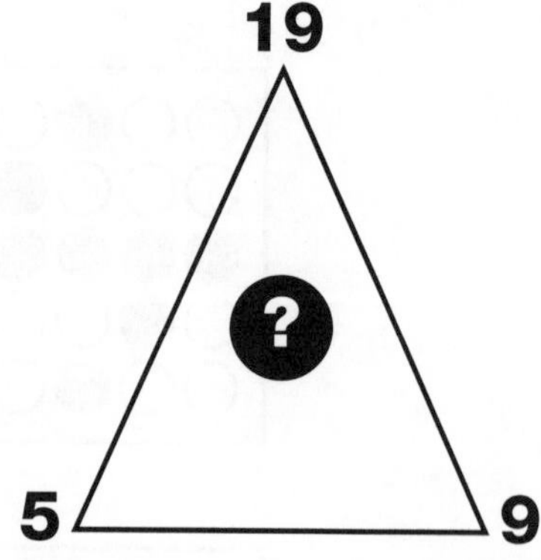

11
PUZZLE

Which number replaces the question mark and completes the puzzle?

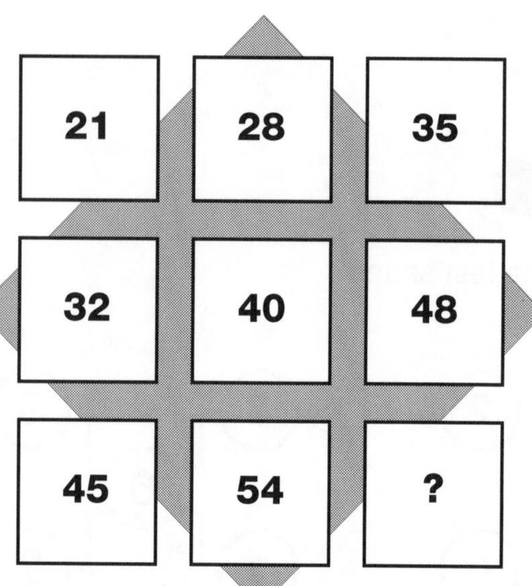

Which number completes this sequence?

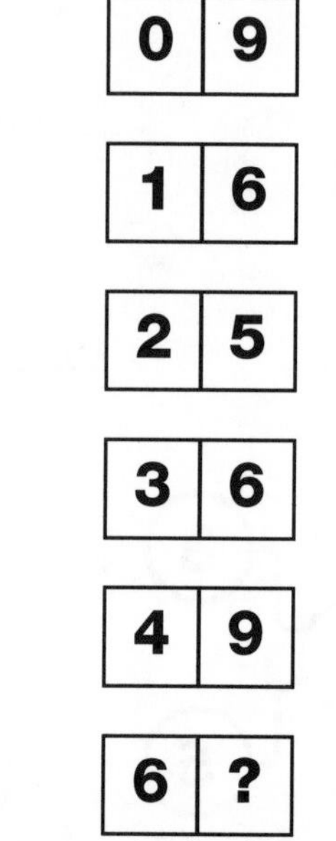

13 PUZZLE

What is missing from this circle?

14 PUZZLE

What completes this pattern?

15 PUZZLE

Which number replaces the question mark and completes the puzzle?

10	11	5
4	6	9
3	0	?

16 PUZZLE

What is needed to make this triangle complete?

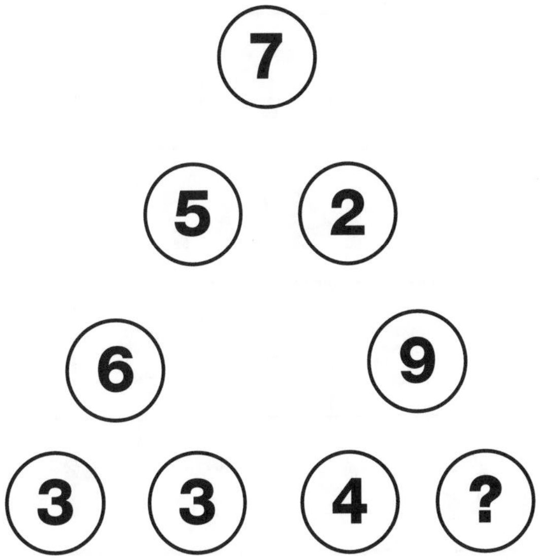

7

5 

6 

3   

LEVEL 3

LEVEL

3

17 PUZZLE

Which number is missing?

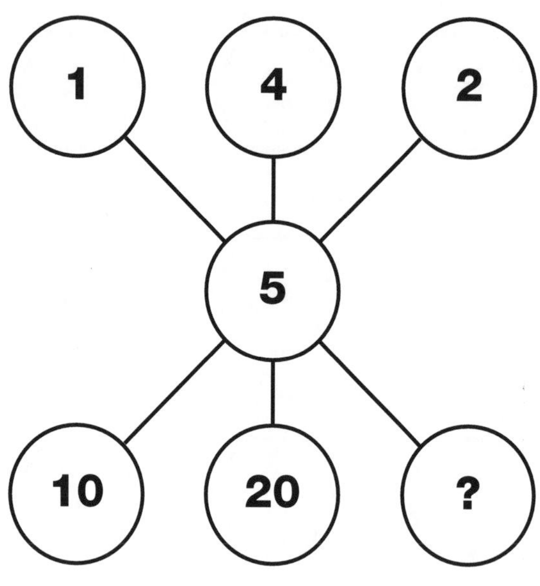

Following a logical sequence, can you complete this puzzle?

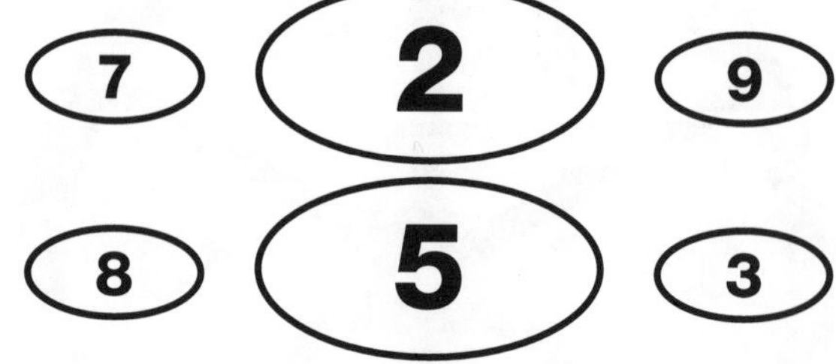

What is needed to complete this pyramid?

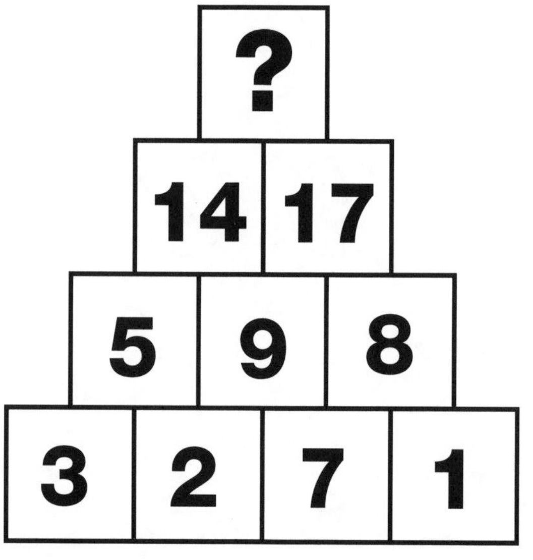

Which number continues the sequence?

Which of the bottom six grids fills the missing gap?

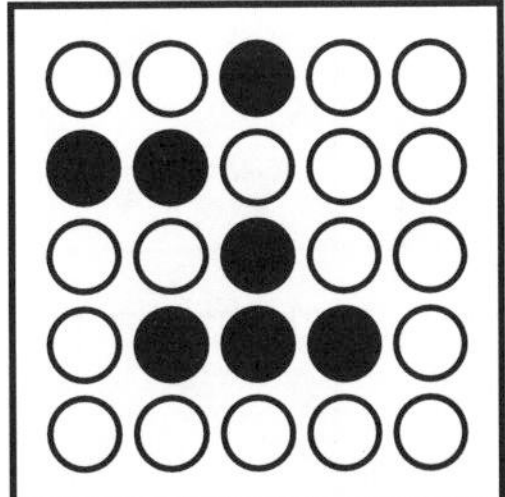
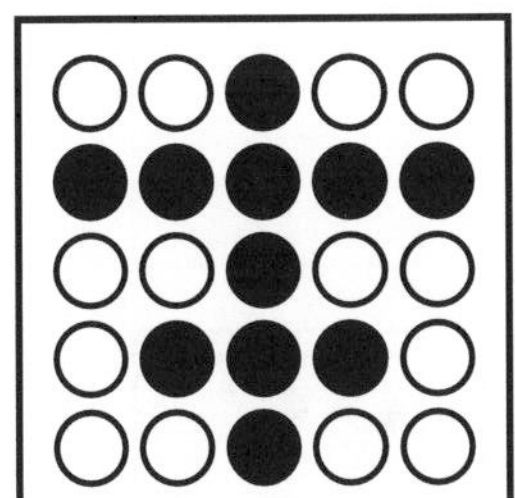
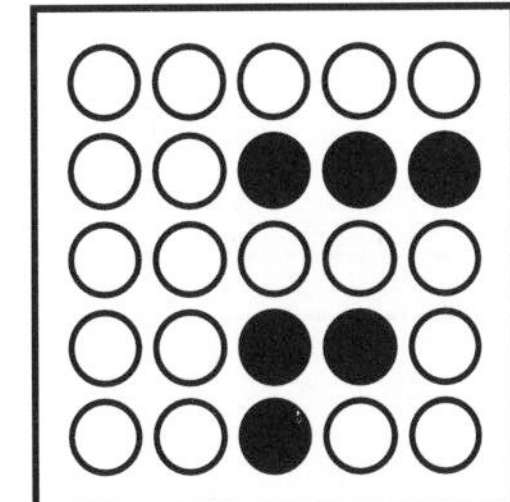
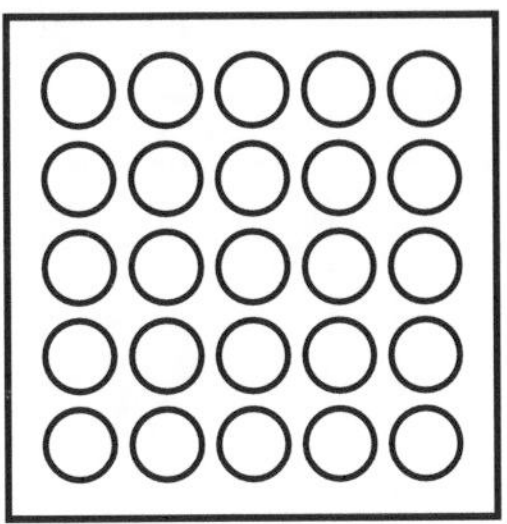
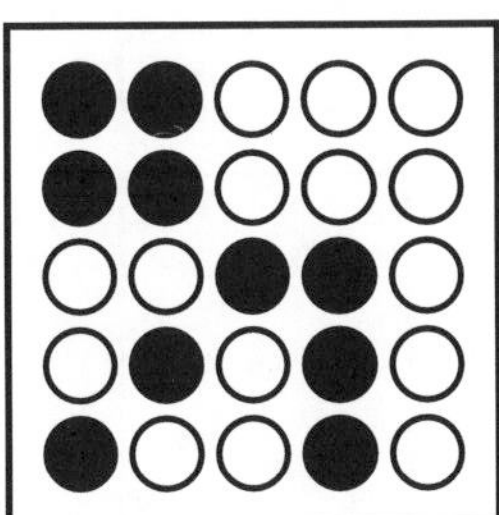
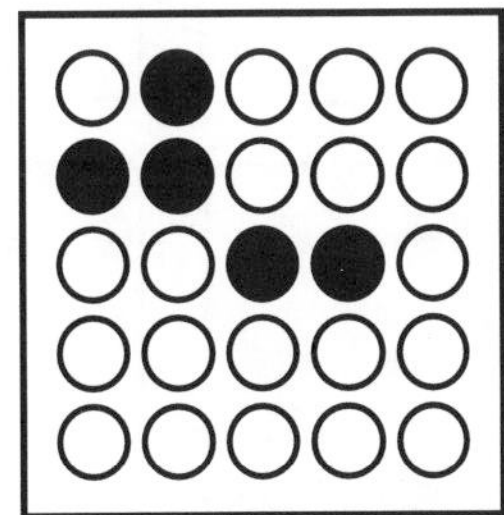

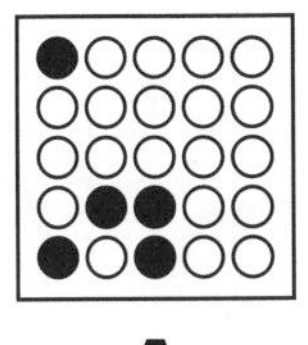
A

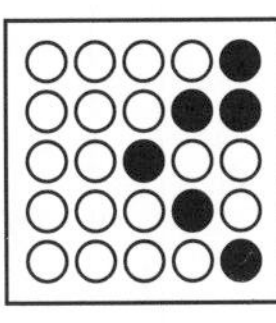
B

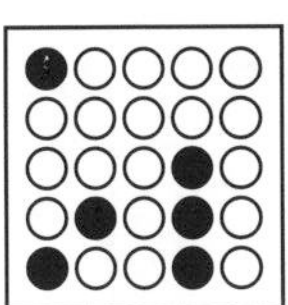
C

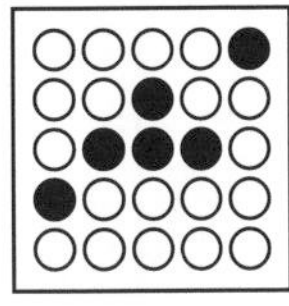
D

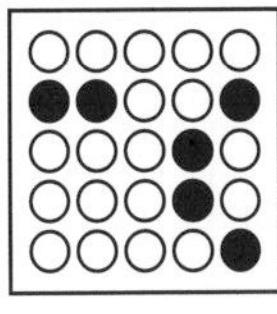
E

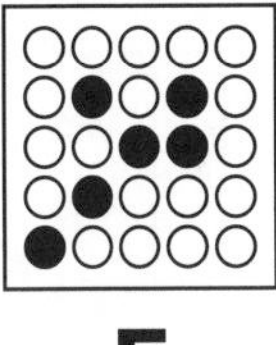
F

22
PUZZLE

Following a logical sequence, can you complete this puzzle?

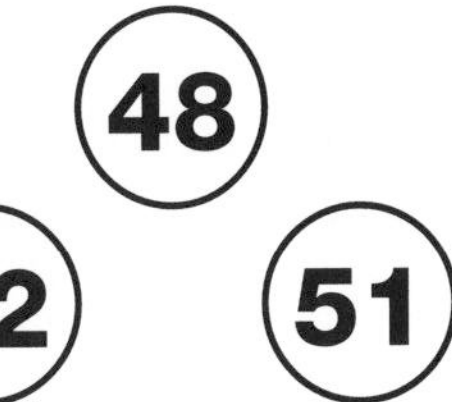

?

LEVEL

3

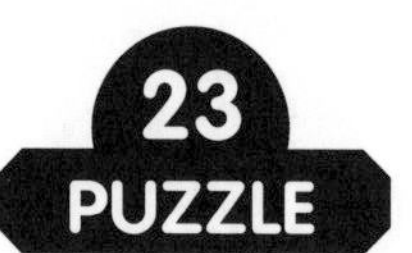

Which playing cards fill the blank spaces?

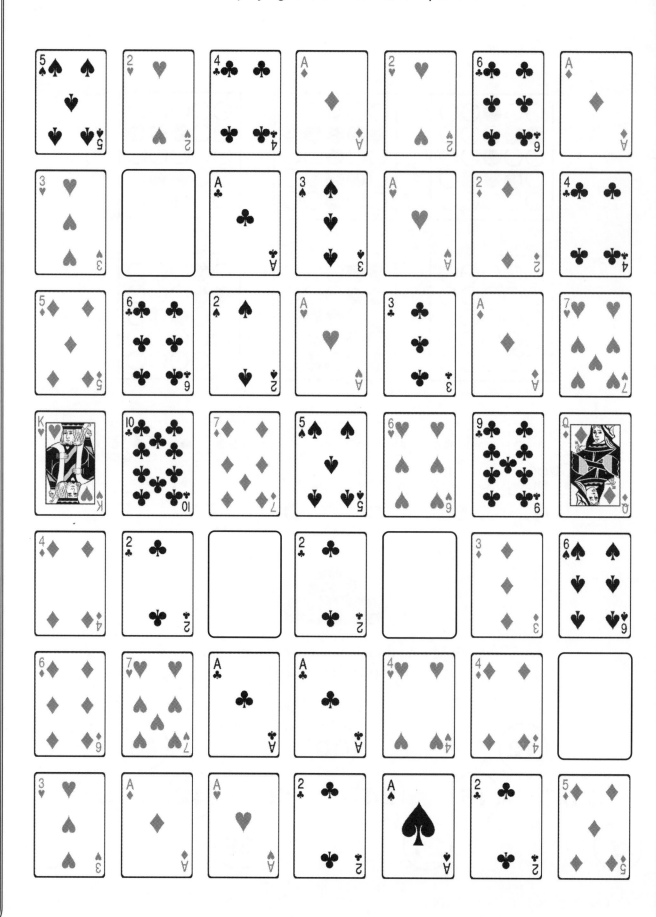

24 PUZZLE

Which number is missing?

25 PUZZLE

Here are 5 matches, which form 2 equilateral triangles, can you add 1 match, and move two others, to form 8 equilateral triangles?

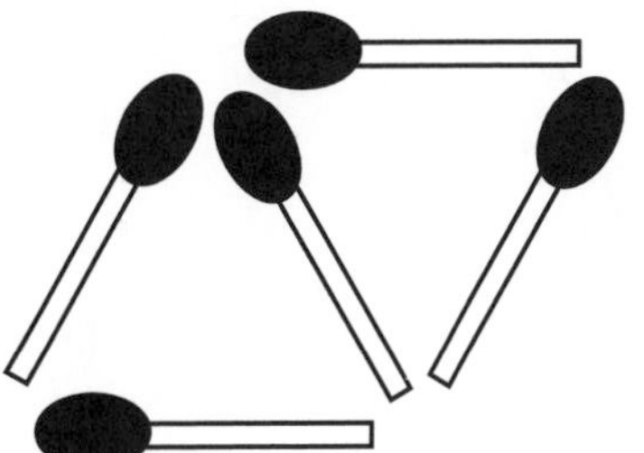

26 PUZZLE

Which letters are the odd ones out?

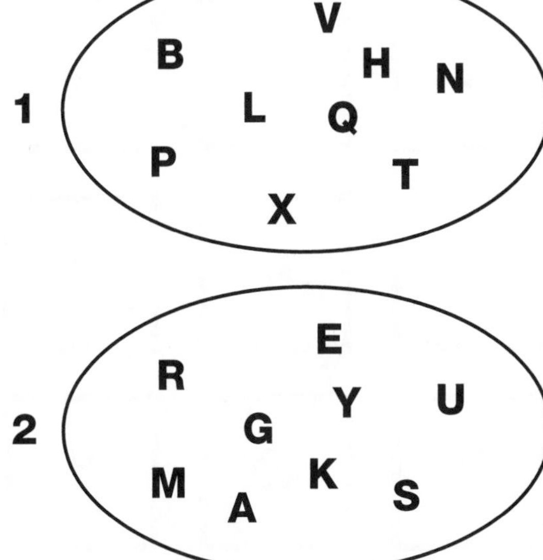

27 PUZZLE

Which number completes this circle?

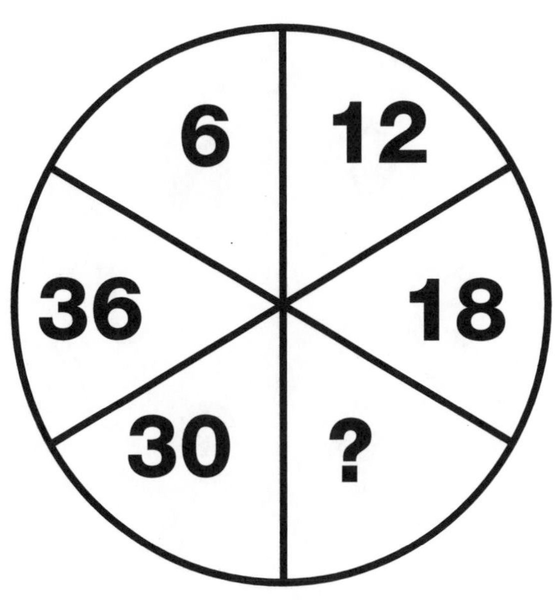

LEVEL 3

Which letter completes the puzzle?

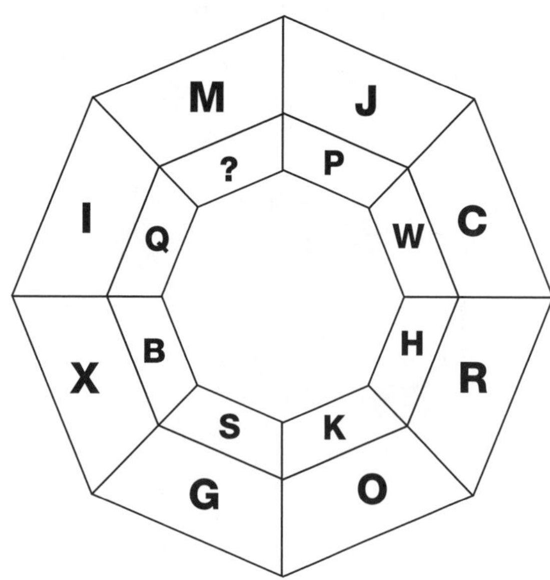

Which number is missing?

3
PUZZLE

Which letter is needed to complete this circle?

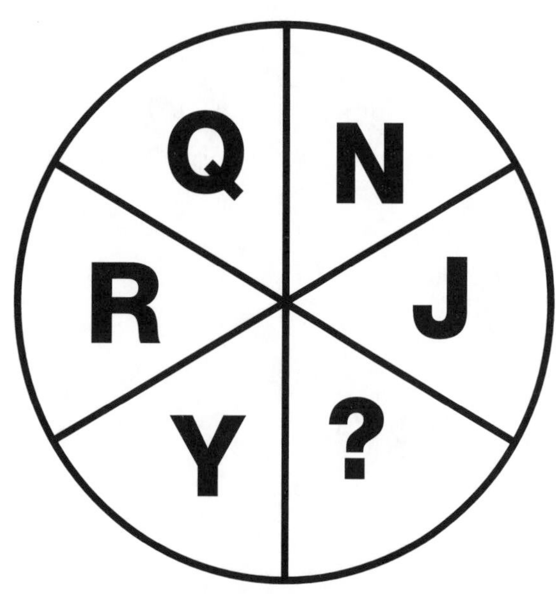

Following a logical sequence, can you complete this puzzle?

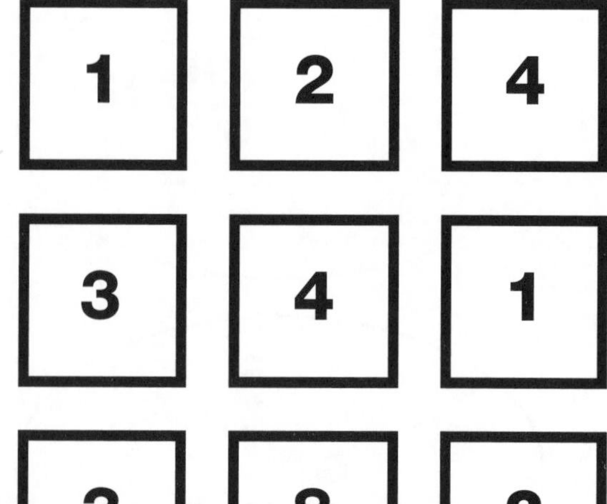

Which of the bottom six grids completes the puzzle?

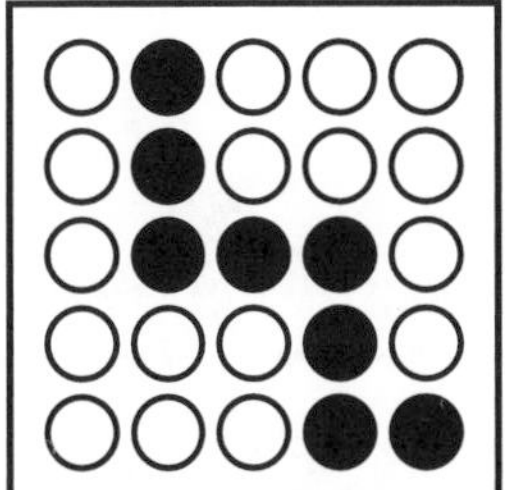
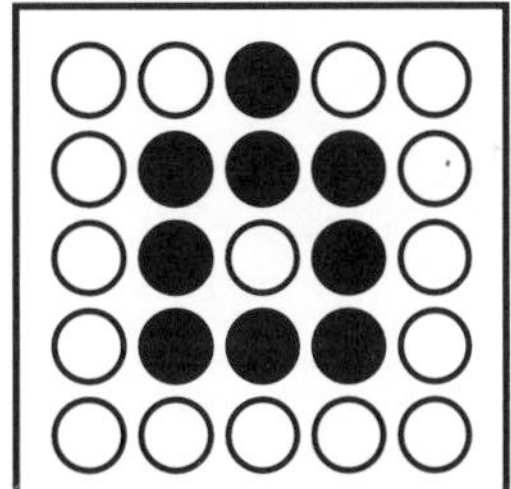
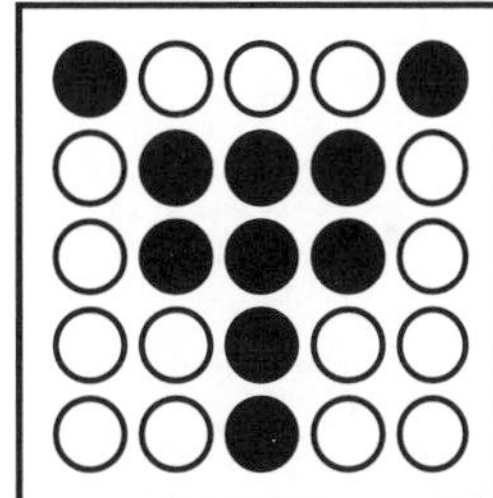
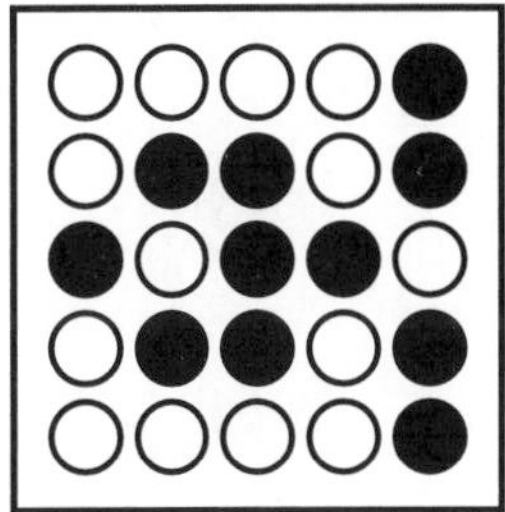
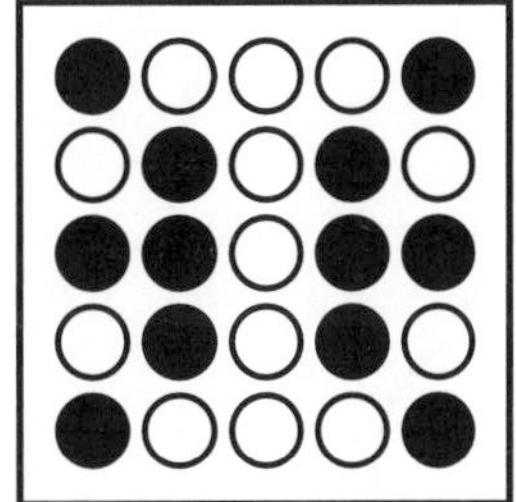

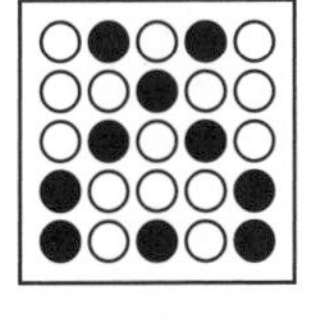
A

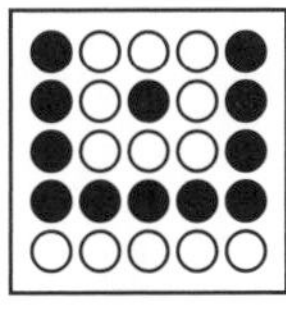
B

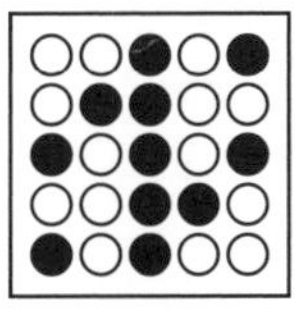
C

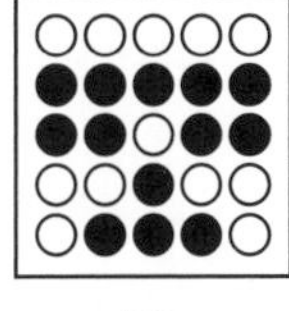
D

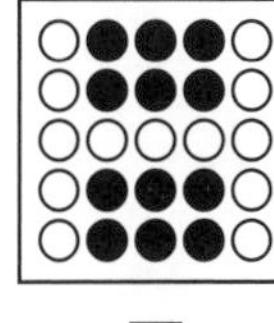
E

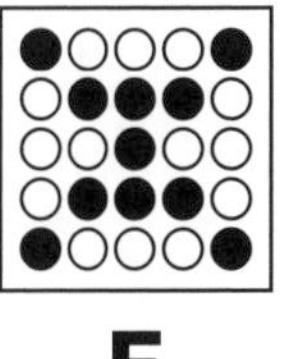
F

What time should the last watch show?

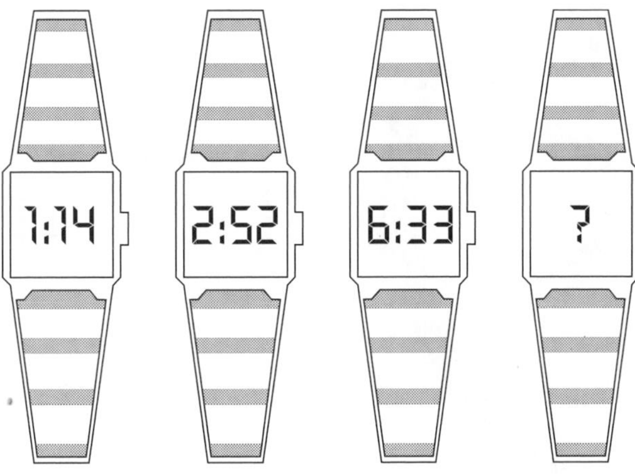

What is missing from the empty circle?

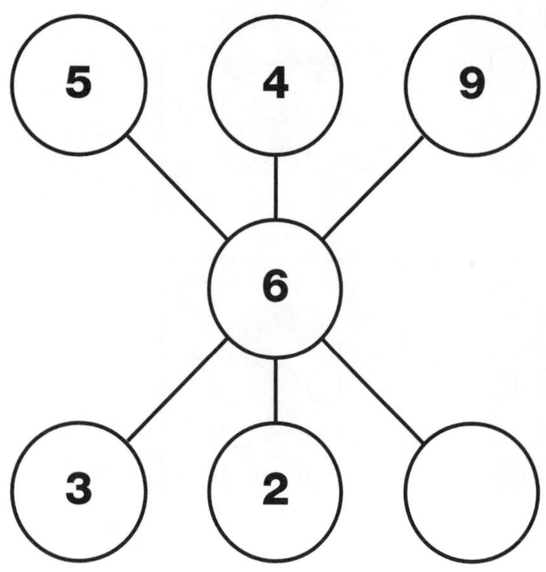

What letter is missing?

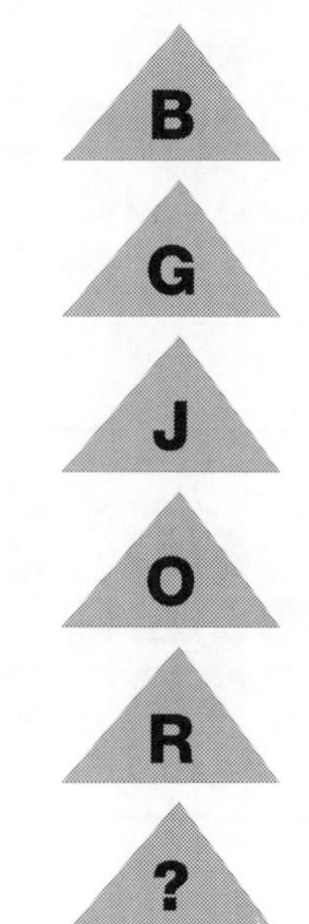

PUZZLE 9

What is missing from the empty segment?

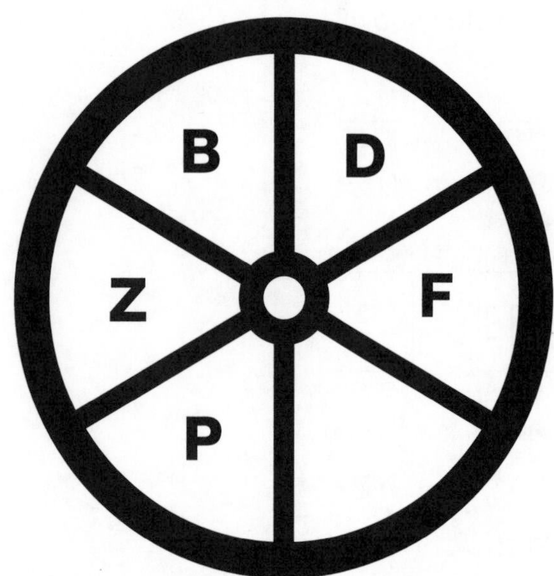

Which letter completes the puzzle?

Following a logical sequence, can you complete this puzzle?

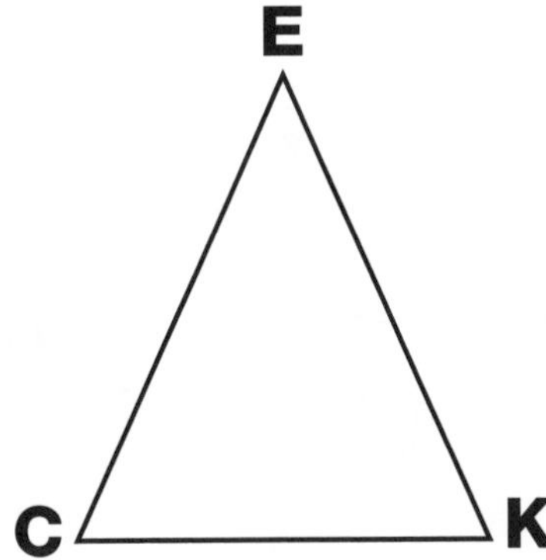

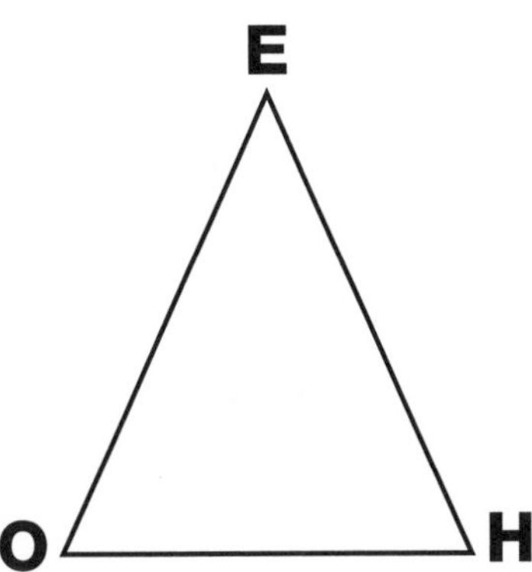

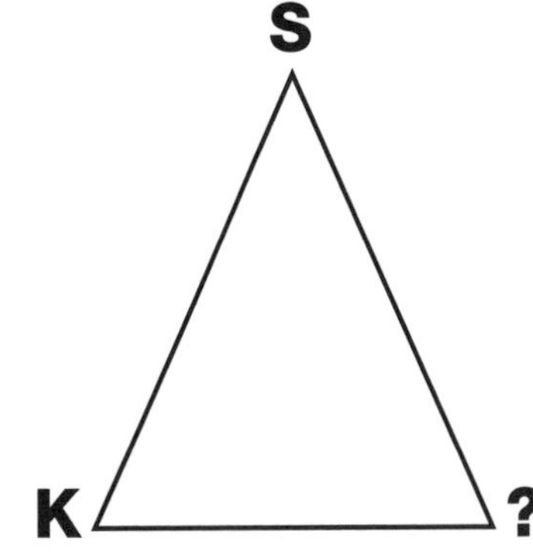

12 PUZZLE

Which three numbers are missing from this pattern?

1	6	2	0	2	4	2	8
2	0	2	?	3	0	3	5
2	4	3	0	3	6	4	2
2	8	3	5	4	?	4	9
3	2	4	0	4	8	5	6
3	6	4	5	5	4	6	?

LEVEL 4

What number is missing?

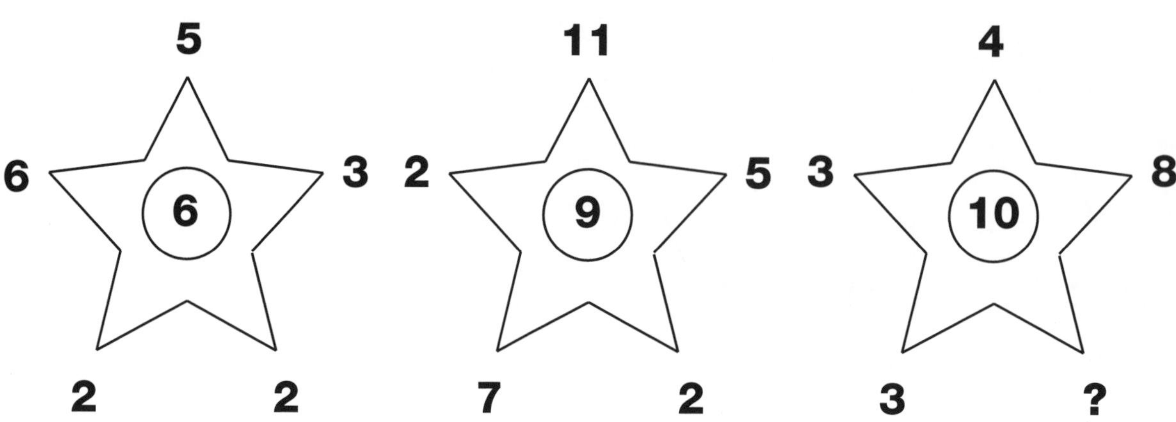

14 PUZZLE

Which letter is missing?

15 PUZZLE

Following a logical sequence, can you complete this puzzle?

16 PUZZLE

What is missing from the last segment?

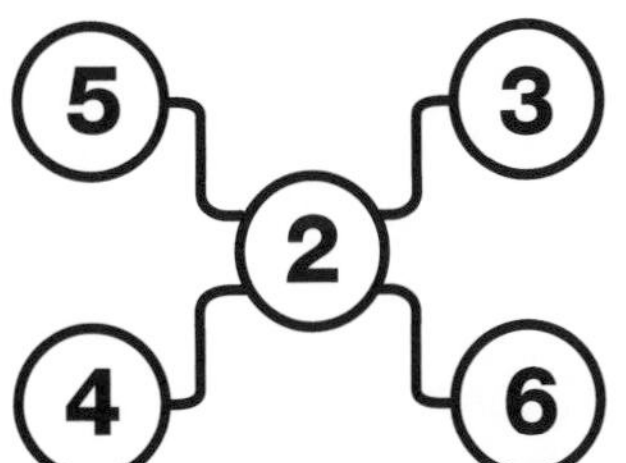

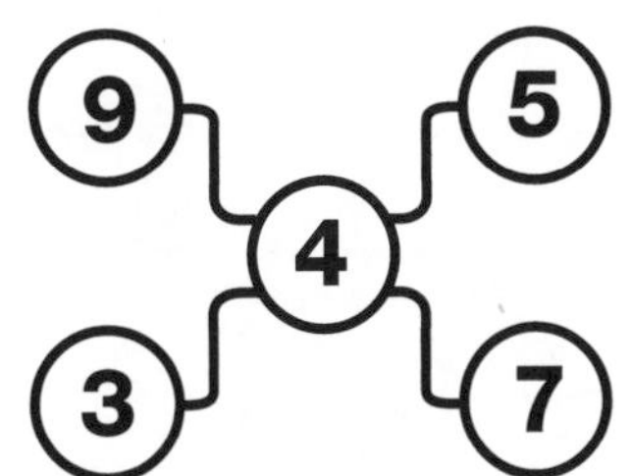

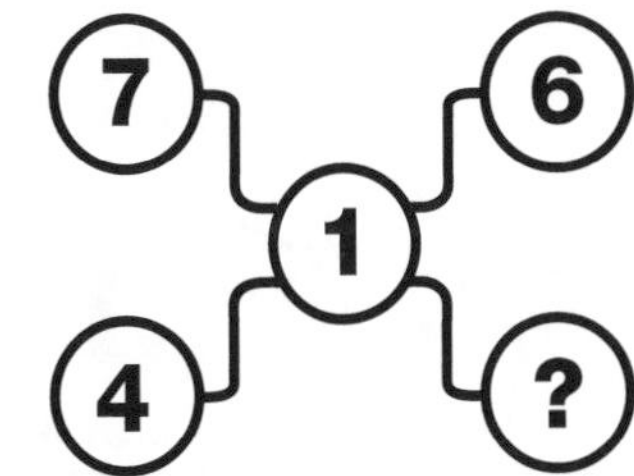

Which number is missing?

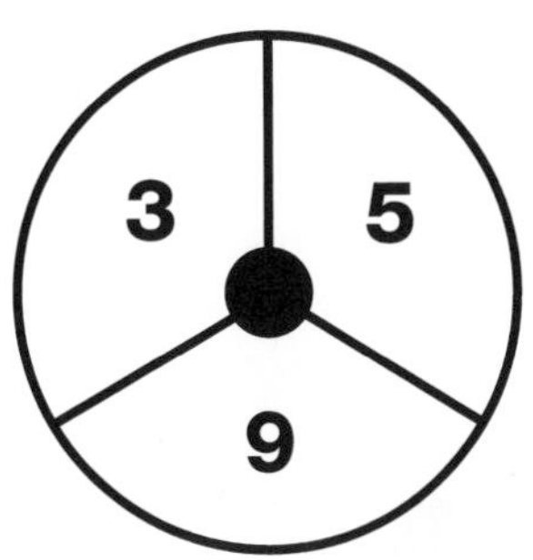

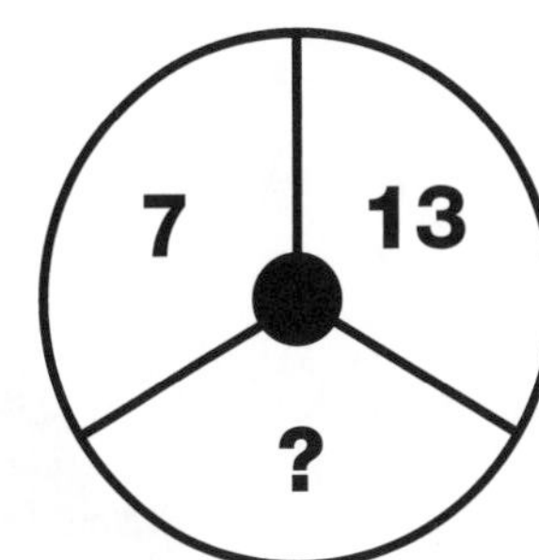

18 PUZZLE

Which letter completes the puzzle?

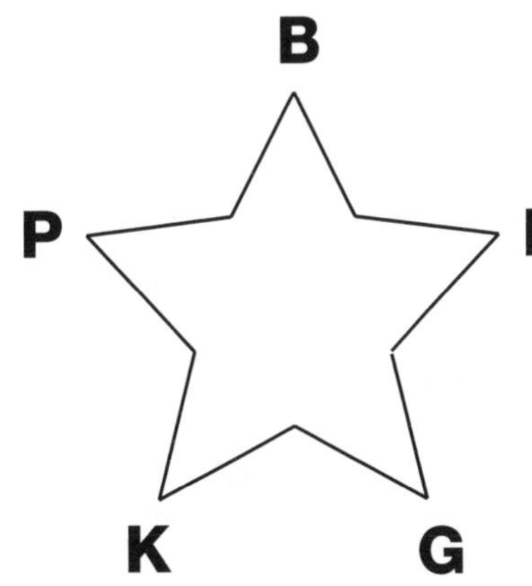

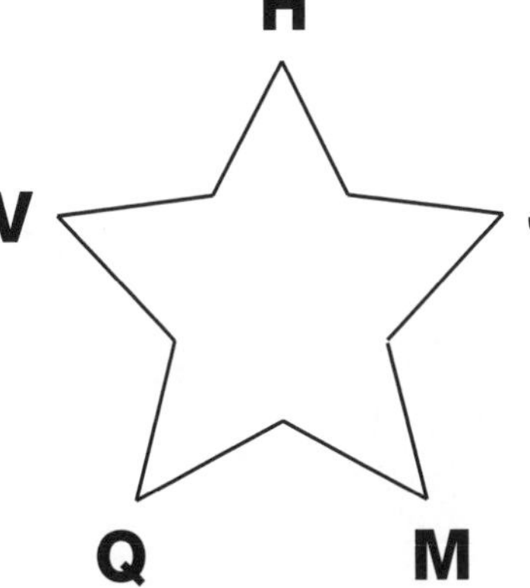

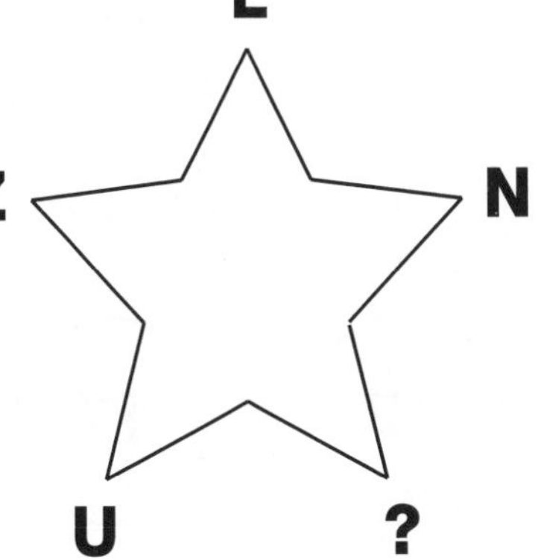

LEVEL 4

LEVEL 4

PUZZLE 19

What completes this sequence?

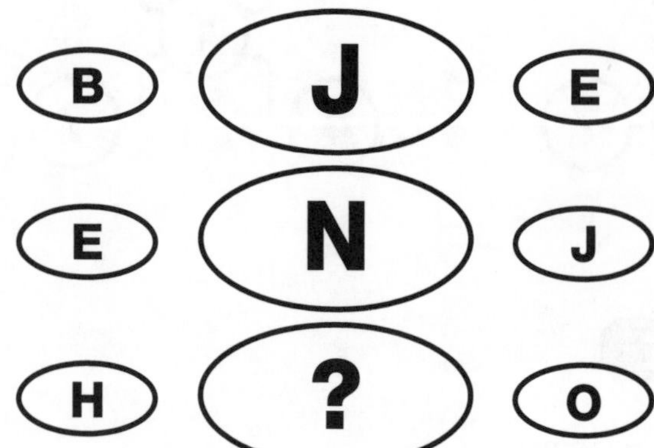

PUZZLE 20

Can you move just 3 coins to make the triangle point upwards?

PUZZLE 21

Which number is missing?

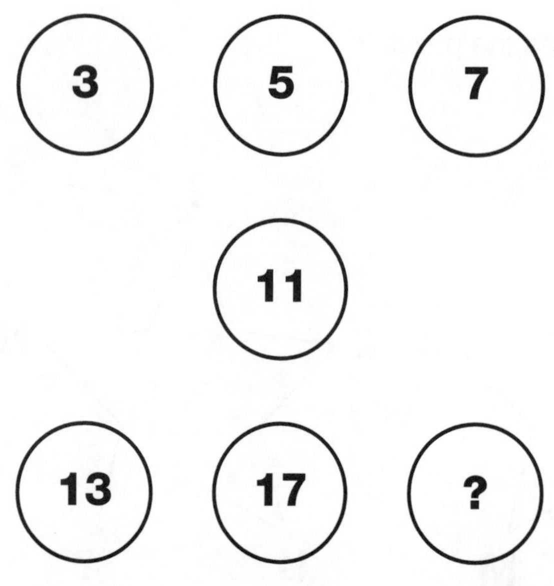

PUZZLE 22

Which number is the odd one out in each shape?

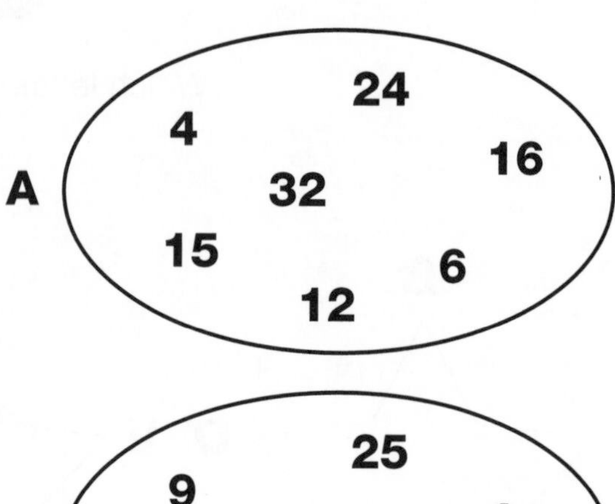

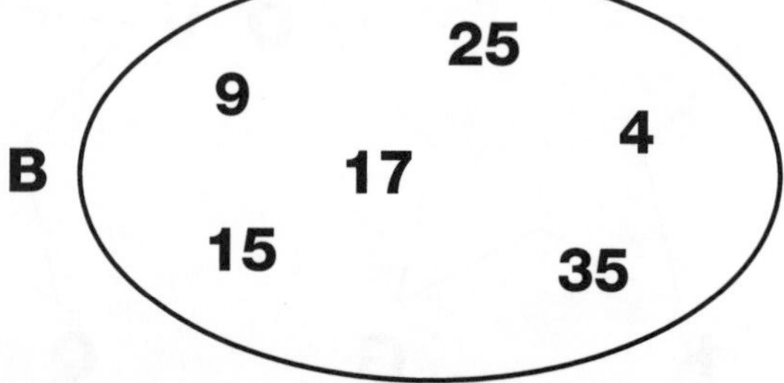

23 PUZZLE

What number is missing?

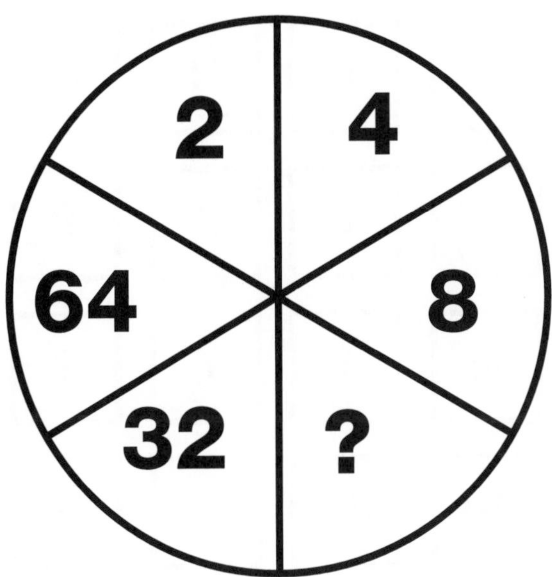

Which letter completes the puzzle?

25 PUZZLE

Following a logical sequence, can you complete this puzzle?

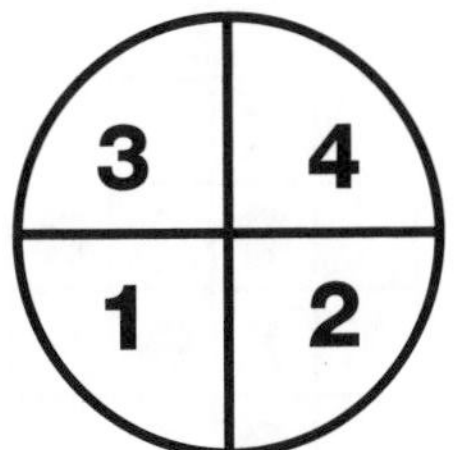

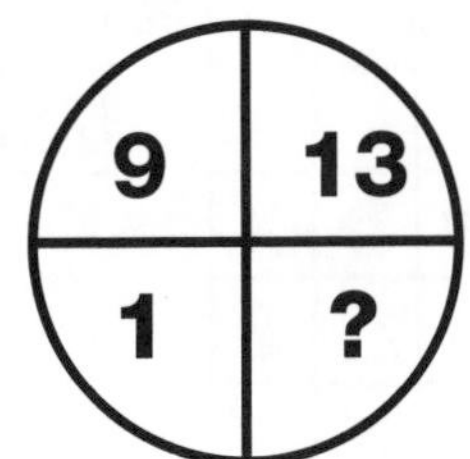

What is missing from the bottom scale to make it balance?

LEVEL 4

LEVEL 4

Where does the missing hand go?

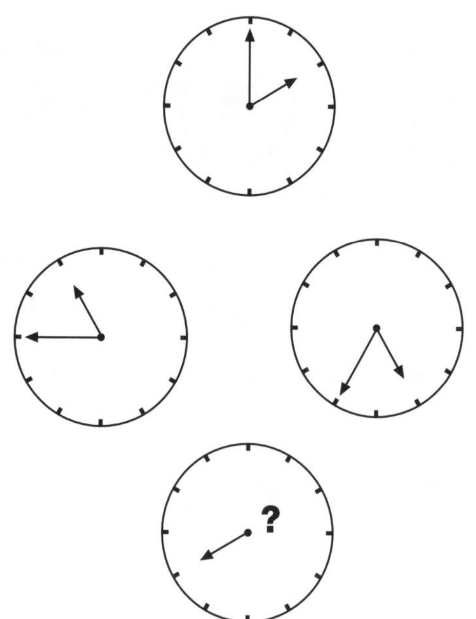

What letter is missing?

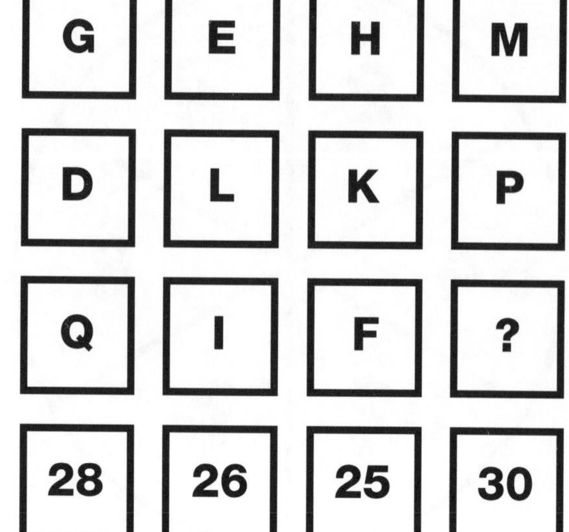

29 PUZZLE

Which piece fits back into the grid to complete the pattern?

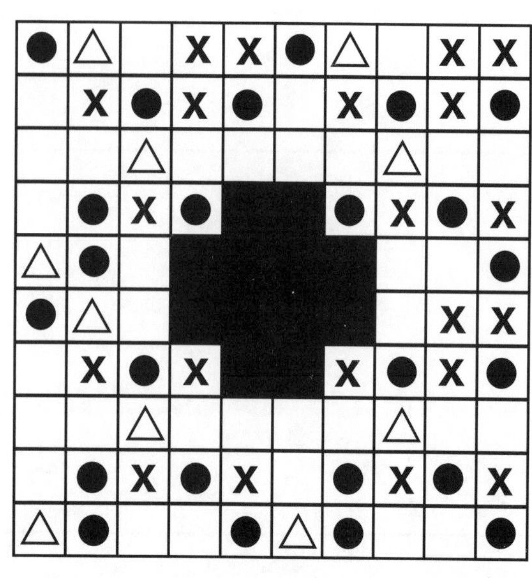

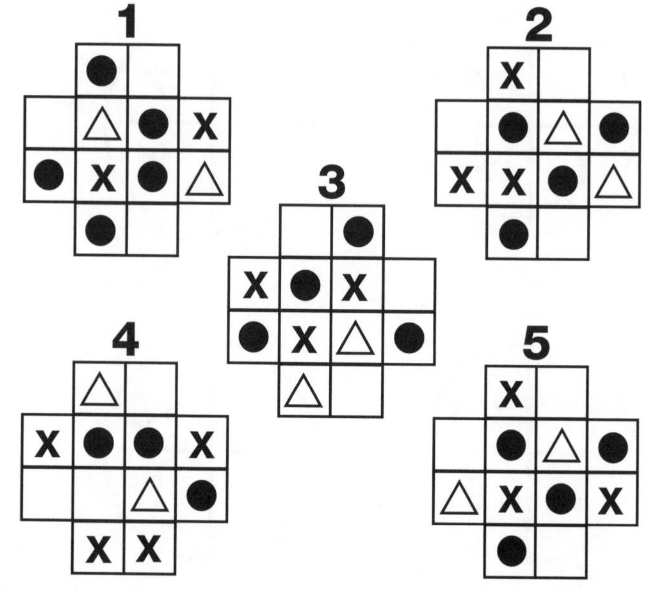

Which number is missing?

Which letter replaces the question mark?

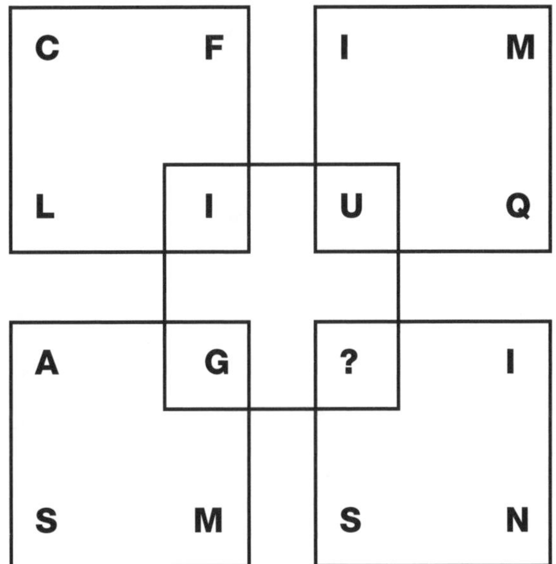

3
PUZZLE

Following a logical sequence, can you complete this puzzle?

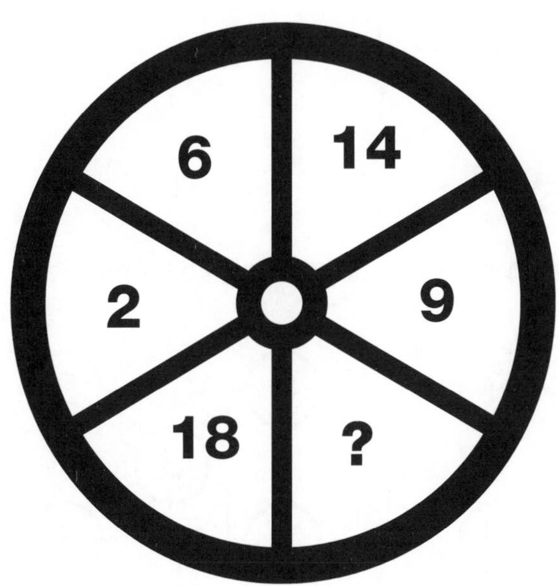

Which letter completes the puzzle?

A	P	E
F	U	J
K	Z	?

LEVEL 5

LEVEL 5

Which playing card will complete the puzzle?

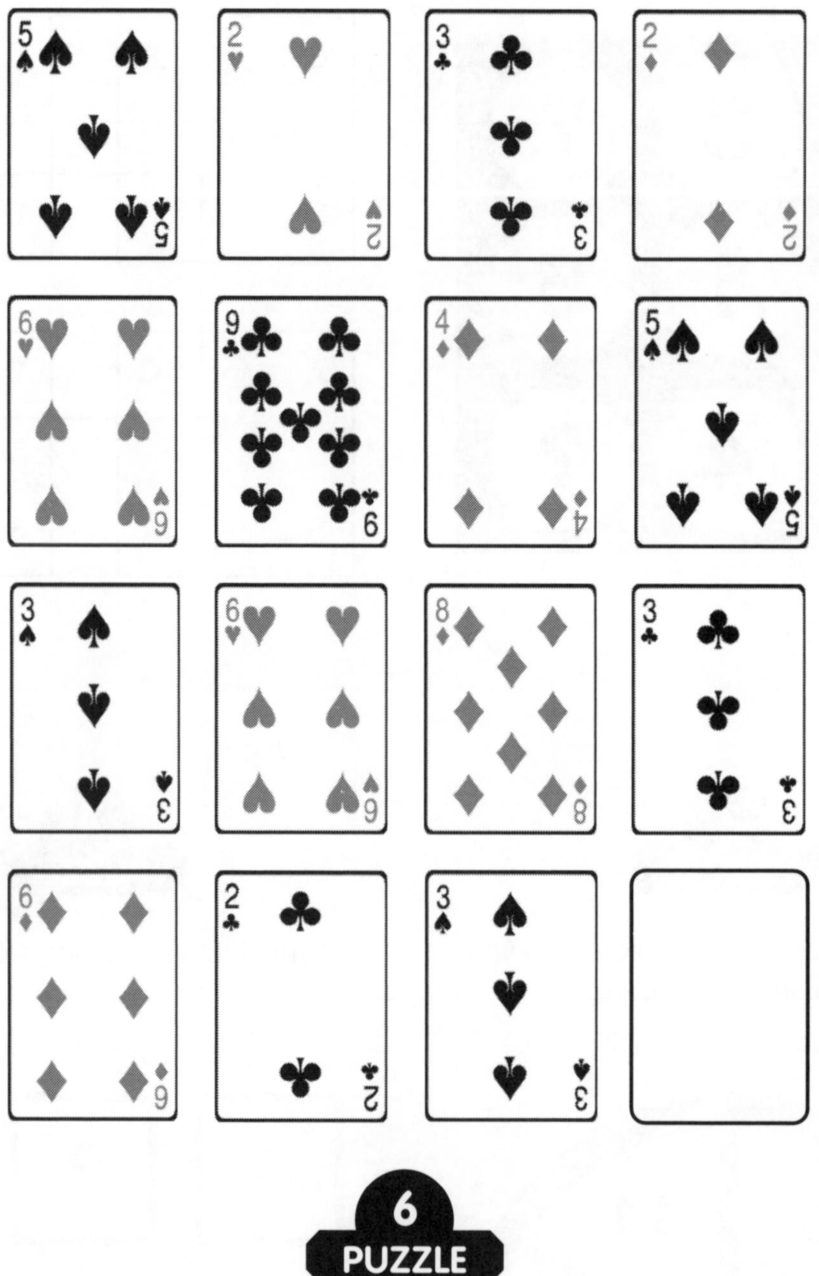

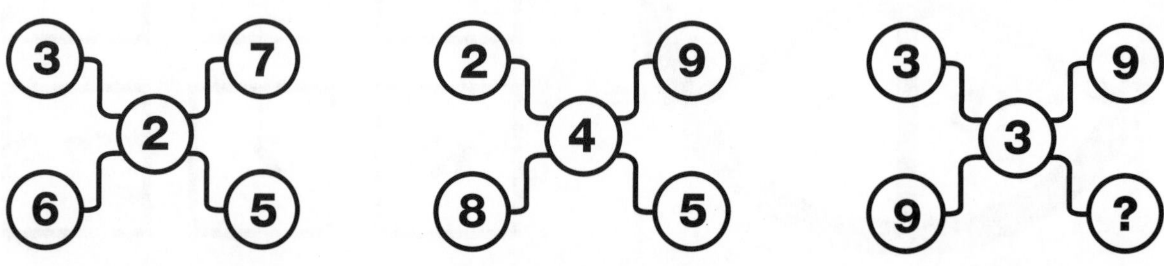

6 PUZZLE

In this sequence of numbers what should go within the last shape to make it complete?

7 PUZZLE

What number is missing?

8 PUZZLE

Which letter completes the puzzle?

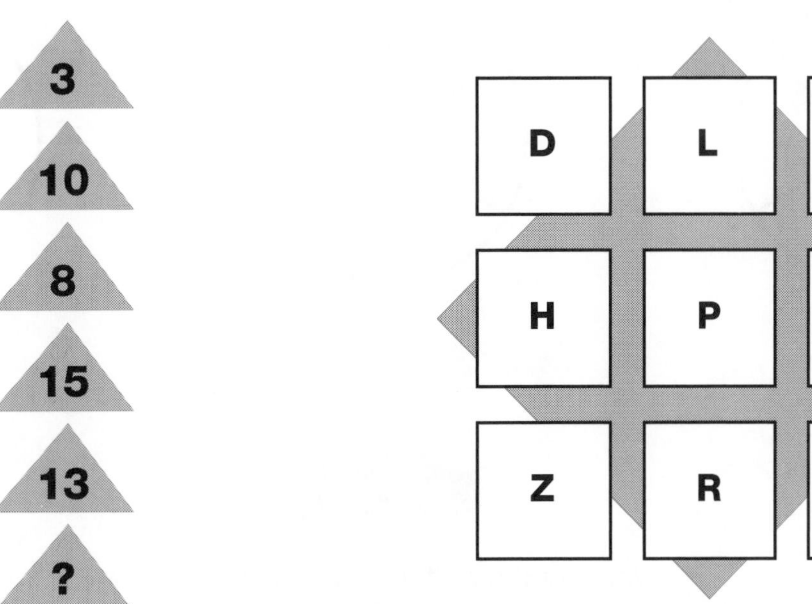

9 PUZZLE

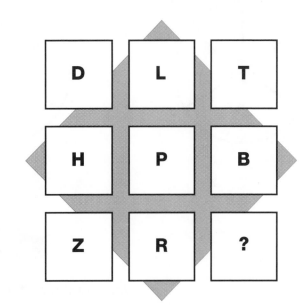

Which watch should go in the missing space to complete the sequence?

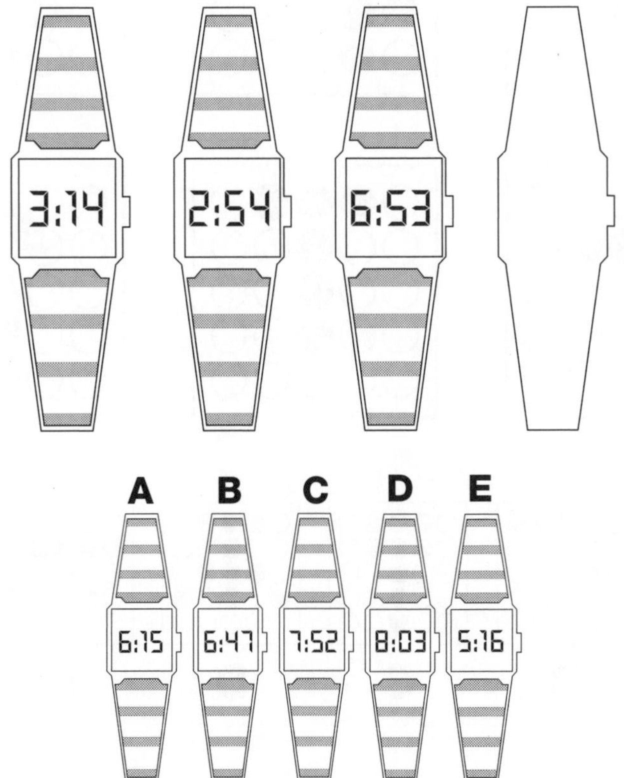

Which number is missing?

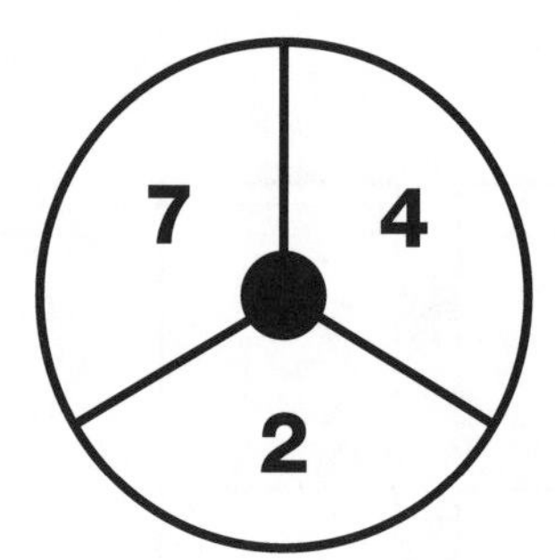

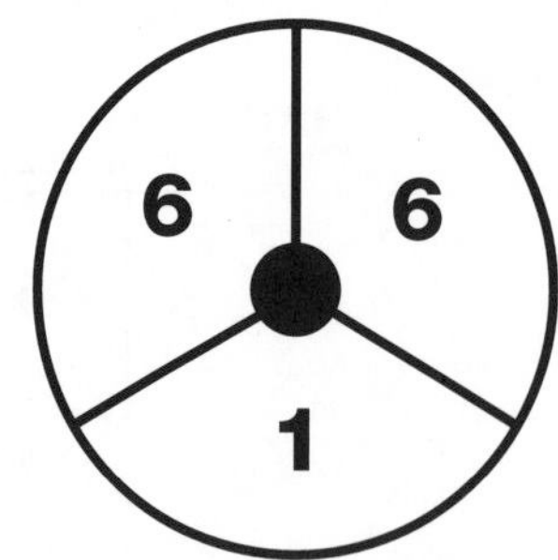

11
PUZZLE

Which of the bottom six grids completes the puzzle?

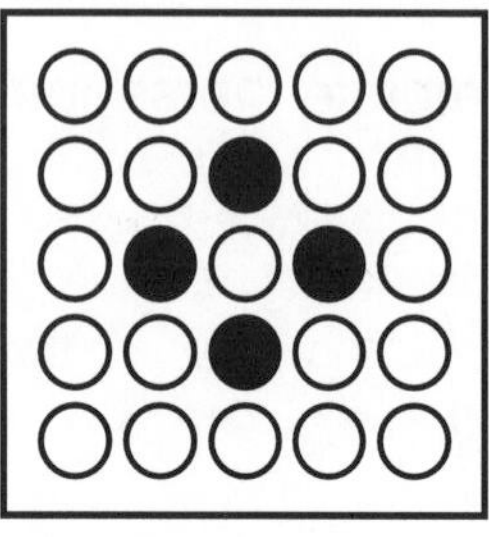
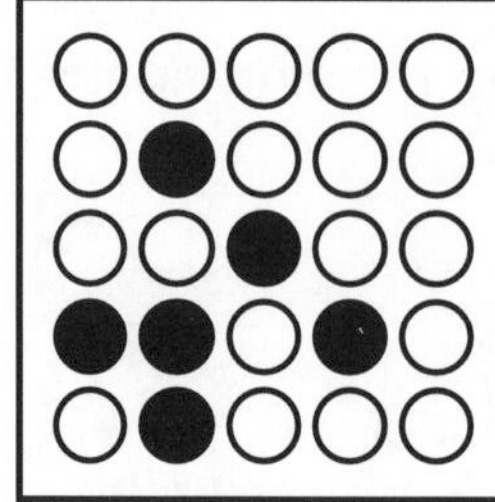
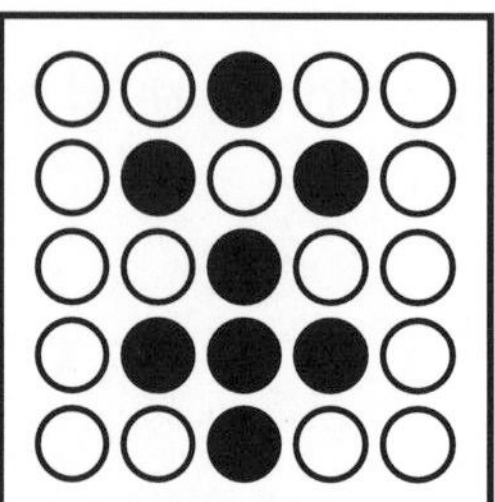

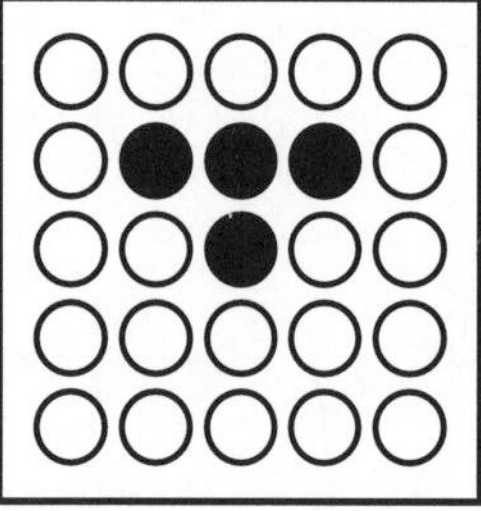
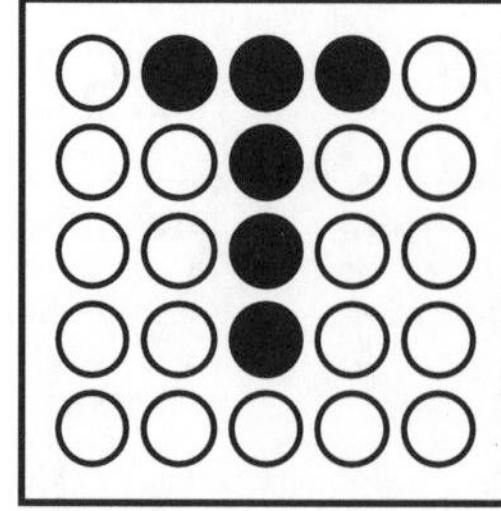

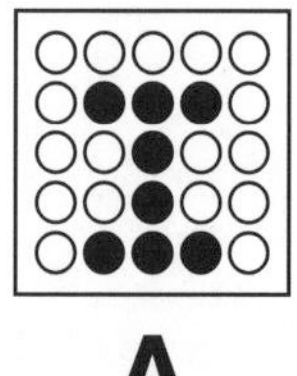
A

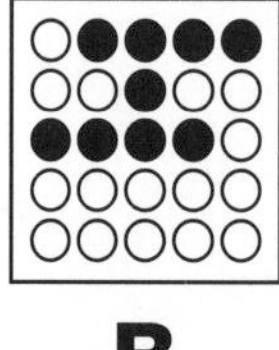
B

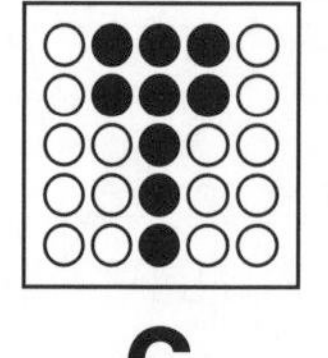
C

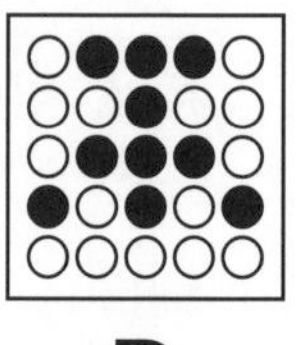
D

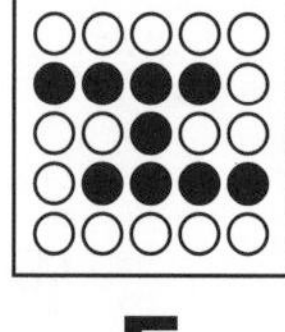
E

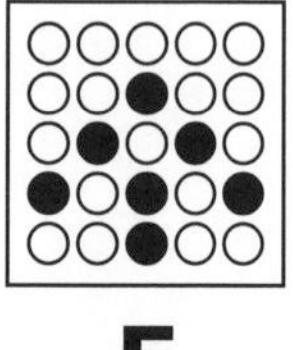
F

12 PUZZLE

What number is missing?

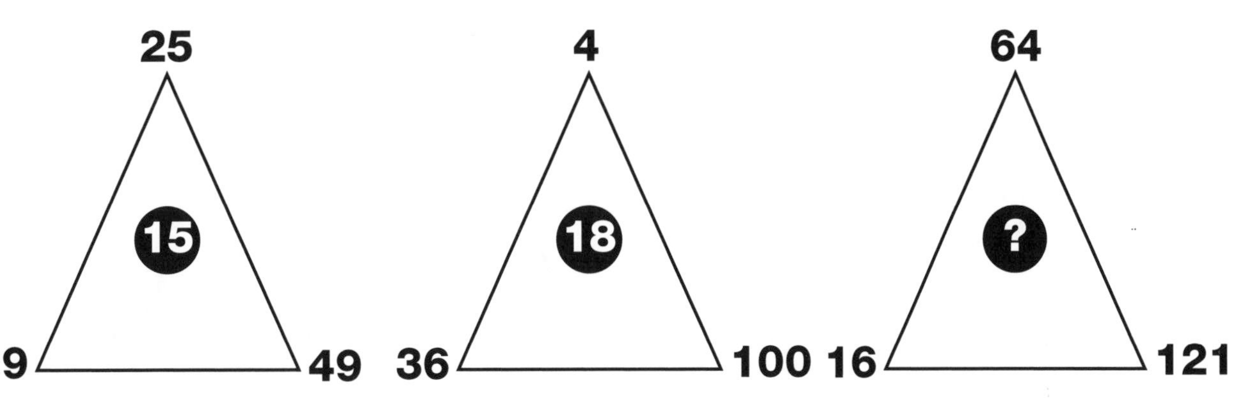

13 PUZZLE

Following a logical sequence, can you complete this puzzle?

24	35	48	63	?

14 PUZZLE

Which numbers are the odd ones out in these selections?

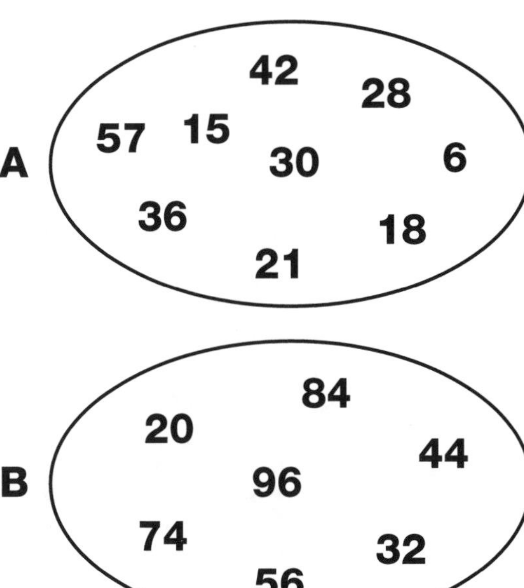

LEVEL 5

What completes this triangle of numbers?

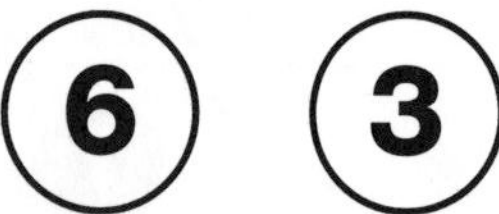

16 PUZZLE

What is missing from this puzzle?

17 PUZZLE

Following a logical sequence, can you complete this puzzle?

18 PUZZLE

Which letter completes the puzzle?

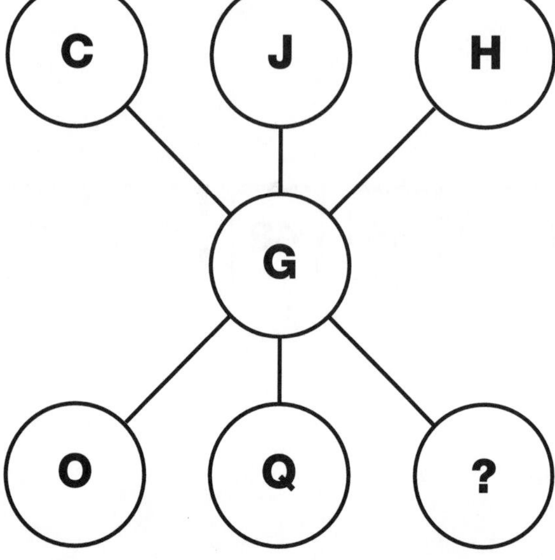

19 PUZZLE

Which number completes this puzzle?

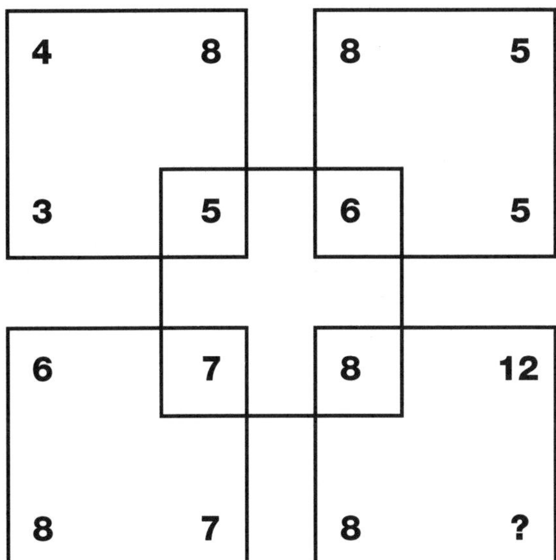

In this logical sequence of letters, what is needed to make it complete?

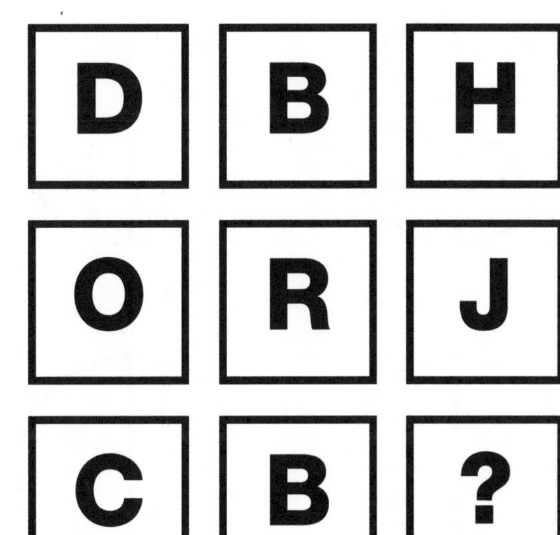

What is missing?

What number is missing?

LEVEL 5

PUZZLE 23

Which number is missing?

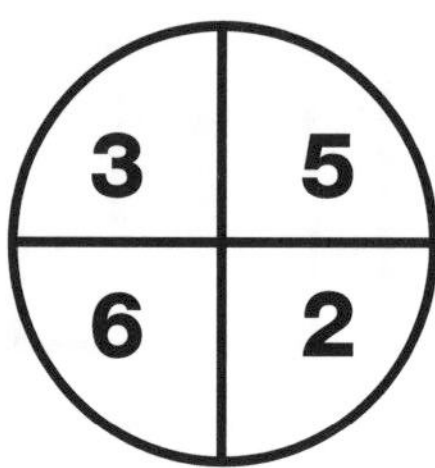

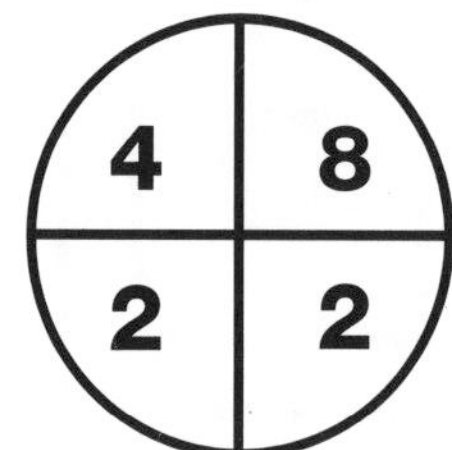

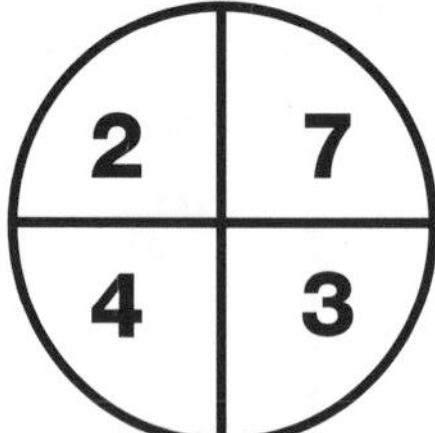

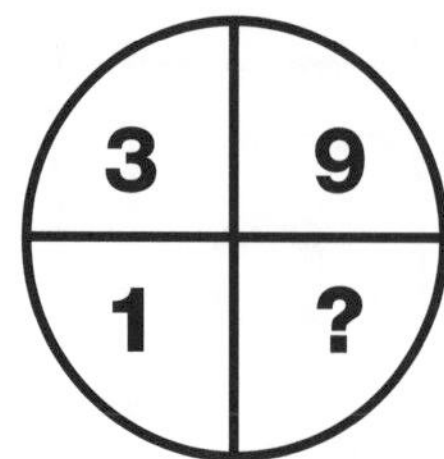

PUZZLE 24

Which value replaces the question mark and balances the scales?

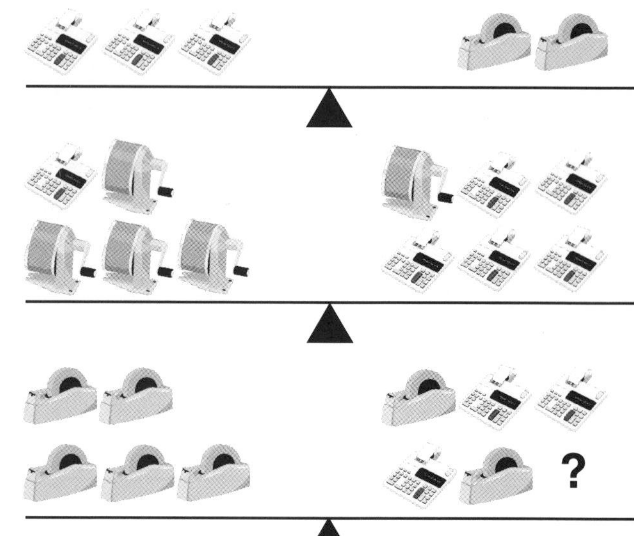

PUZZLE 25

Which playing card completes the puzzle?

PUZZLE 26

What three numbers are missing from this grid?

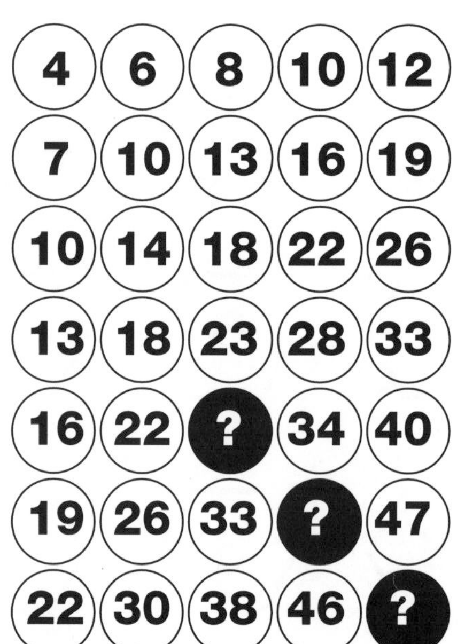

4	6	8	10	12
7	10	13	16	19
10	14	18	22	26
13	18	23	28	33
16	22	?	34	40
19	26	33	?	47
22	30	38	46	?

Which pattern completes this sequence?

1 2 3 4 5

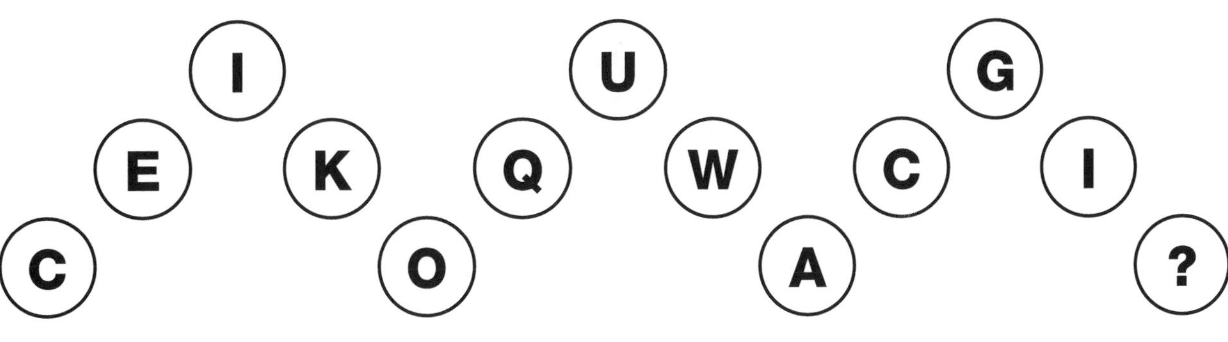

28 PUZZLE

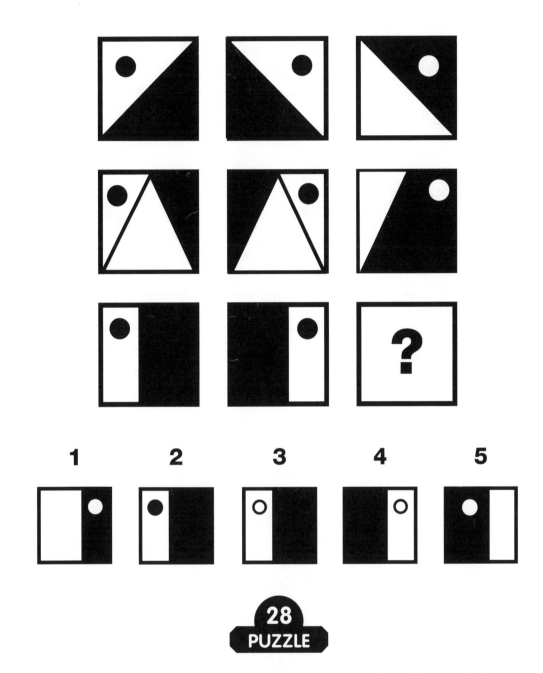

Following a logical sequence, can you complete this puzzle?

LEVEL 5

Which of the lower six grids completes the sequence?

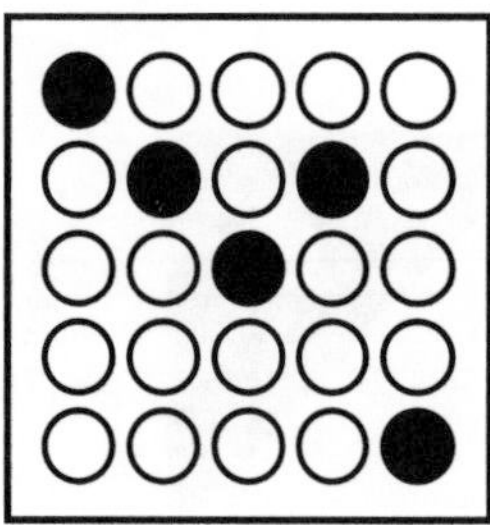
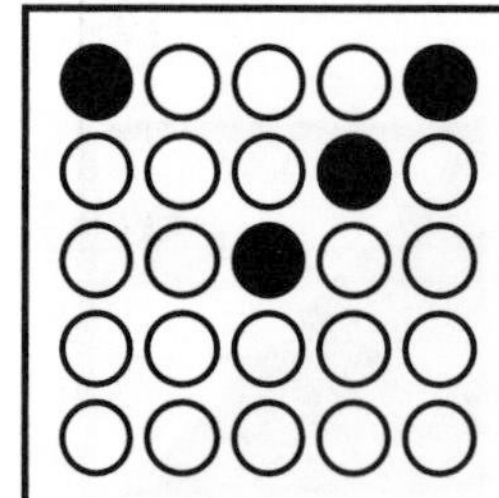
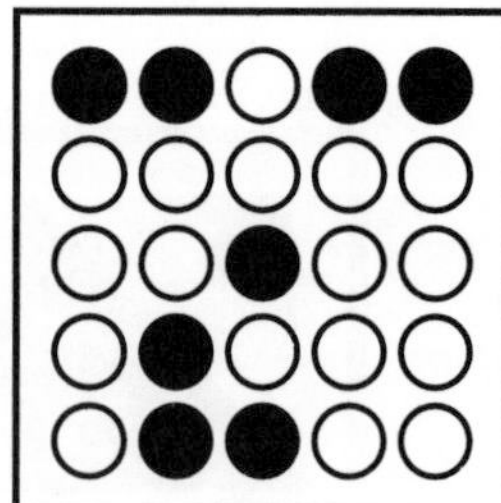
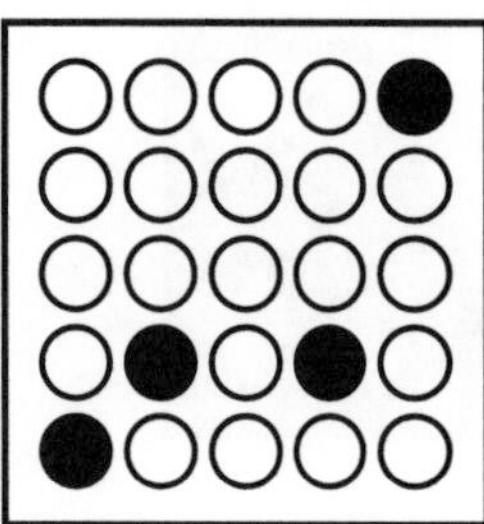
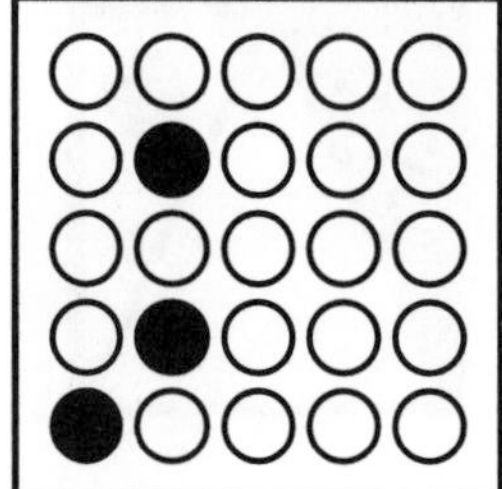

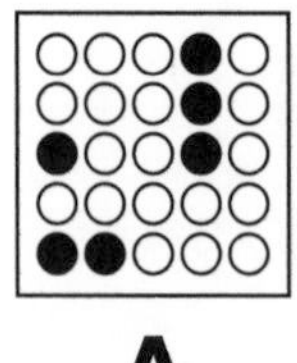
A

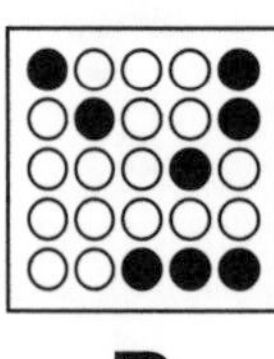
B

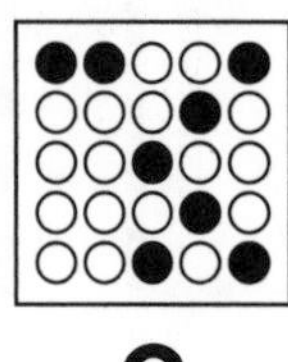
C

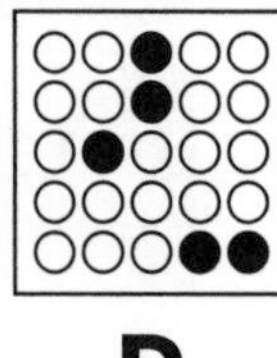
D

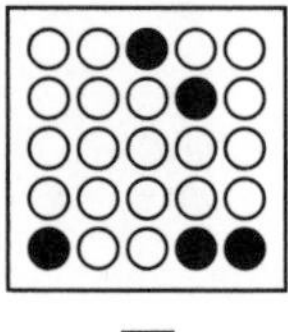
E

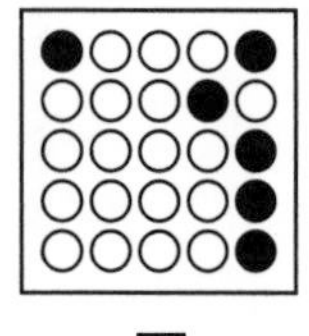
F

2
PUZZLE

What is missing from the last triangle?

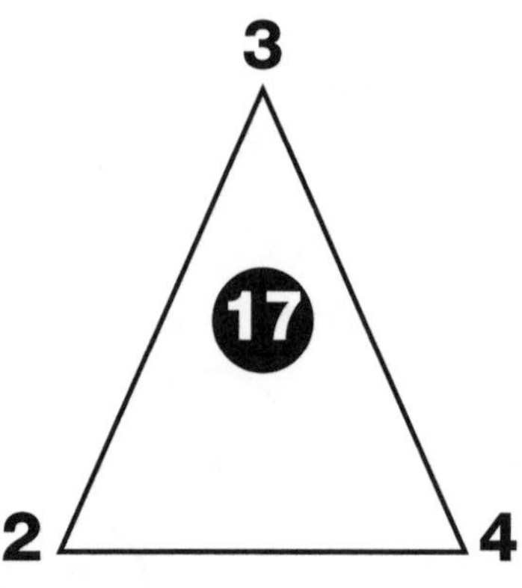

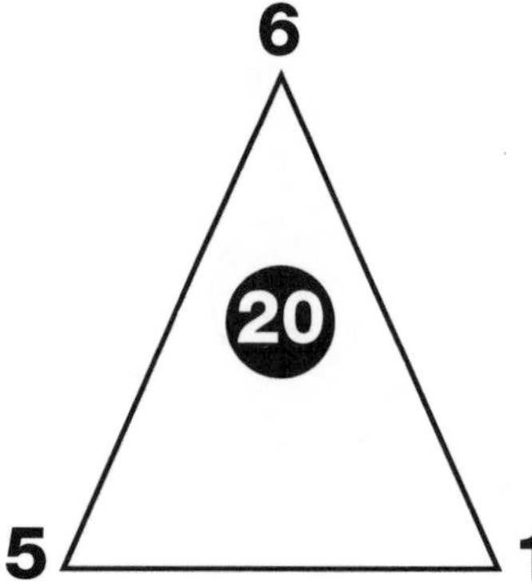

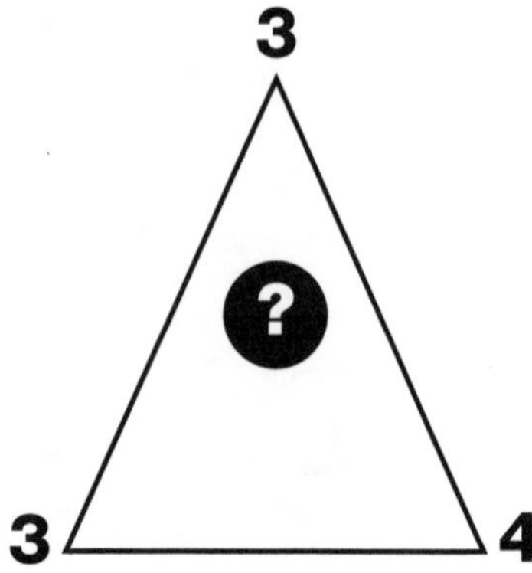

3 PUZZLE

What number is missing?

4 PUZZLE

Which number completes this sequence?

5 PUZZLE

Which letter completes the puzzle?

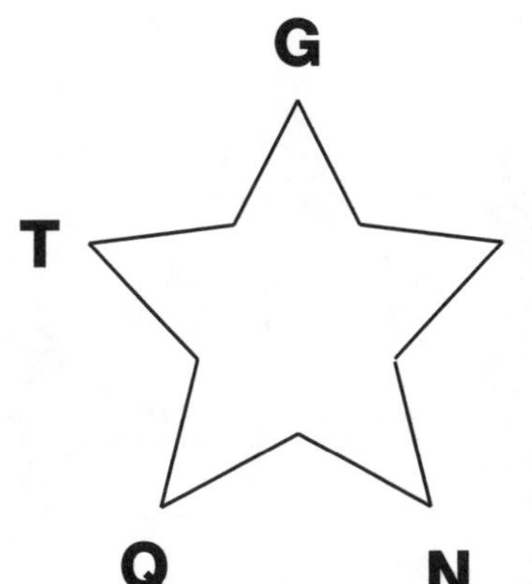

LEVEL 6

LEVEL 6

PUZZLE 6

Following a logical sequence, can you complete this puzzle?

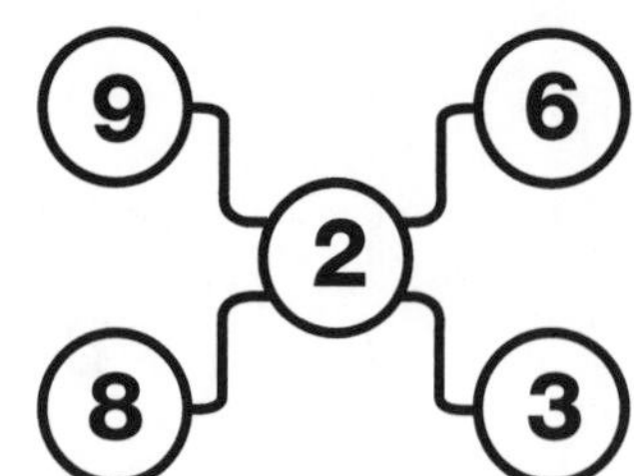

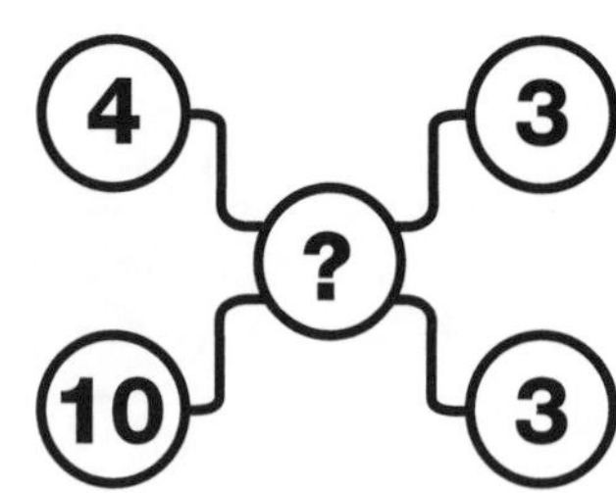

PUZZLE 7

What is missing from the last shape?

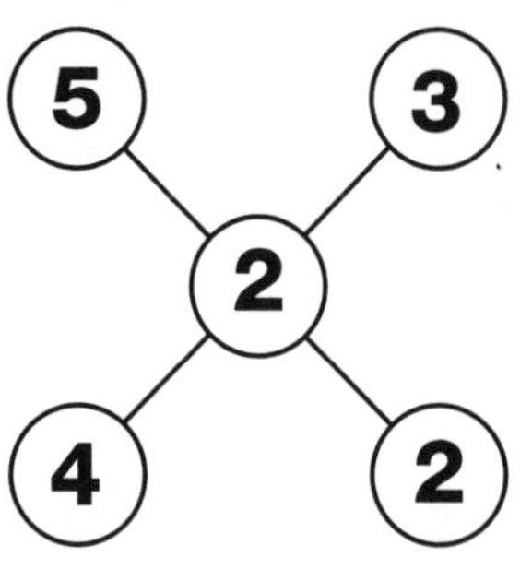

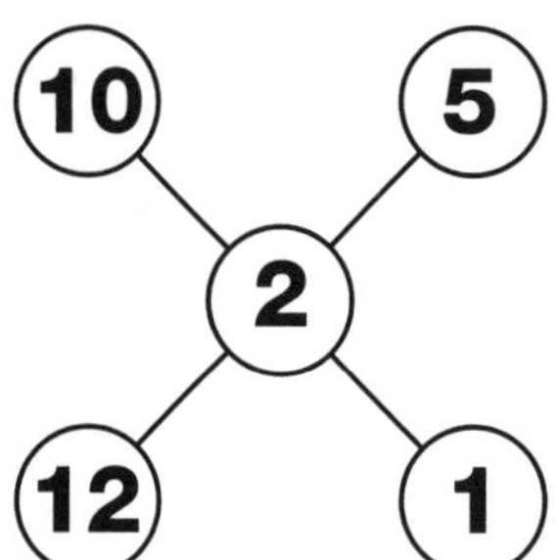

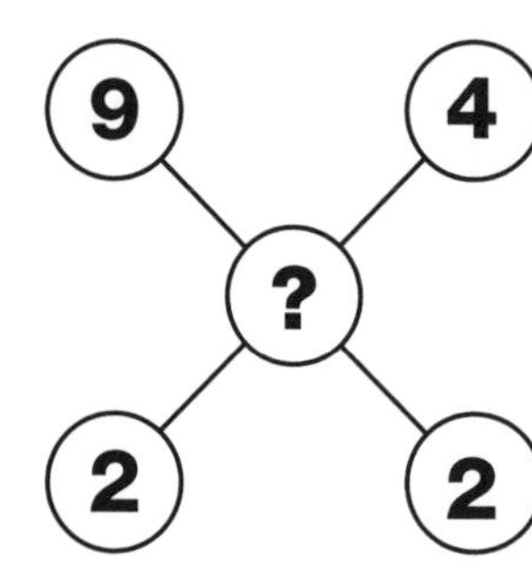

PUZZLE 8

Which number fits within the bottom right hand circle to complete the puzzle?

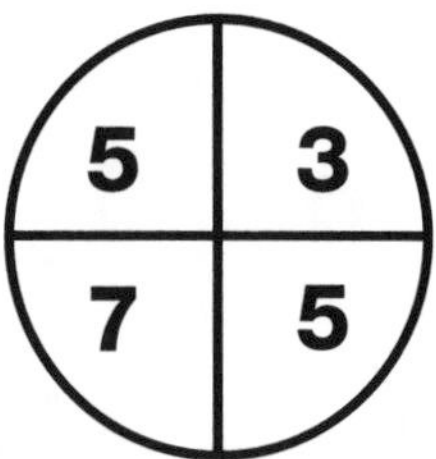

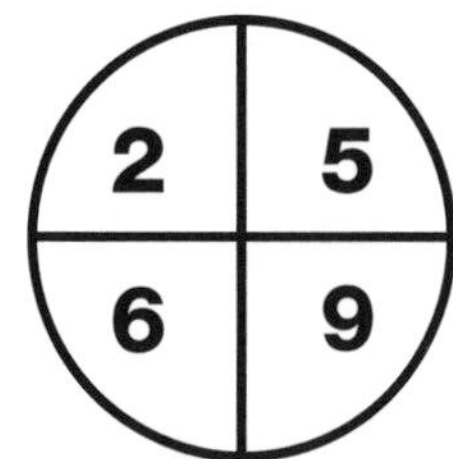

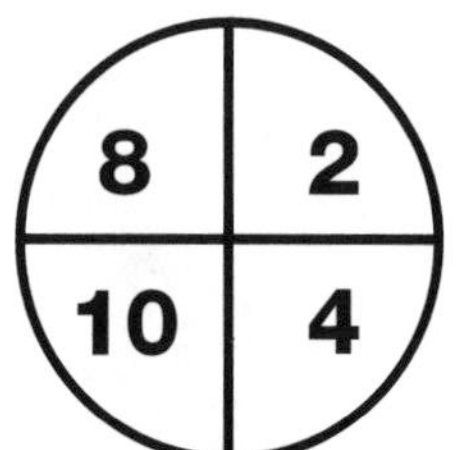

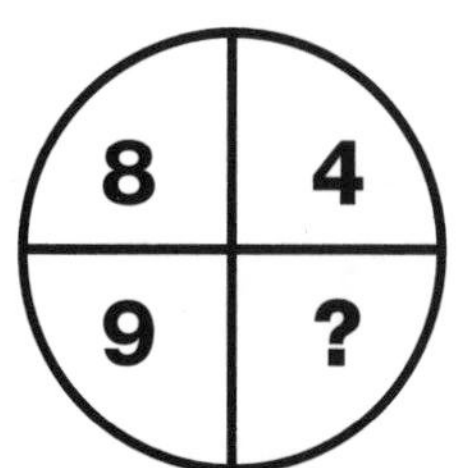

PUZZLE 9

Which letter completes the puzzle?

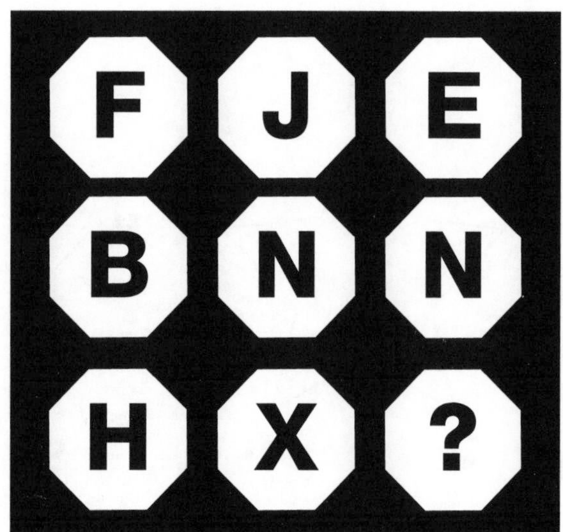

10 PUZZLE

Which number is missing from the last circle?

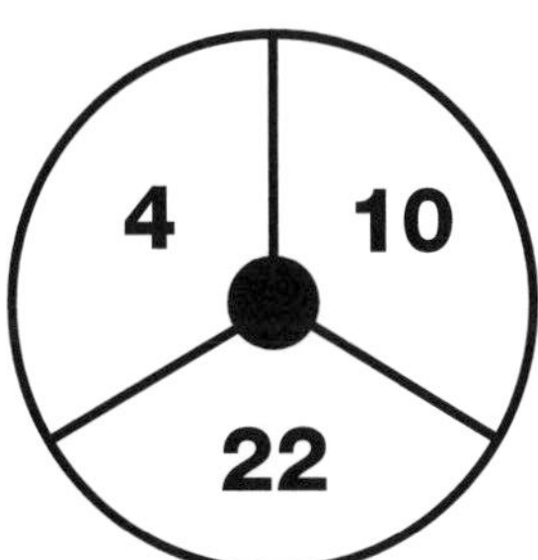

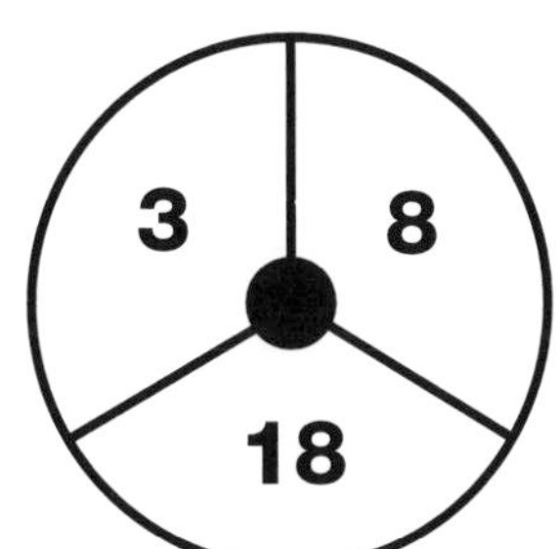

11 PUZZLE

What number is missing?

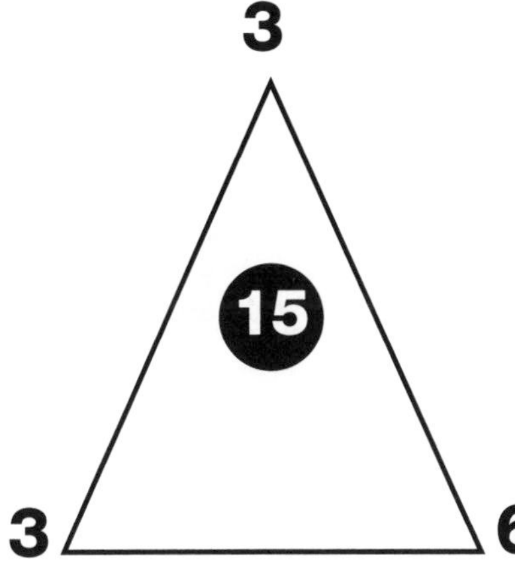

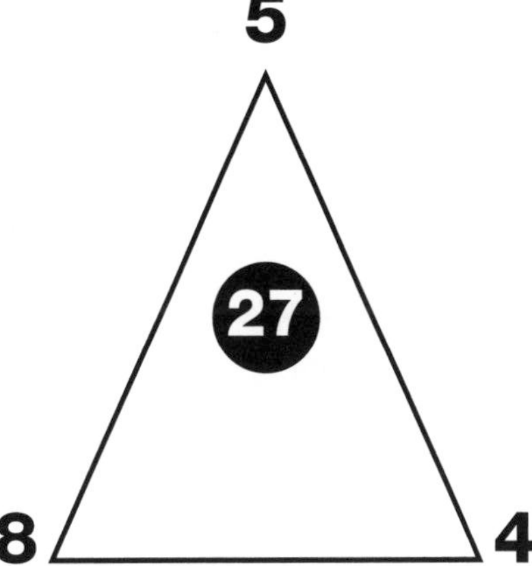

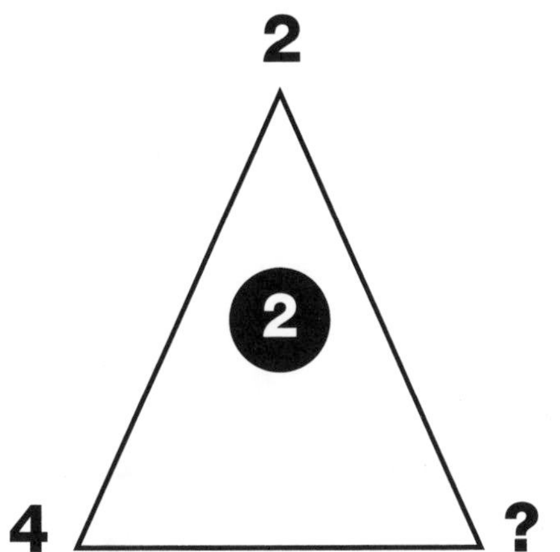

LEVEL 6

LEVEL 6

12 PUZZLE

Which number completes this puzzle?

3	3	7
1	5	1
1	8	?

13 PUZZLE

In this sequence of letters, what is needed to complete the puzzle?

J	K
M	P
T	Y
E	L
T	C
M	?

14 PUZZLE

What is needed to complete this pyramid of numbers?

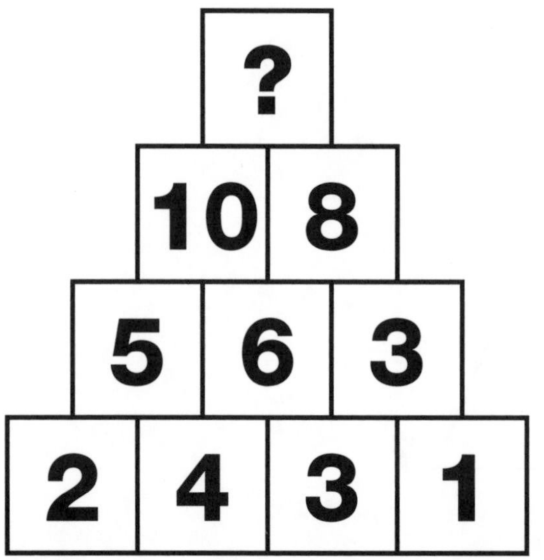

15 PUZZLE

Which letter completes the puzzle?

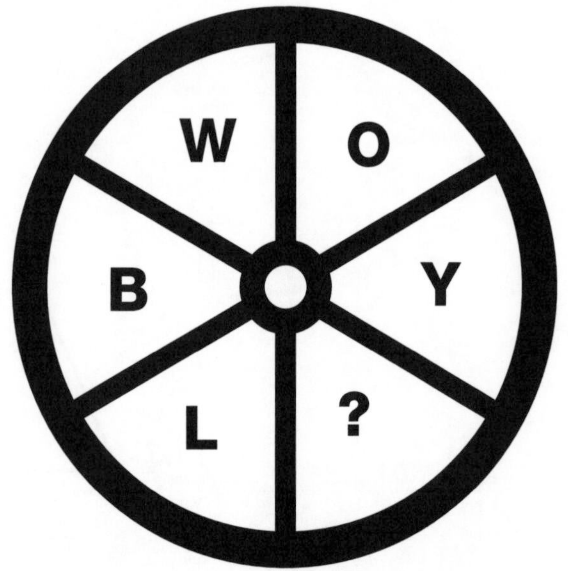

16 PUZZLE

Which letter goes within this triangle?

17 PUZZLE

What is missing from this sequence?

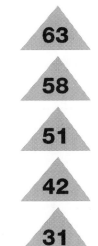

18 PUZZLE

Following a logical sequence, can you complete this puzzle?

19 PUZZLE

What letter is missing?

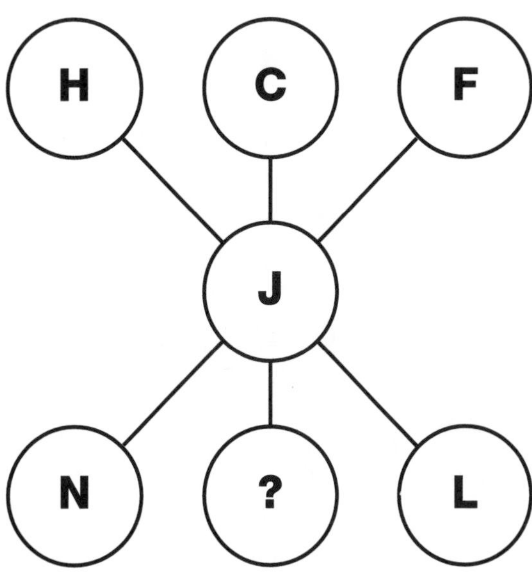

LEVEL 6

20 PUZZLE

What is needed to complete this puzzle?

R

W

C

J

?

21 PUZZLE

Which letter completes the puzzle?

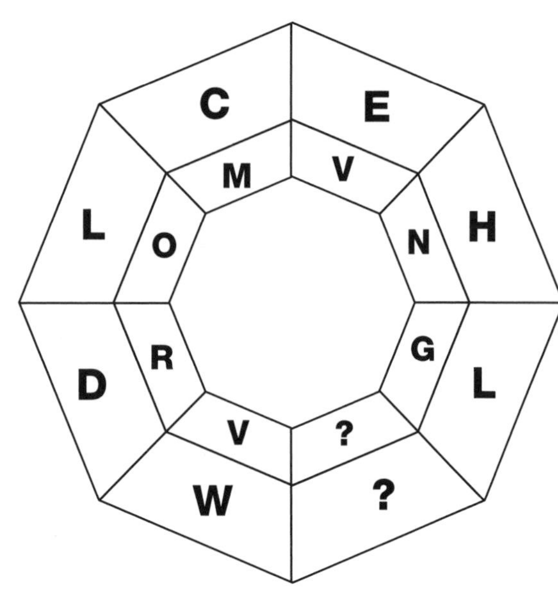

22 PUZZLE

What letter completes this pyramid?

23 PUZZLE

Can you move just 4 matches to make 3 equilateral triangles?

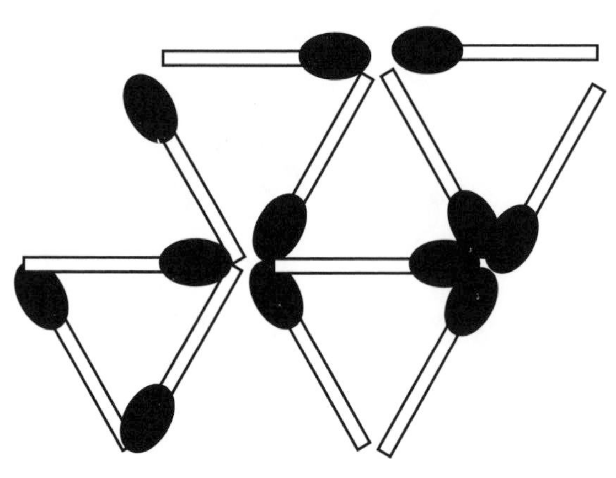

24 PUZZLE

Which letter is the odd one out in each oval?

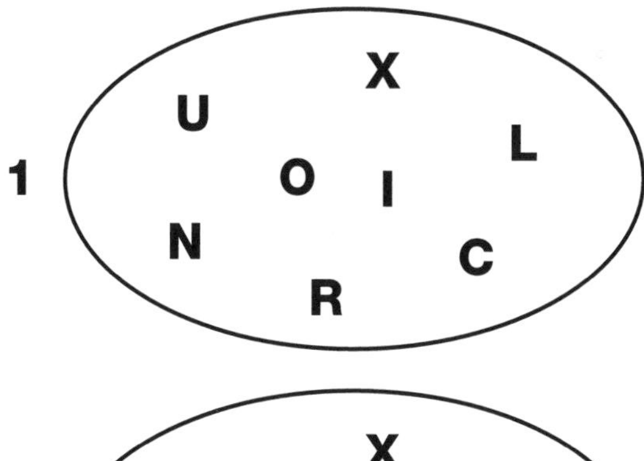

Where does the missing hand go?

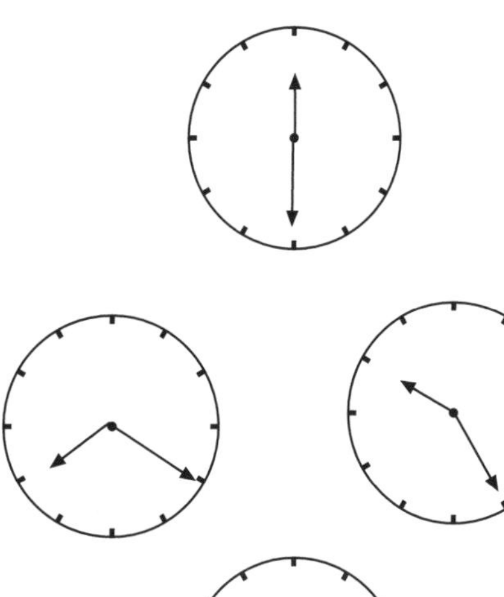

26 PUZZLE

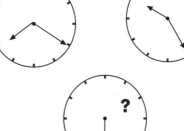

Following a logical sequence, can you complete this puzzle?

27 PUZZLE

What goes in the empty segment?

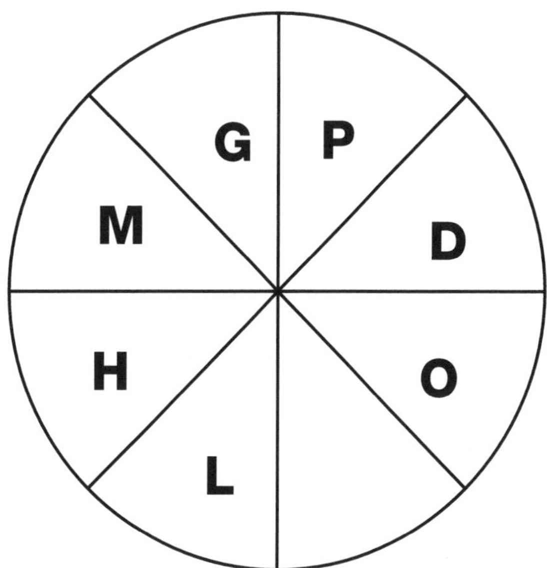

LEVEL 6

28 PUZZLE

What number is missing?

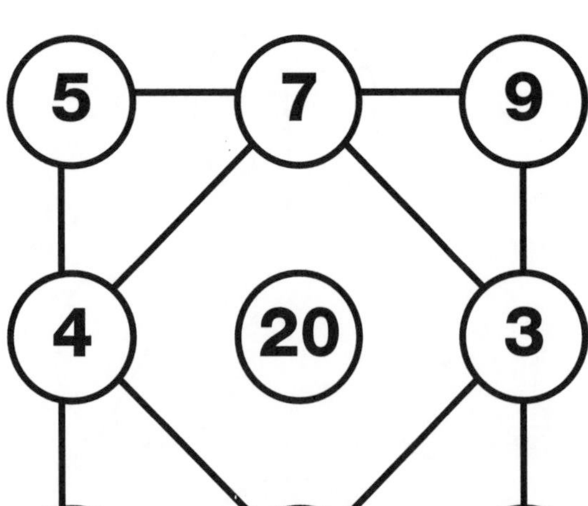

29 PUZZLE

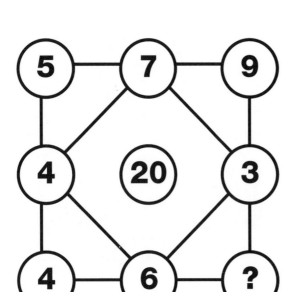

Following a logical sequence, can you complete this puzzle?

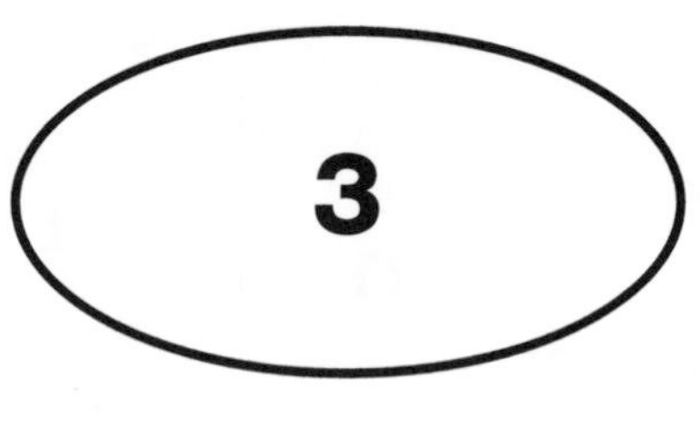

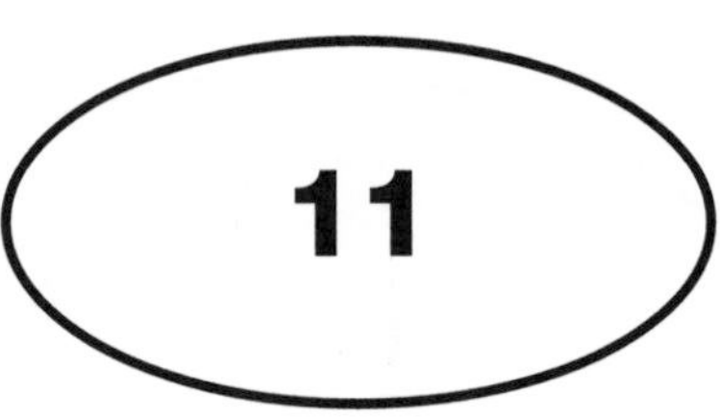

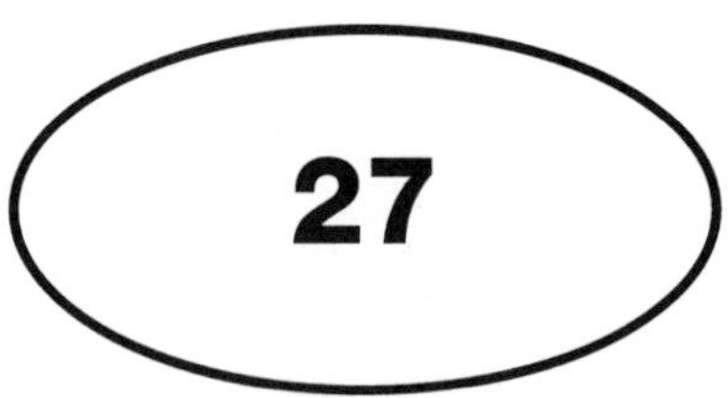

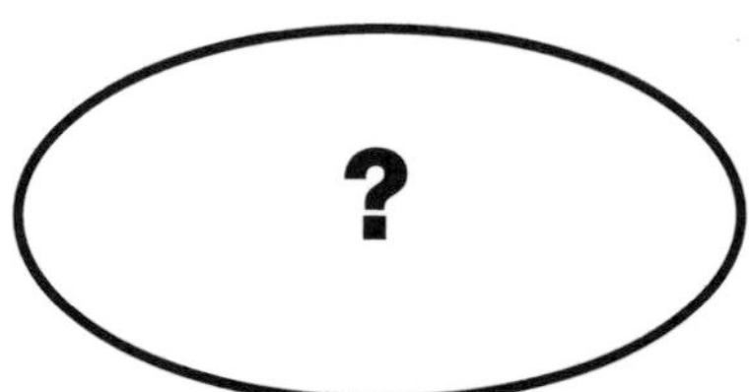

30 PUZZLE

What needs to be added to the third set of scales to make it balance perfectly?

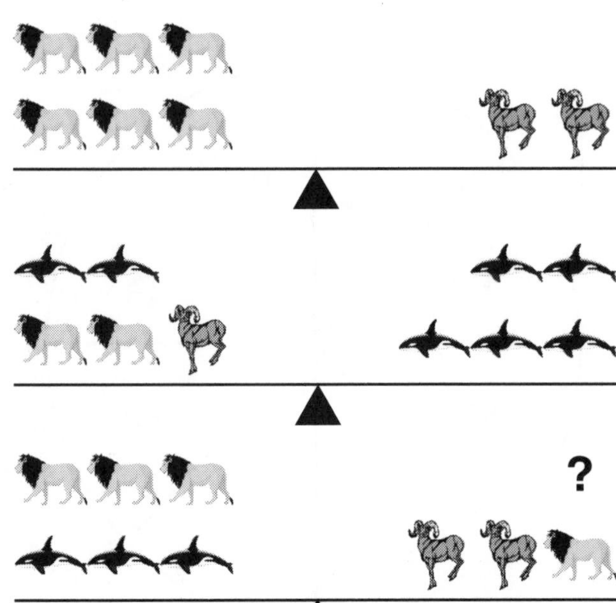

1 PUZZLE

What completes this puzzle?

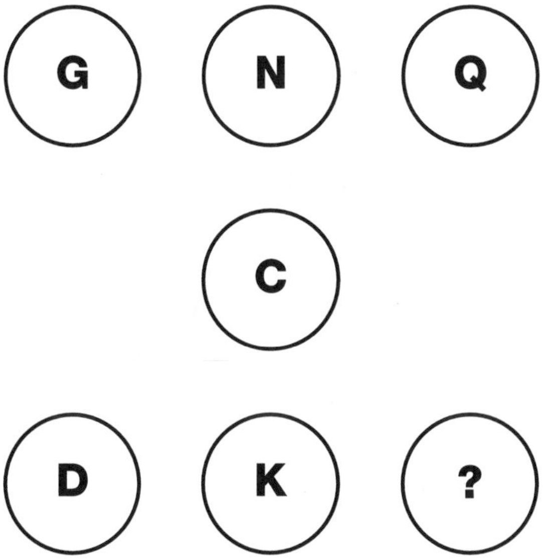

C

Which letter completes the puzzle?

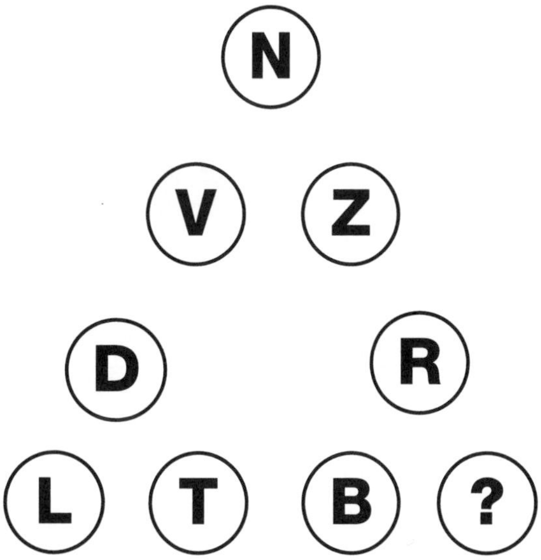

3 PUZZLE

Which of the lower patterns replaces the question mark to continue the sequence?

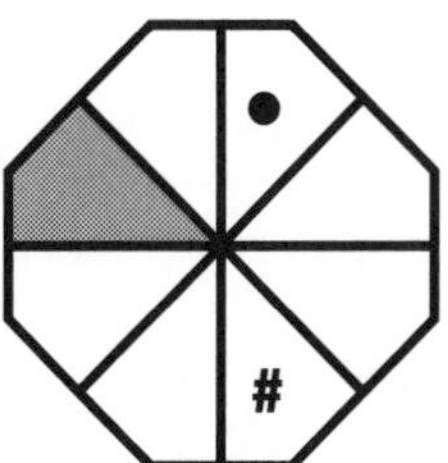

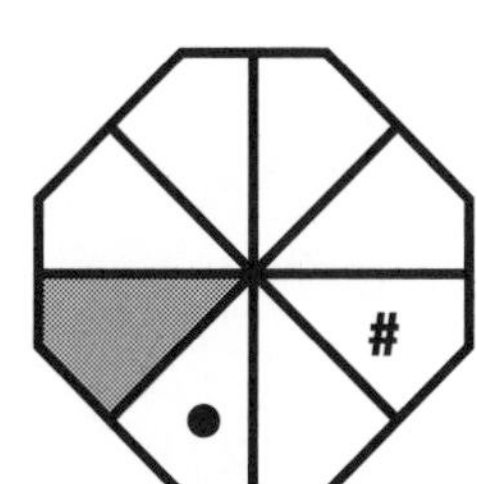

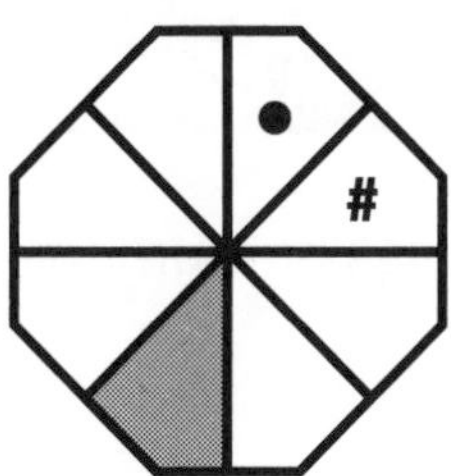

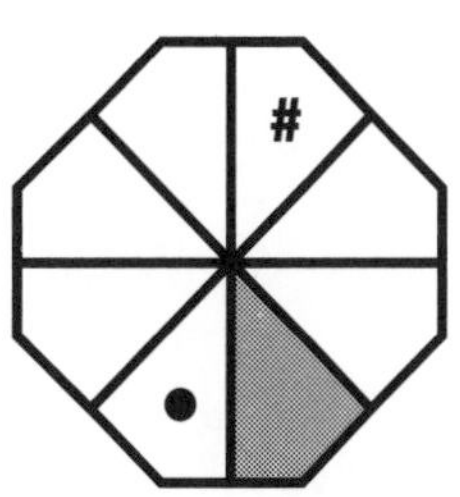

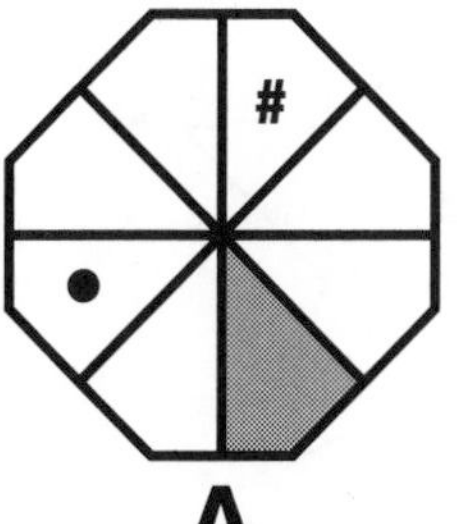

A

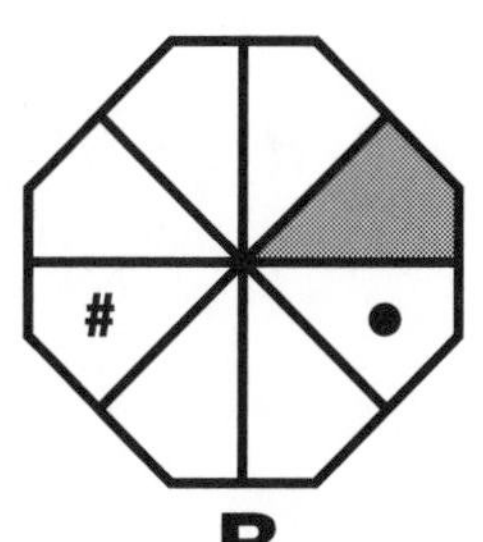

B

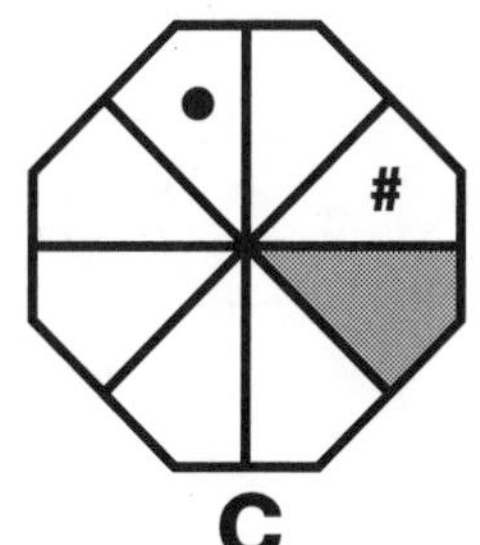

C

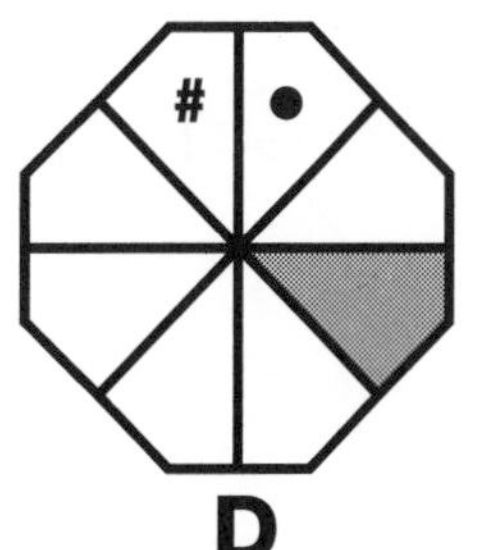

D

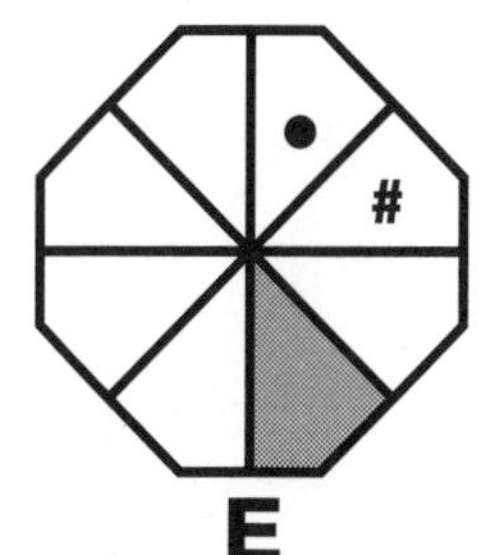

E

LEVEL

What number is missing?

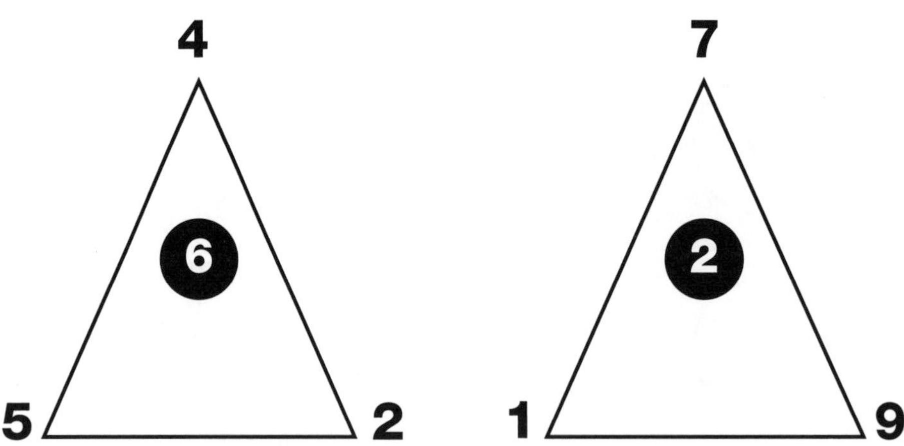

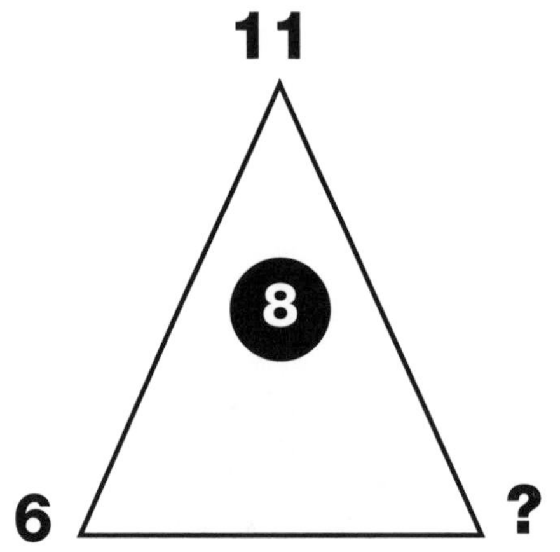

What is missing from the last star?

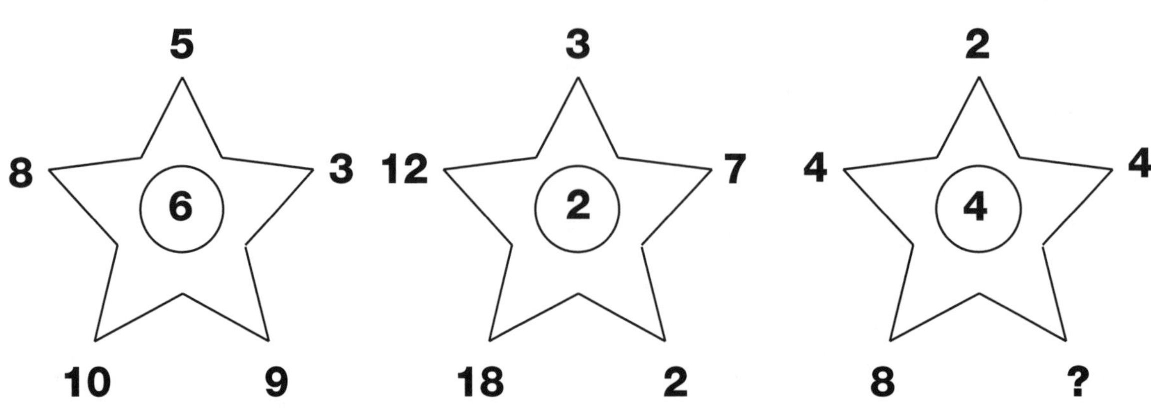

Which letter completes the puzzle?

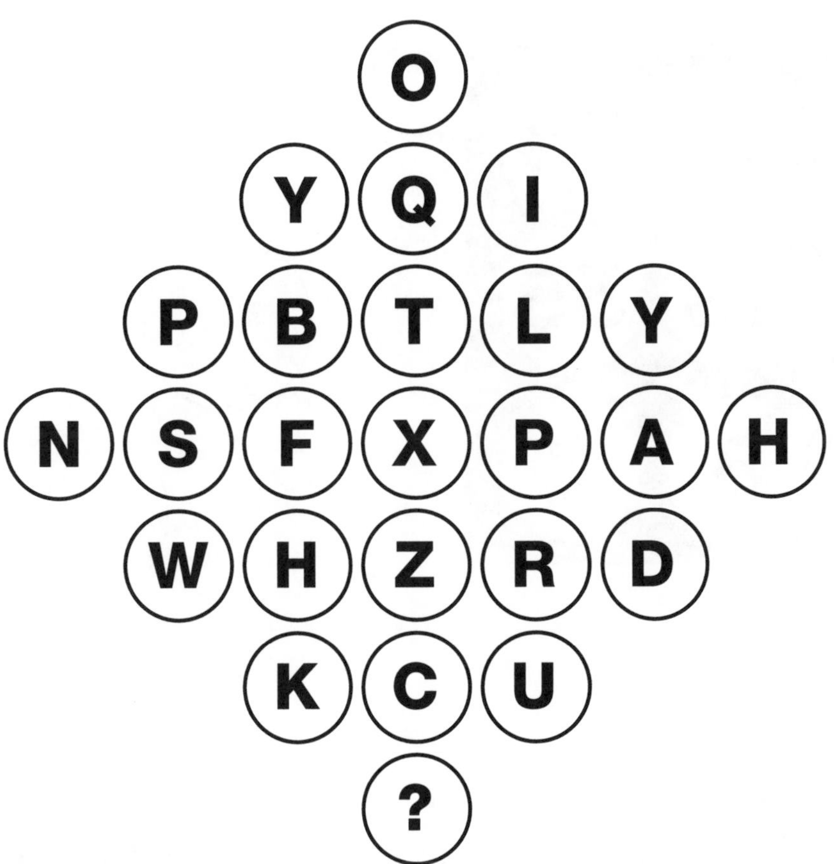

Following a logical sequence, can you complete this puzzle?

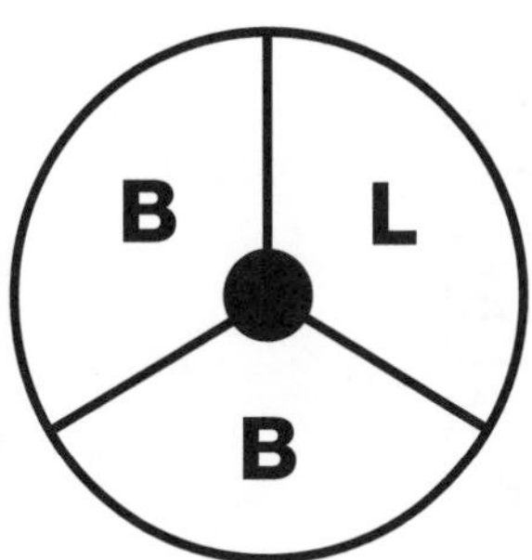

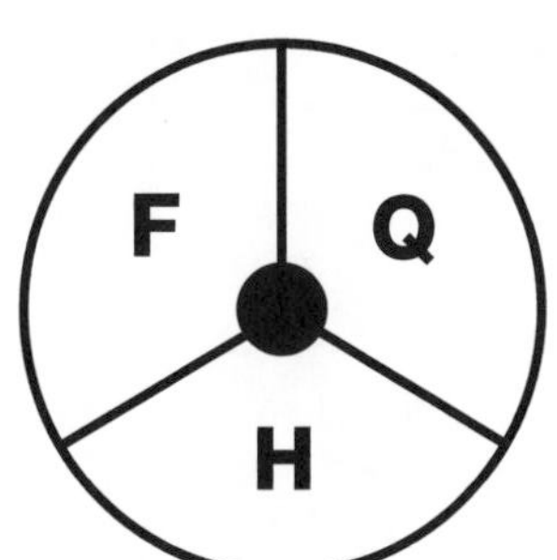

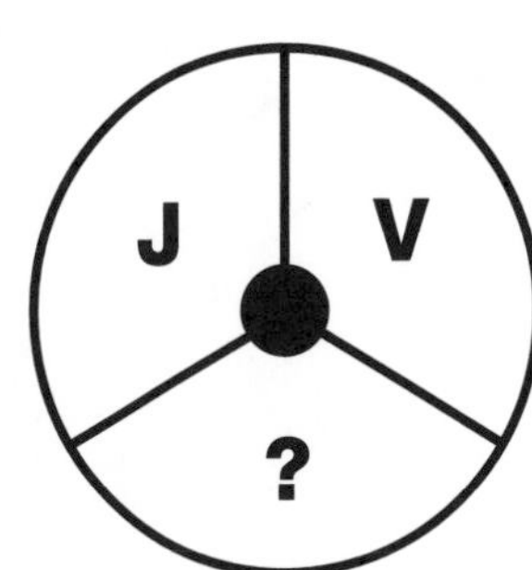

LEVEL 7

LEVEL

7

Which number completes this puzzle?

Where does the missing hand go?

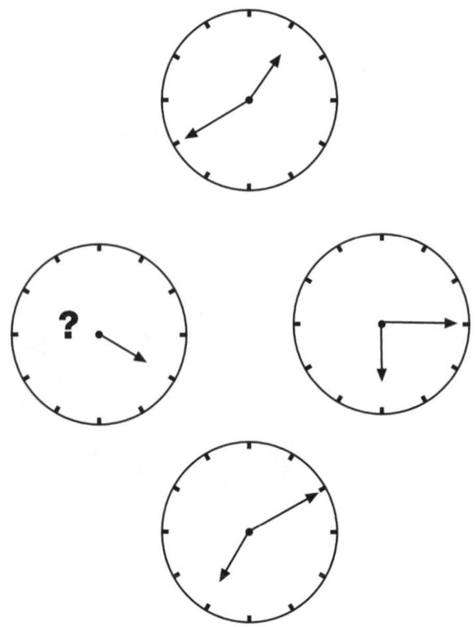

10 PUZZLE

Which letter follows? (Clue: this is the first time you have needed to think like this)

B C D G ?

11 PUZZLE

In this sequence of numbers, what completes the puzzle?

5	7
7	10
11	16
19	28
35	52
67	?

What number is missing?

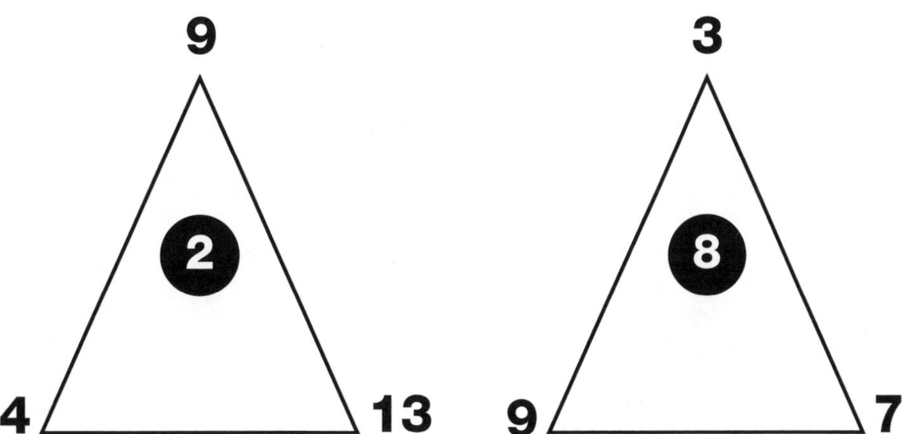

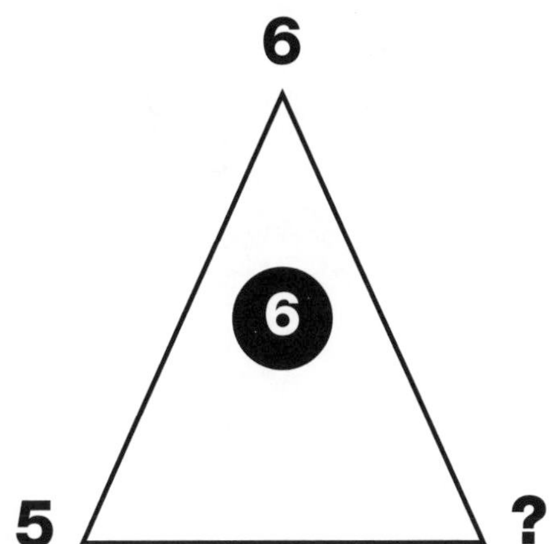

What is missing from the last triangle?

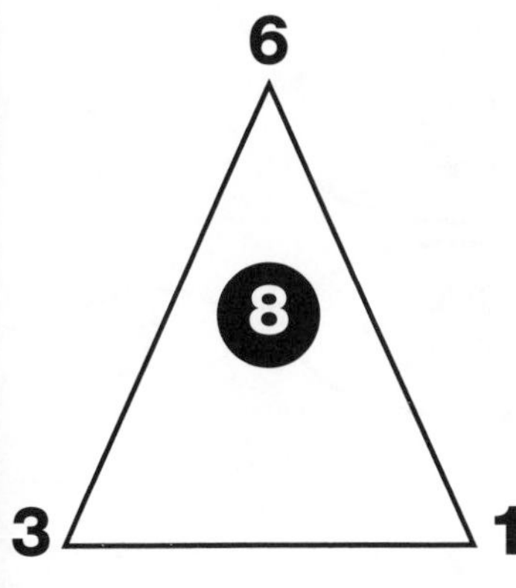

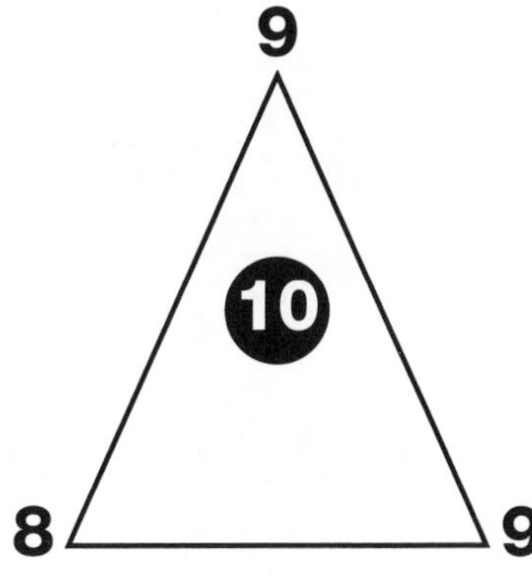

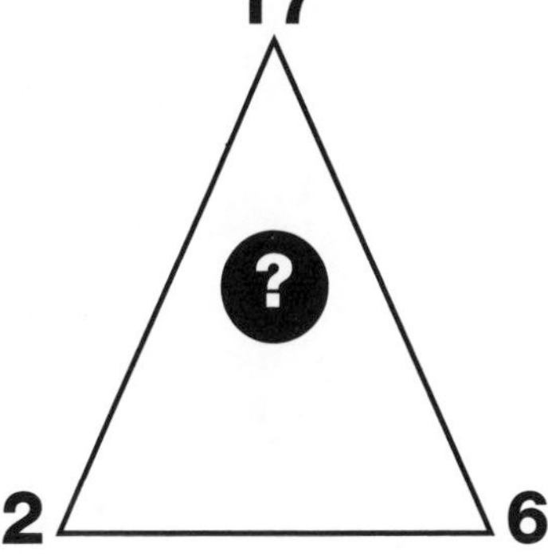

LEVEL

7

LEVEL

7

14 PUZZLE

What is needed in this triangle to complete the puzzle?

Which letter completes the puzzle?

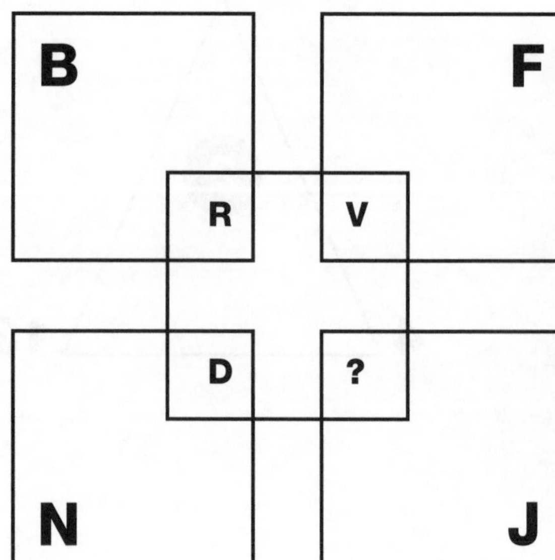

16 PUZZLE

Following a logical sequence, can you complete this puzzle?

92

22

What letter is missing?

18 PUZZLE

Which number goes in the lower right hand segment?

What replaces the question mark?

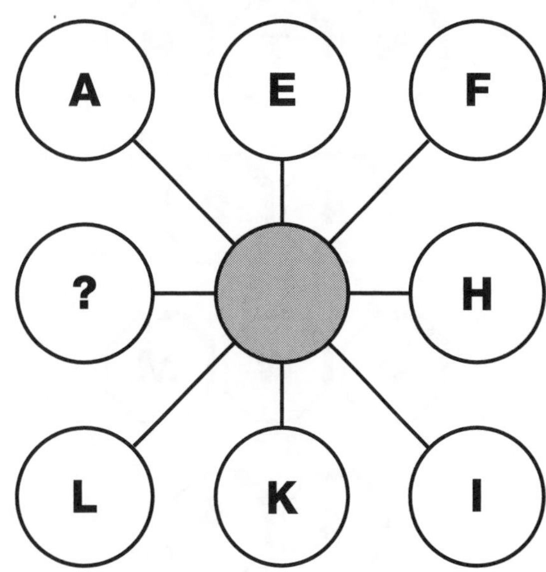

20 PUZZLE

Following a logical sequence, can you complete this puzzle?

Can you remove three matches to leave three squares?

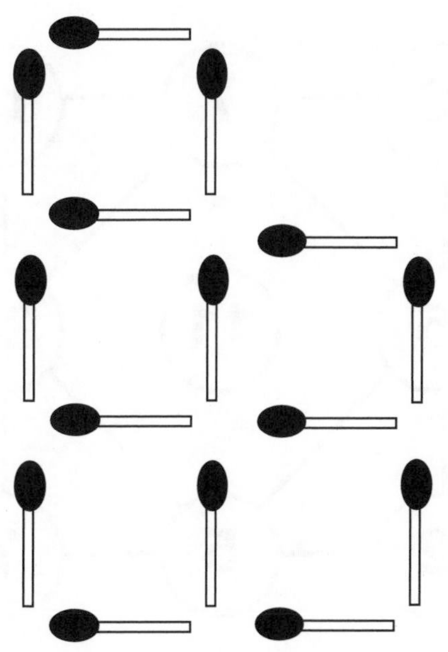

LEVEL 7

What completes this sequence?

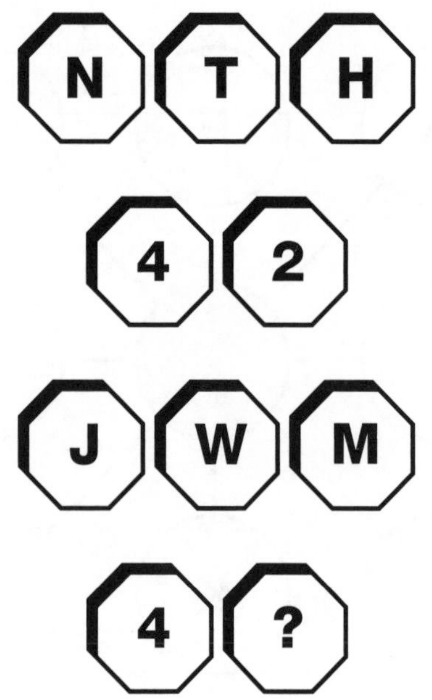

Which letter completes the puzzle?

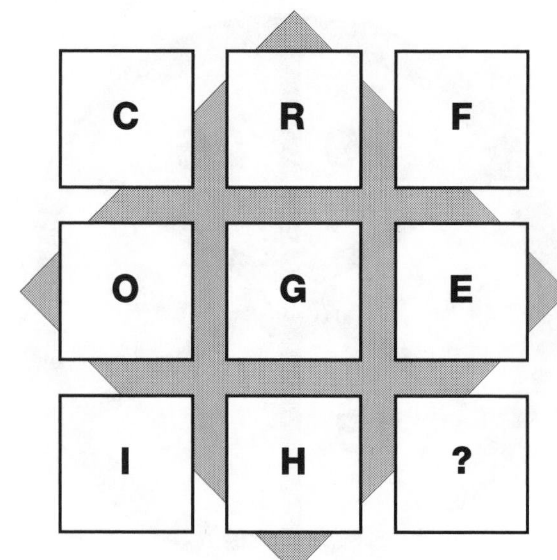

24
PUZZLE

What number is missing?

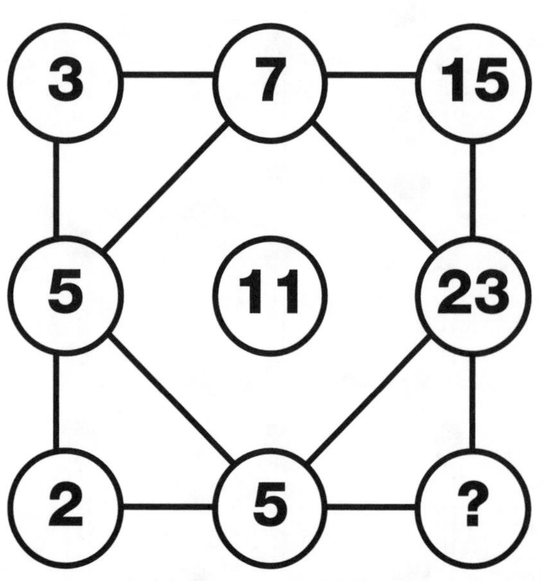

Can you trace around this figure using only 10 straight lines, without lifting your pen off the paper, or drawing over any line twice?

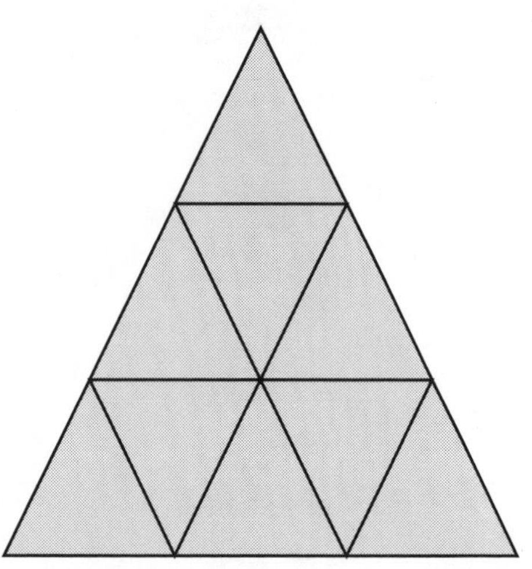

Complete this puzzle.

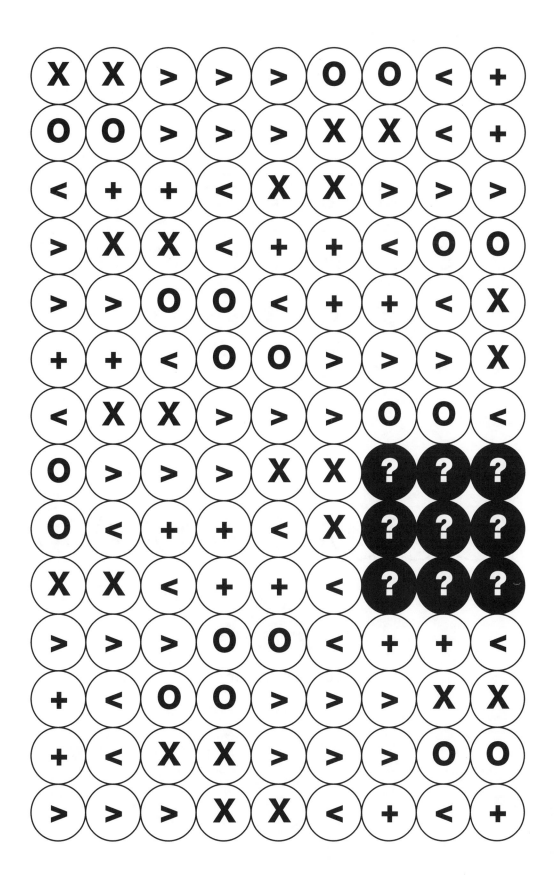

X	X	>	>	>	O	O	<	+
O	O	>	>	>	X	X	<	+
<	+	+	<	X	X	>	>	>
>	X	X	<	+	+	<	O	O
>	>	O	O	<	+	+	<	X
+	+	<	O	O	>	>	>	X
<	X	X	>	>	>	O	O	<
O	>	>	>	X	X	?	?	?
O	<	+	+	<	X	?	?	?
X	X	<	+	+	<	?	?	?
>	>	>	O	O	<	+	+	<
+	<	O	O	>	>	>	X	X
+	<	X	X	>	>	>	O	O
>	>	>	X	X	<	+	<	+

LEVEL

8

Which letter completes the puzzle?

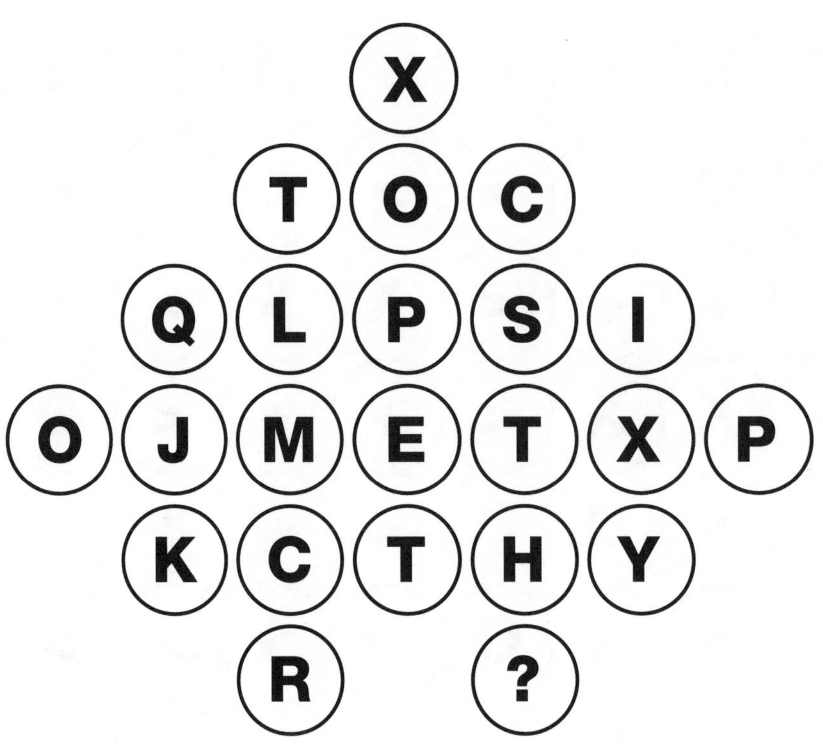

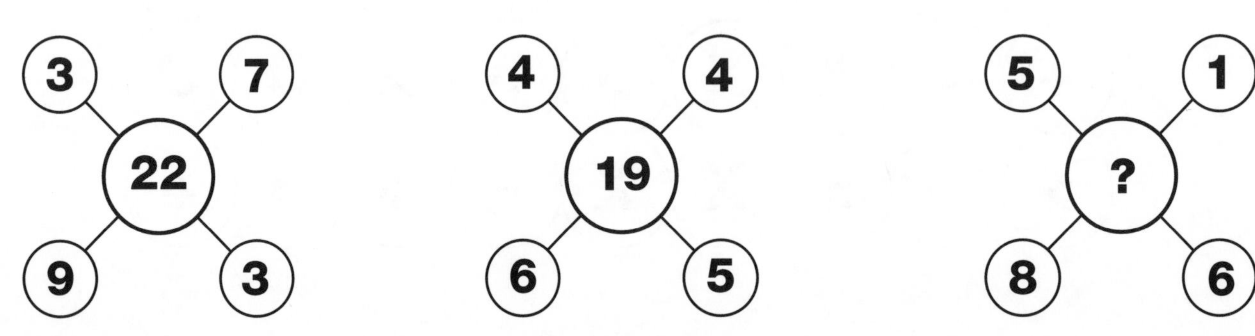

Which number is missing?

What number is missing?

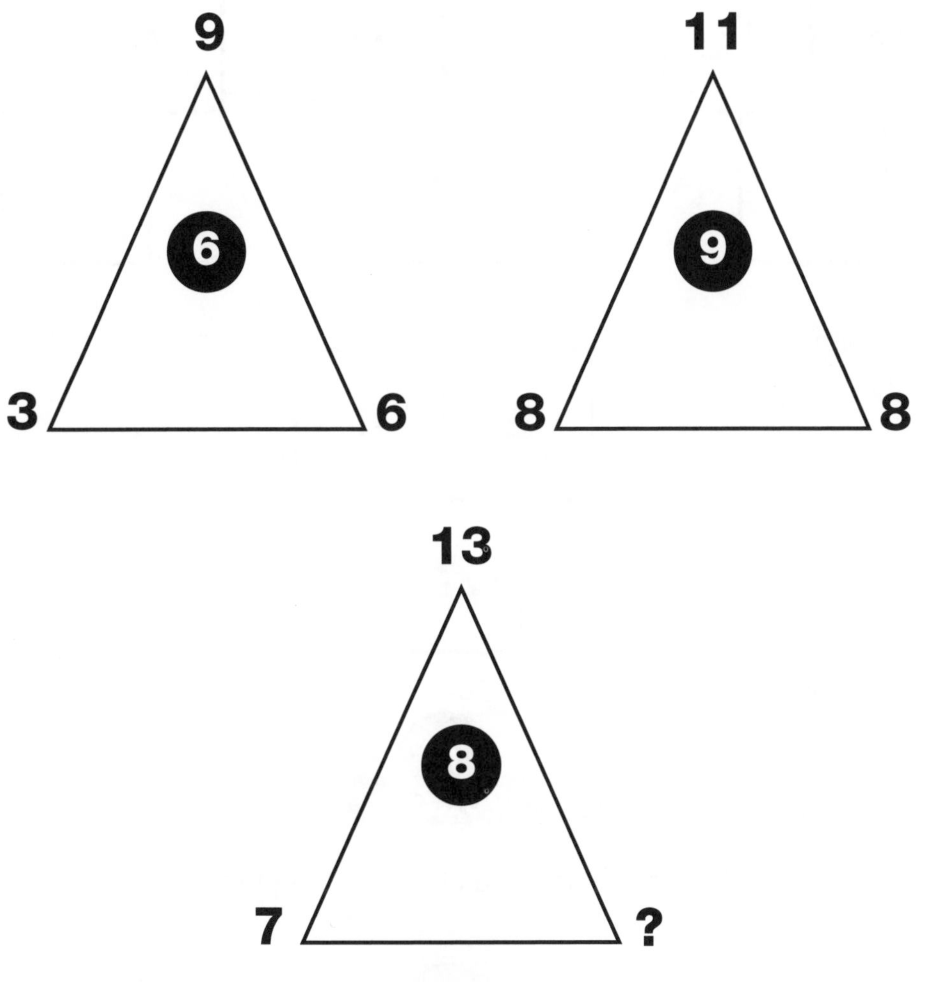

4 PUZZLE

Which number replaces the question mark?

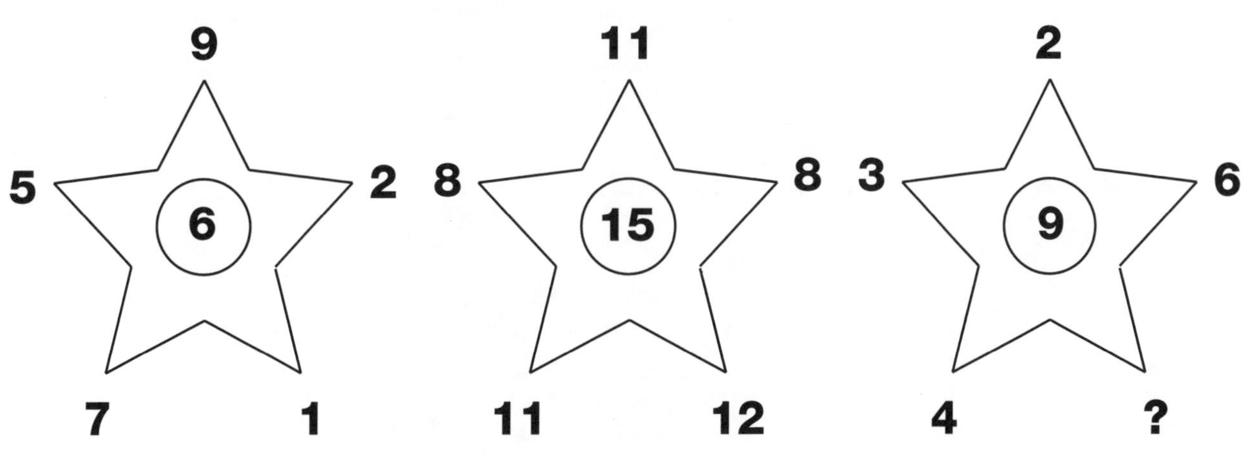

LEVEL 8

What is missing from the bottom square?

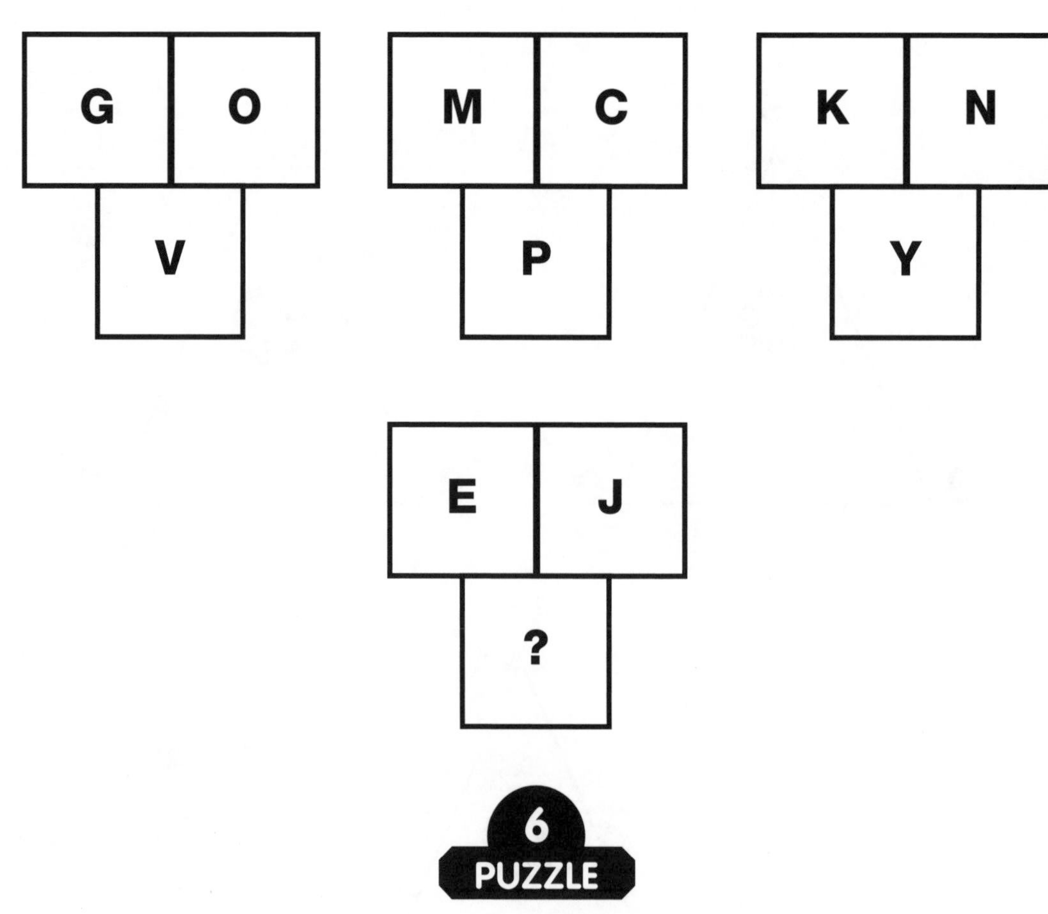

6 PUZZLE

Which of the bottom watches fills the empty space?

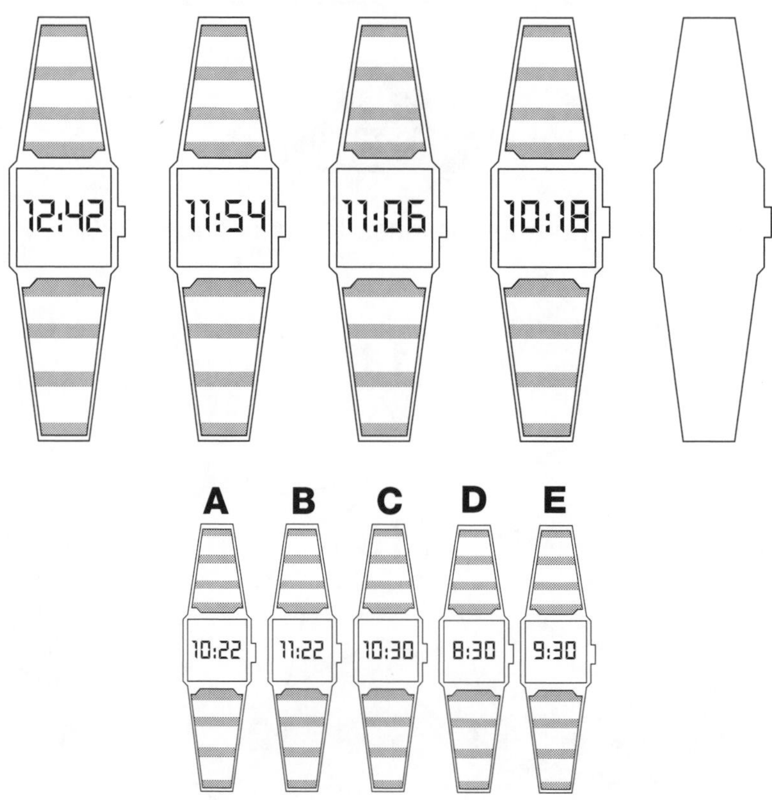

7 PUZZLE

Following a logical sequence, can you complete this puzzle?

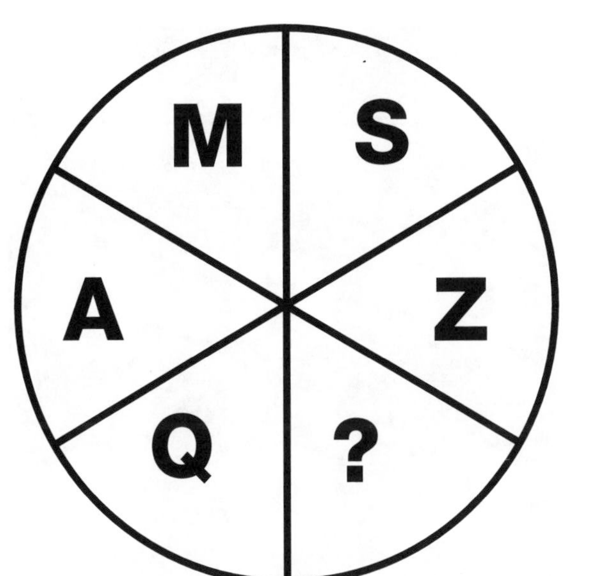

8 PUZZLE

What letter is missing?

9 PUZZLE

Which two letters complete this puzzle?

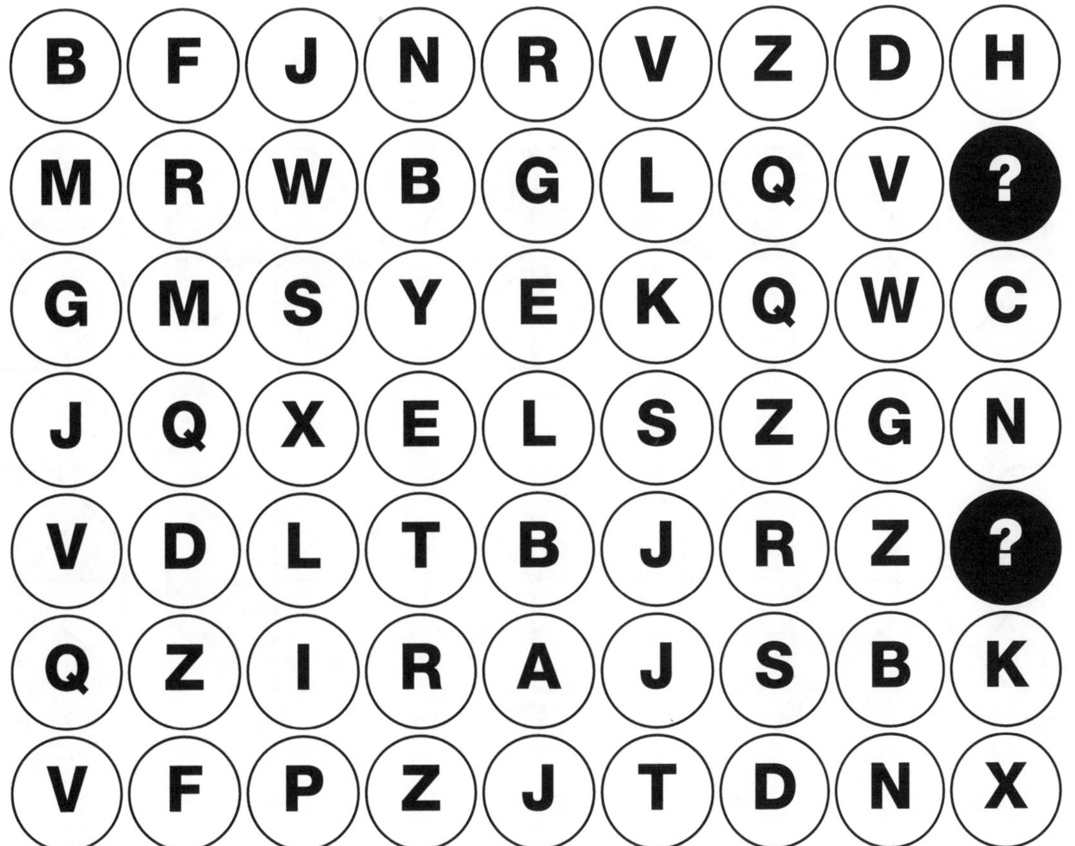

LEVEL

8

10 PUZZLE

What completes this puzzle?

11 PUZZLE

Which letter is needed to complete the puzzle?

12 PUZZLE

Which of the lower patterns finishes the sequence?

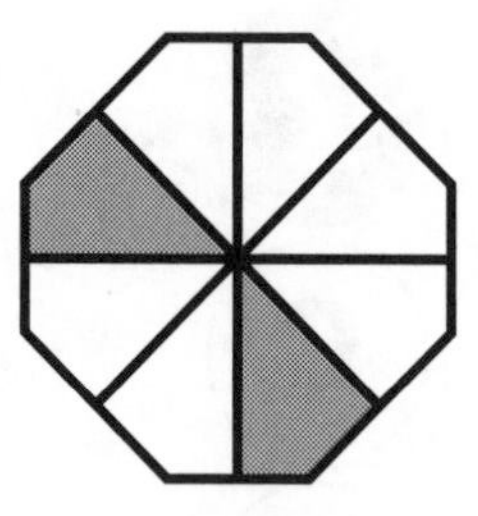
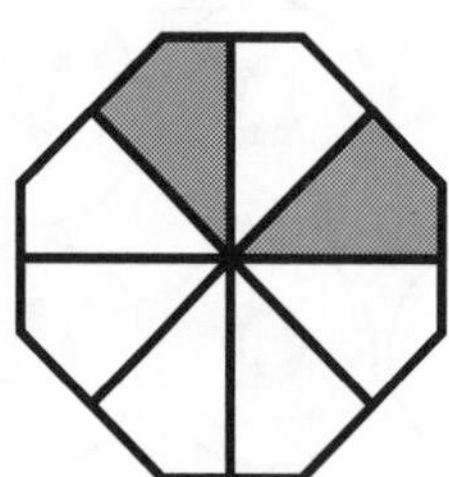
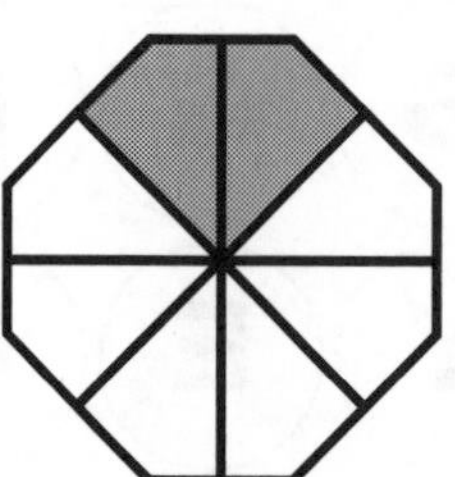
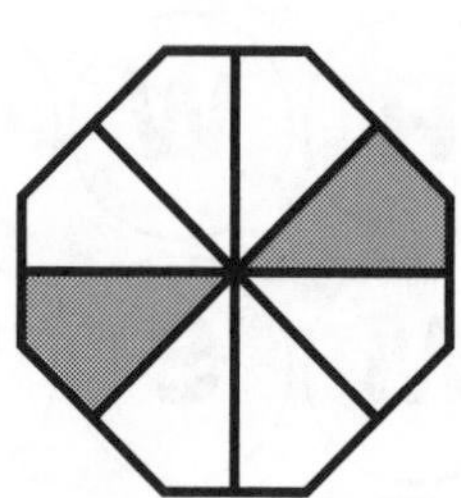

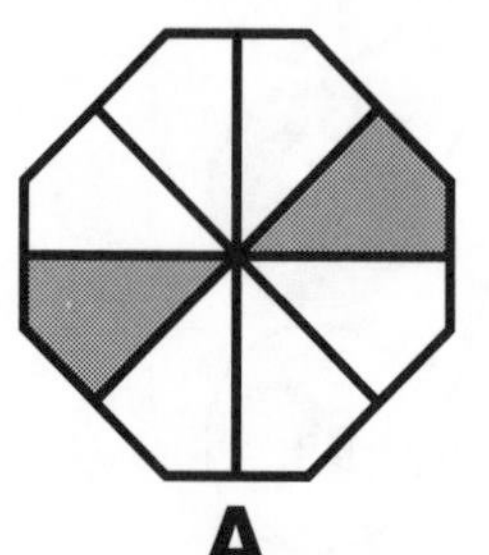
A

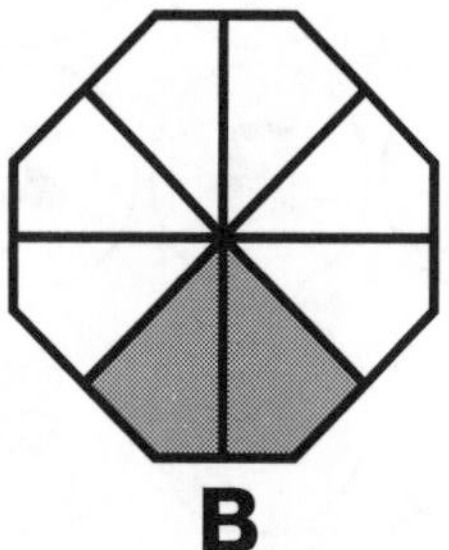
B

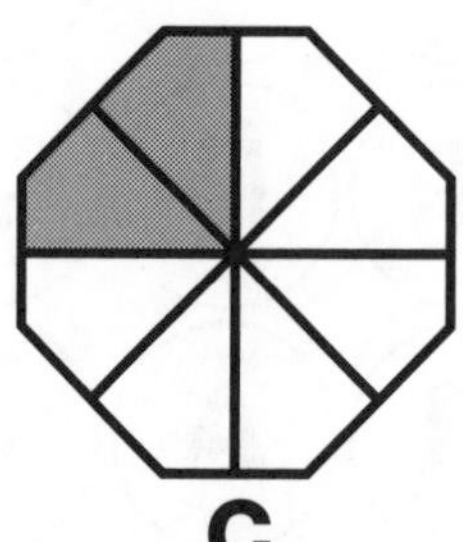
C

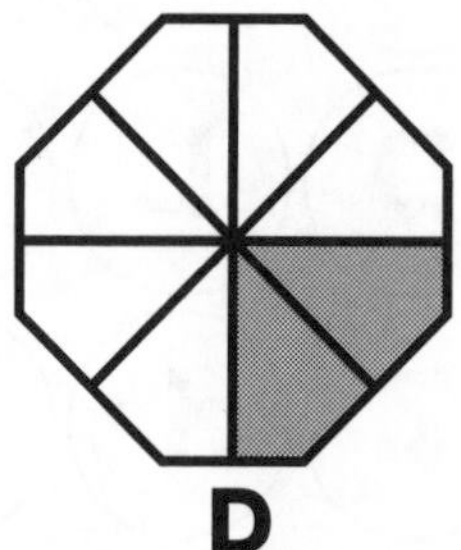
D

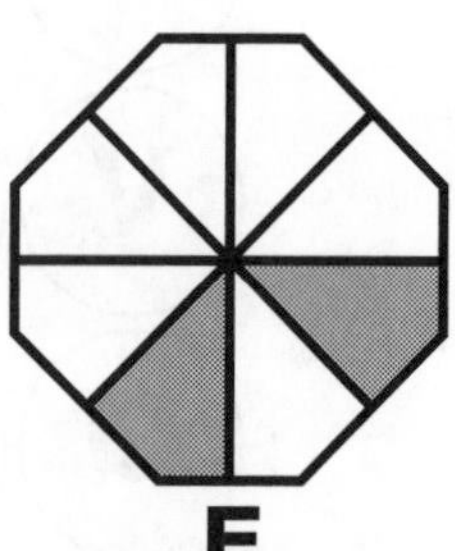
E

LEVEL 8

13 PUZZLE

What number is missing?

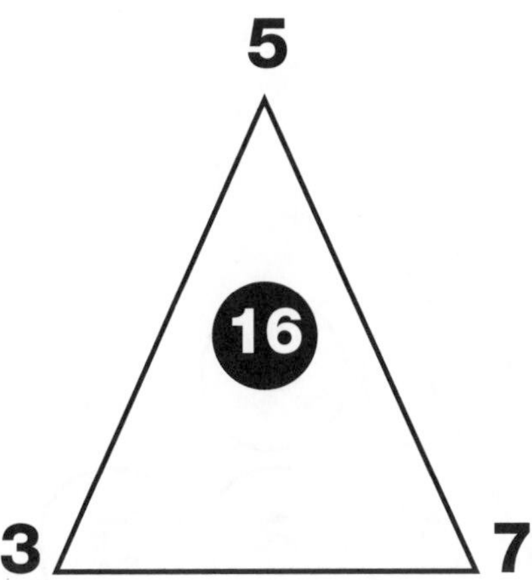

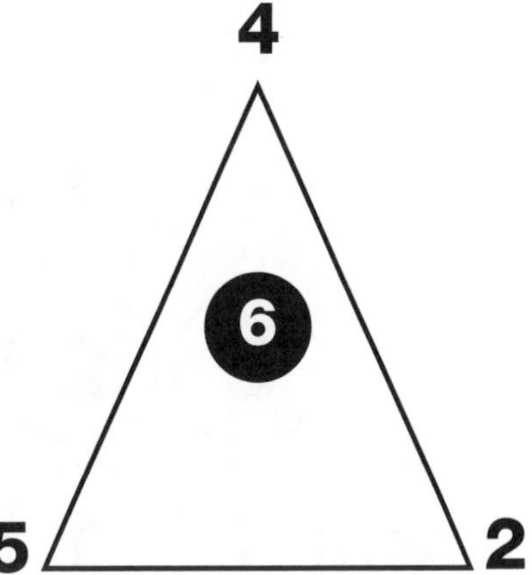

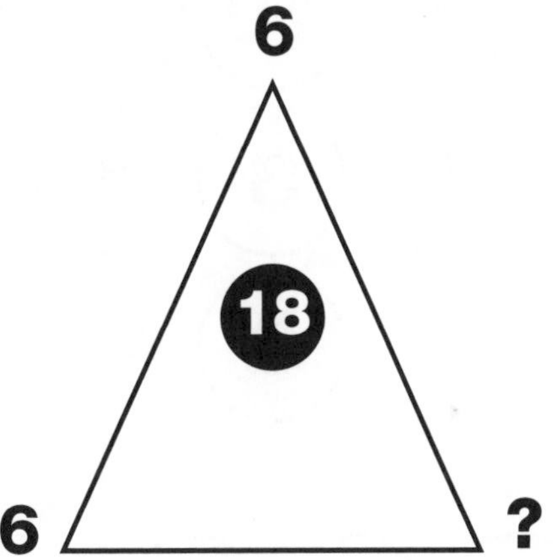

Following a logical sequence, can you complete this puzzle?

What is needed to complete this sequence?

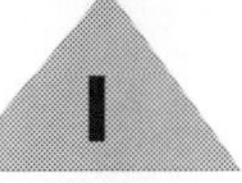

LEVEL 8

What number is missing from the centre?

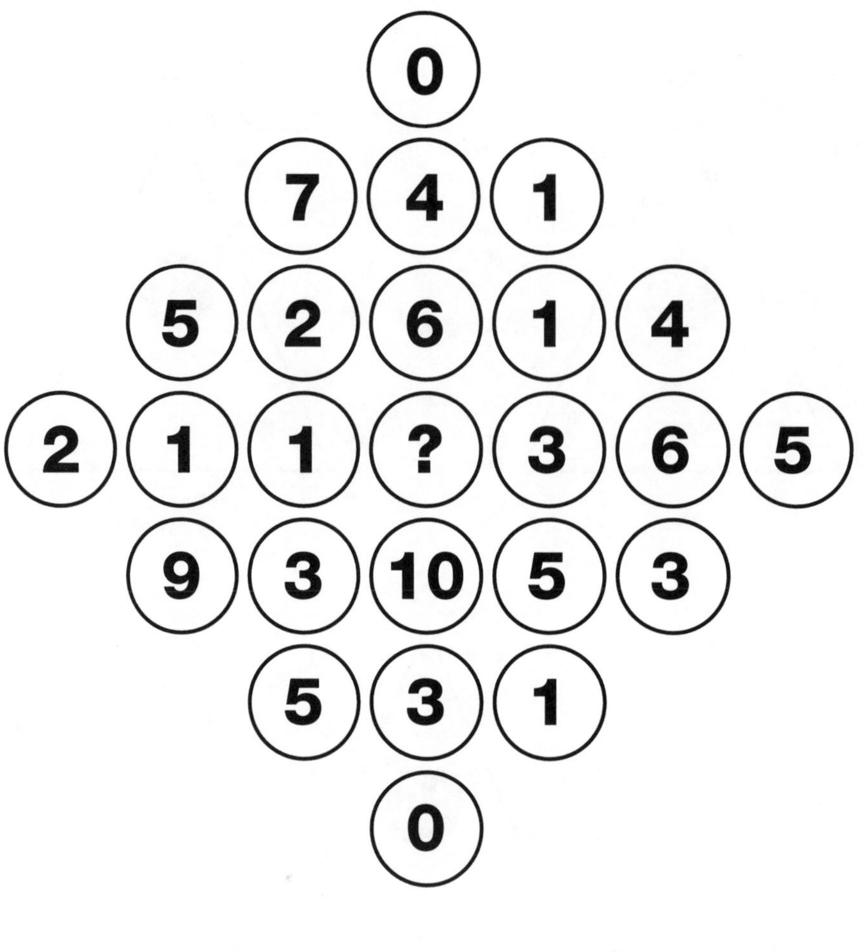

17 PUZZLE

Move two matches only to make this sum correct.

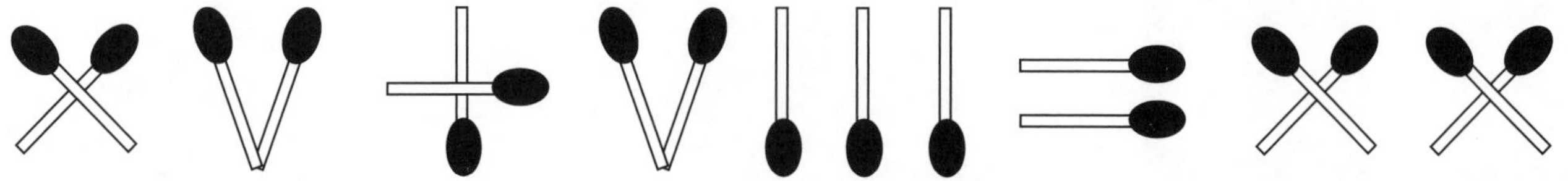

18 PUZZLE

Which letter is missing?

A

D

I

P

?

19 PUZZLE

Which number completes this wheel?

20 PUZZLE

Which number completes the puzzle?

D		K
19		12
16		?
O		H

21 PUZZLE

What is needed to complete this sequence?

5	9
14	4
18	10
28	8
36	20
56	?

LEVEL 8

LEVEL 8

22 PUZZLE

Following a logical sequence, can you complete this puzzle?

What number is missing?

24 PUZZLE

What number is missing from the bottom right hand circle?

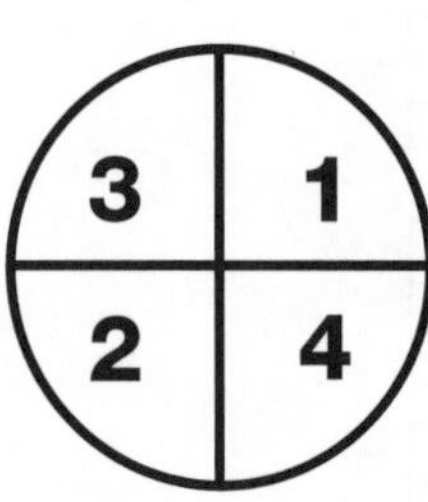

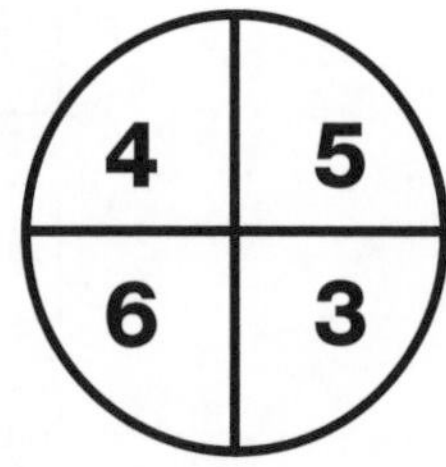

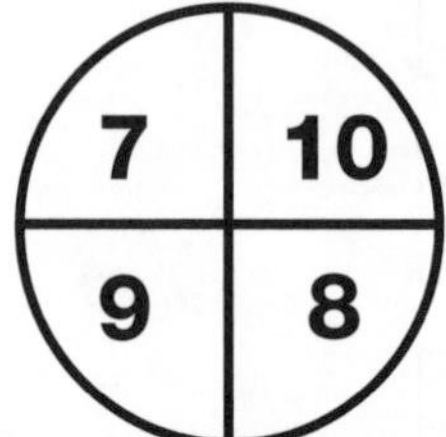

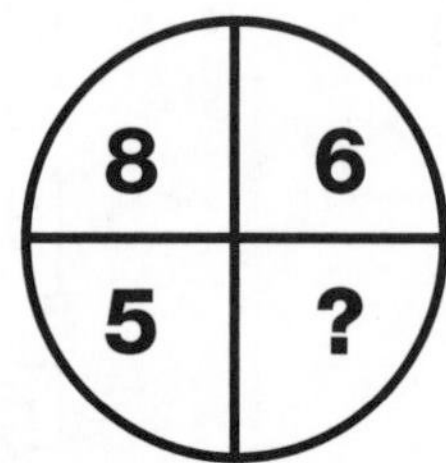

Where should the missing hand go?

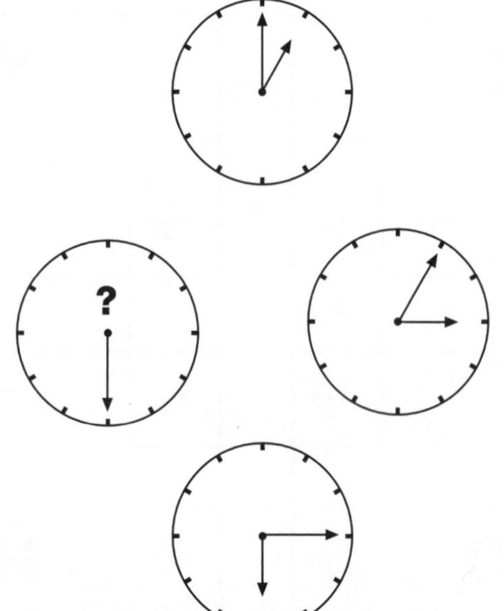

What is missing from this wheel?

Which letter completes the puzzle?

B F J P ?

3
PUZZLE

What number is missing?

4
PUZZLE

What is needed to complete this puzzle?

LEVEL

9

5 PUZZLE

What number is missing from the bottom triangle?

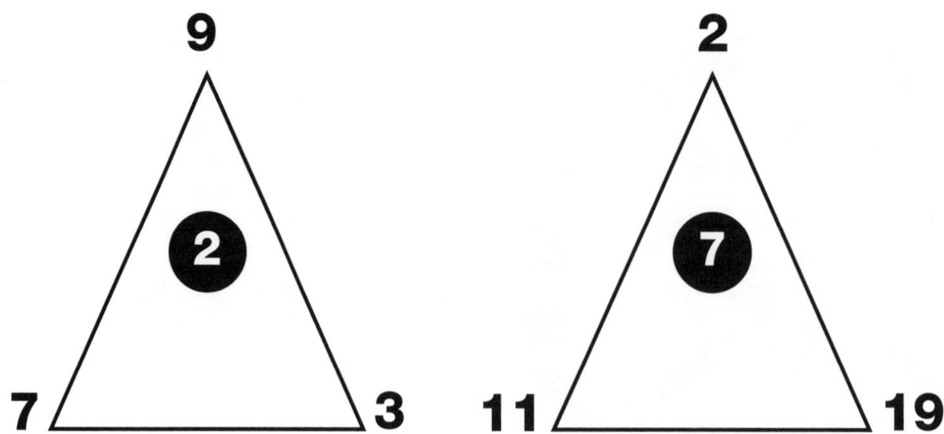

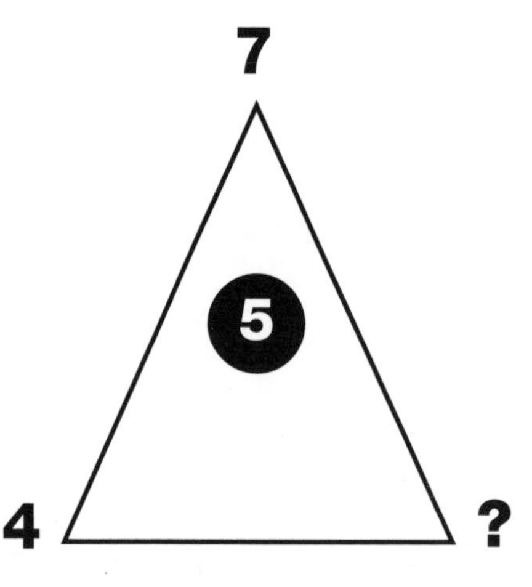

Which letter should go on top of the last star?

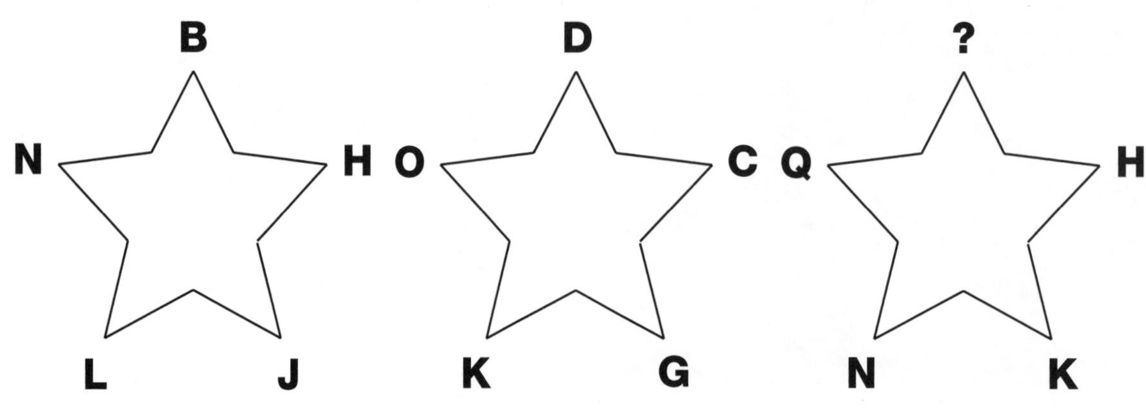

PUZZLE 7

What number completes this grid?

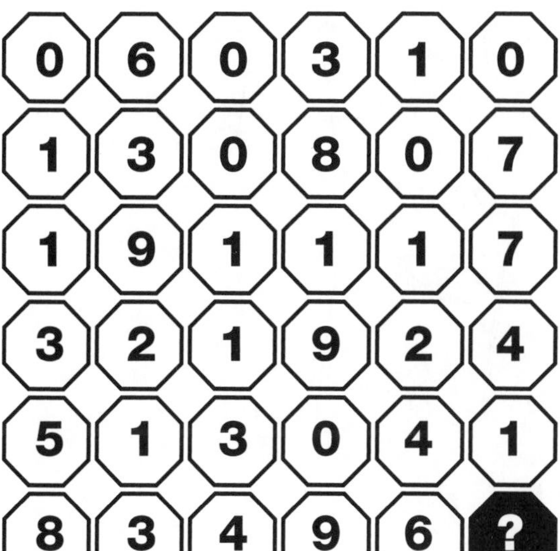

PUZZLE 8

Following a logical sequence, can you complete this puzzle?

6
9
15
27
?

PUZZLE 9

Which piece fits back into the grid?

5	3	6	8	1	1	7	4	7	0
9	2	1	3	7	8	3	6	3	8
1	3	0	6	4	6	1	0	5	9
6	4	5	3			2	3	4	7
4	7	9					1	6	4
4	6	1					9	7	4
7	4	3	2			3	5	4	6
9	5	0	1	6	4	6	0	3	1
8	3	6	3	8	7	3	1	2	9
0	7	4	7	1	1	8	6	3	5

1

	9	8	
3	5	0	7
7	0	5	3
	8	9	

2

	8	7	
8	0	3	9
0	5	3	5
	9	7	

3

	9	7	
3	5	1	8
8	1	5	3
	7	9	

4

	4	8	
3	1	0	7
7	9	4	6
	2	7	

5

	7	3	
8	0	5	9
9	5	0	8
	3	7	

LEVEL

9

Which of the bottom watches fills the gap?

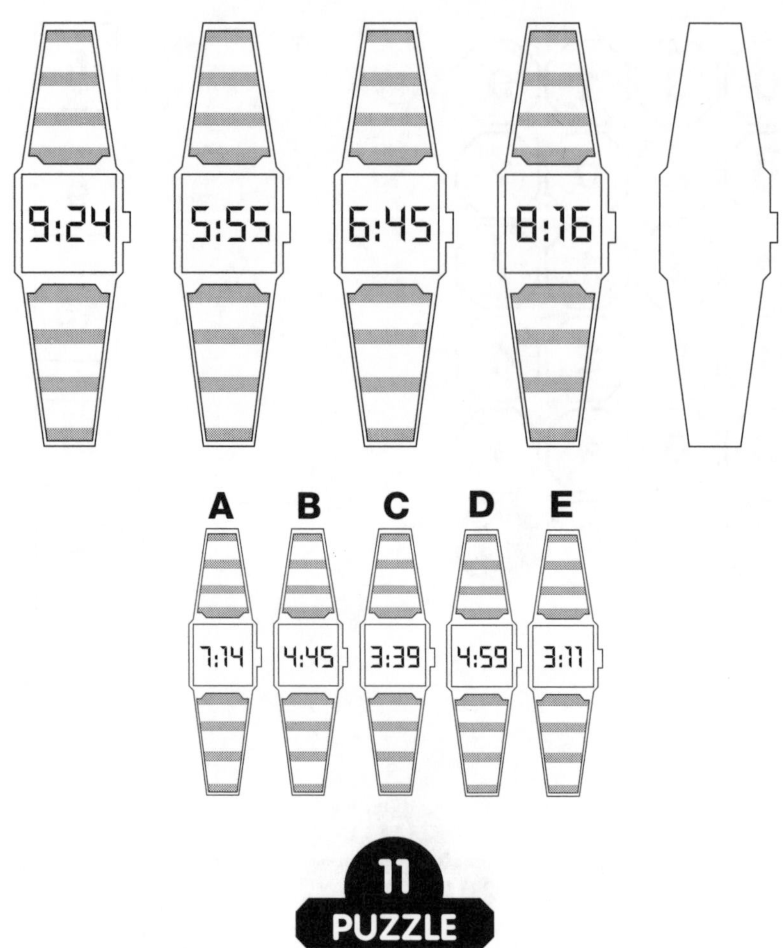

11

PUZZLE

Which of the bottom patterns replaces the question mark?

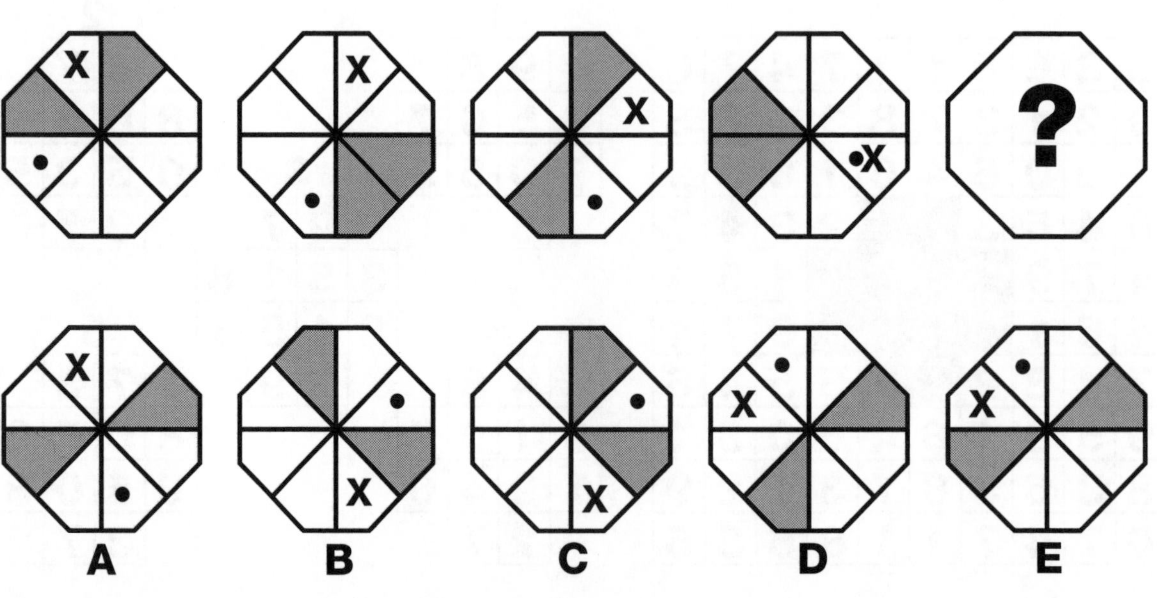

Following a logical sequence, can you complete this puzzle?

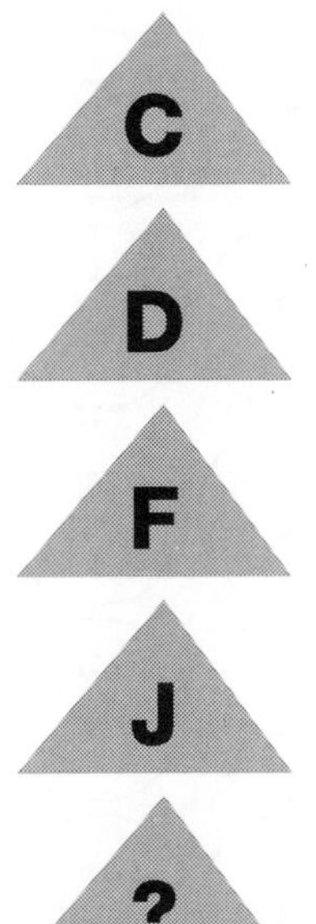

What number is missing?

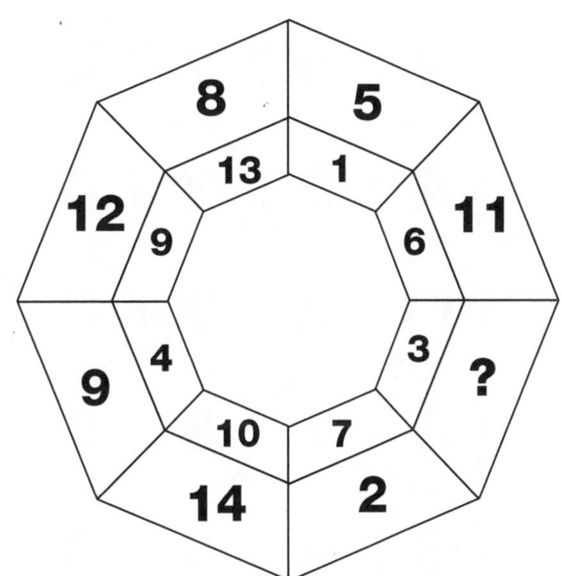

14 PUZZLE

What number completes the puzzle?

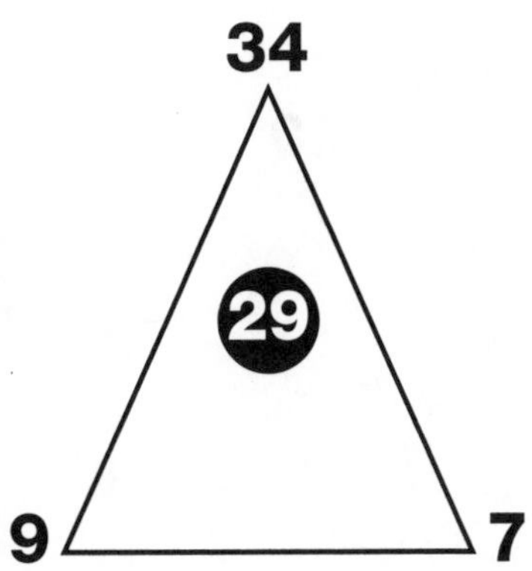

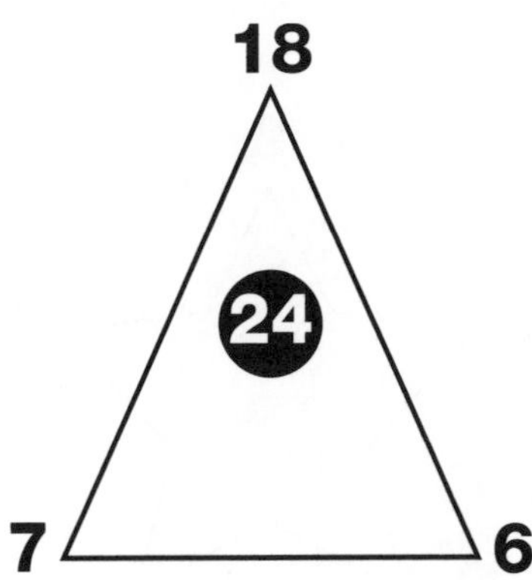

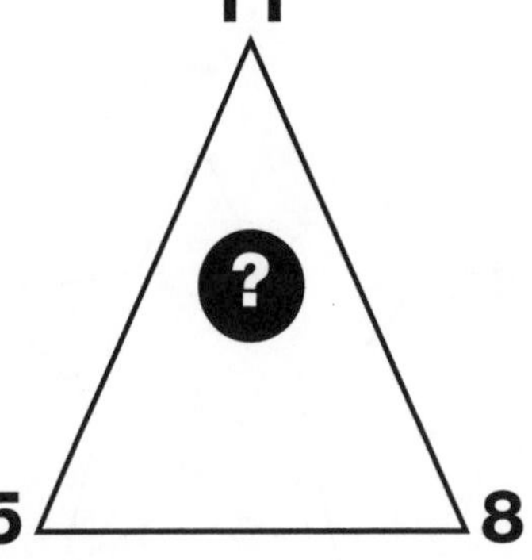

LEVEL 9

LEVEL 9

What is needed to complete this grid?

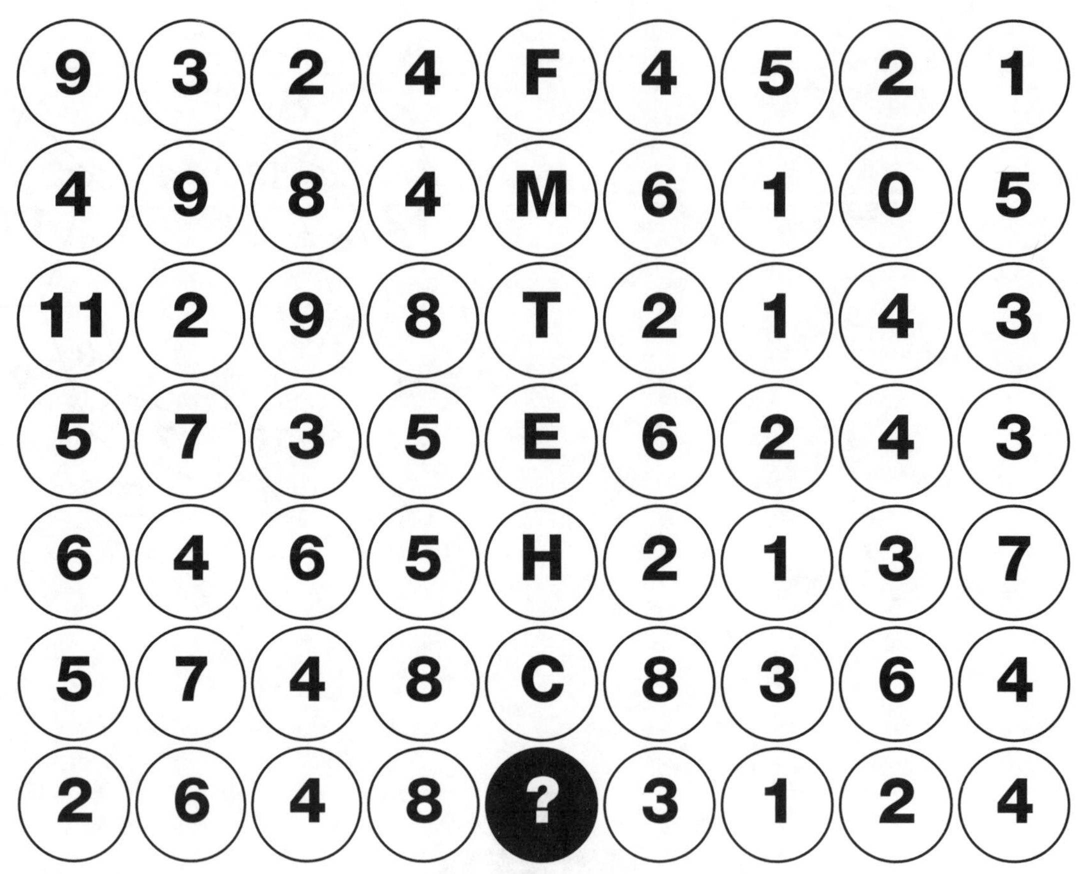

16 PUZZLE

Which number is missing from the last star?

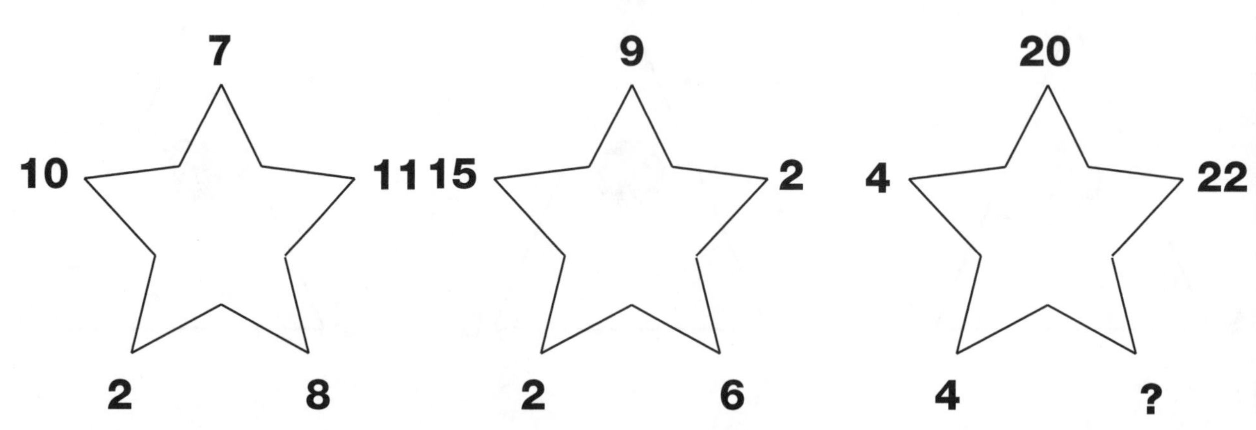

Which letter is missing?

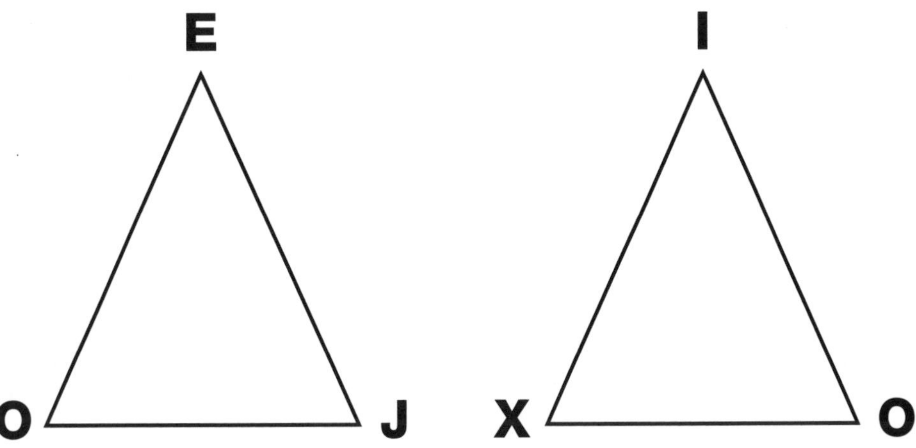

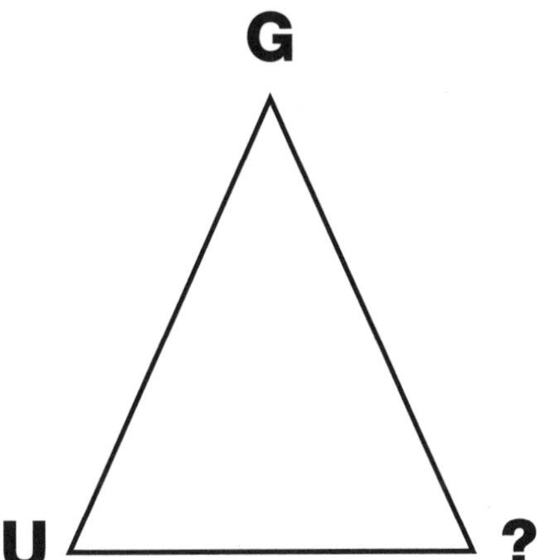

What number is missing?

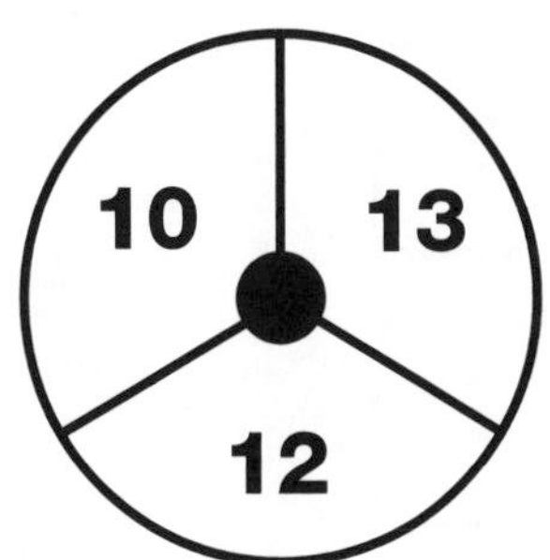

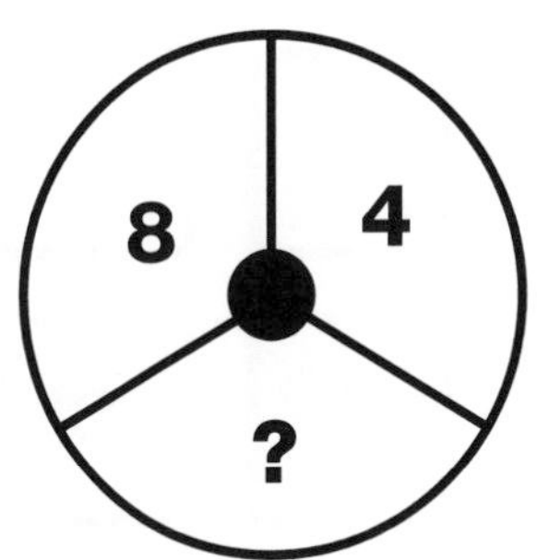

LEVEL 9

LEVEL 9

19 PUZZLE

What is missing from the last shape?

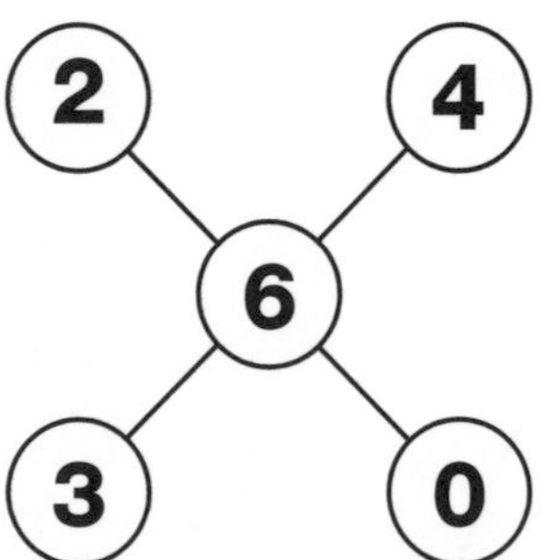

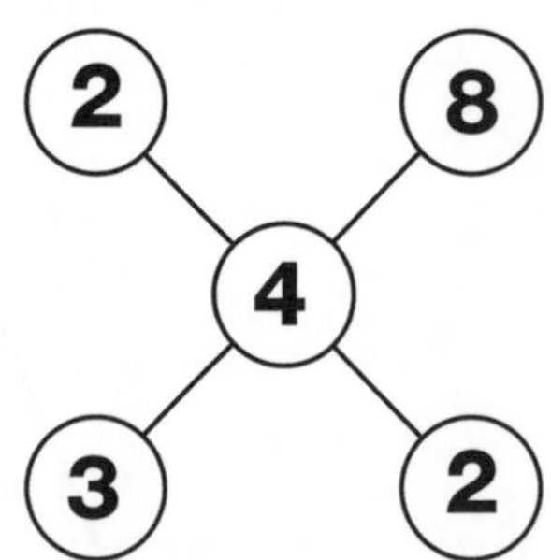

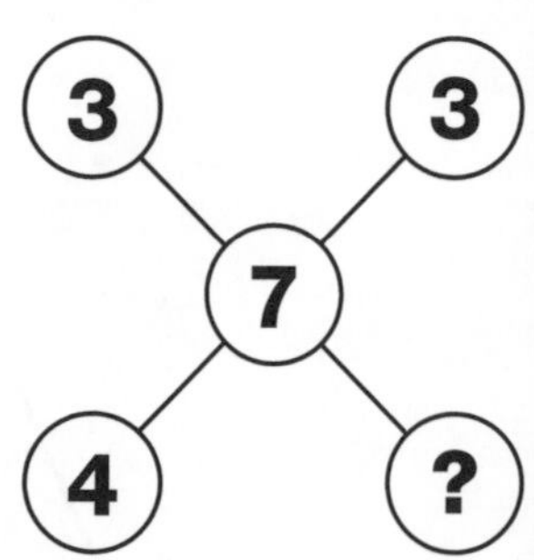

20 PUZZLE

Following a logical sequence, can you complete this puzzle?

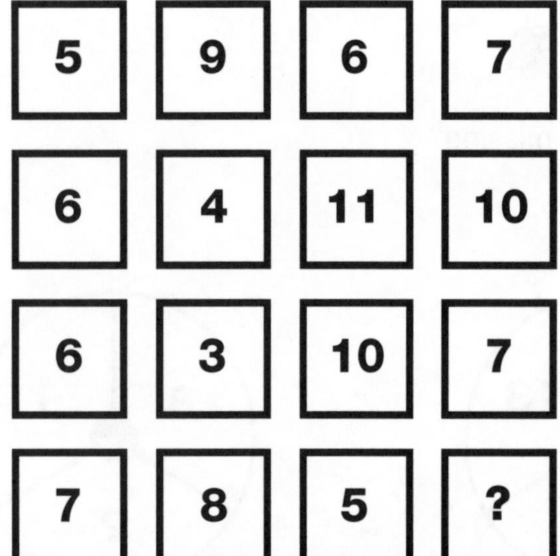

5	9	6	7
6	4	11	10
6	3	10	7
7	8	5	?

Move just four matches to reduce the area of this triangle by exactly half.

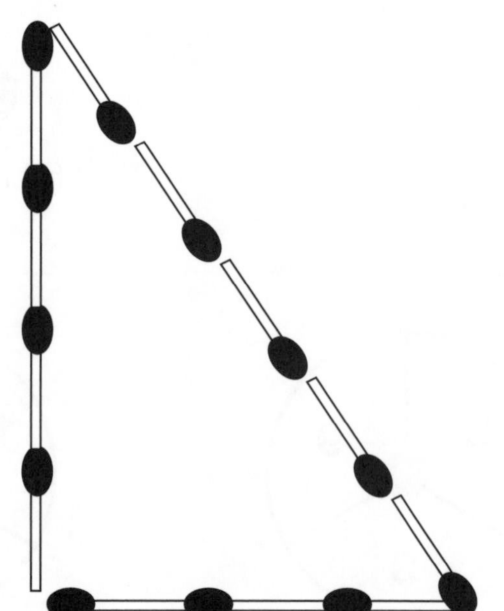

What number is missing?

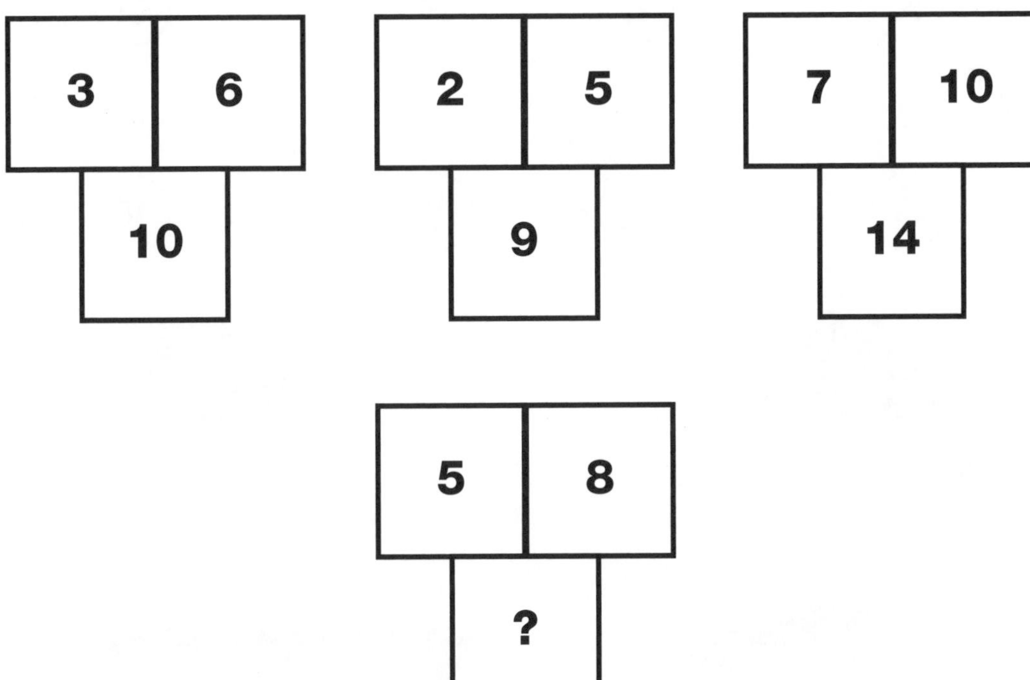

23 PUZZLE

Which letter completes the wheel?

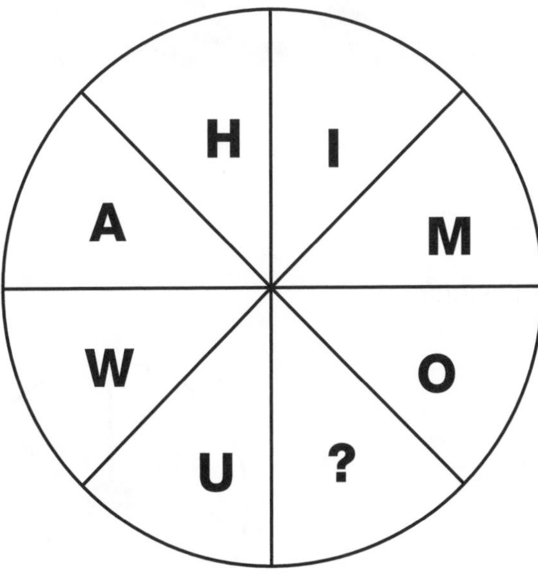

24 PUZZLE

Place every digit 1 to 9, in this puzzle, so that all horizontal, vertical and diagonal lines add up to the same number.

	3	
1		
		2

LEVEL

9

LEVEL

10

1 PUZZLE

Which letter completes the puzzle?

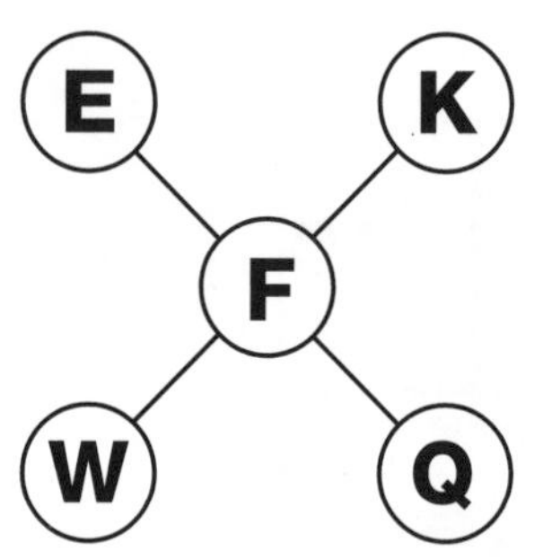

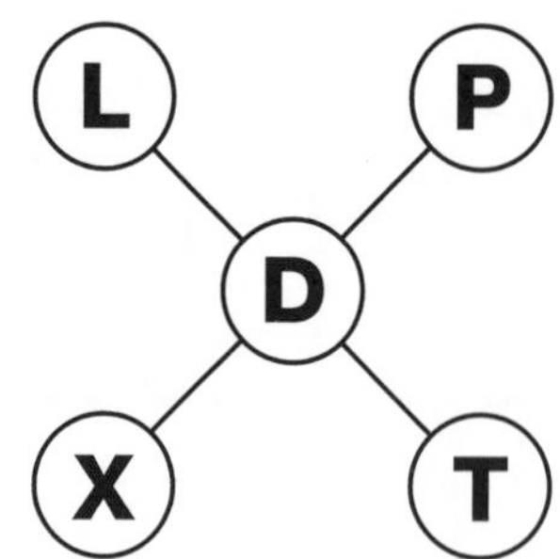

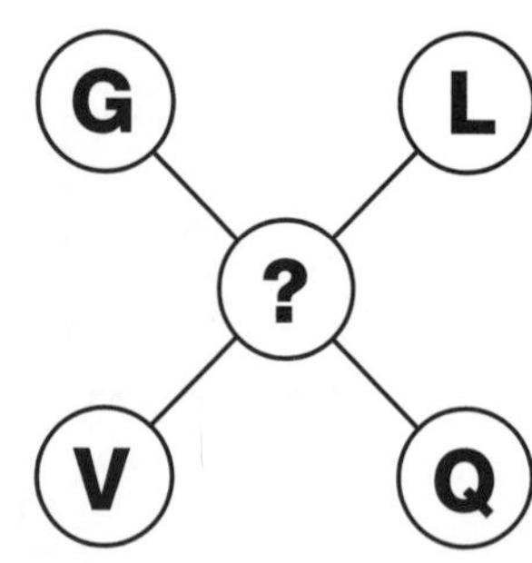

2 PUZZLE

Fill in the empty segment.

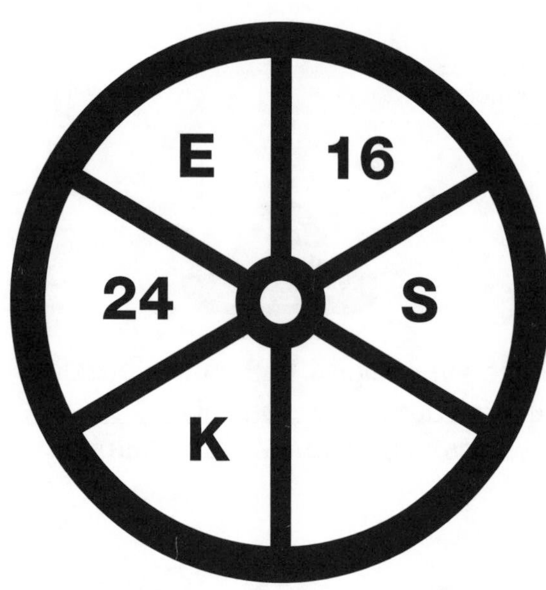

3 PUZZLE

What letter is missing?

4 PUZZLE

What number is missing?

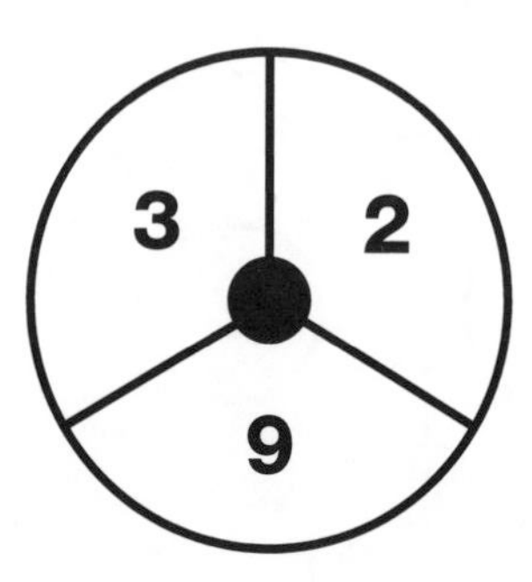

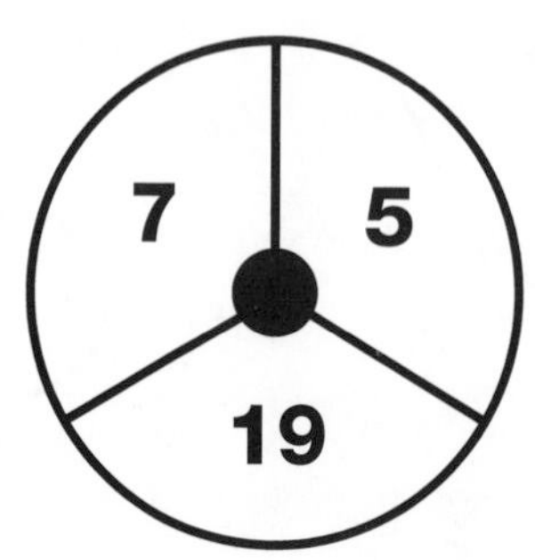

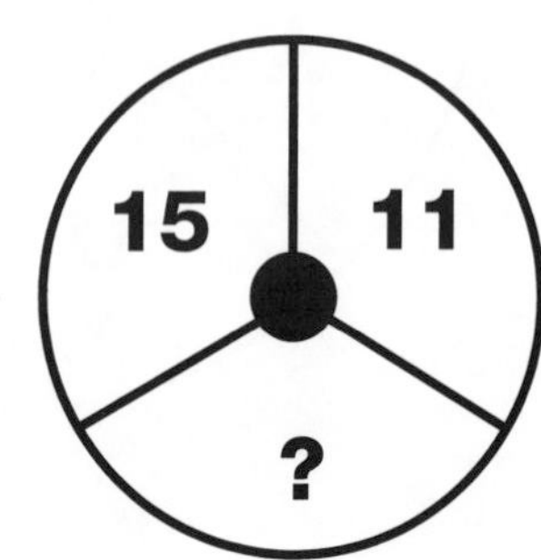

5 PUZZLE

What number goes in the centre of the bottom triangle?

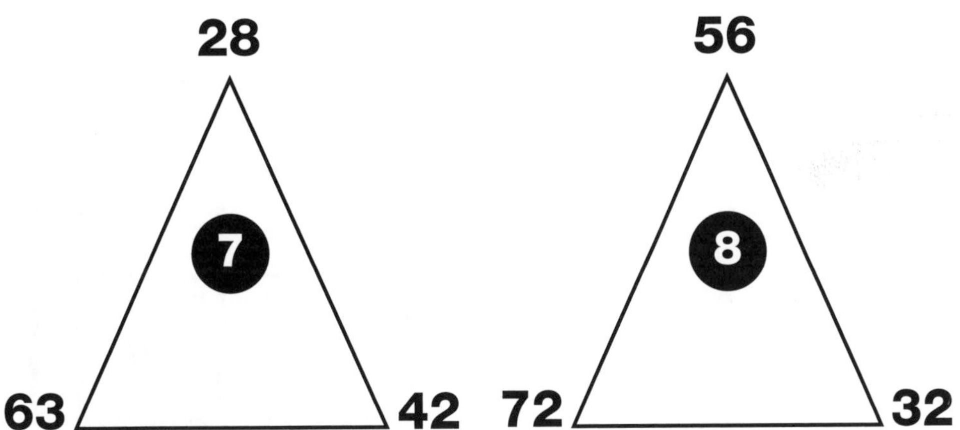

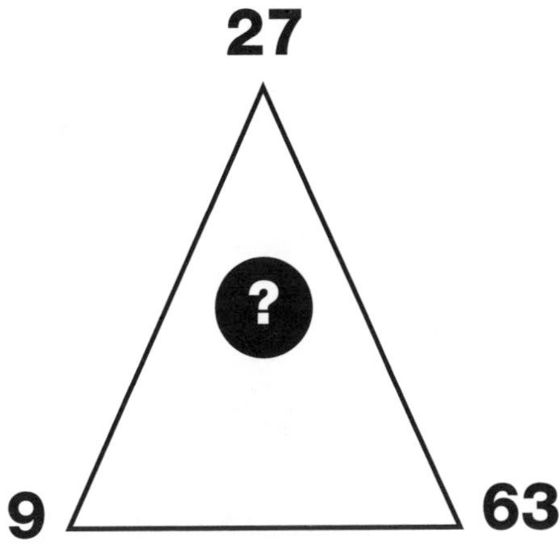

Following a logical sequence, can you complete this puzzle?

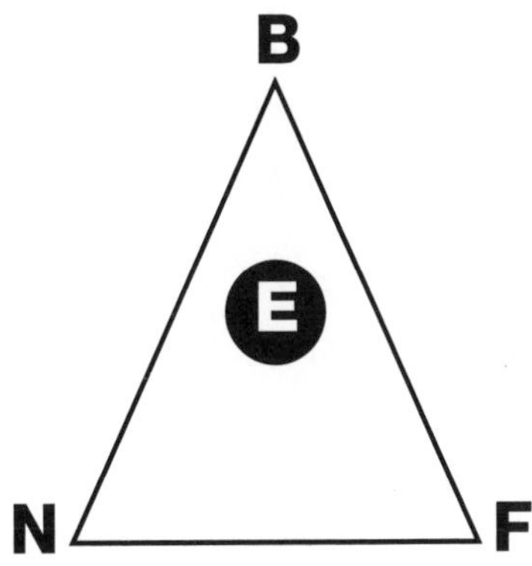

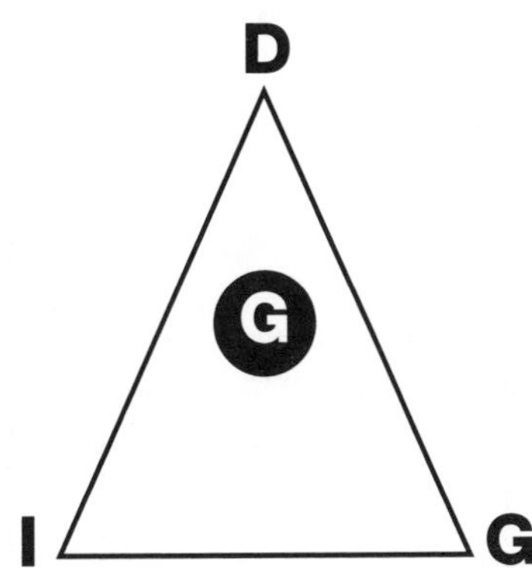

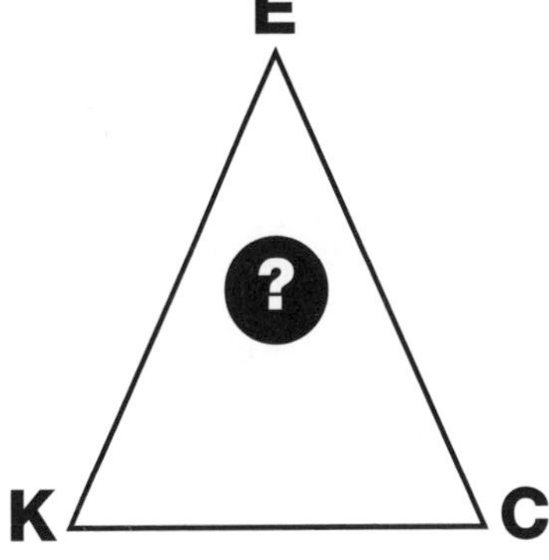

7 PUZZLE

Where does the missing hand go?

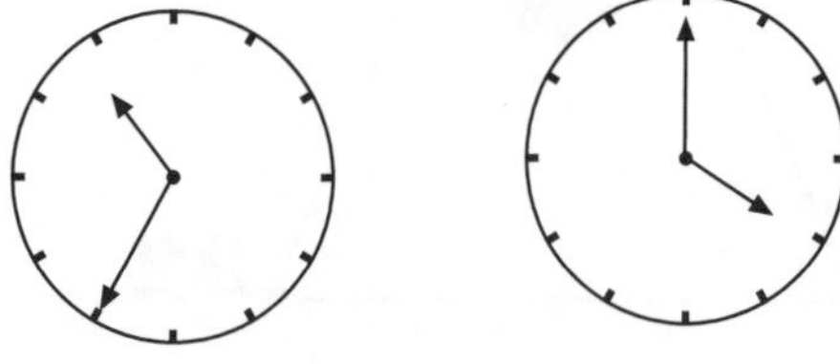

8 PUZZLE

Which letter completes the puzzle?

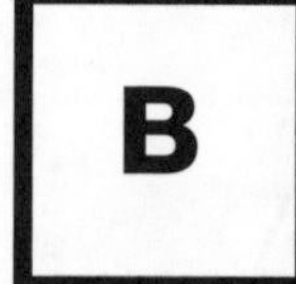

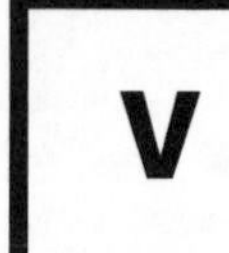

9 PUZZLE

What number is missing?

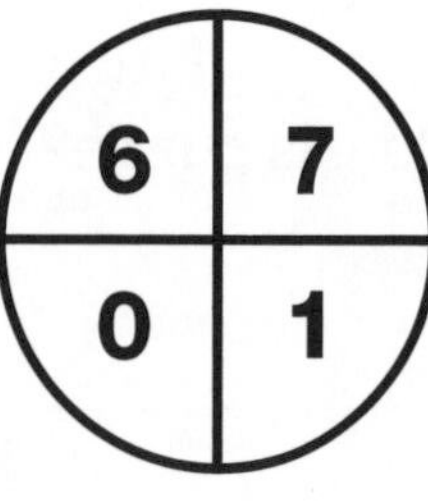

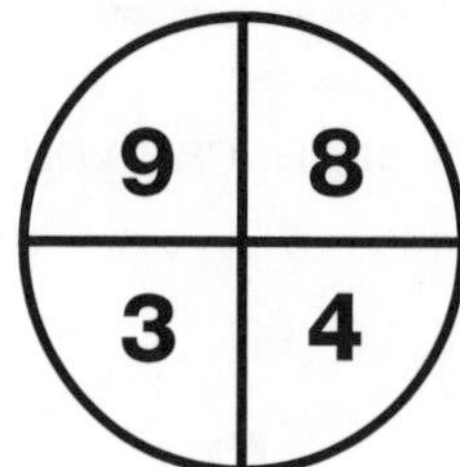

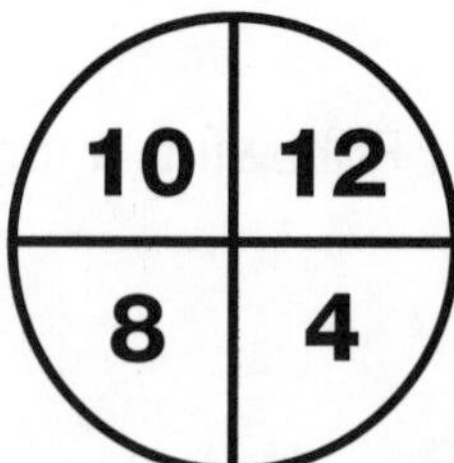

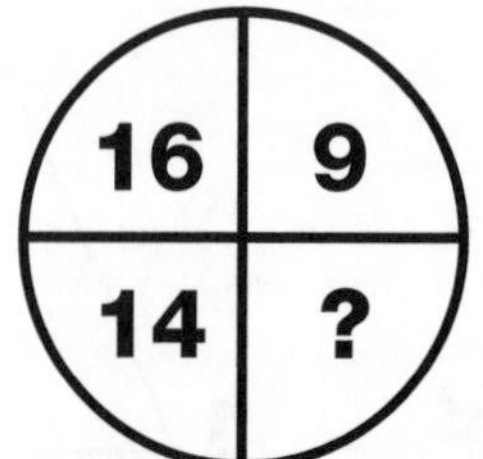

PUZZLE 10

Which letter completes the puzzle?

PUZZLE 11

What number is missing?

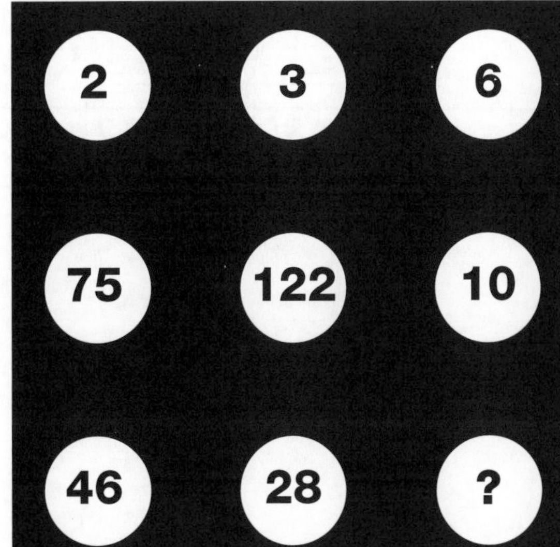

PUZZLE 12

Which letter completes this puzzle?

G

C

K

PUZZLE 13

Following a logical sequence, can you complete this puzzle?

13

17

19

23

?

LEVEL 10

Which of the bottom watches completes the sequence?

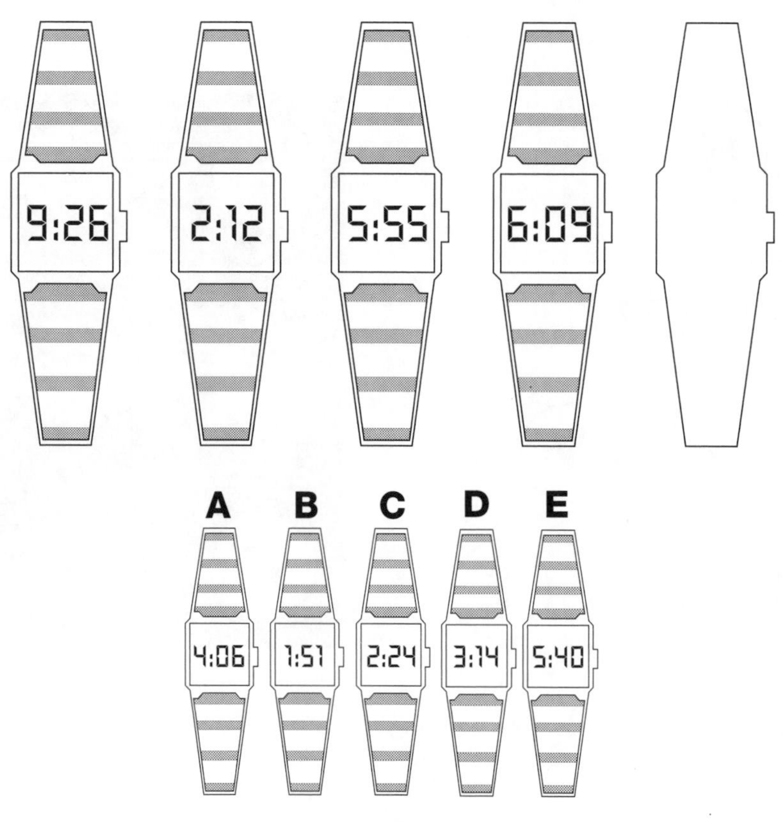

15 PUZZLE

What is missing from this puzzle?

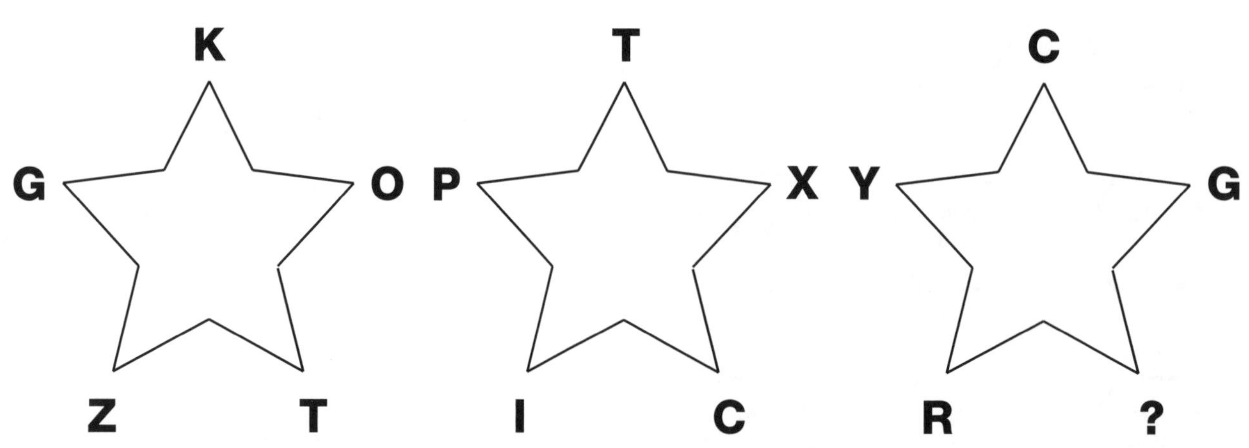

16 PUZZLE

Which letter completes this puzzle?

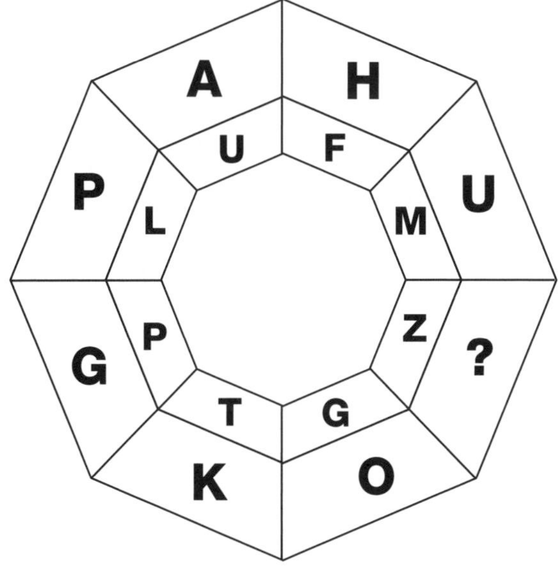

17 PUZZLE

What is missing from this sequence of numbers?

18 PUZZLE

What number is missing?

3	1	4	2	7	5
4	3	2	3	2	6
6	3	5	4	8	10
9	5	6	6	9	15
14	7	10	9	16	24
22	11	15	14	24	?

19 PUZZLE

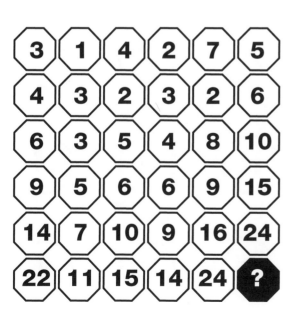

What completes this puzzle?

8	12	9
10	7	20
3	10	?

LEVEL 10

LEVEL 10

20 PUZZLE

What completes this pyramid?

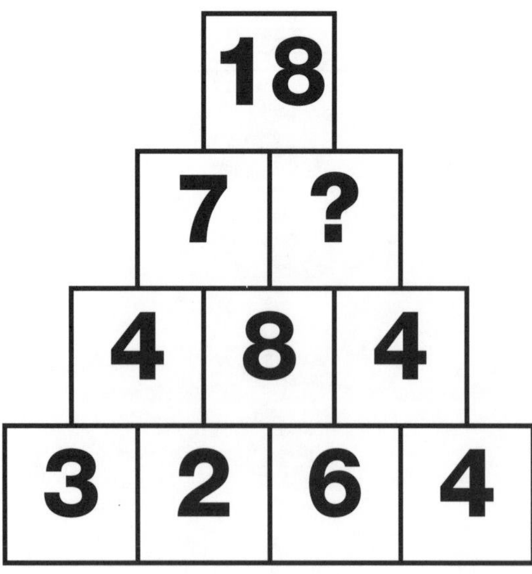

21 PUZZLE

What is missing from the wheel?

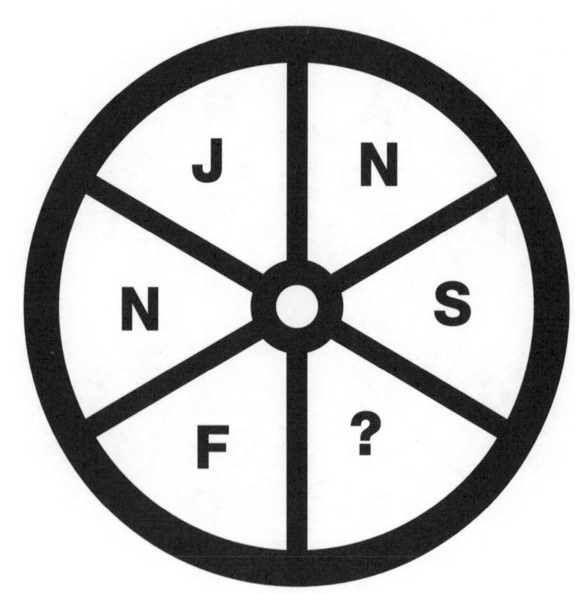

22 PUZZLE

What is missing from the empty segment?

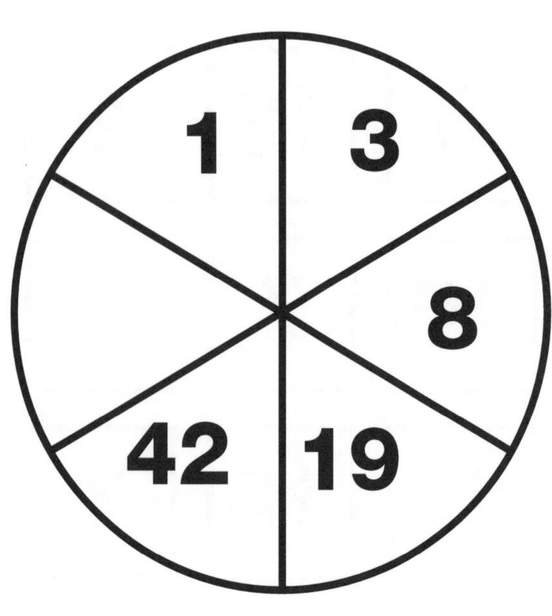

23 PUZZLE

What completes this puzzle?

24 PUZZLE

Following a logical sequence, can you complete this puzzle?

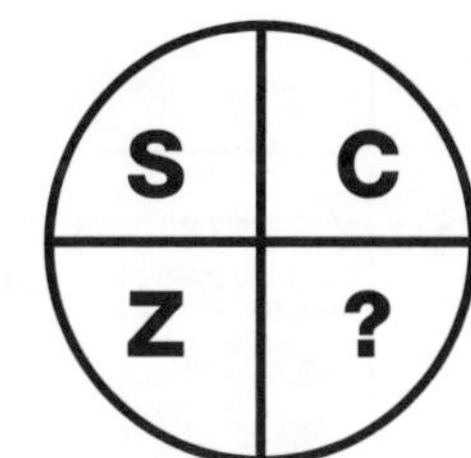

Which three letters complete this puzzle?

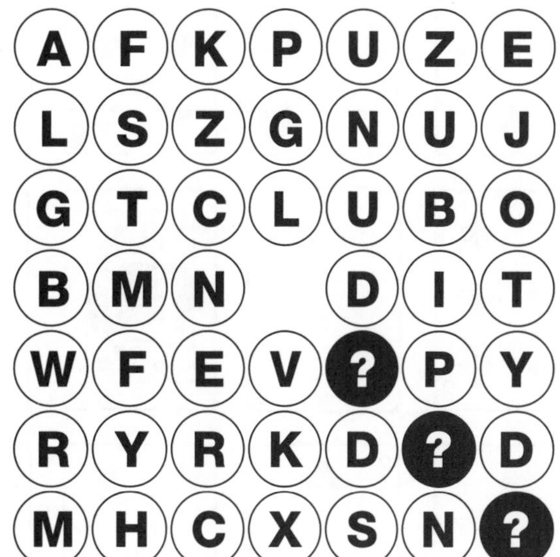

26 PUZZLE

Can you draw 4 straight lines, without lifting your pencil, which will pass through the middle of each of these dots?

Can you fill in the blank boxes in the diagram, so that all horizontal, vertical and diagonal lines add up to 33?

LEVEL 10

Which playing cards fill in the missing gaps?

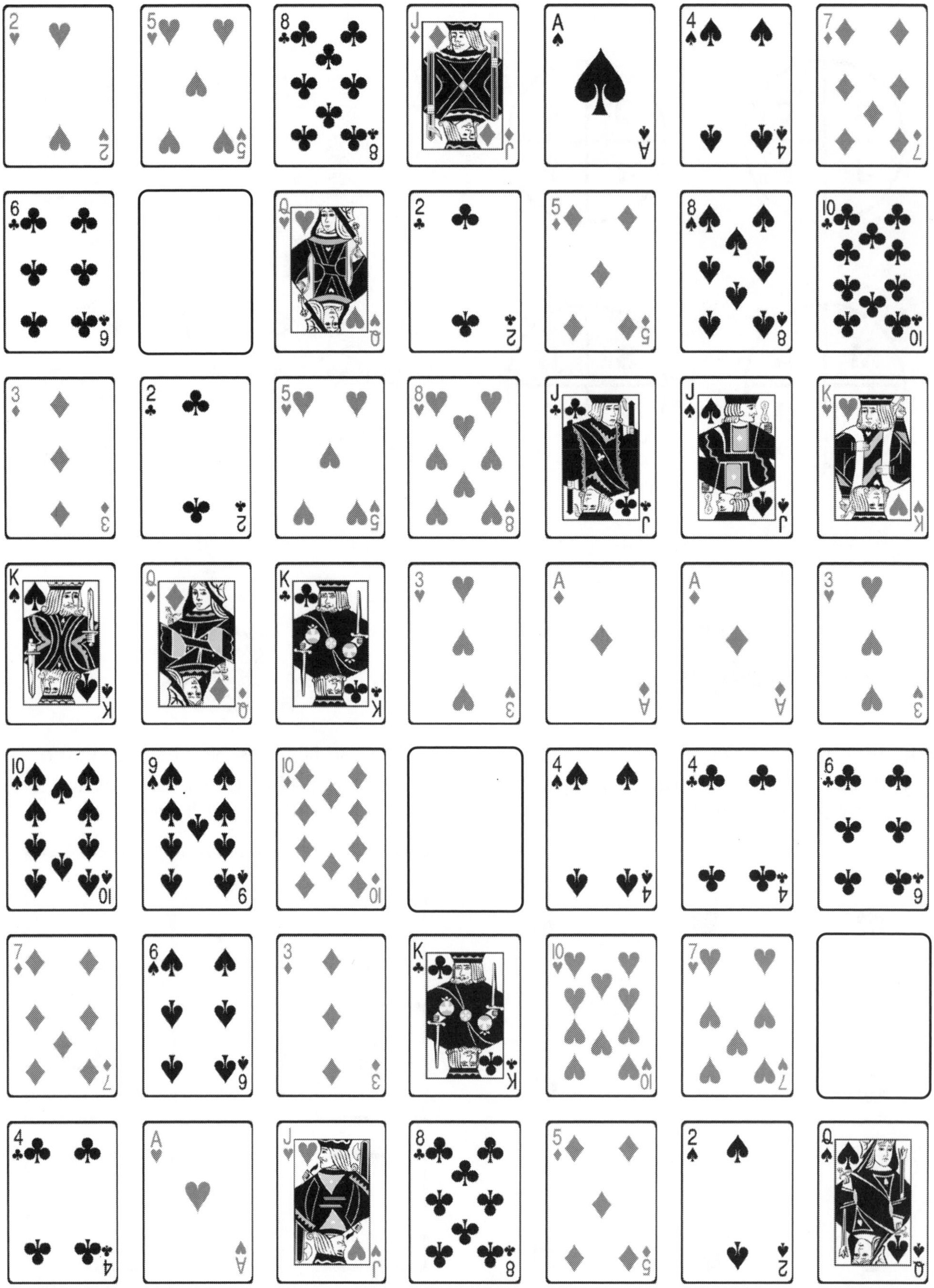

What is missing from this arrangement of circles?

Following a logical sequence, can you complete this puzzle?

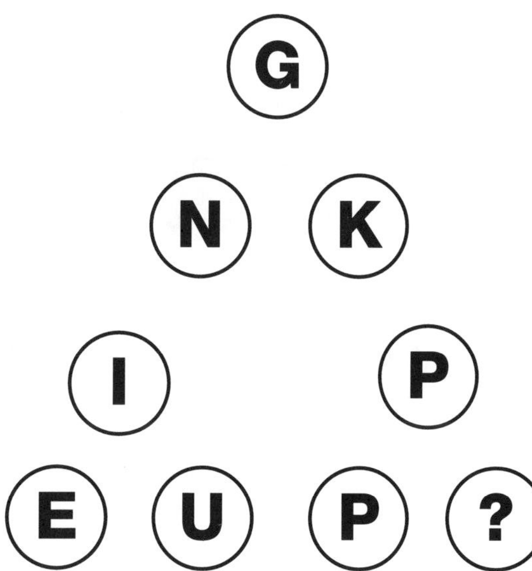

Which number completes the puzzle?

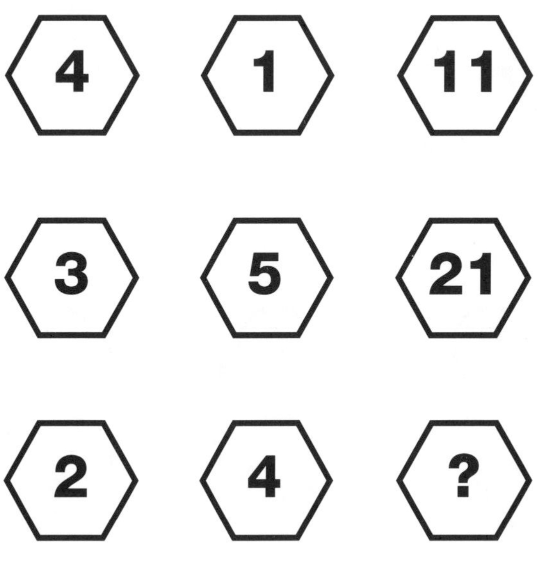

Which letter completes the puzzle?

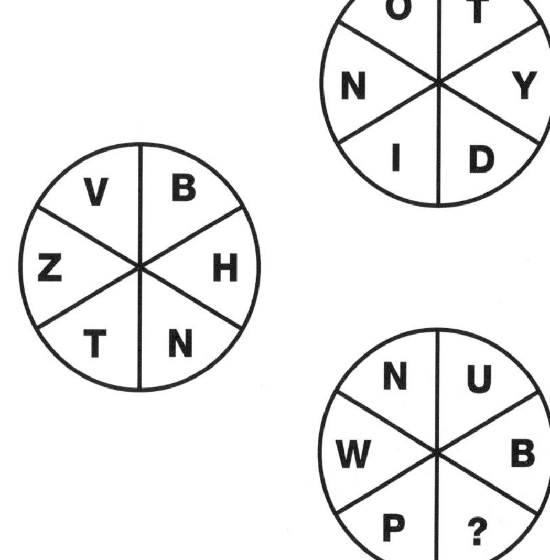

LEVEL

11

What is missing from the bottom triangle?

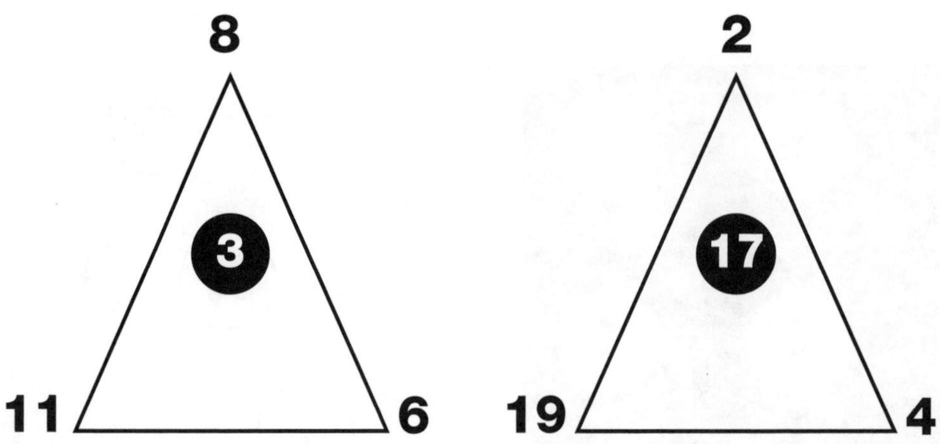

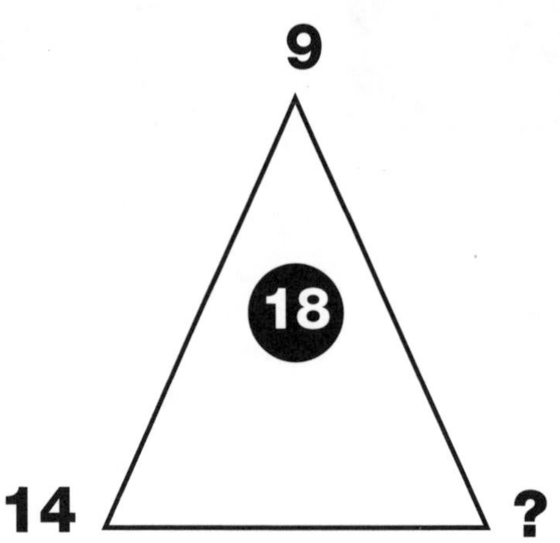

Which number completes the puzzle?

Which two letters are needed to complete this puzzle?

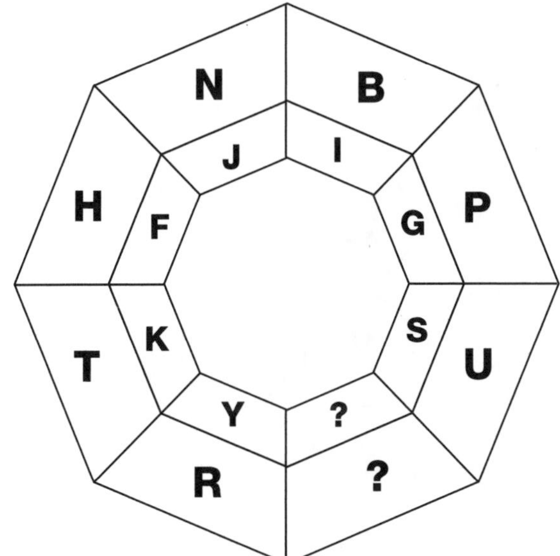

Following a logical sequence, can you complete this puzzle?

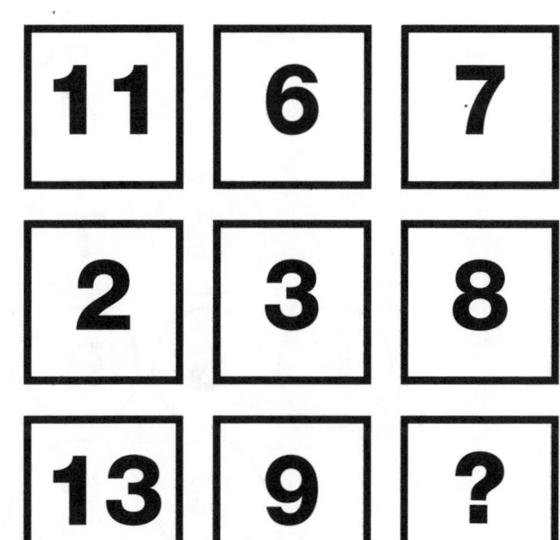

11	6	7
2	3	8
13	9	?

What is missing from this arrangement of circles?

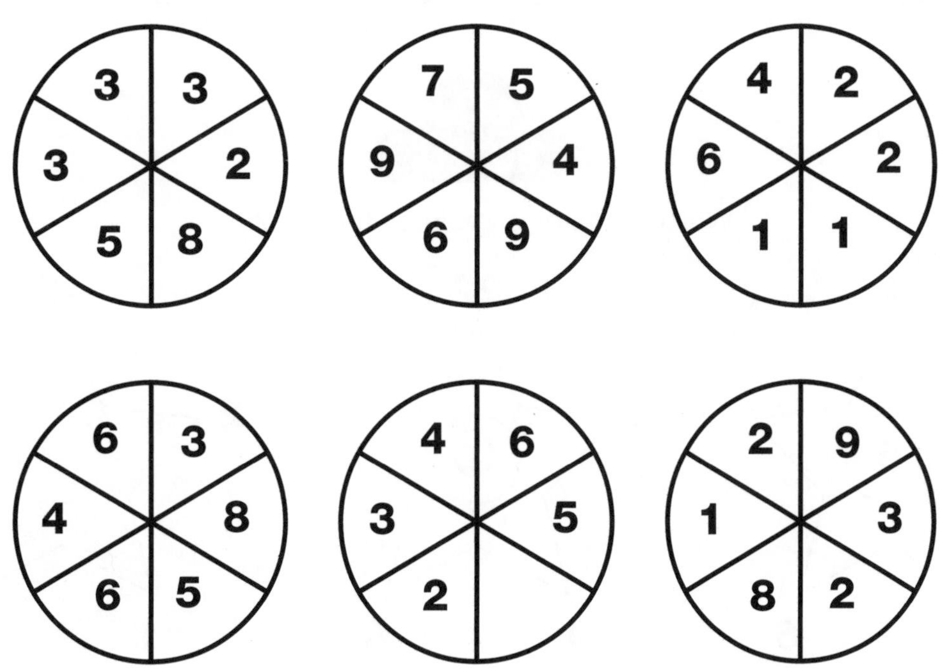

LEVEL

11

Which letter completes the puzzle?

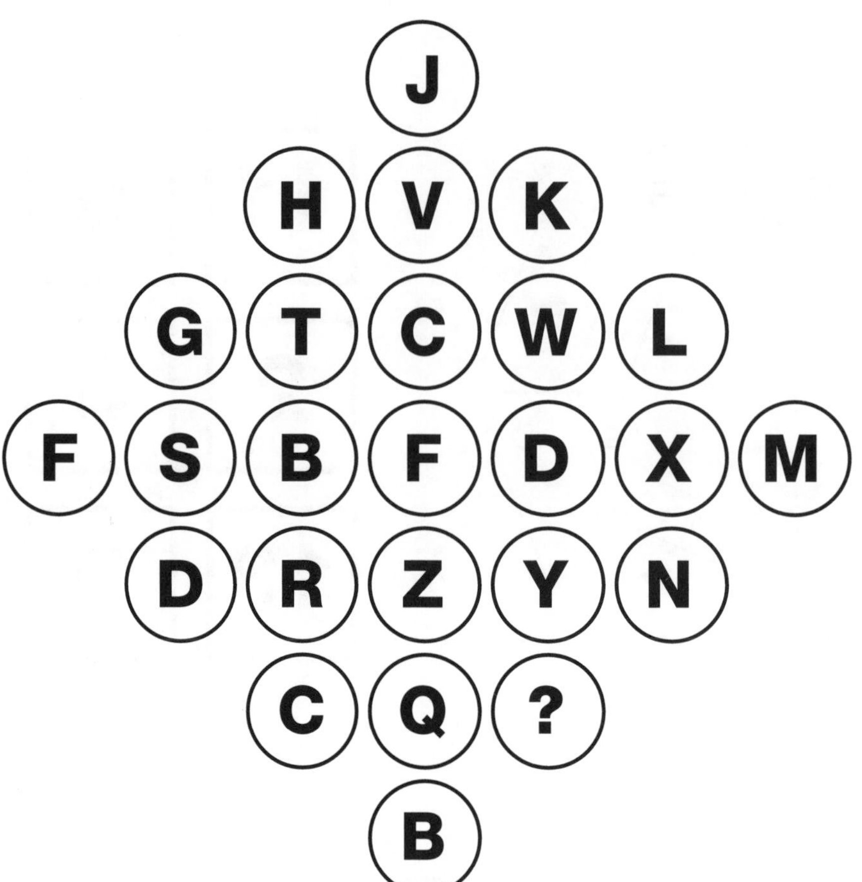

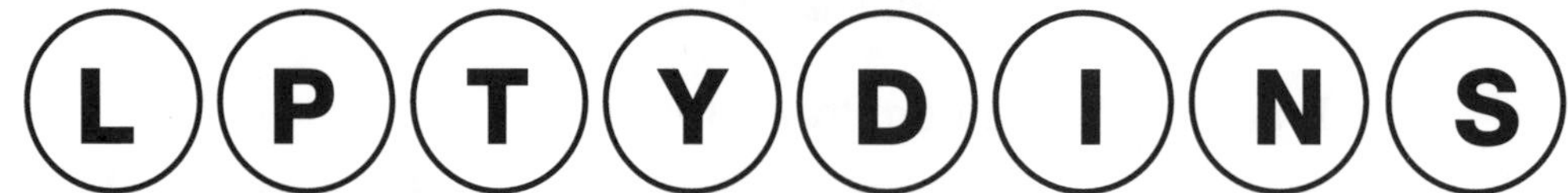

Which number completes the puzzle?

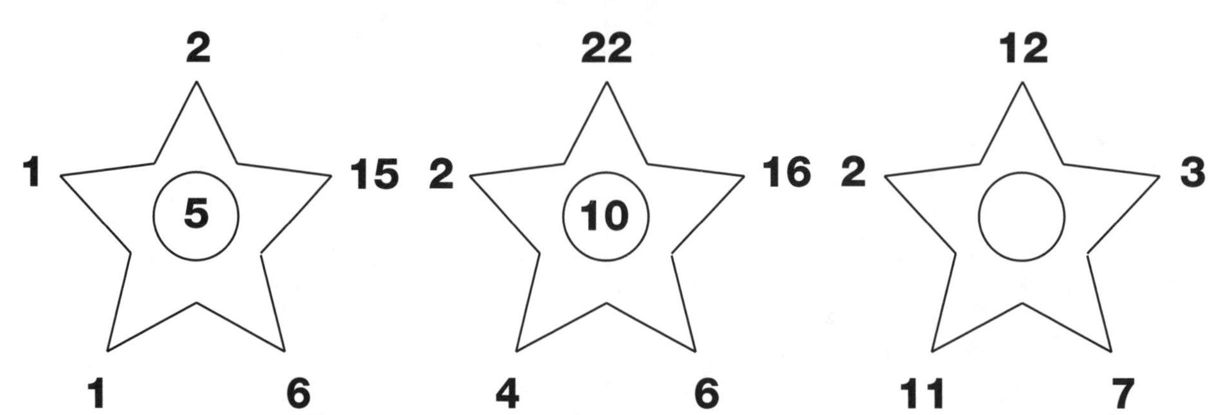

Following a logical sequence, can you complete this puzzle?

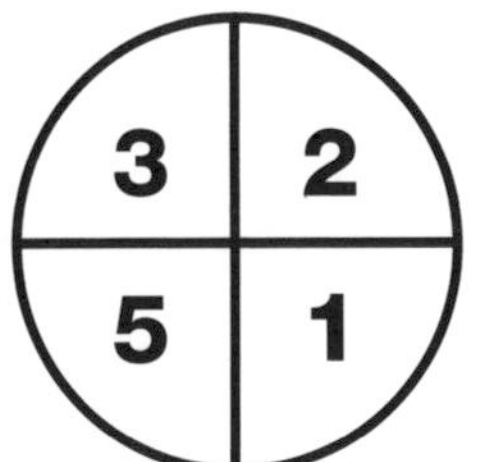

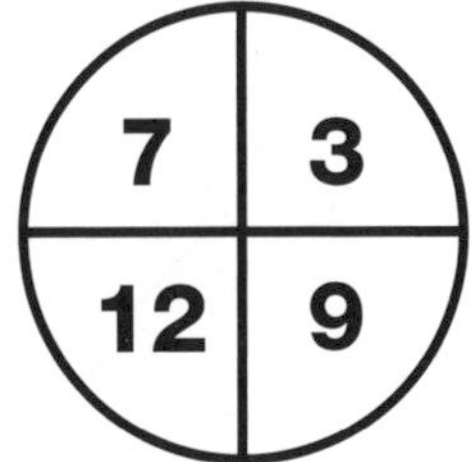

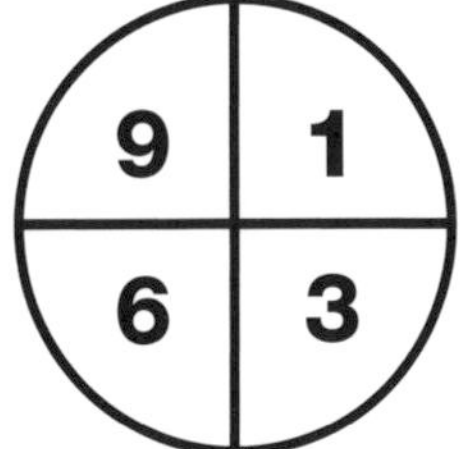

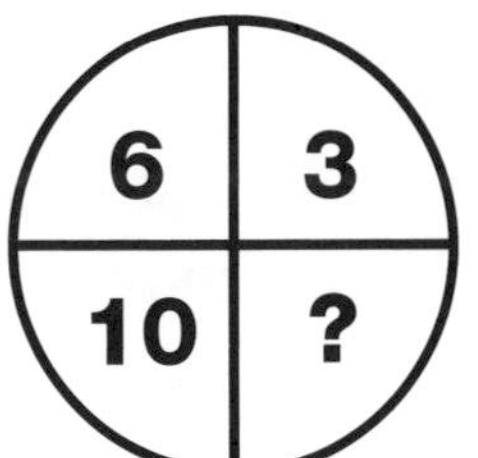

13 PUZZLE

Which of the lower patterns continues the sequence?

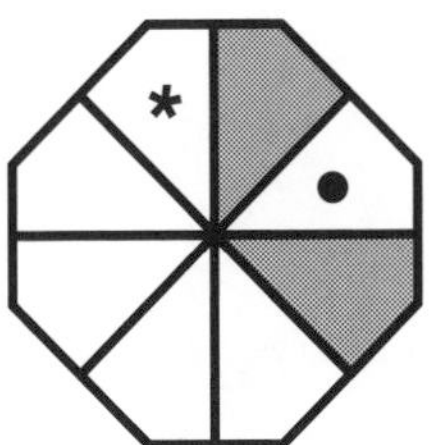
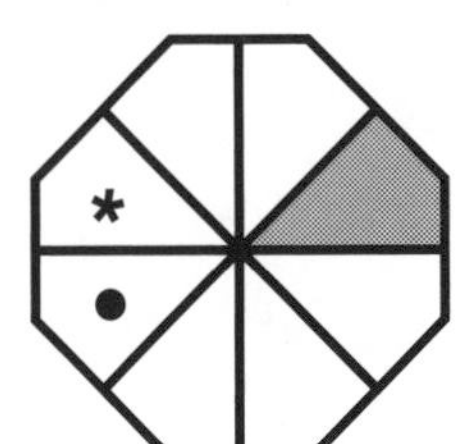
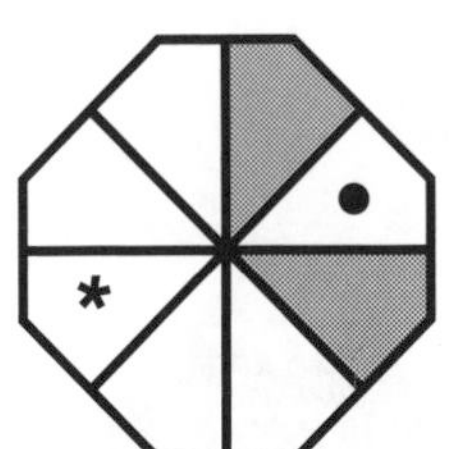
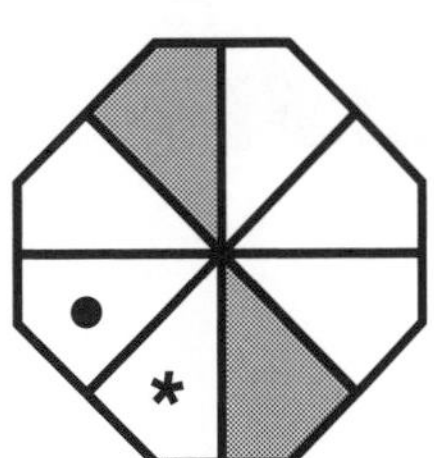

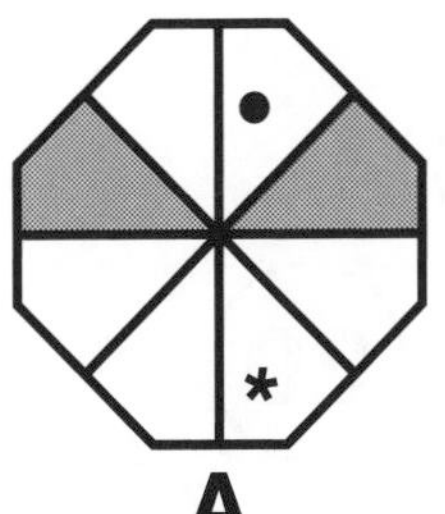
A

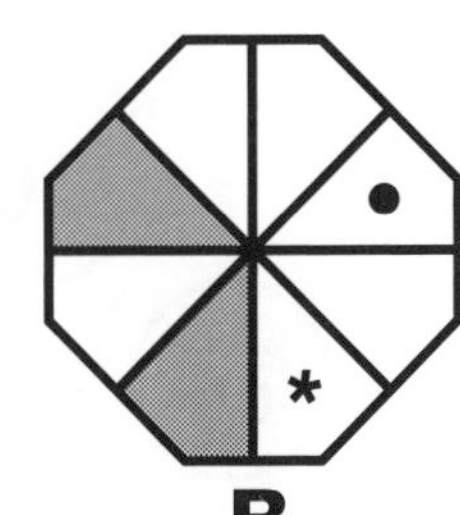
B

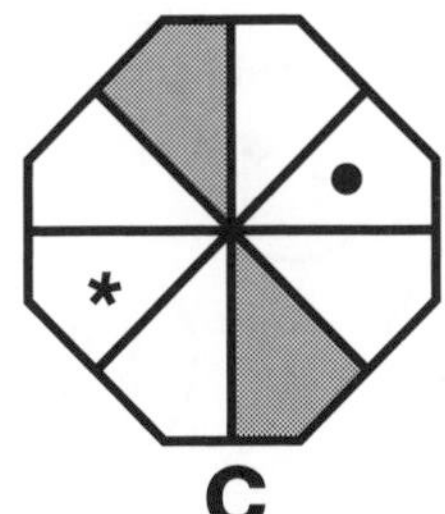
C

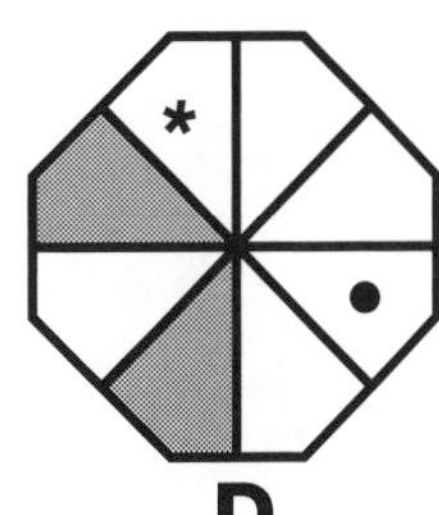
D

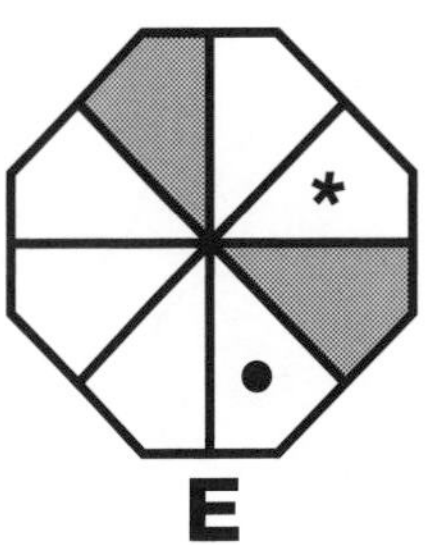
E

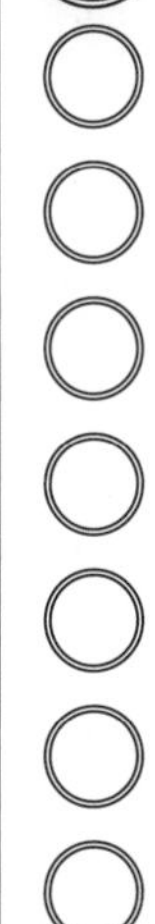

LEVEL

11

14 PUZZLE

Which letter completes the puzzle?

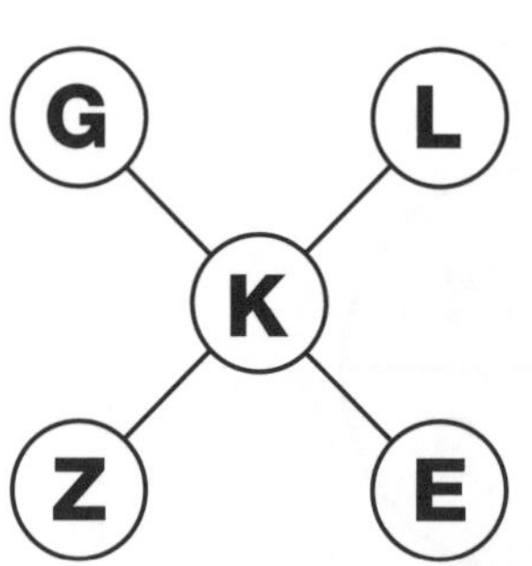

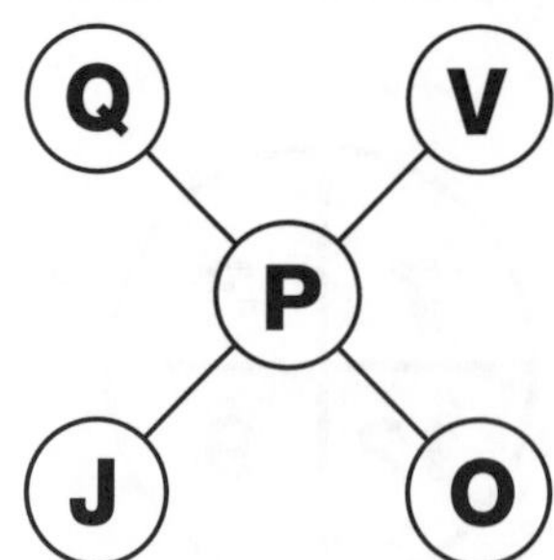

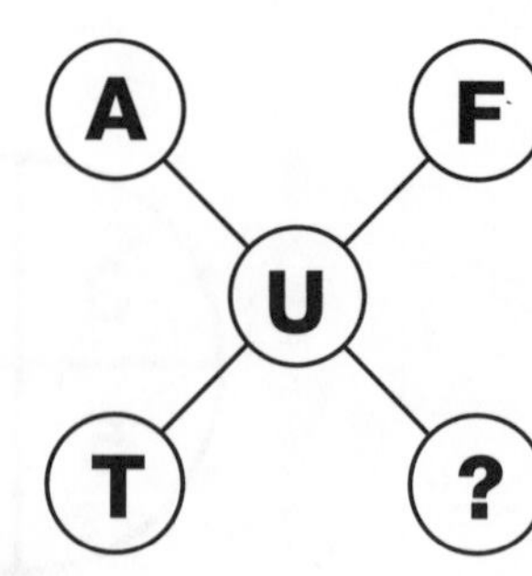

15 PUZZLE

In this sequence of letters what needs to be added to make the puzzle correct?

16 PUZZLE

This arrangement of 9 matches makes 5 equilateral triangles, can you produce another 4 triangles, but using only 6 matches?

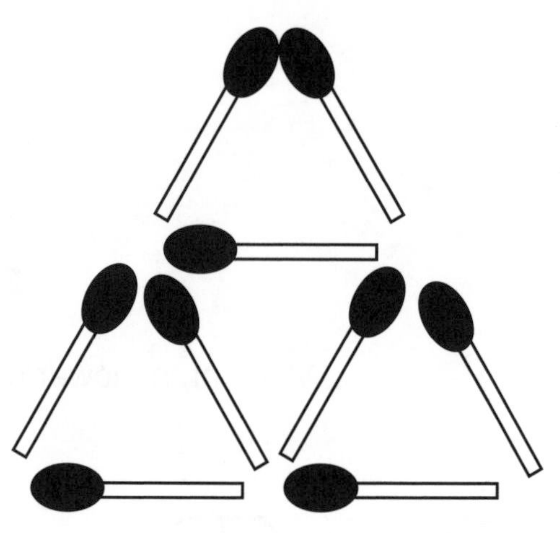

17 PUZZLE

Which number completes the puzzle?

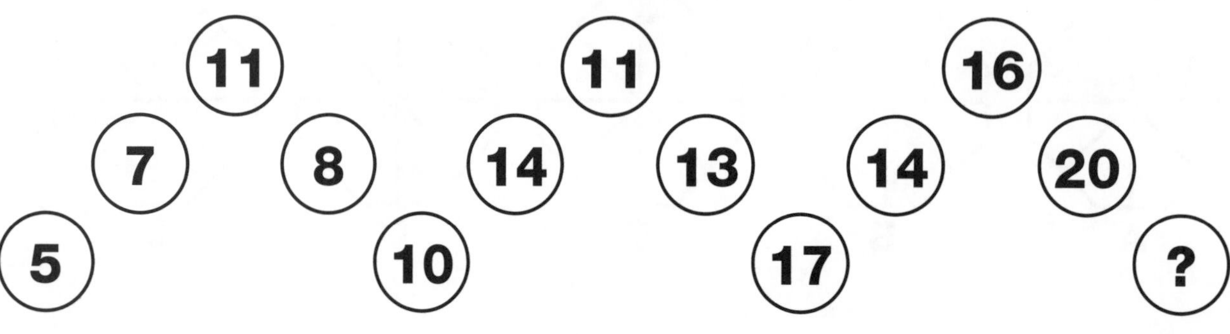

18 PUZZLE

Can you place the given dominos in this grid, so that each horizontal, vertical and diagonal line has a spot total of 10?

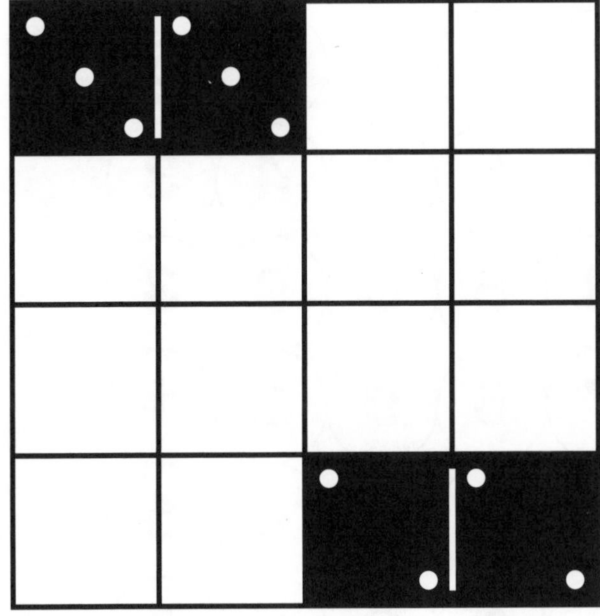

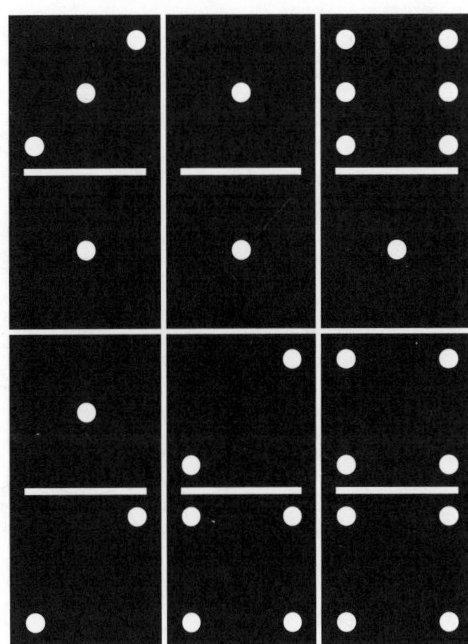

19 PUZZLE

Which number is the odd one out in each shape?

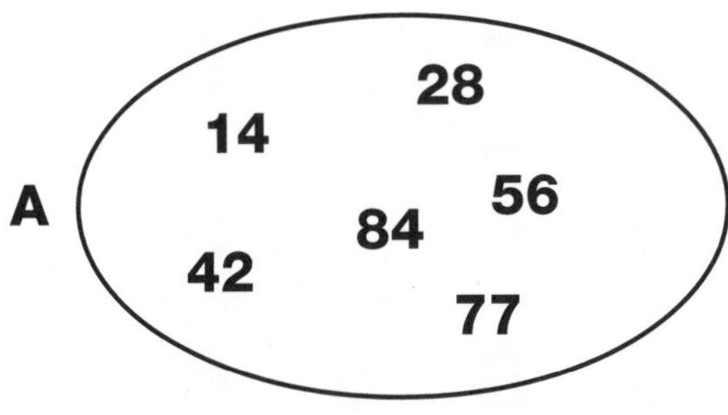

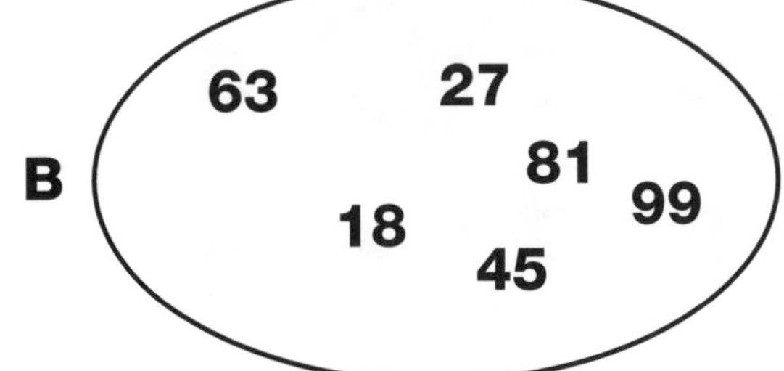

20 PUZZLE

Following a logical sequence, can you complete this puzzle?

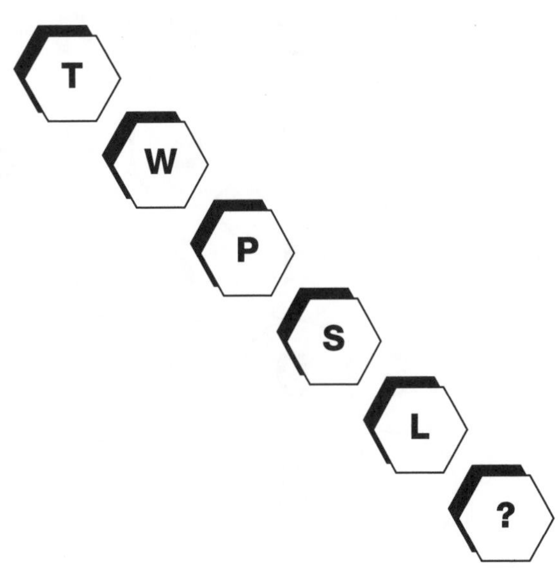

LEVEL 11

Which three numbers are needed to complete this puzzle?

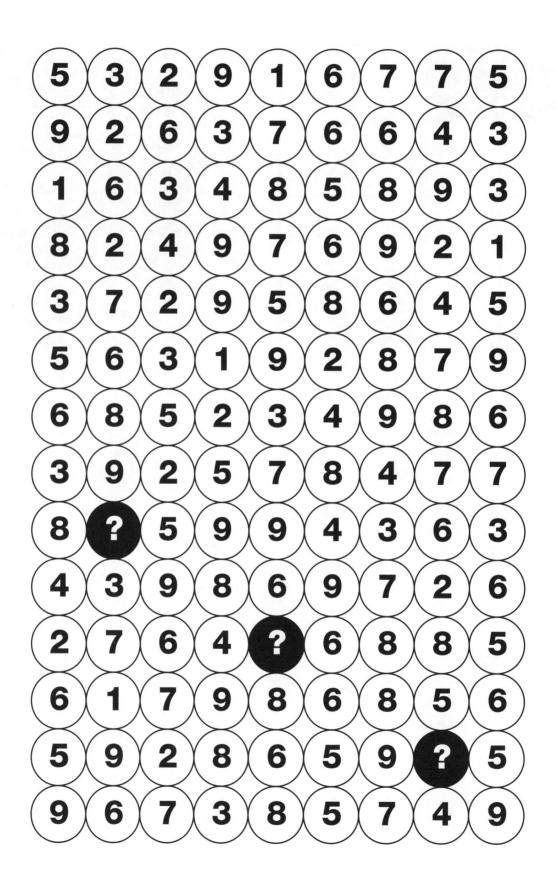

5	3	2	9	1	6	7	7	5
9	2	6	3	7	6	6	4	3
1	6	3	4	8	5	8	9	3
8	2	4	9	7	6	9	2	1
3	7	2	9	5	8	6	4	5
5	6	3	1	9	2	8	7	9
6	8	5	2	3	4	9	8	6
3	9	2	5	7	8	4	7	7
8	?	5	9	9	4	3	6	3
4	3	9	8	6	9	7	2	6
2	7	6	4	?	6	8	8	5
6	1	7	9	8	6	8	5	6
5	9	2	8	6	5	9	?	5
9	6	7	3	8	5	7	4	9

Which two dominos are missing from this puzzle?

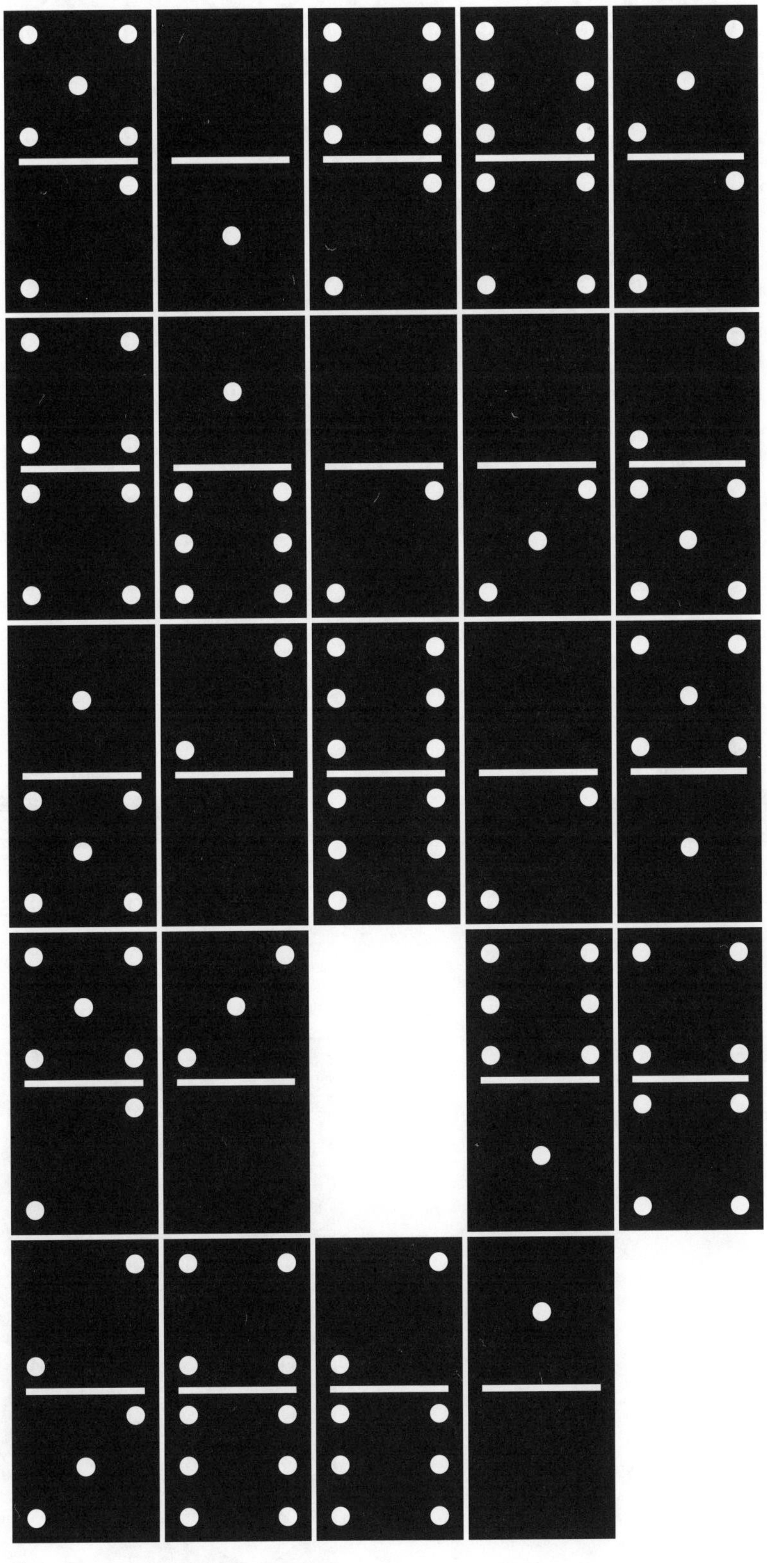

LEVEL

11

Which of the bottom patterns continues the sequence?

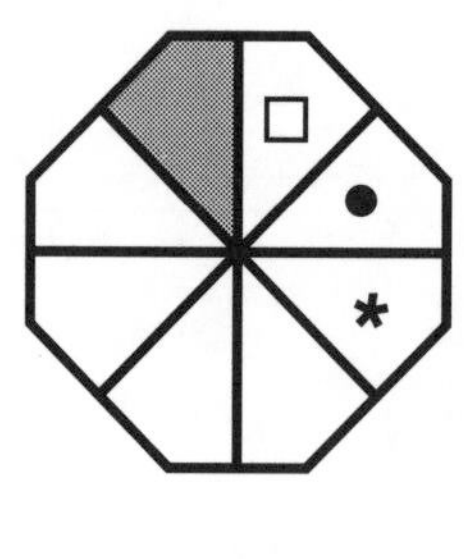
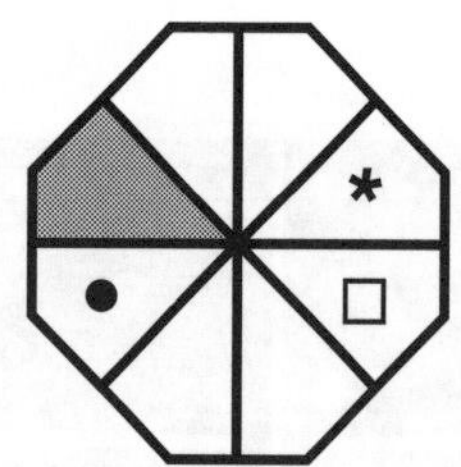
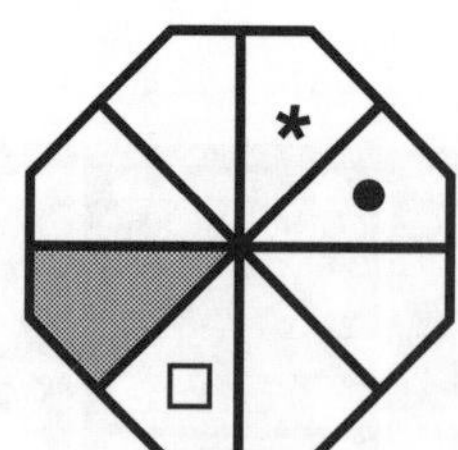
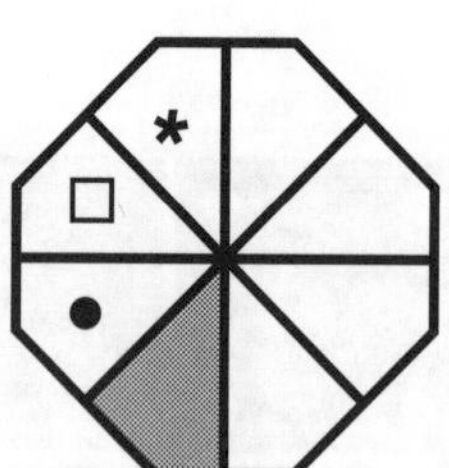

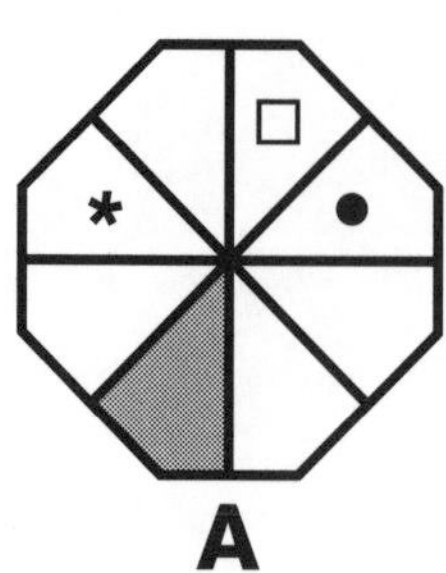

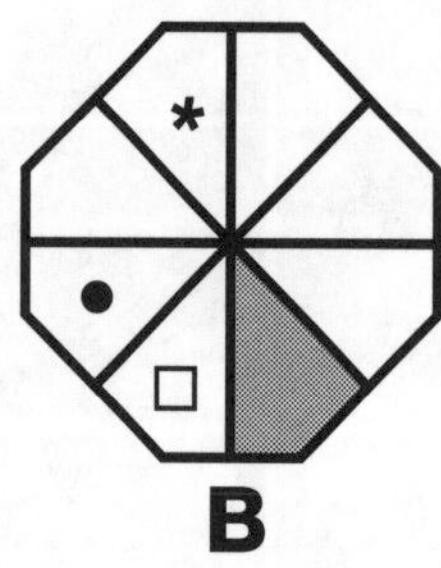

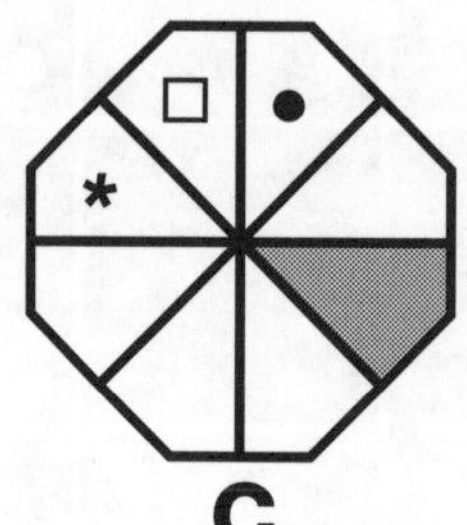

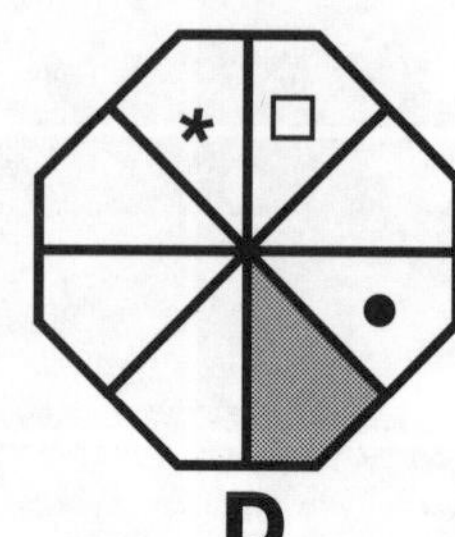

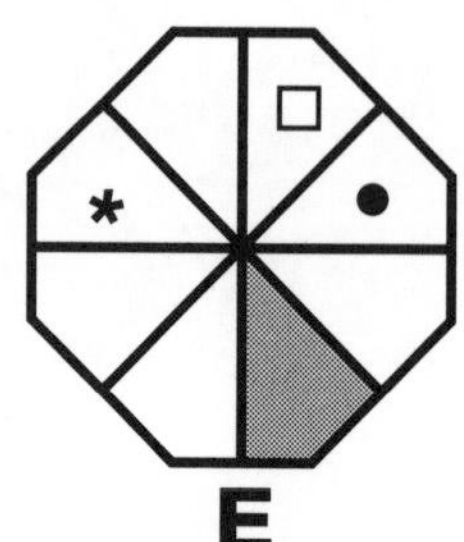

2
PUZZLE

Where does the missing hand go?

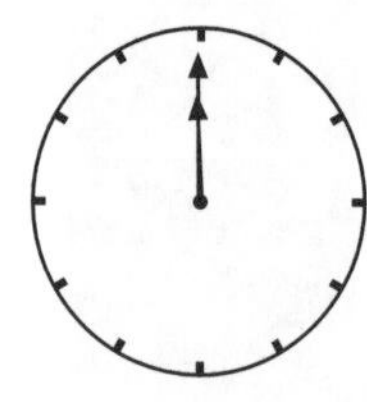
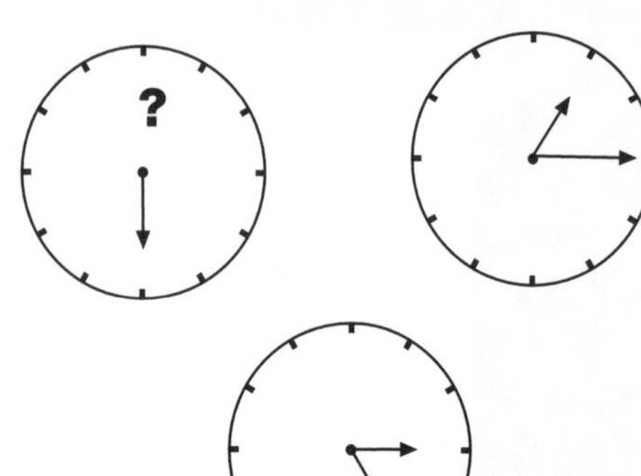

What is missing from this arrangement of circles?

4 PUZZLE

Which number completes the puzzle?

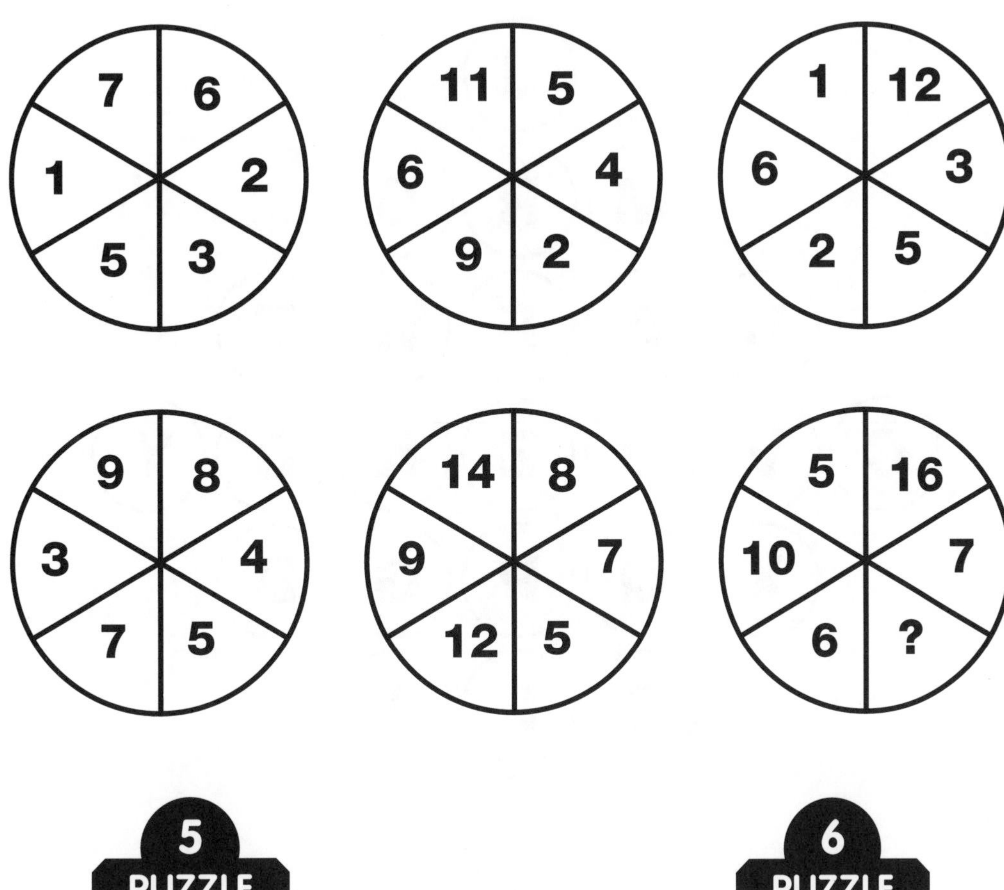

5 PUZZLE

Following a logical sequence, can you complete this puzzle?

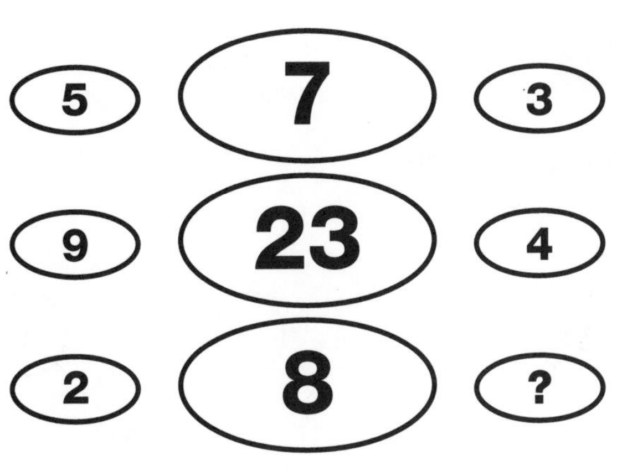

6 PUZZLE

What is missing from this pyramid?

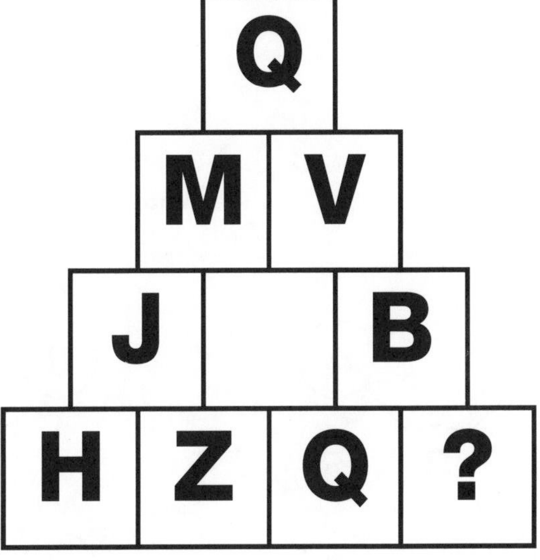

LEVEL 12

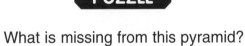

LEVEL

12

Which letter completes the puzzle?

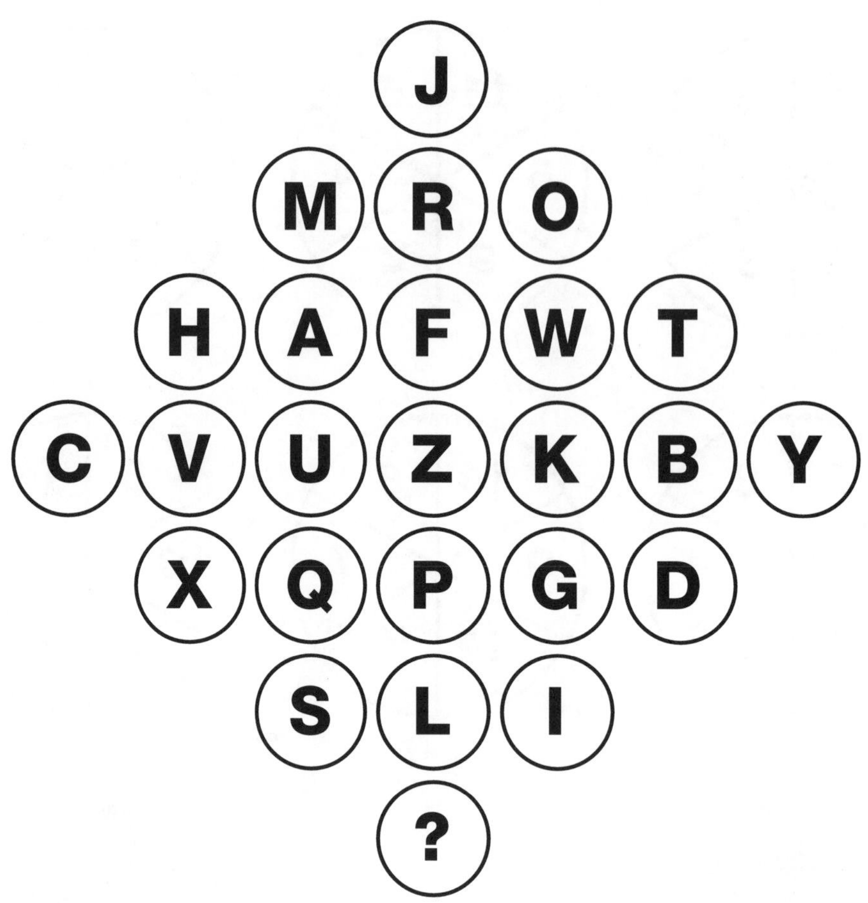

8
PUZZLE

What is missing from the last shape?

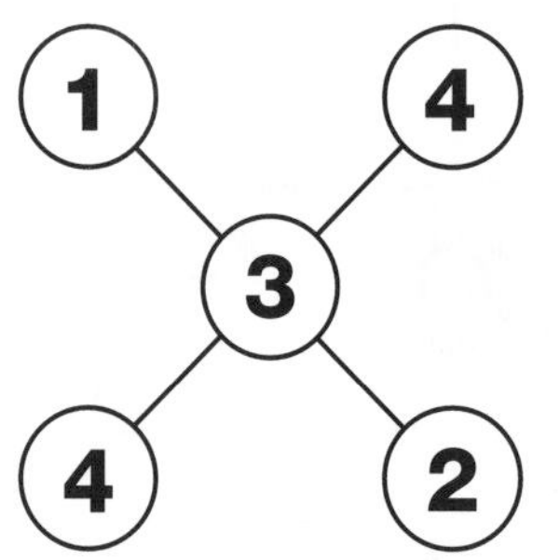

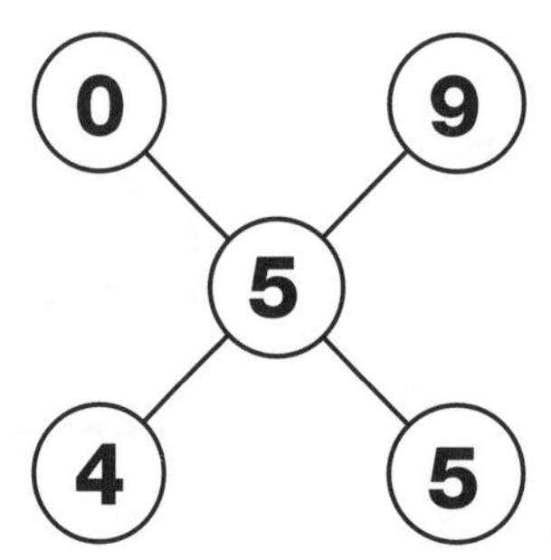

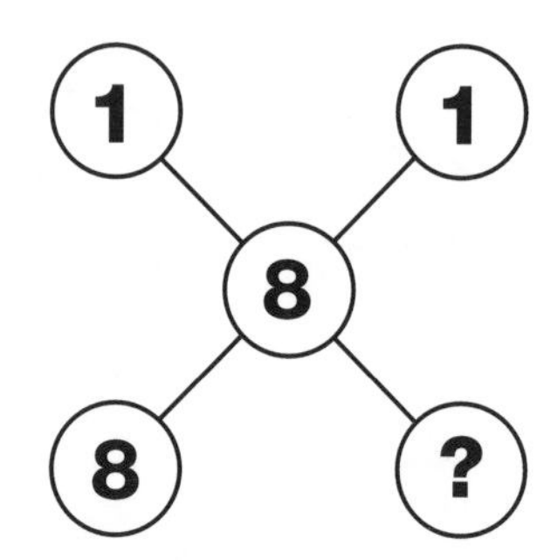

9 PUZZLE

Following a logical sequence, can you complete this puzzle?

125
216
343
512
729
?

10 PUZZLE

Which number completes the puzzle?

11 PUZZLE

What is missing from this arrangement of circles?

12 PUZZLE

What is missing from this sequence?

5	3
7	2
11	6
17	9
27	16
43	?

Which letter completes the puzzle?

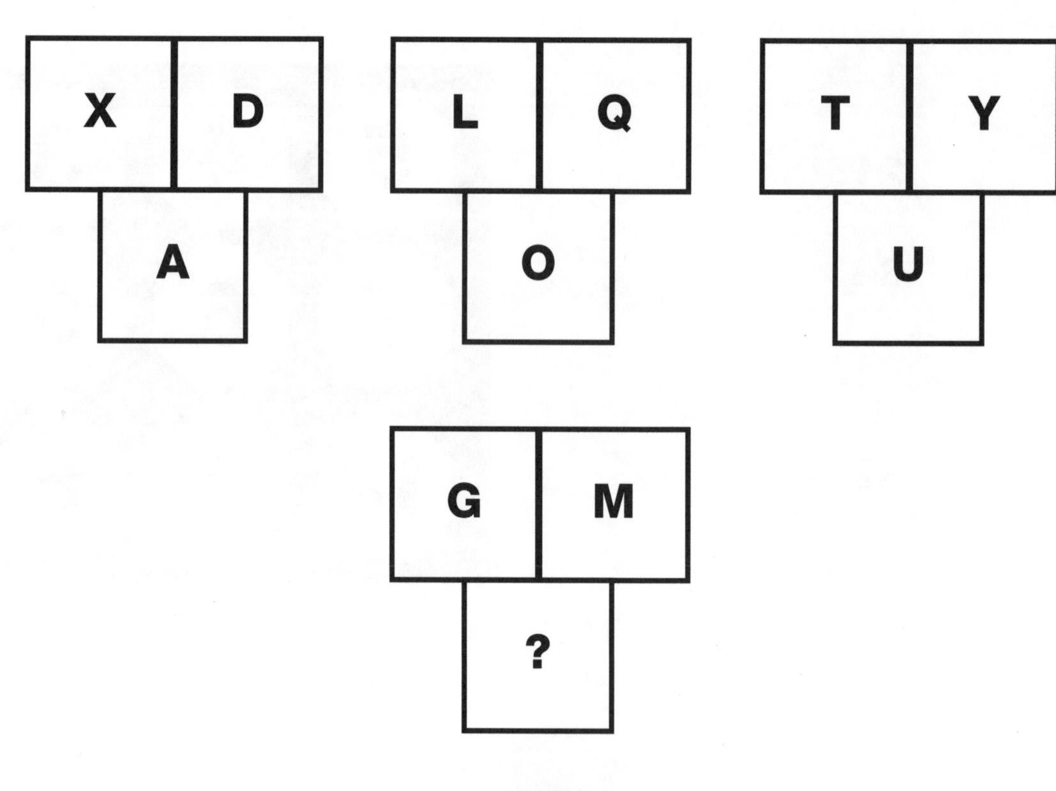

14 PUZZLE

Following a logical sequence, can you complete this puzzle?

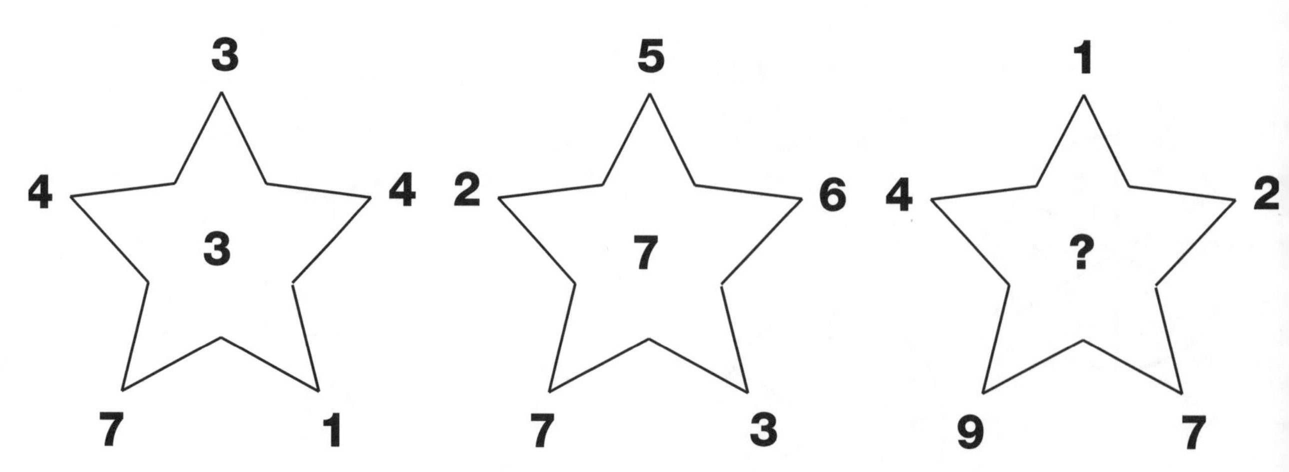

15 PUZZLE

In this sequence of letters what needs to be added to make the puzzle correct?

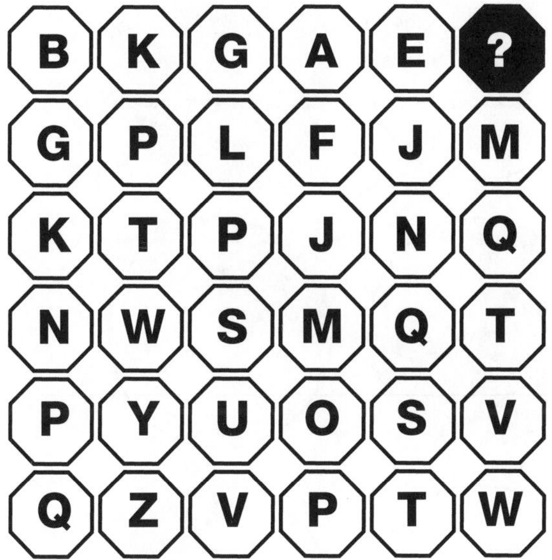

16 PUZZLE

What is the minimum number of matches you can remove from this diagram to leave just 2 squares?

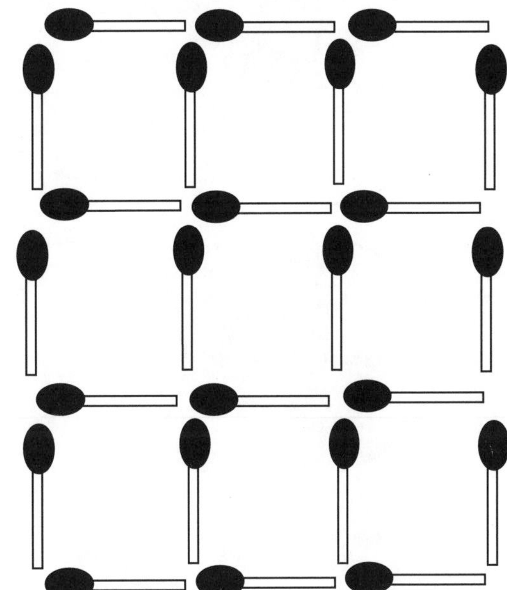

17 PUZZLE

Which letter is the odd one out in each ellipse?

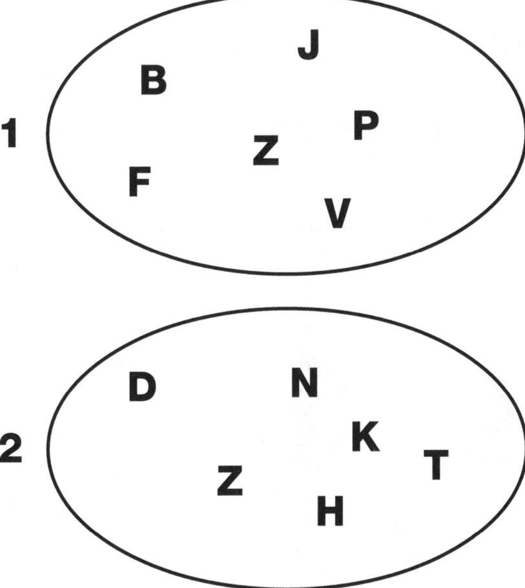

18 PUZZLE

Which two numbers complete the puzzle?

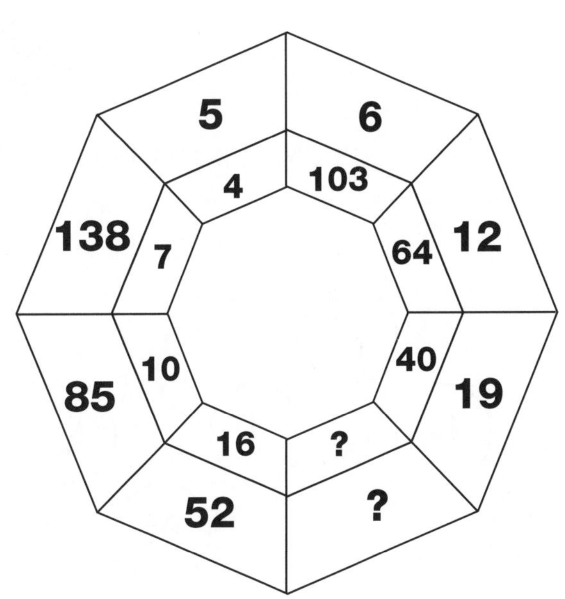

LEVEL 12

LEVEL 12

Which patterns replace the question marks?

?
?

20 PUZZLE

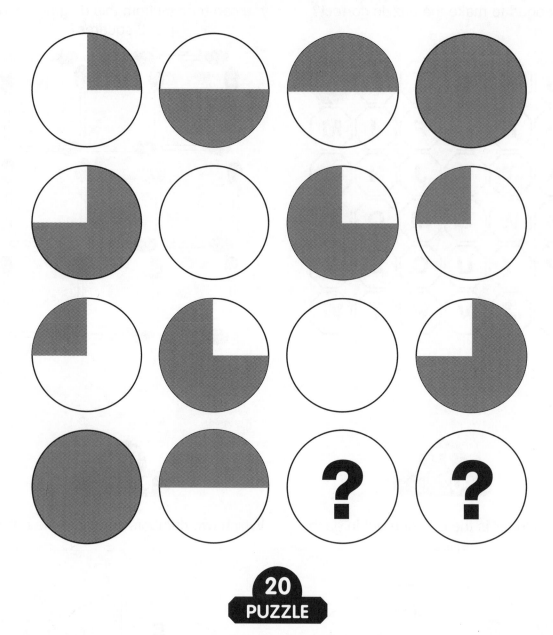

What is missing from this arrangement of circles?

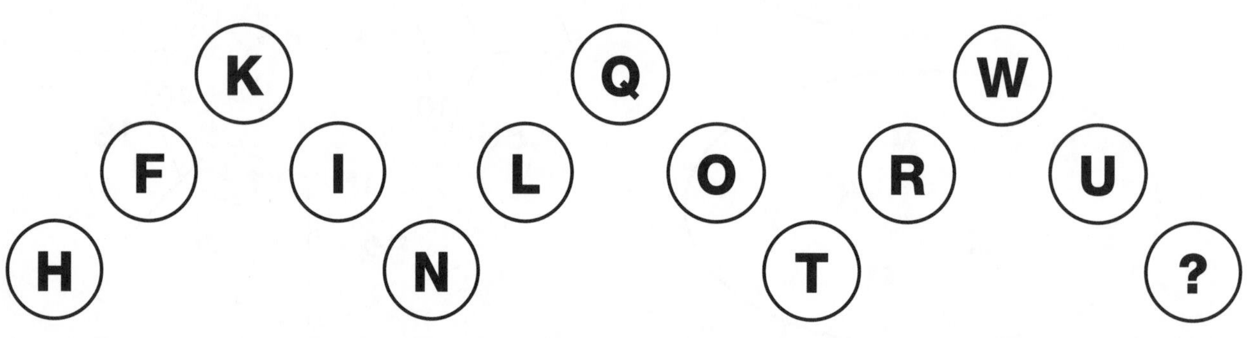

PUZZLE 21

Following a logical sequence, can you complete this puzzle?

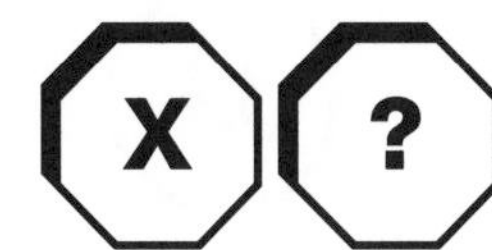

PUZZLE 22

Which letter completes the puzzle?

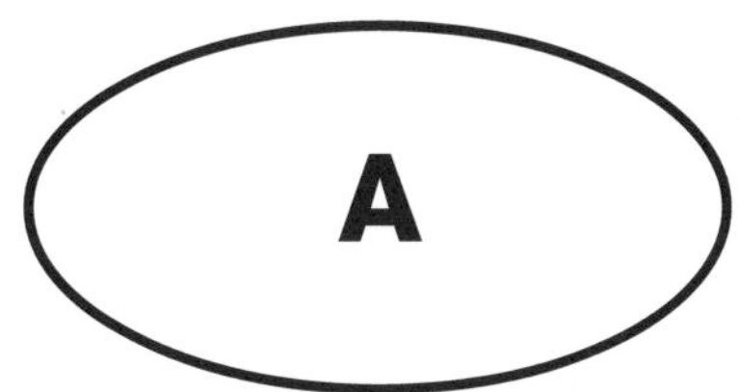

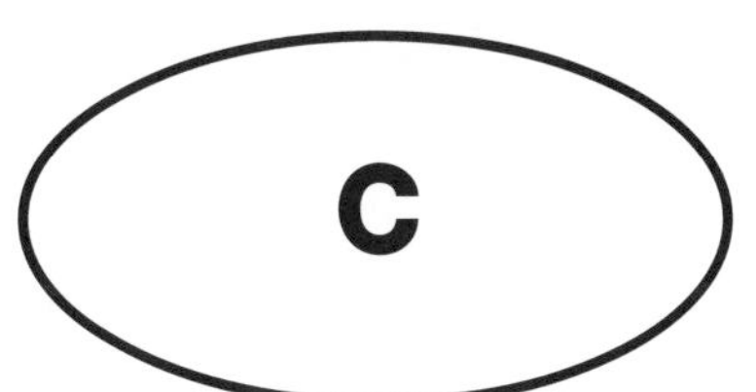

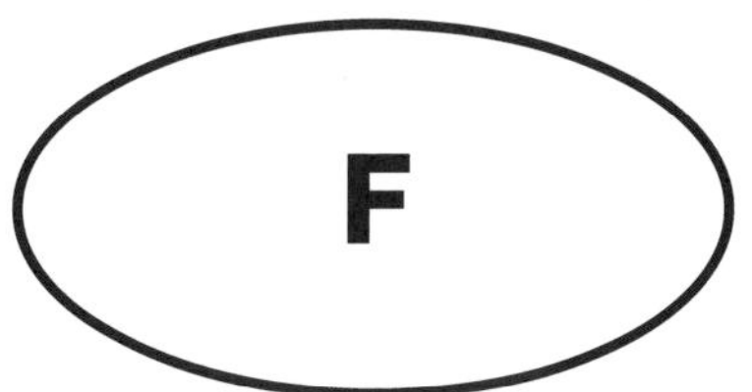

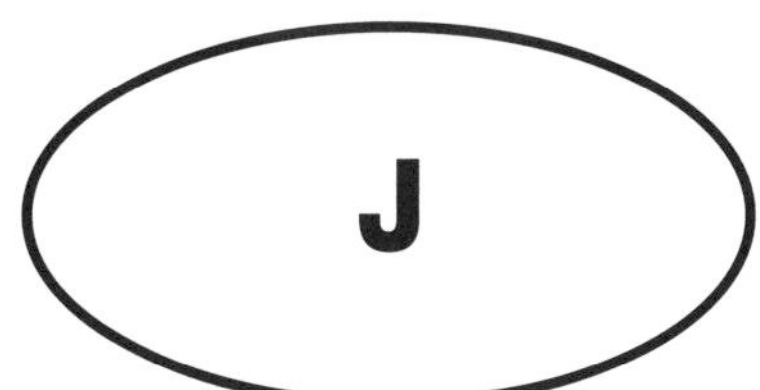

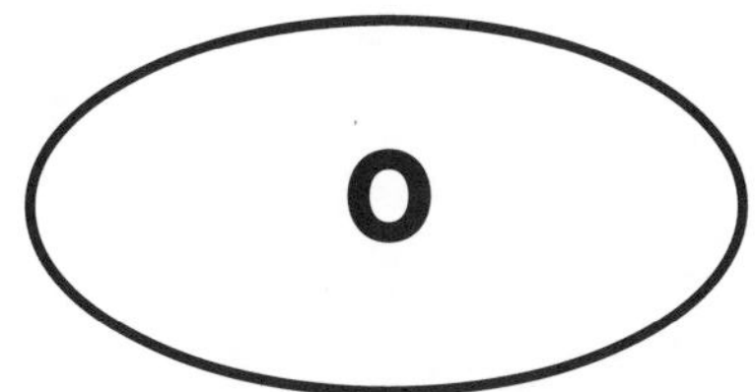

PUZZLE 23

In this sequence of letters what needs to be added to make the puzzle correct?

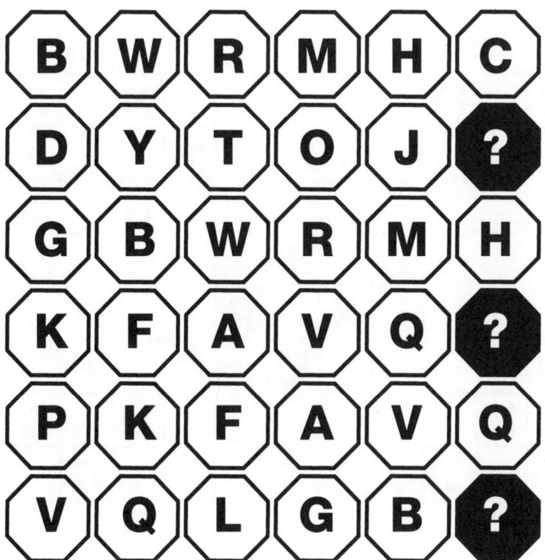

24 PUZZLE

Following a logical sequence, can you complete this puzzle?

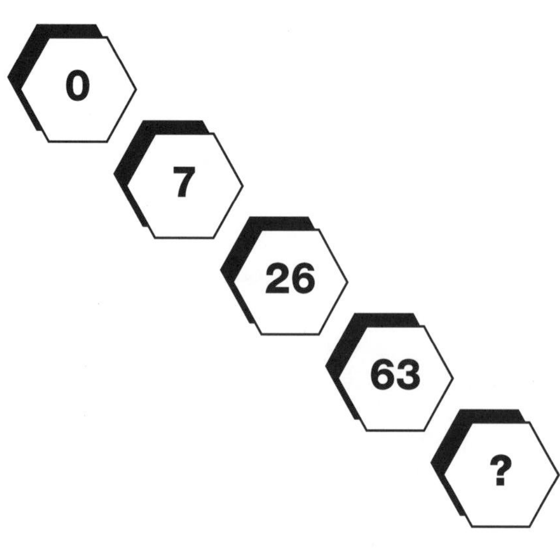

25 PUZZLE

Which letter completes the puzzle?

26 PUZZLE

Which grid fills the gap in the middle?

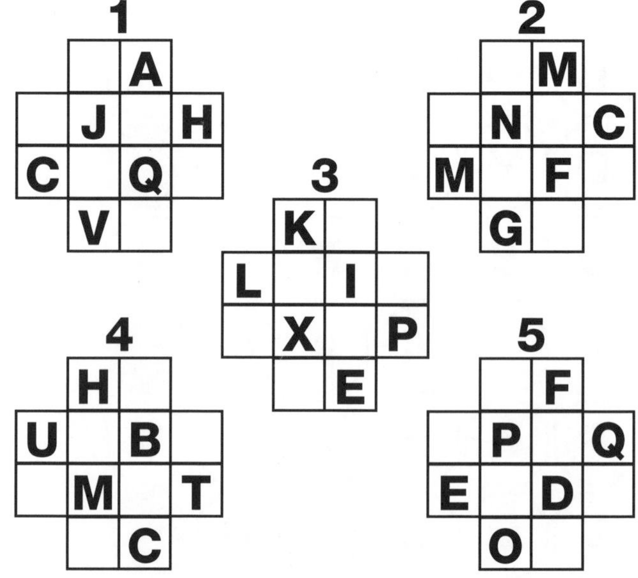

What sequence of letters will complete this puzzle?

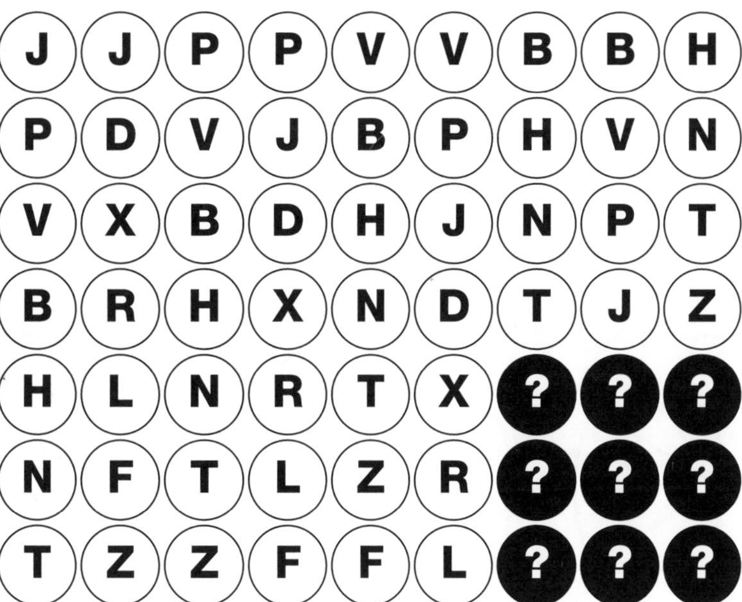

2 PUZZLE

Which number completes the puzzle?

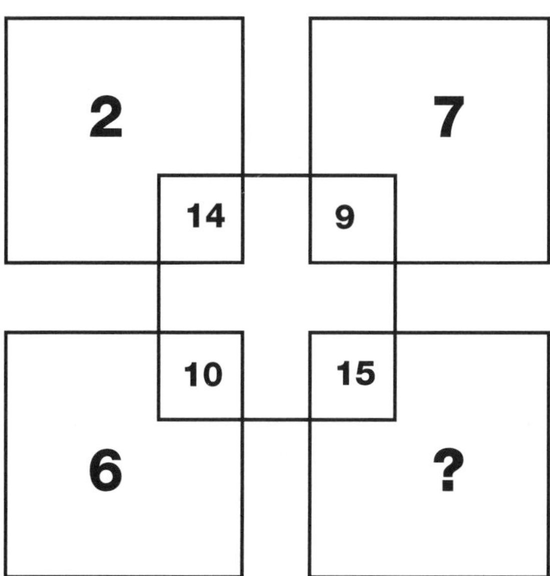

3 PUZZLE

Following a logical sequence, can you complete this puzzle?

A
E
F
H
?

LEVEL 13

4 PUZZLE

What is missing from this arrangement of circles?

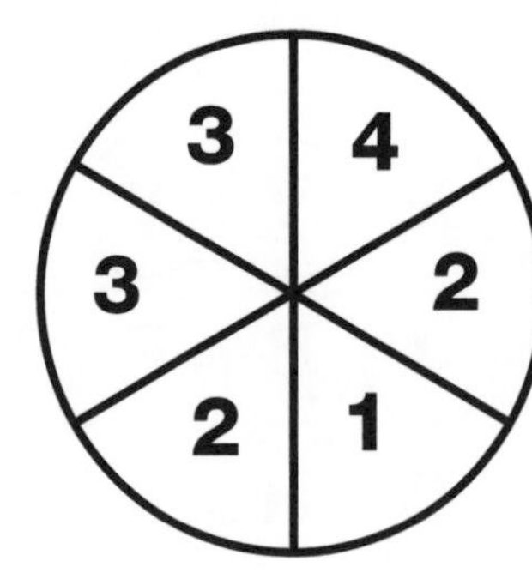

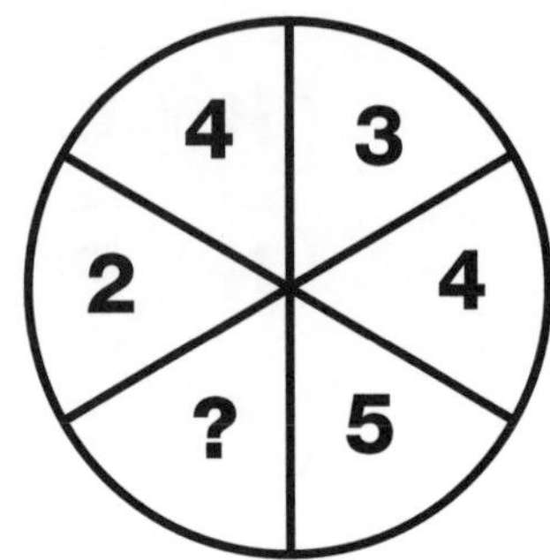

5 PUZZLE

Which number completes the puzzle?

6 PUZZLE

Following a logical sequence, can you complete this puzzle?

3	2
7	7
11	12
17	15
19	22
27	?

What is missing from this pyramid?

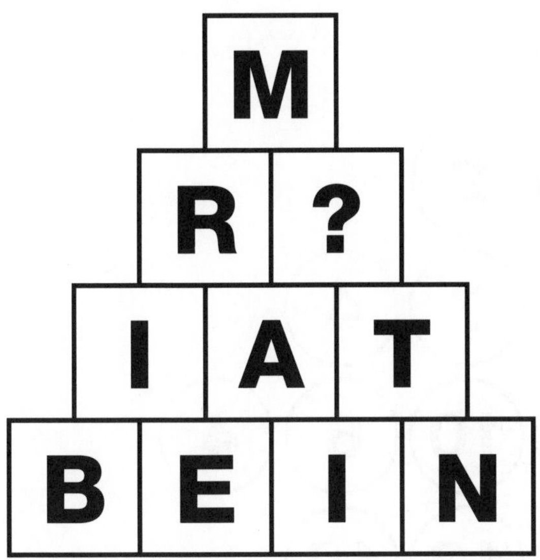

8
PUZZLE

Which letter completes the puzzle?

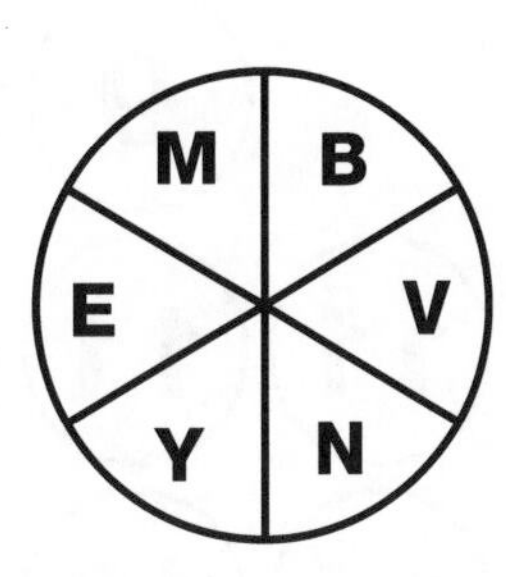

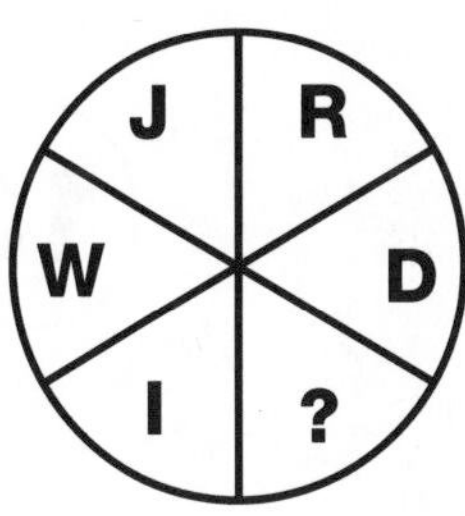

9
PUZZLE

In this sequence of letters what needs to be added to make the puzzle correct?

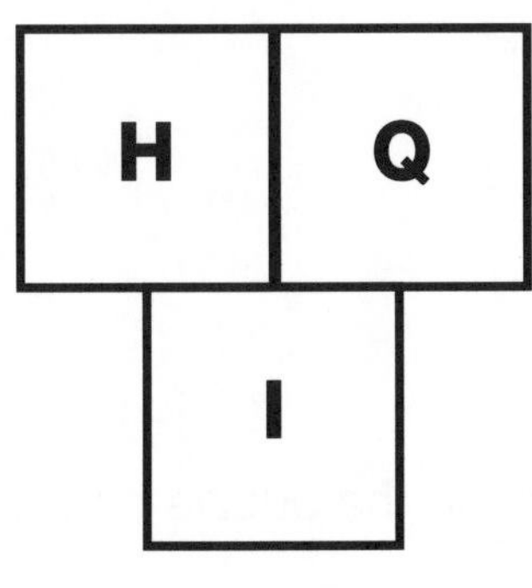

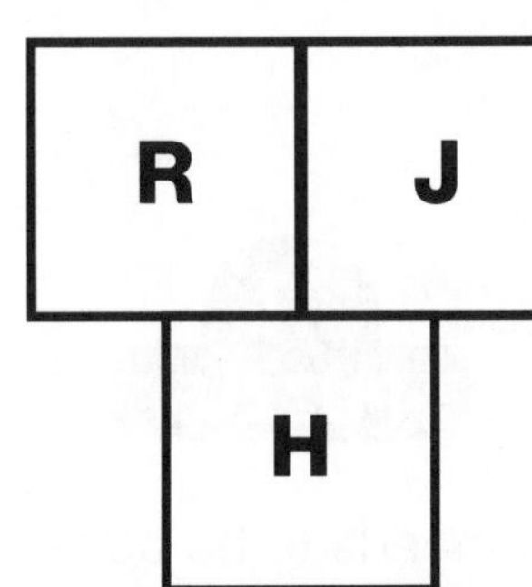

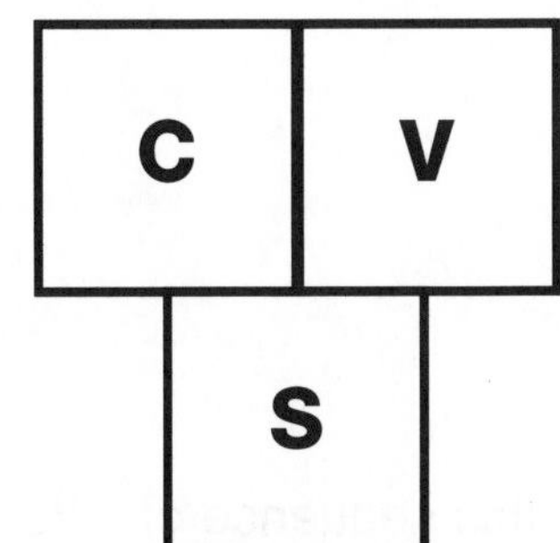

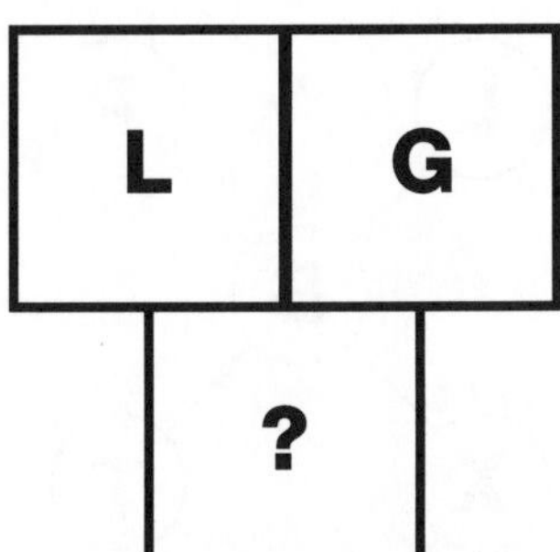

LEVEL 13

10 PUZZLE

Which numbers complete the puzzle?

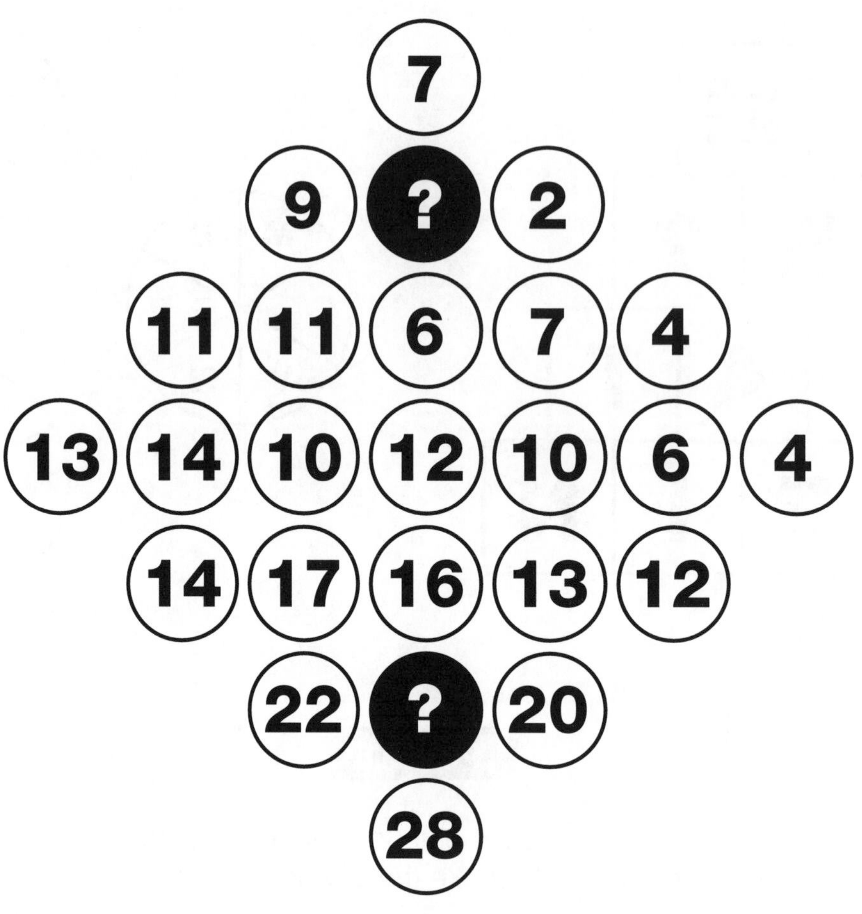

11 PUZZLE

In this sequence of letters what needs to be added to make the puzzle correct?

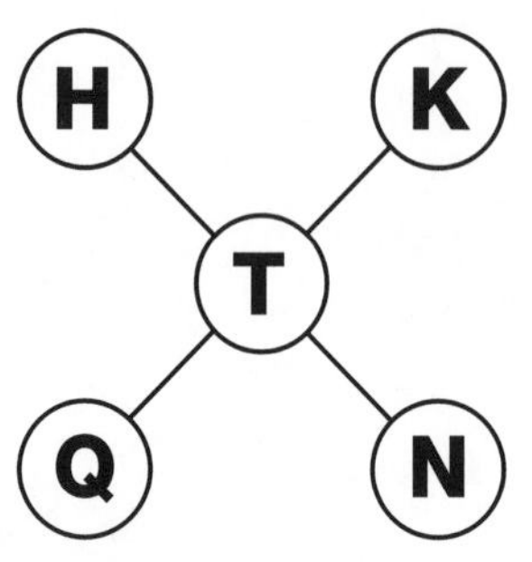

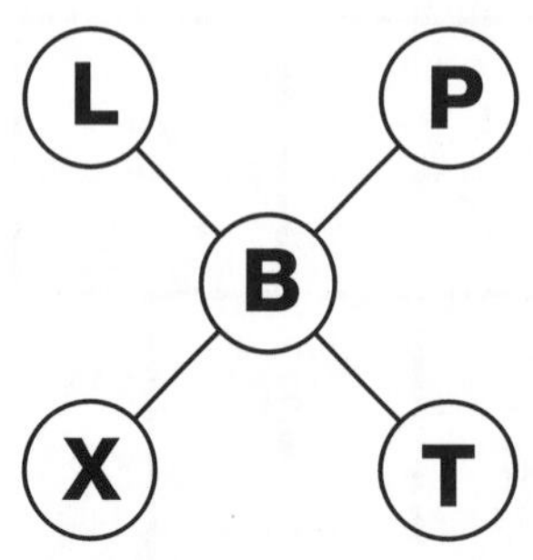

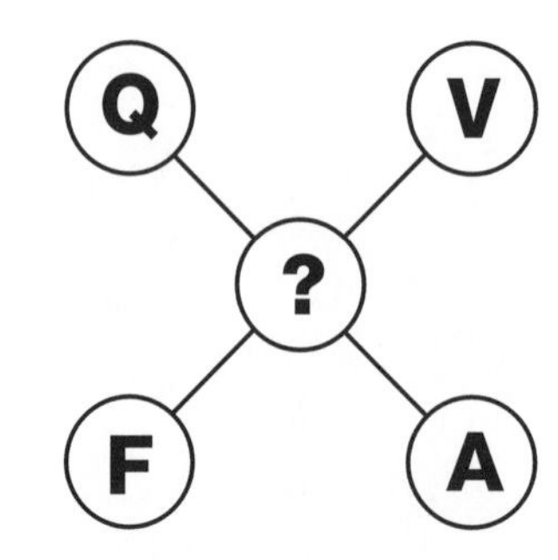

12 PUZZLE

What is missing from the last star?

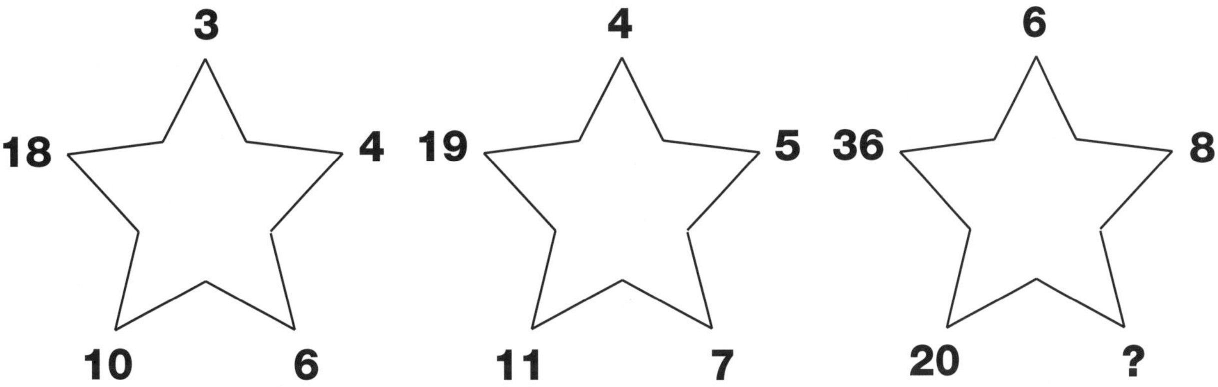

13 PUZZLE

Which letter completes the puzzle?

14 PUZZLE

Following a logical sequence, can you complete this puzzle?

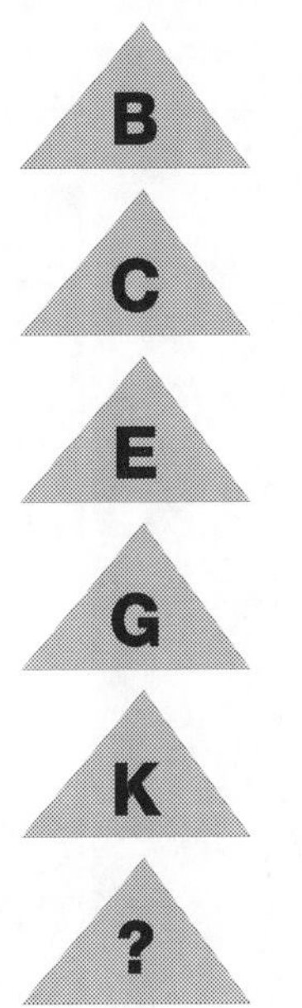

What number is missing?

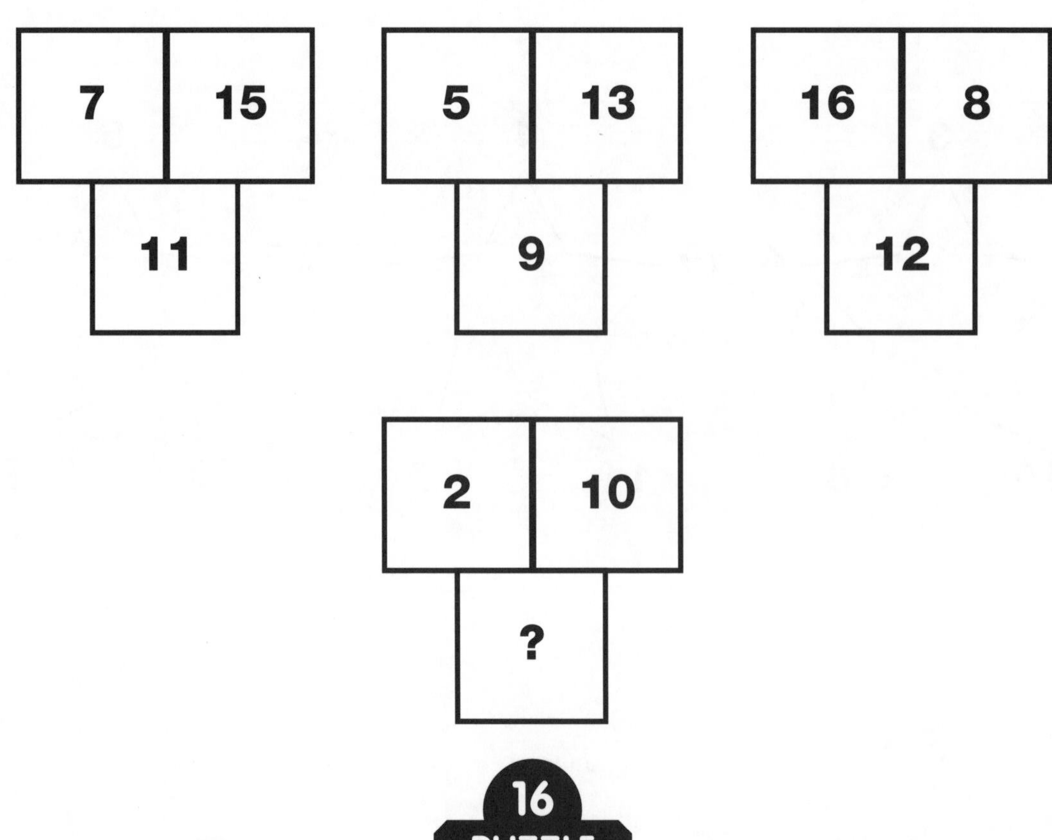

16 PUZZLE

Which dominos are missing from this group?

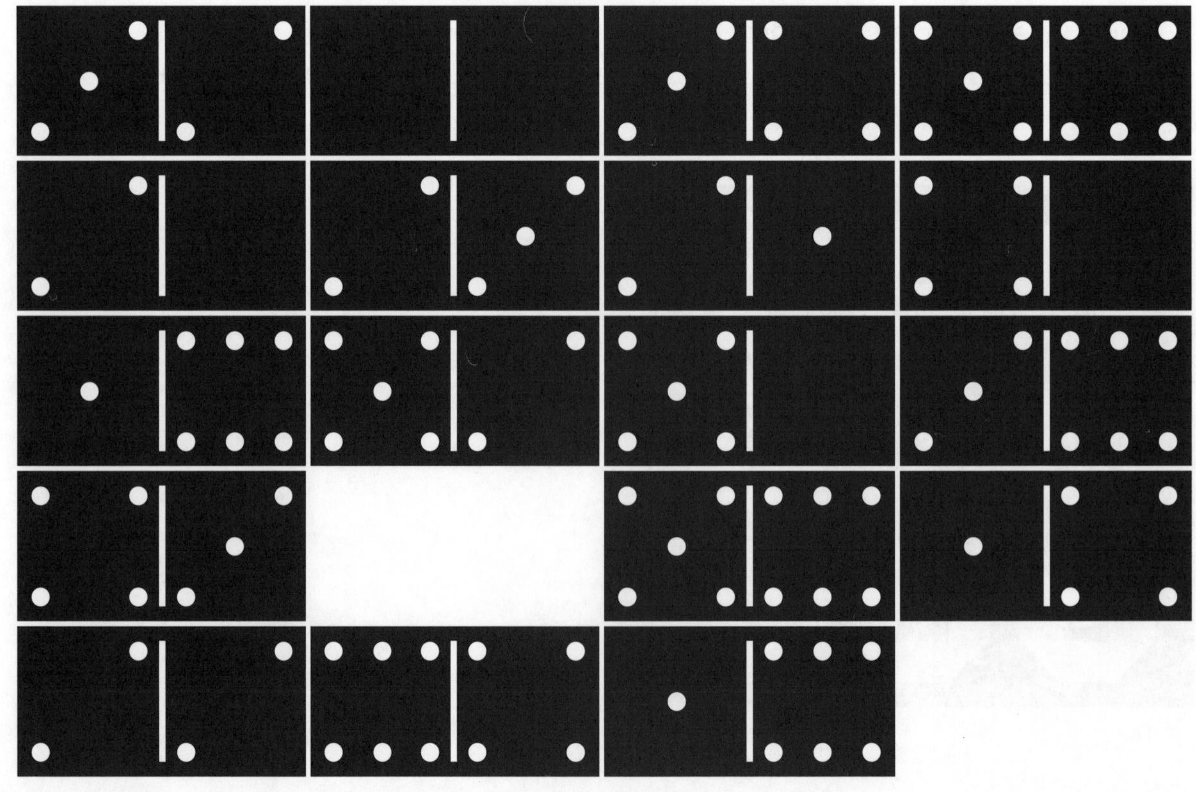

17 PUZZLE

Remove two matches from this arrangement, to leave just four squares. If you can do that, can you remove 4 matches from the original arrangement to leave only 3 squares?

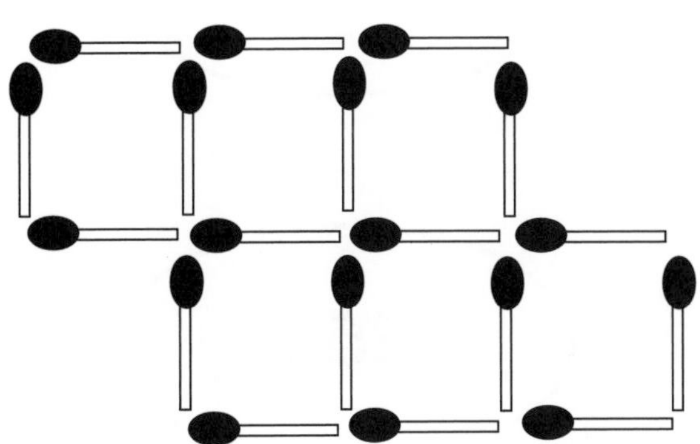

18 PUZZLE

Following a logical sequence, can you complete this puzzle?

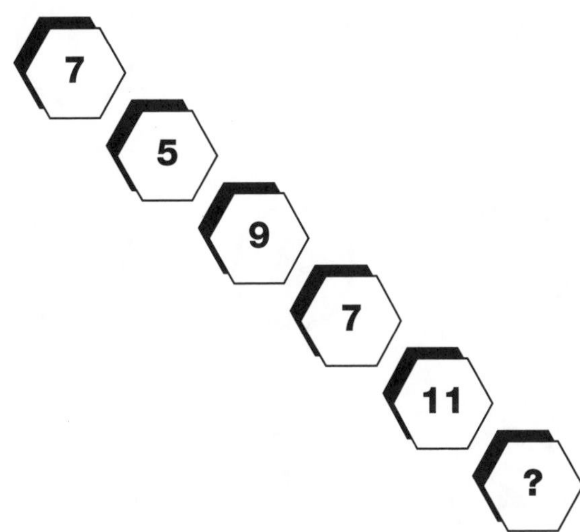

19 PUZZLE

Which letter completes the puzzle?

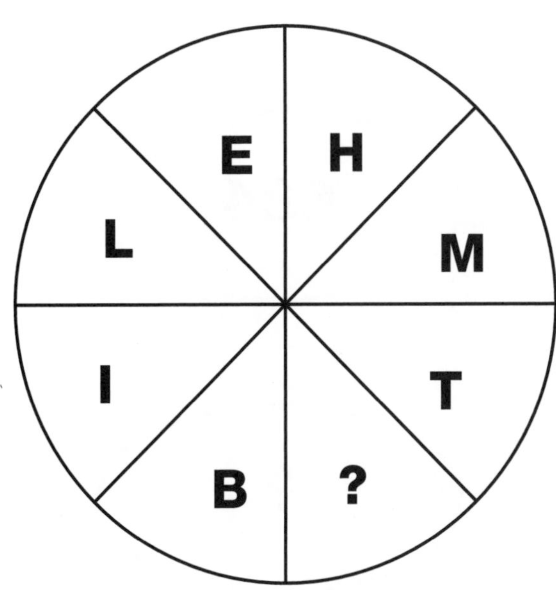

20 PUZZLE

Which number completes the puzzle?

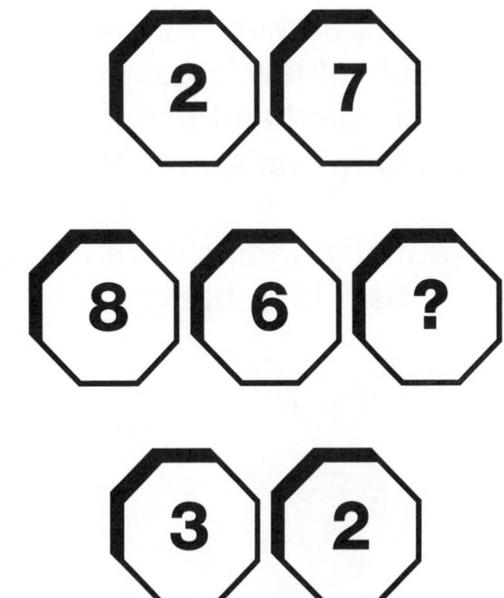

LEVEL

13

21 PUZZLE

Which number completes the puzzle?

Following a logical sequence, can you complete this puzzle?

366

479

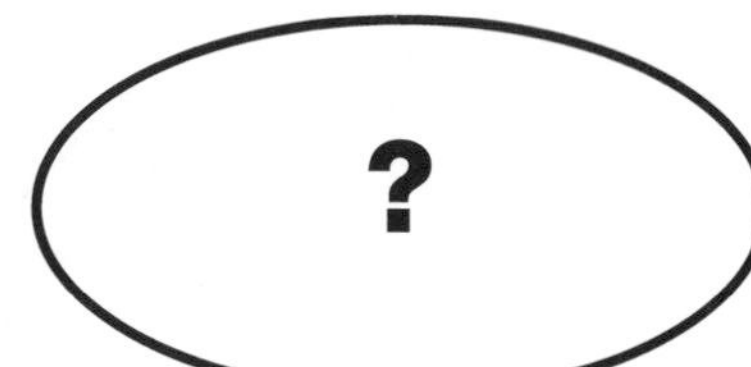

John bought a bag of apples from the supermarket, but when he got them home, he found that two-thirds of them were bruised, half had mildew, a quarter were both bruised and had mildew, and only one was fit to eat.

How many apples were in the bag John bought?

24 PUZZLE

Which playing cards fill in the missing gaps to complete the puzzle?

LEVEL 13

What is missing from this puzzle?

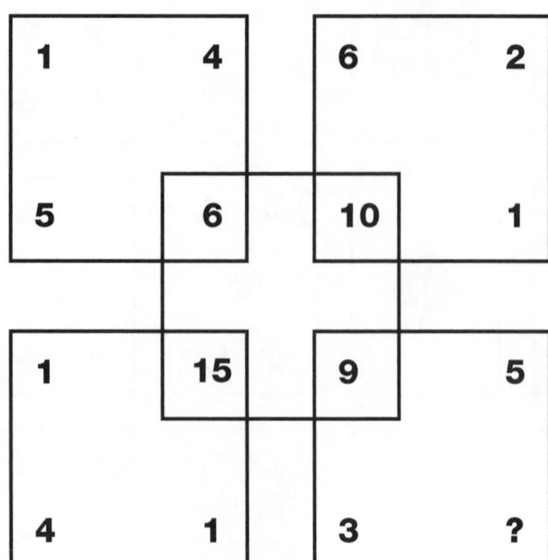

2
PUZZLE

Following a logical sequence, can you complete this puzzle?

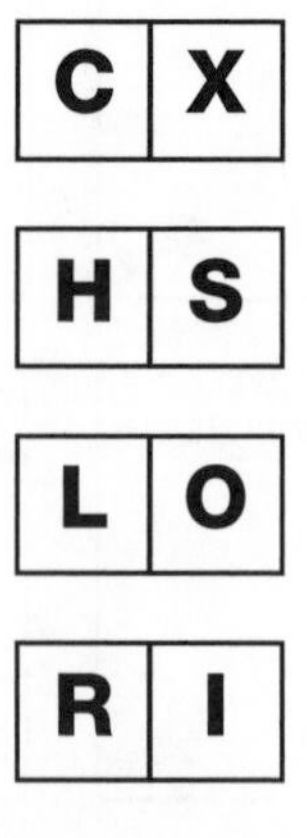

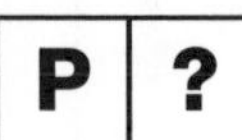

Which number completes this wheel?

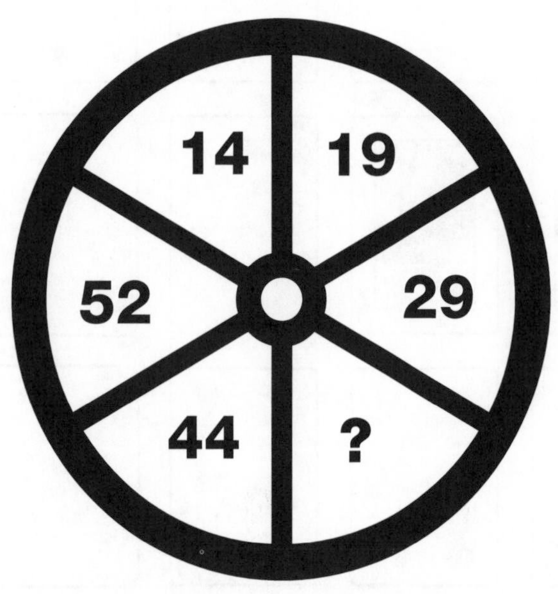

4
PUZZLE

Which letter completes the puzzle?

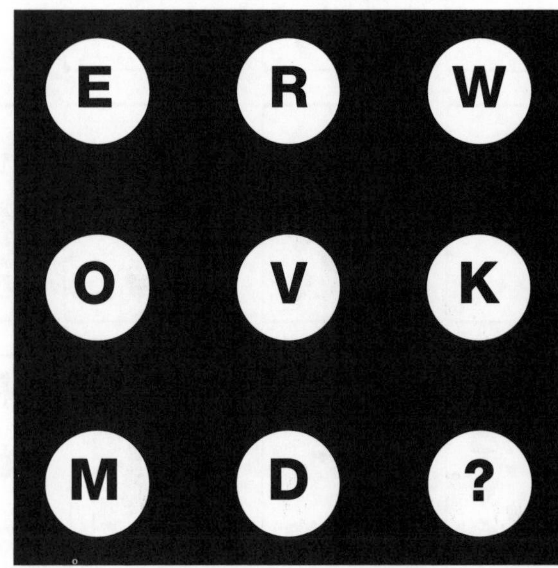

5
PUZZLE

Which number completes the puzzle?

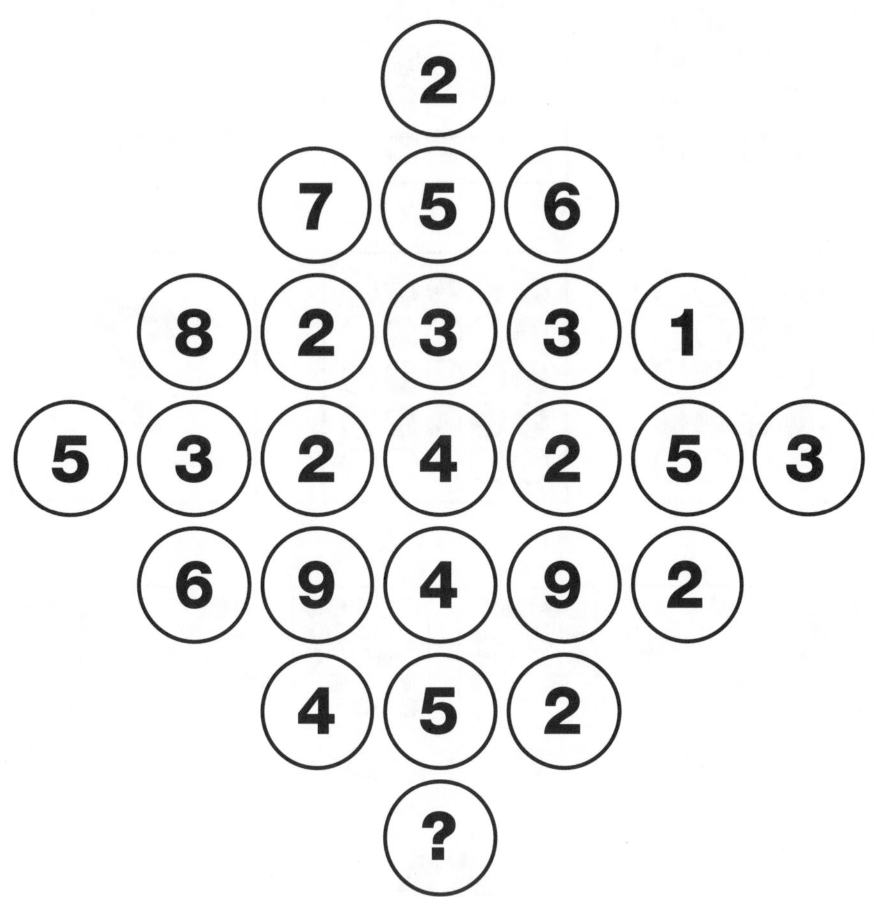

6
PUZZLE

What is missing from this arrangement of circles?

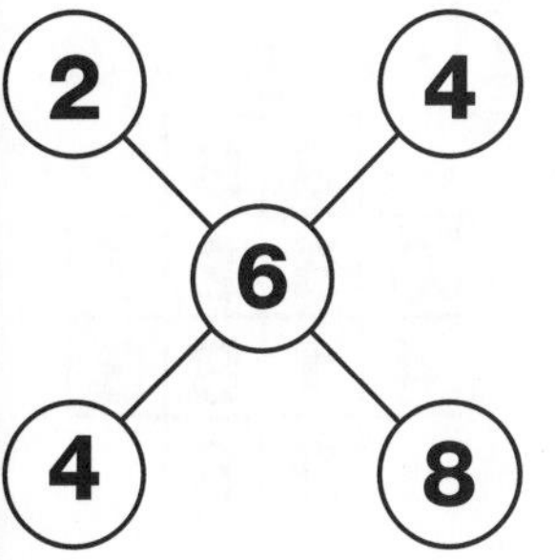

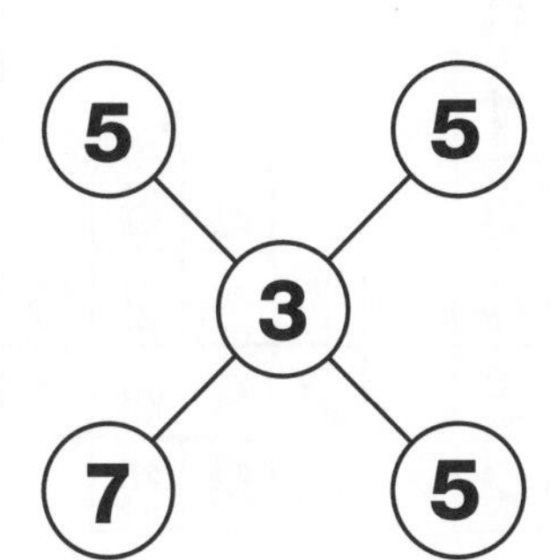

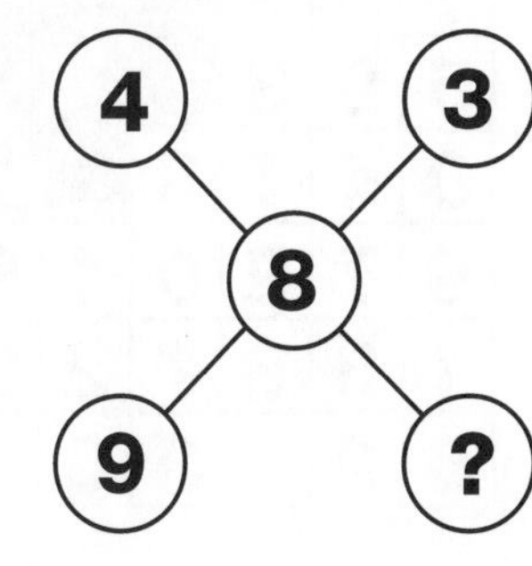

LEVEL

Which of the bottom patterns continues the sequence?

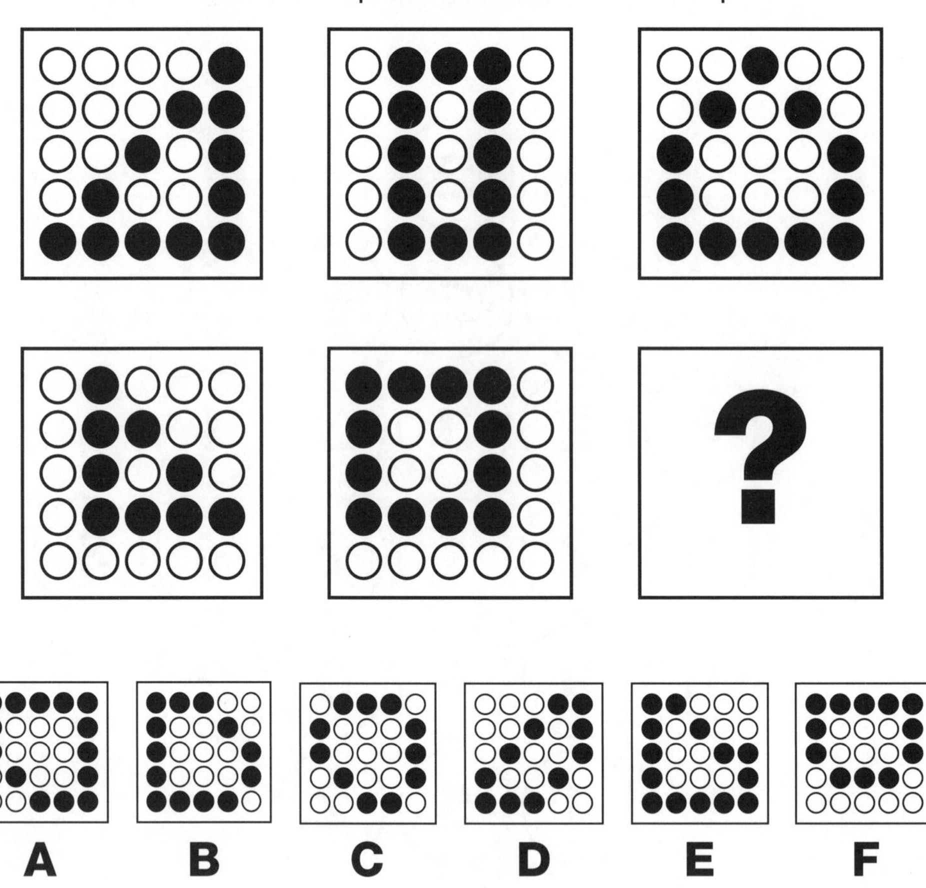

8
PUZZLE

Which grid fills the missing gap?

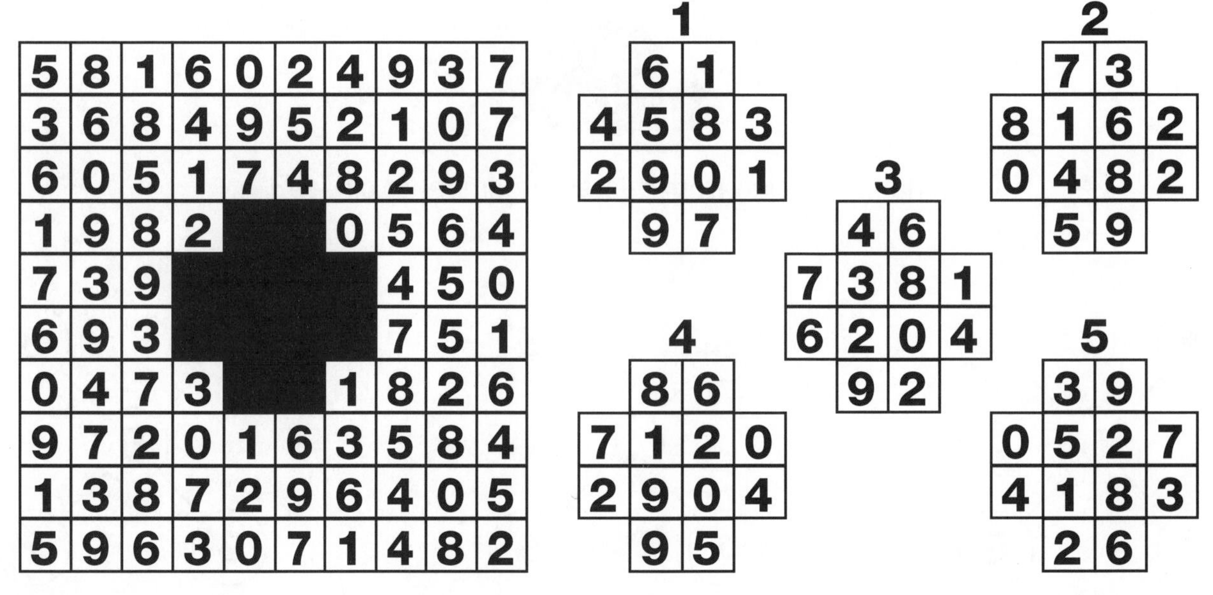

9 PUZZLE

What three letters need to be added to this puzzle?

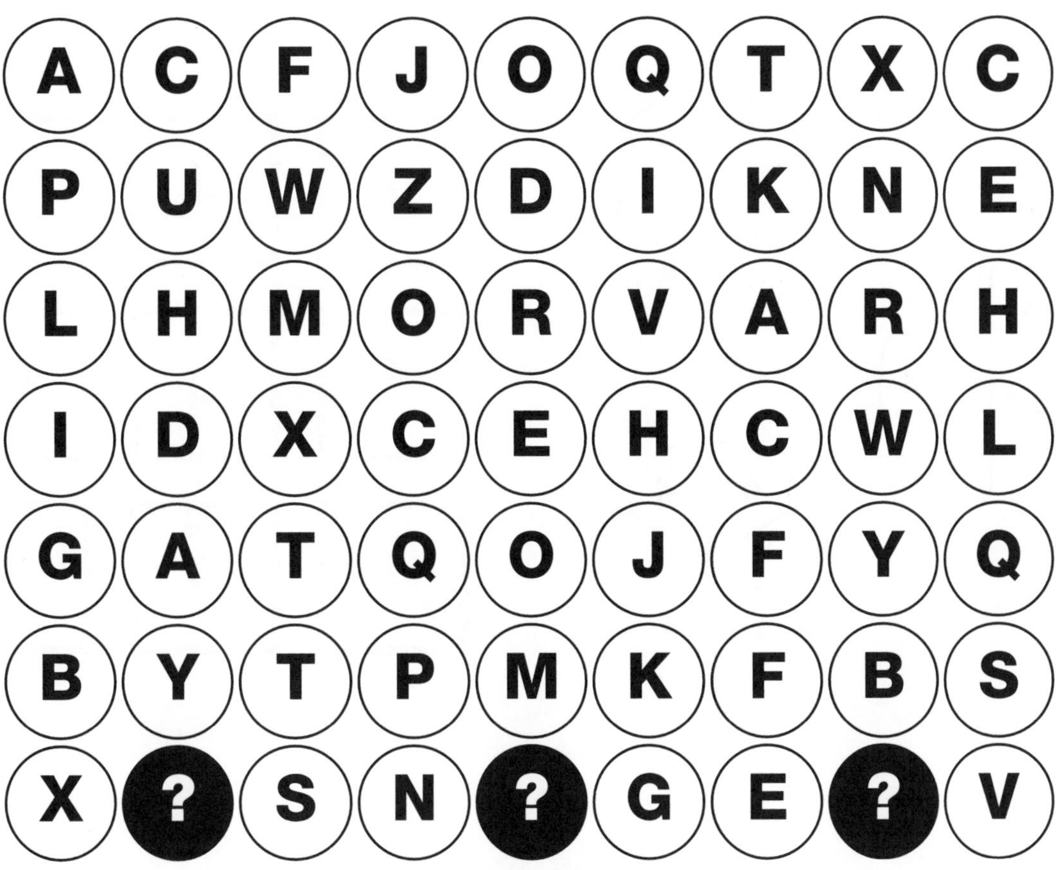

10 PUZZLE

Following a logical sequence, can you complete this puzzle?

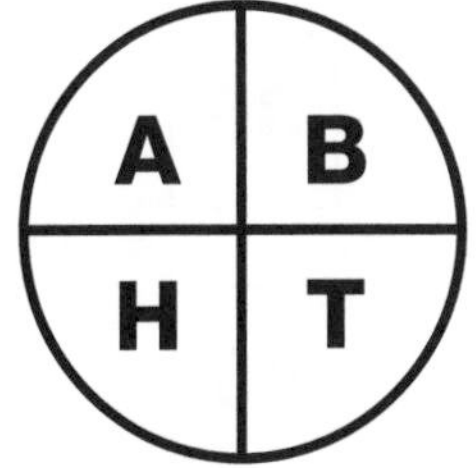

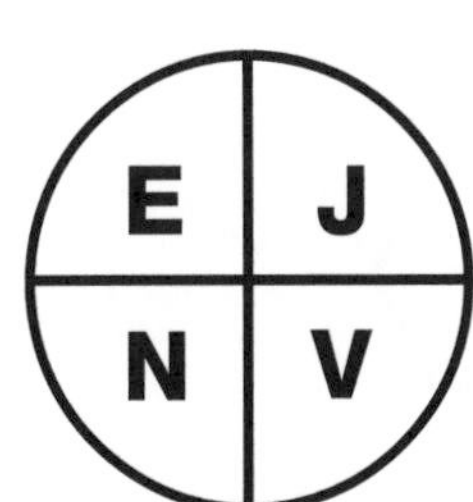

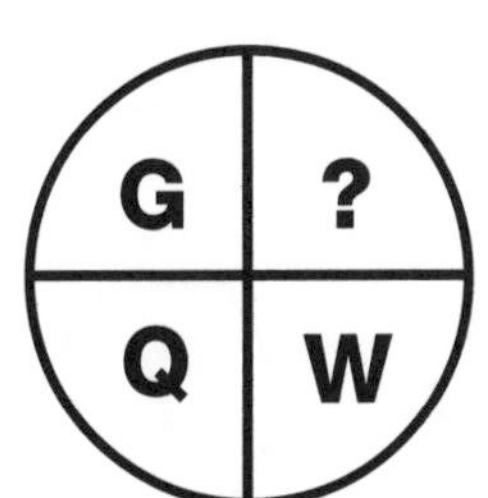

LEVEL

14

11 PUZZLE

Which number completes the puzzle?

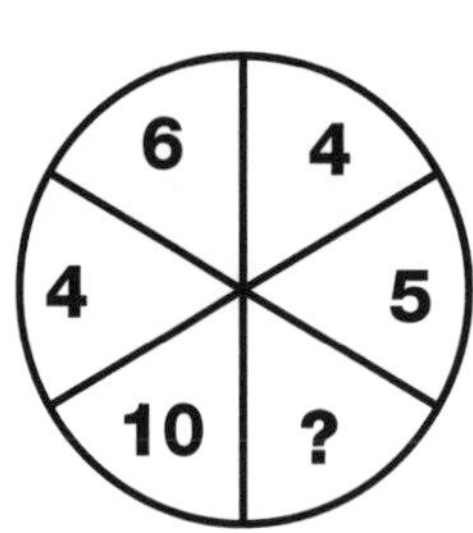

12 PUZZLE

Which number completes this puzzle?

1	9	?

13 PUZZLE

Which number goes in the bottom right hand shape?

2

14 PUZZLE

Following a logical sequence, can you complete this puzzle?

35

48

63

80

?

15 PUZZLE

What is missing from the last star?

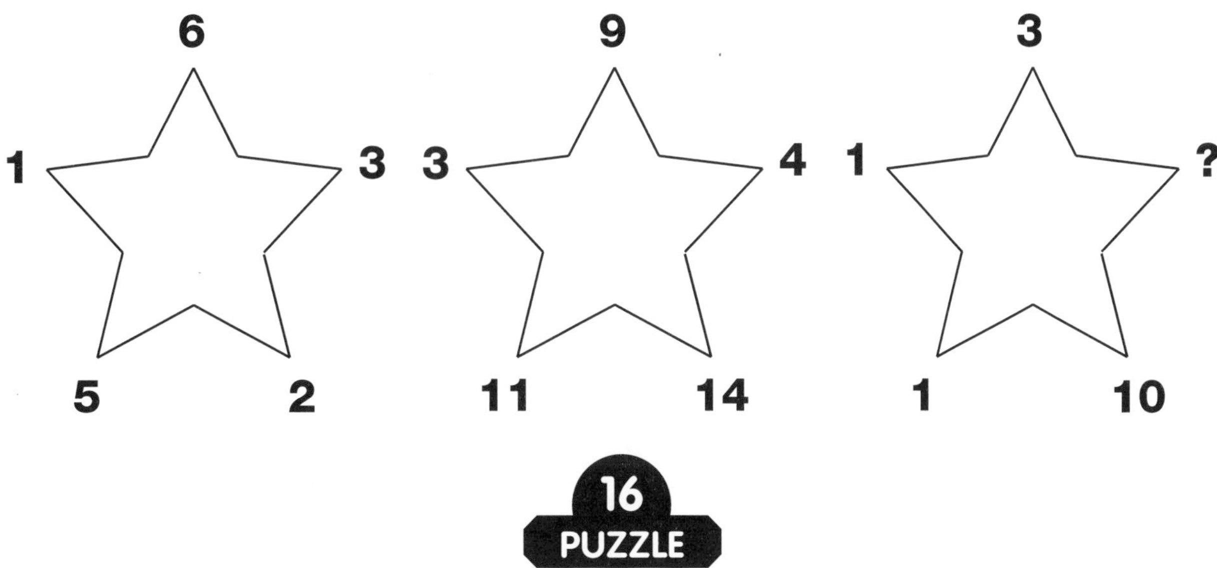

16 PUZZLE

Which patterns replace the two question marks to complete the sequence?

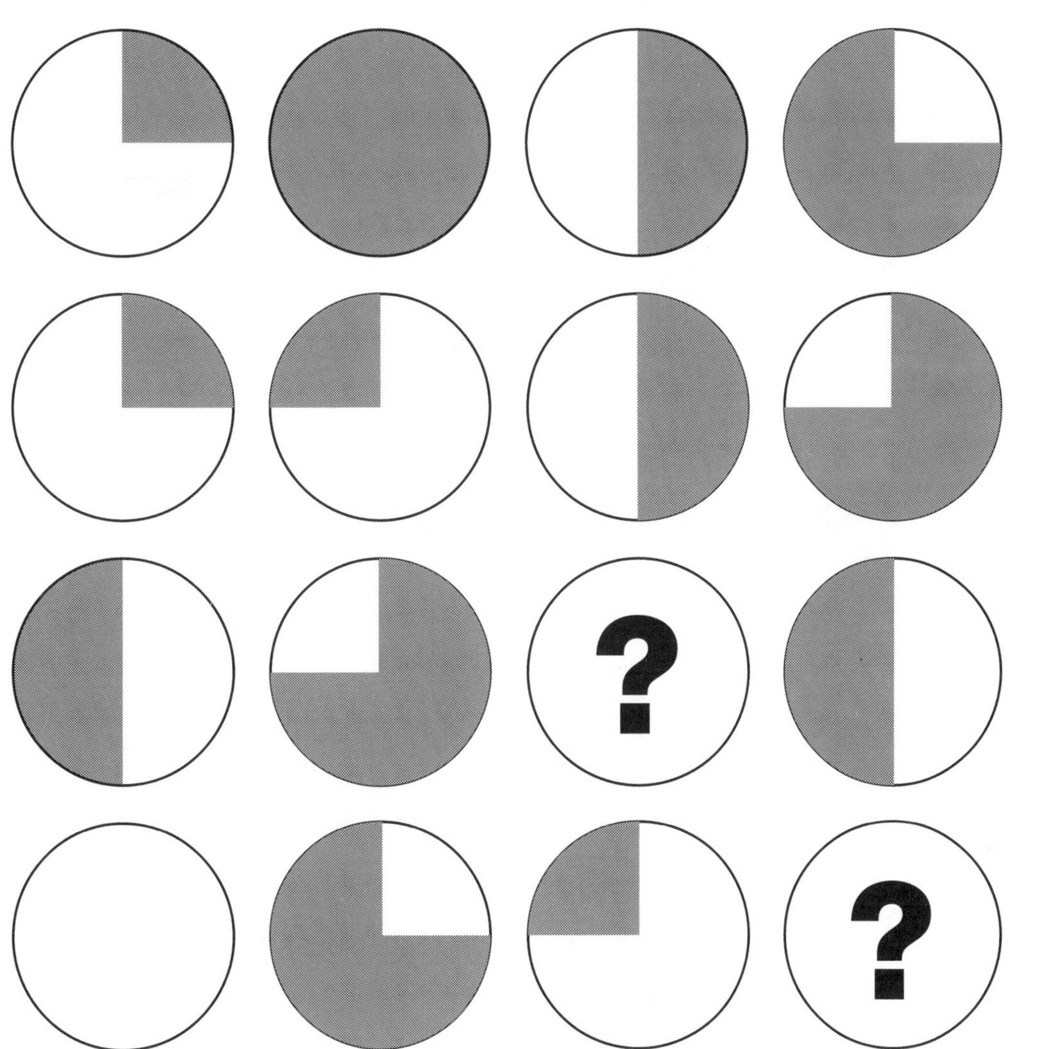

LEVEL

14

LEVEL

14

17 PUZZLE

Which letter completes this wheel?

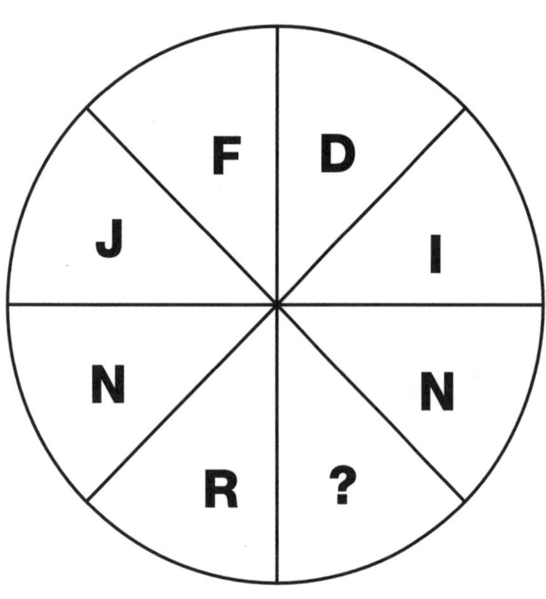

Which letter completes the puzzle?

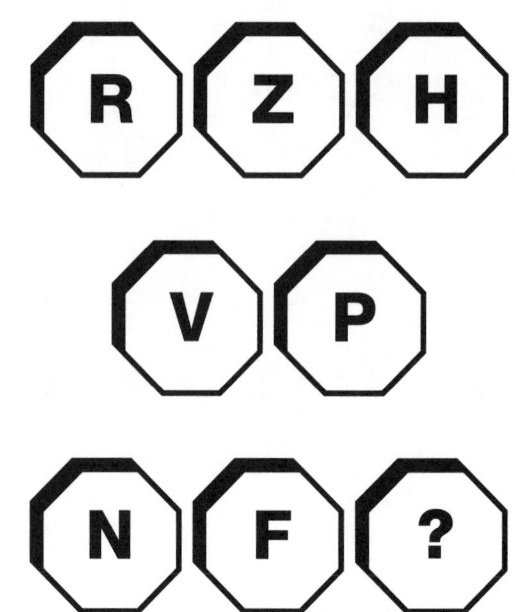

19 PUZZLE

In this sequence of letters what needs to be added to make the puzzle correct?

20 PUZZLE

Can you arrange these 12 matches, to form 6 equilateral triangles?

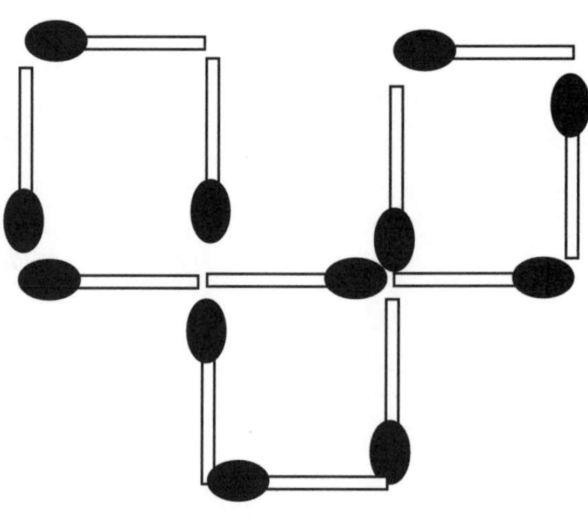

Which letter is missing?

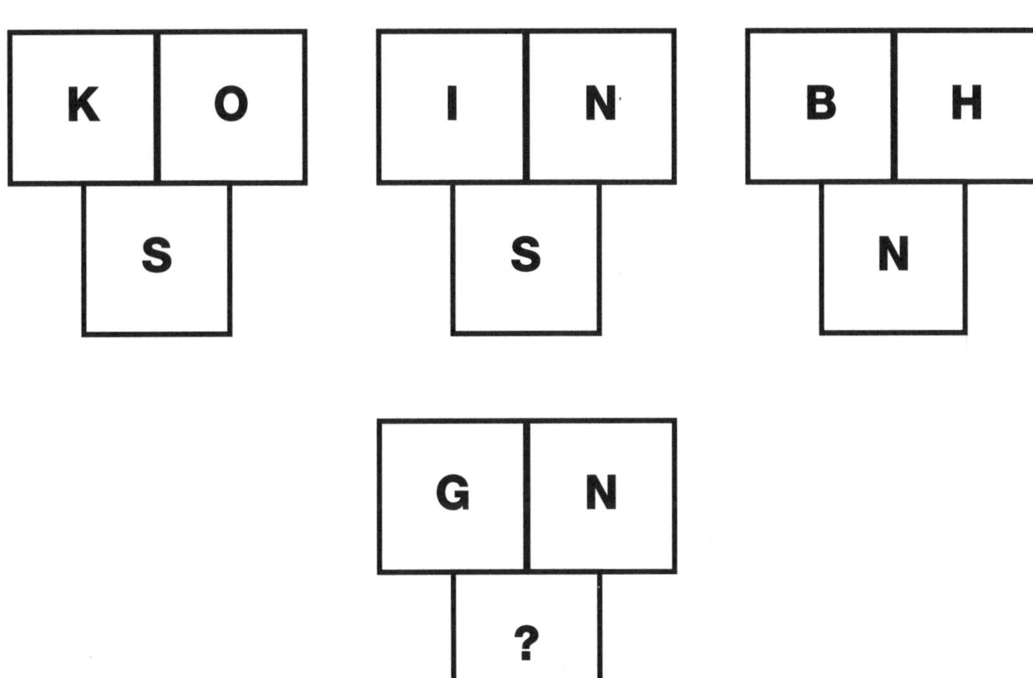

22 PUZZLE

Which grid fills the missing gap?

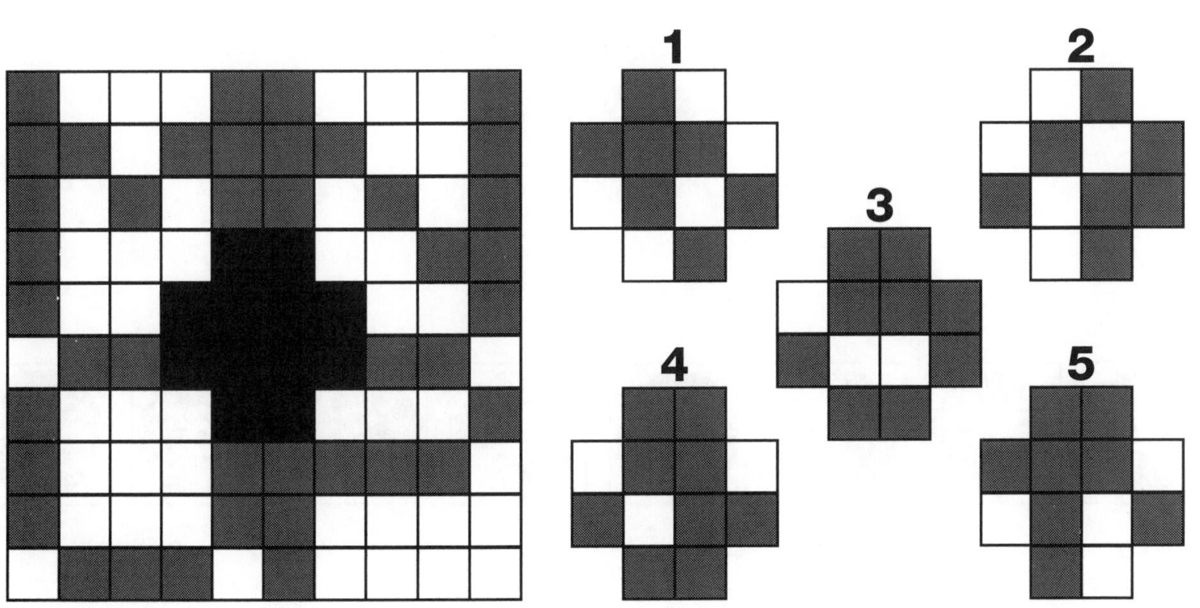

Puzzle 23

Which of the lower patterns completes this puzzle?

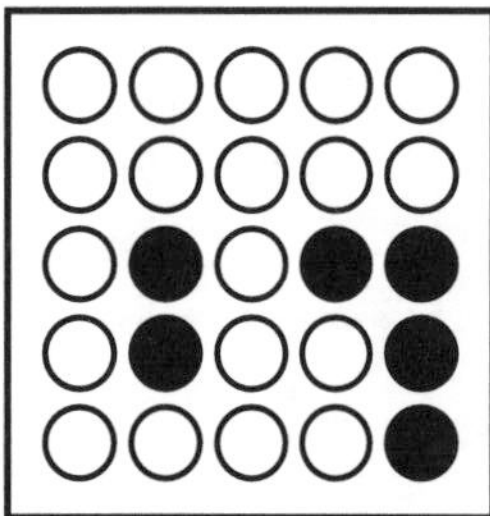
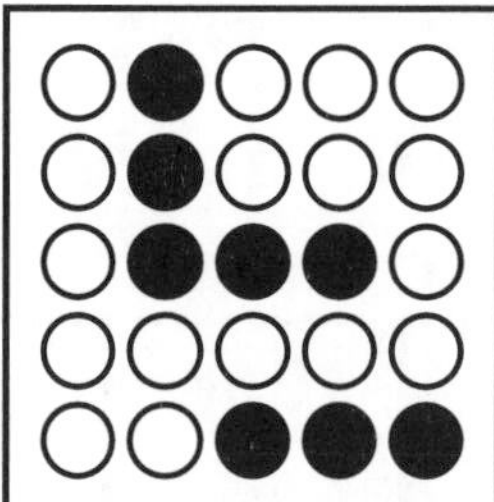
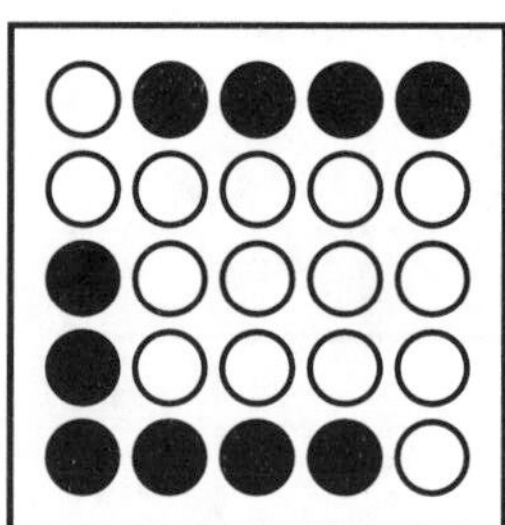
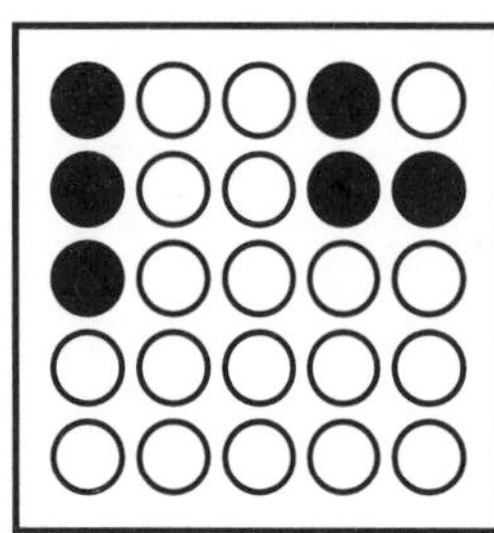
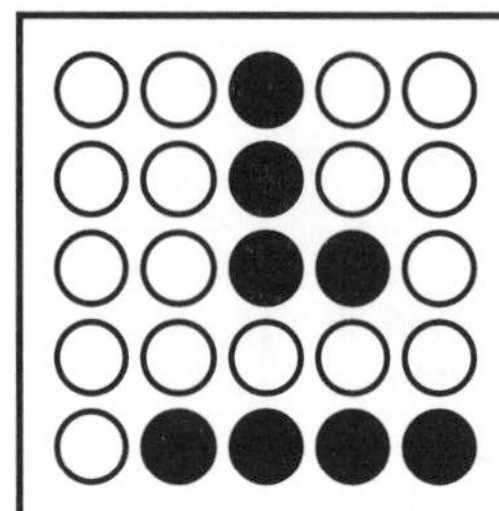

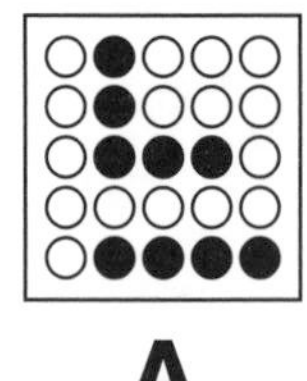
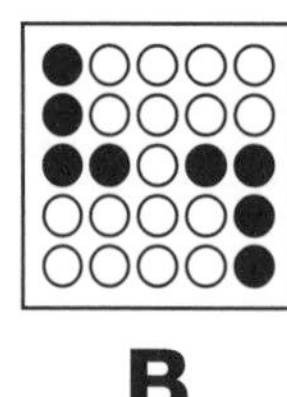
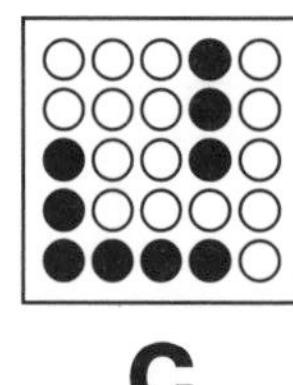
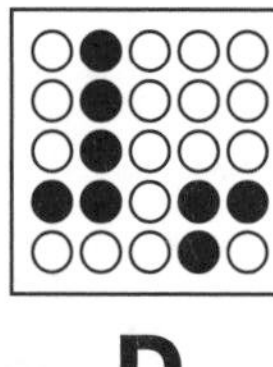
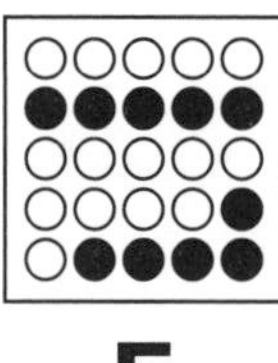
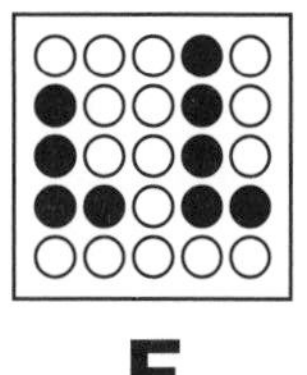

A B C D E F

24 PUZZLE

What is missing from this arrangement of circles?

Which number completes the puzzle?

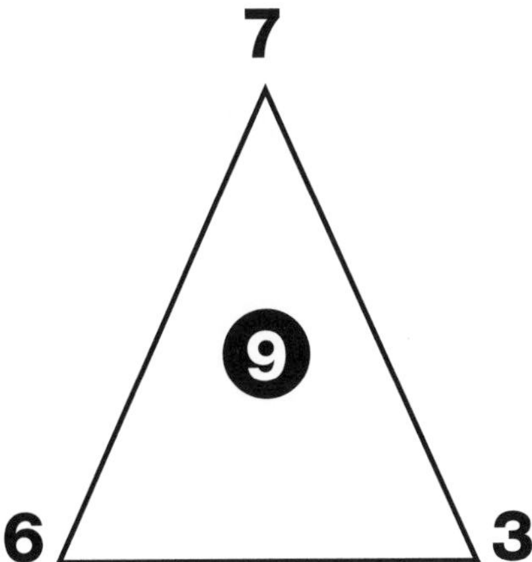

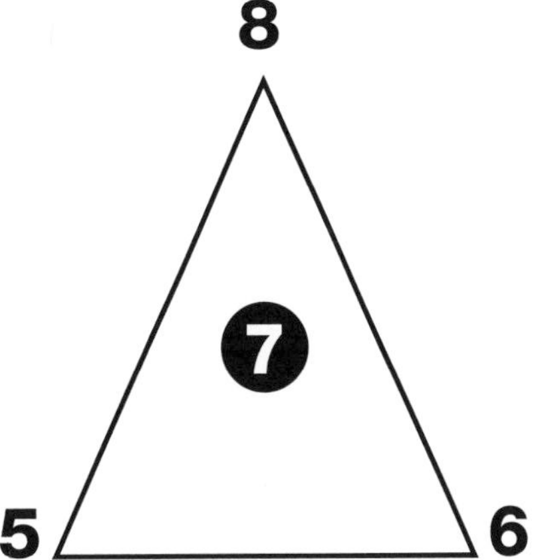

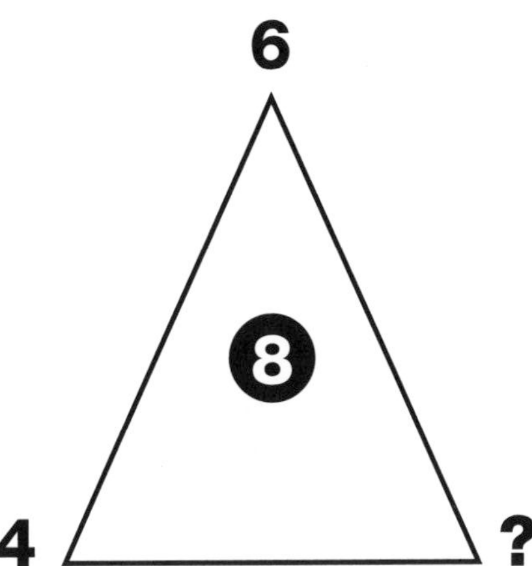

2 PUZZLE

Following a logical sequence, can you complete this puzzle?

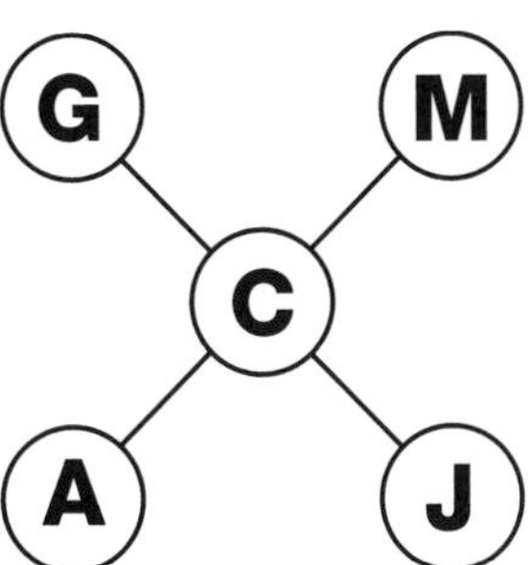

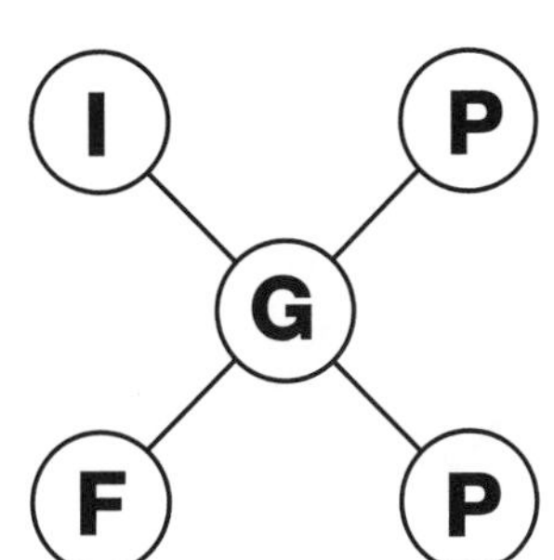

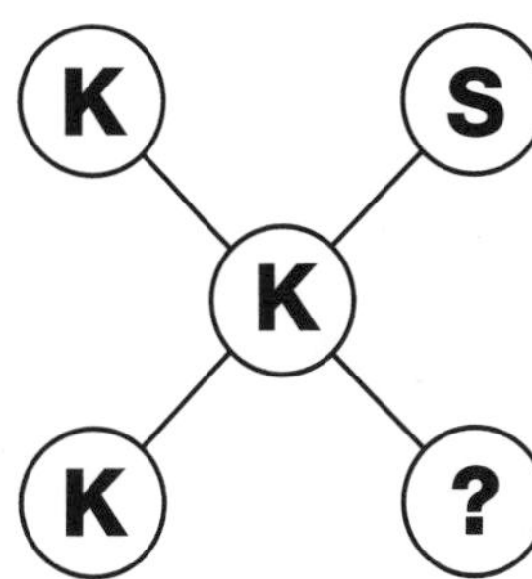

LEVEL

15

3 PUZZLE

What completes this puzzle?

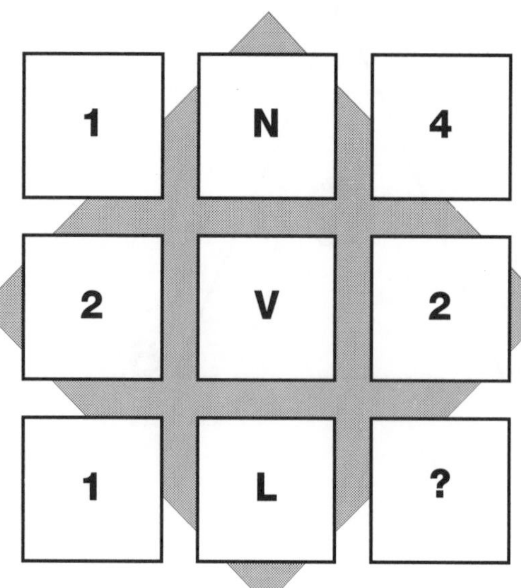

4 PUZZLE

Which number completes the puzzle?

5 PUZZLE

Which of the lower patterns completes the sequence?

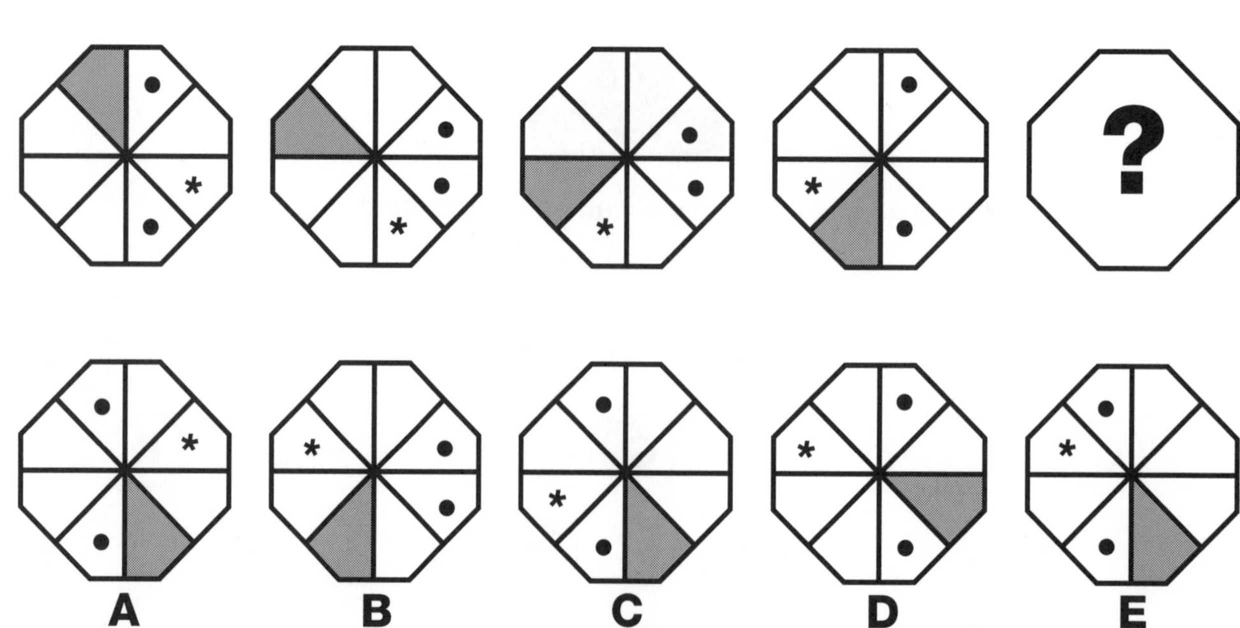

Following a logical sequence, can you complete this puzzle?

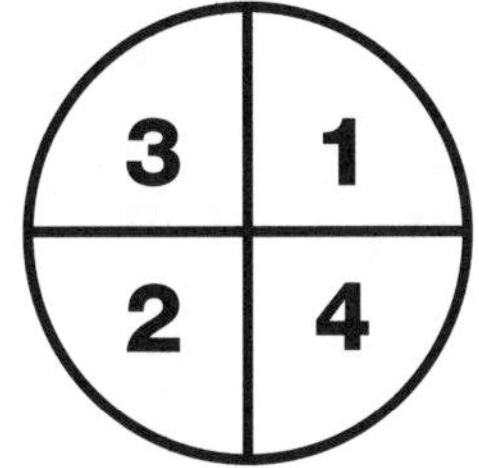

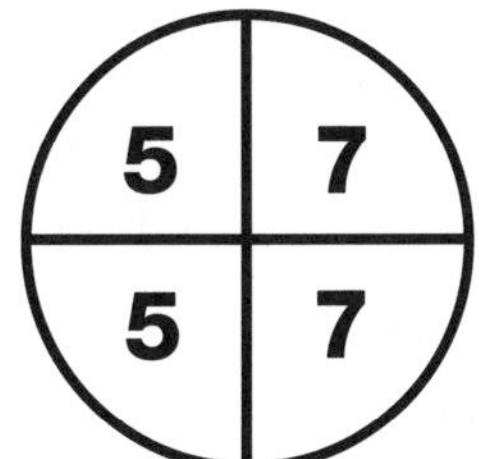

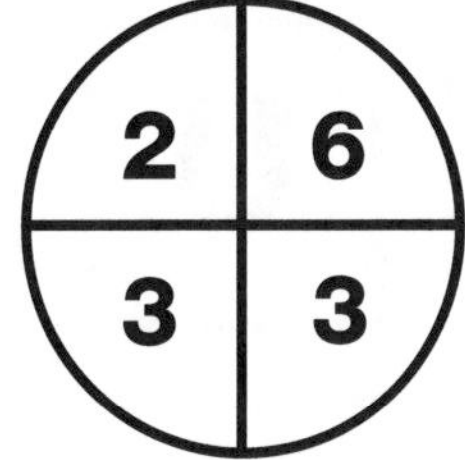

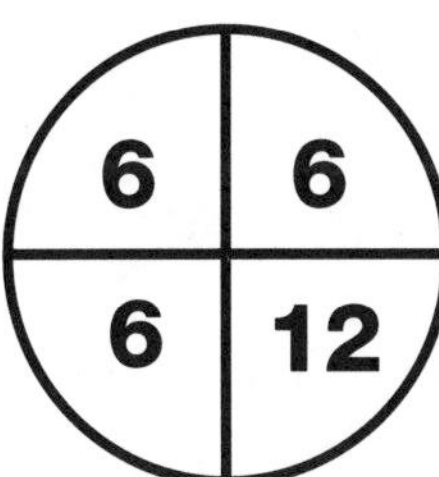

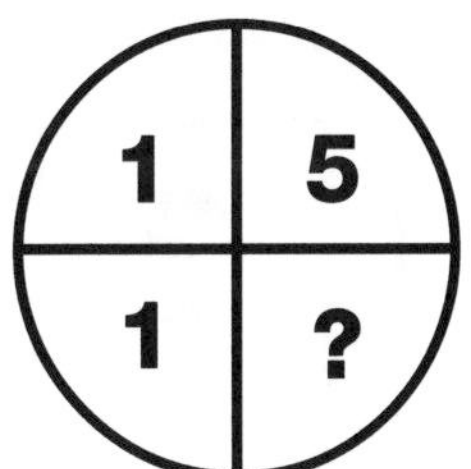

Which of the lower watches fills the missing space?

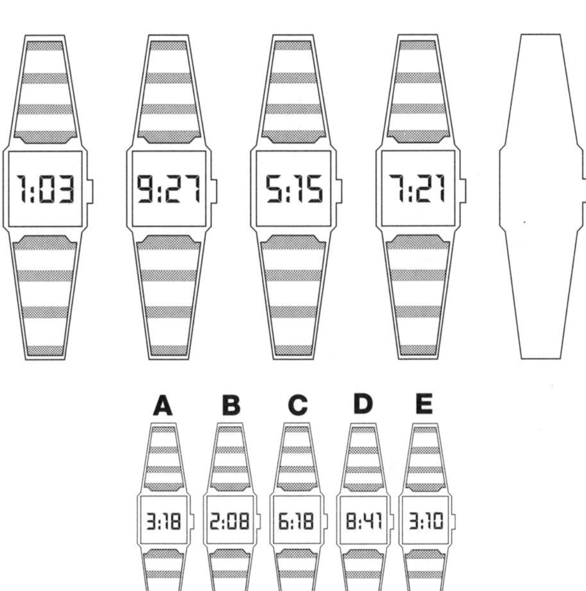

LEVEL 15

Which letter completes the puzzle?

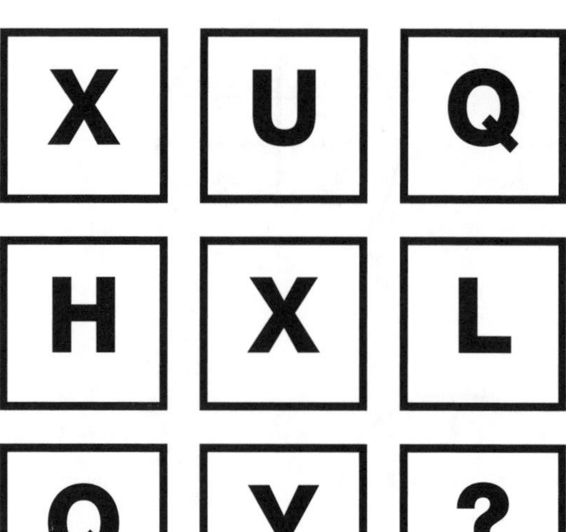

Which number completes the puzzle?

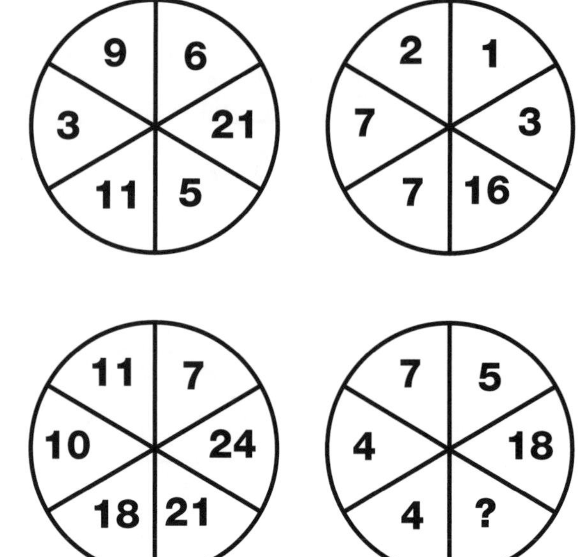

What is missing from the last star?

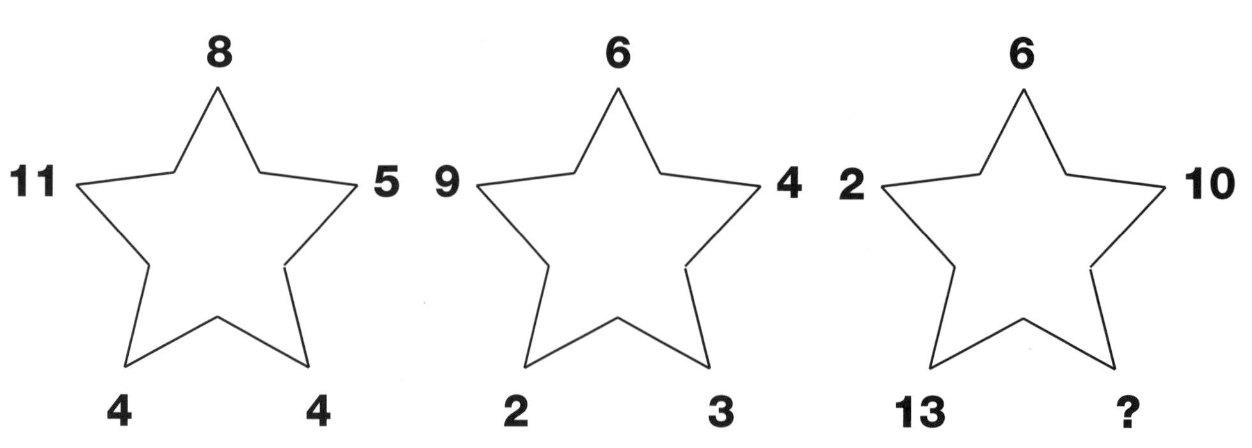

Following a logical sequence, can you complete this puzzle?

4	1
5	1
6	8
9	?

What is missing from this arrangement of circles?

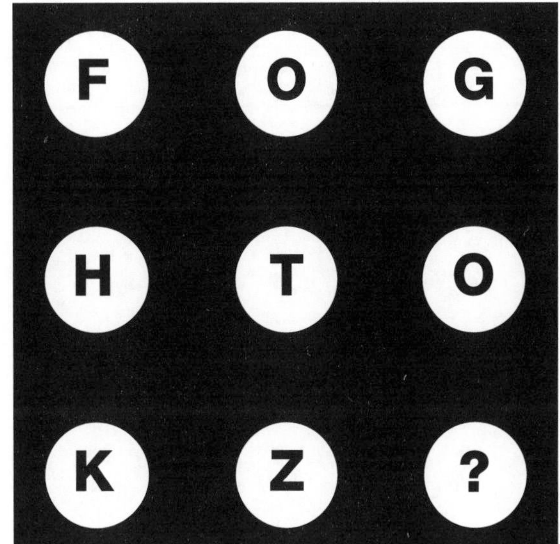

13 PUZZLE

In this sequence of letters what needs to be added to make the puzzle correct?

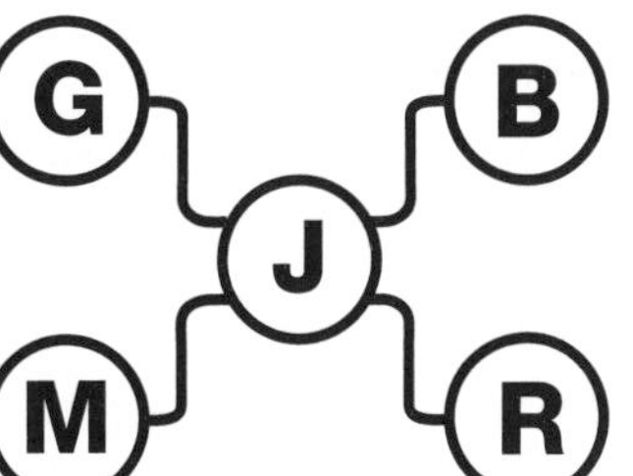

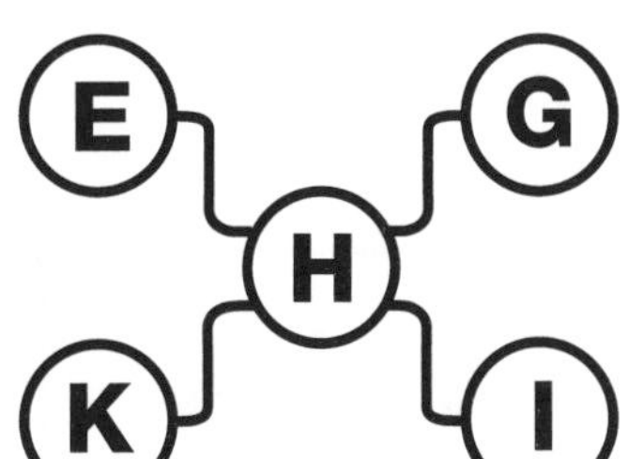

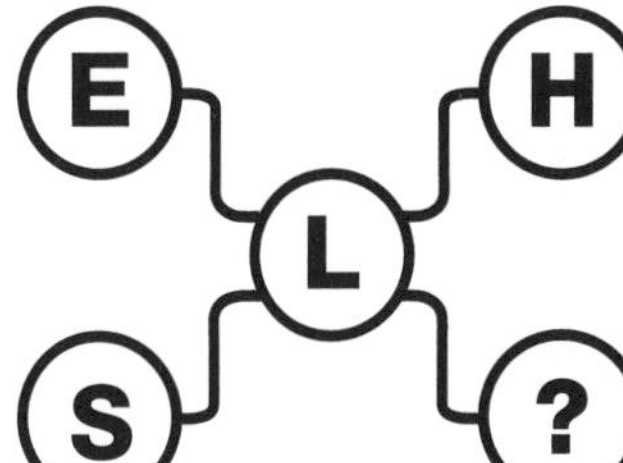

LEVEL

15

14 PUZZLE

Which number is missing?

Which number completes the puzzle?

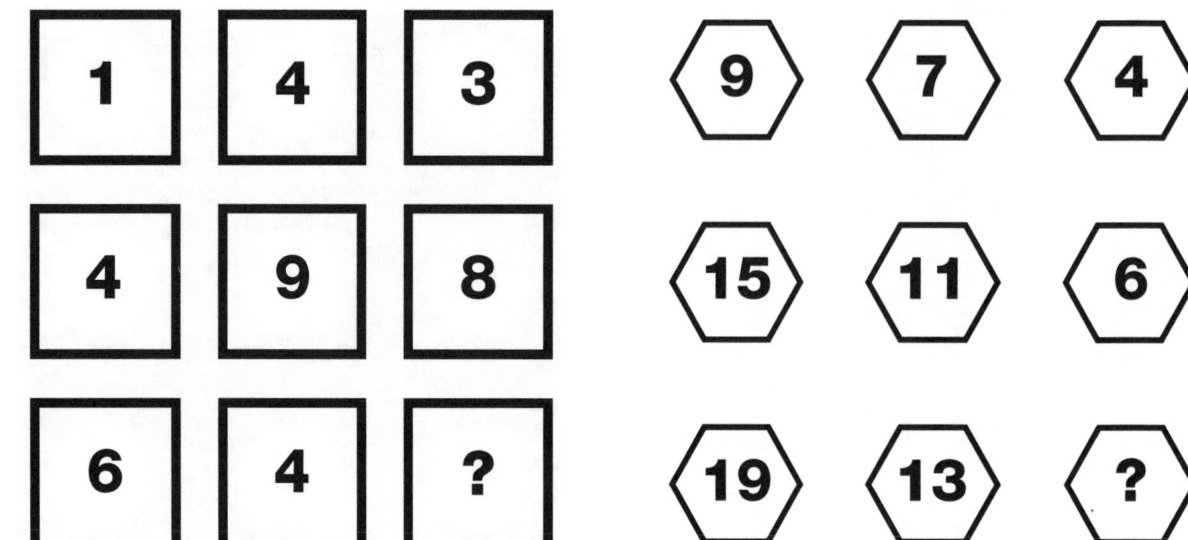

16 PUZZLE

In this sequence of letters what needs to be added to make the puzzle correct?

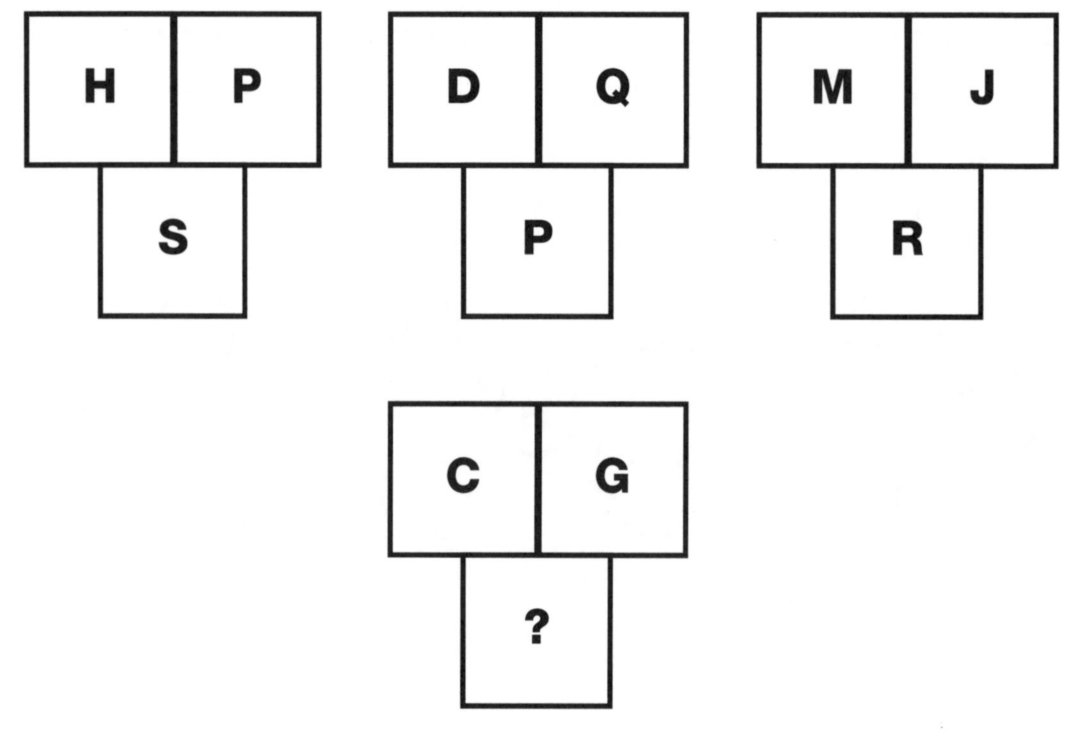

17 PUZZLE

Which letter completes the puzzle?

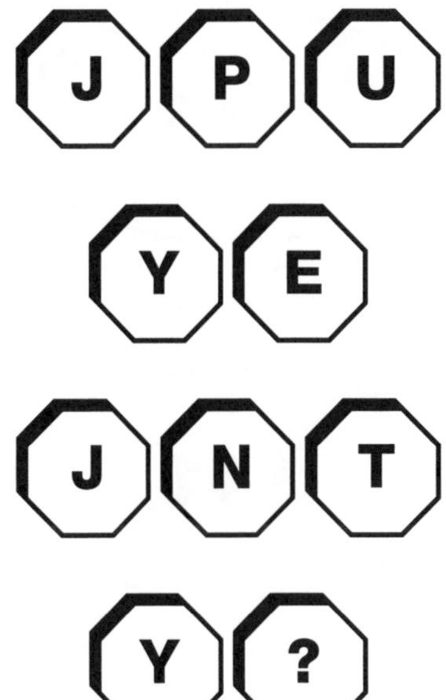

Which number completes this wheel?

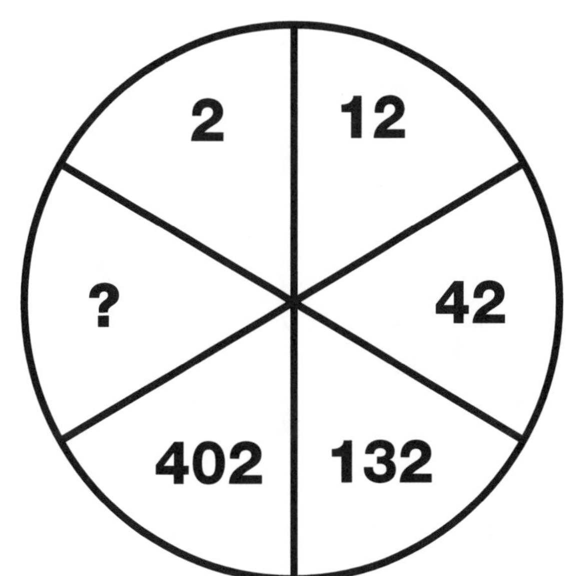

19 PUZZLE

Following a logical sequence, can you complete this puzzle?

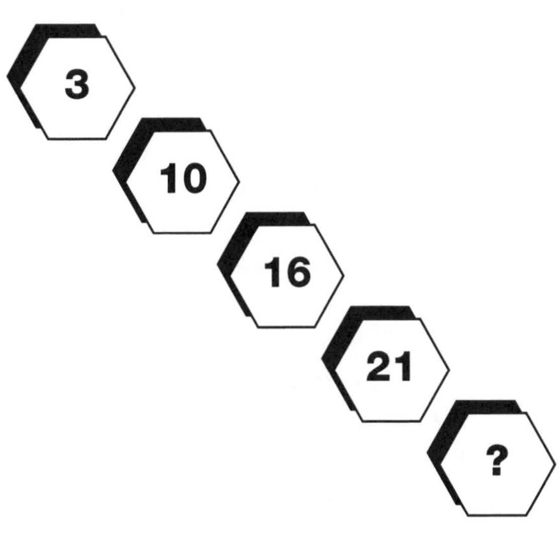

20 PUZZLE

What is missing from this arrangement of circles?

LEVEL

How many jigsaws are needed to balance the bottom scales?

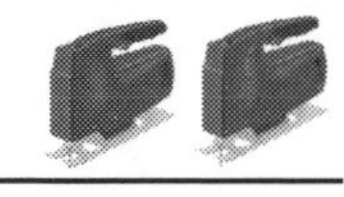

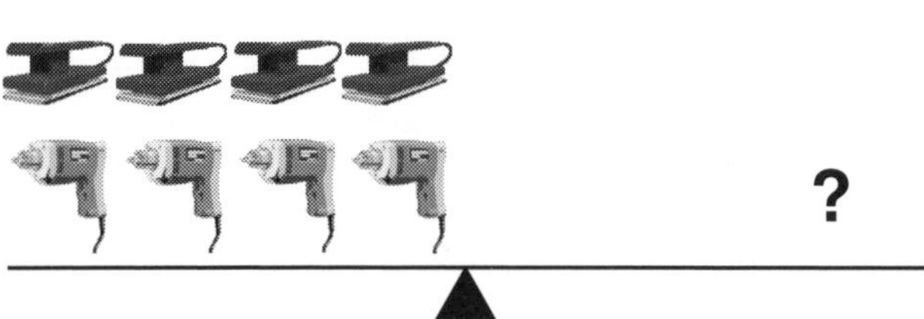

Which letter completes the puzzle?

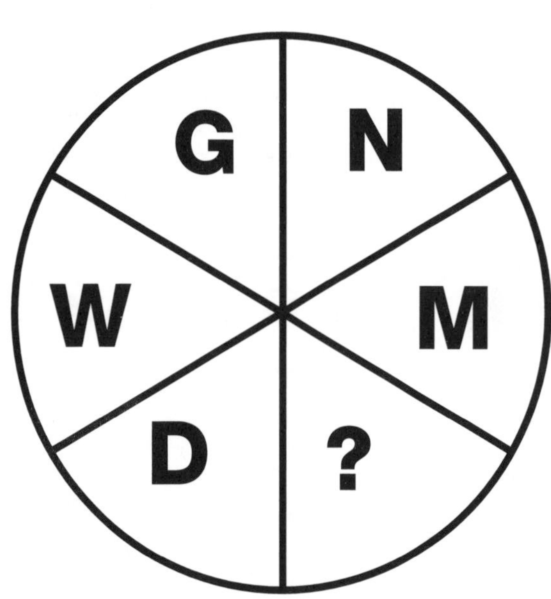

Which number completes the puzzle?

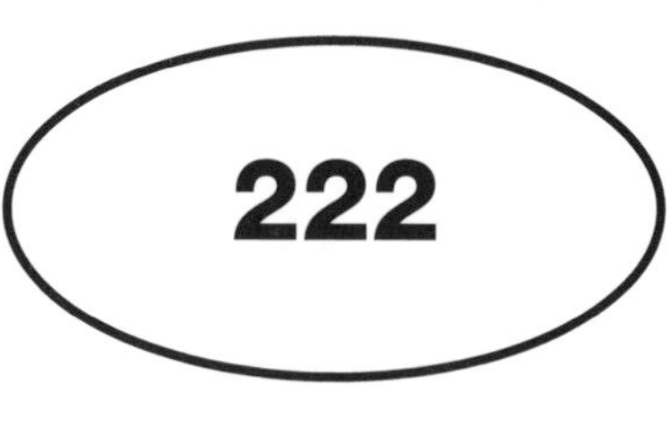

15

24 PUZZLE

Following a logical sequence, can you complete this puzzle?

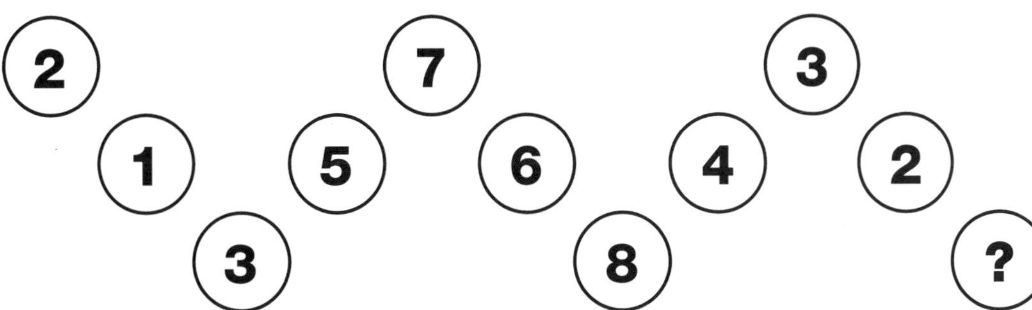

25 PUZZLE

What is the missing pattern?

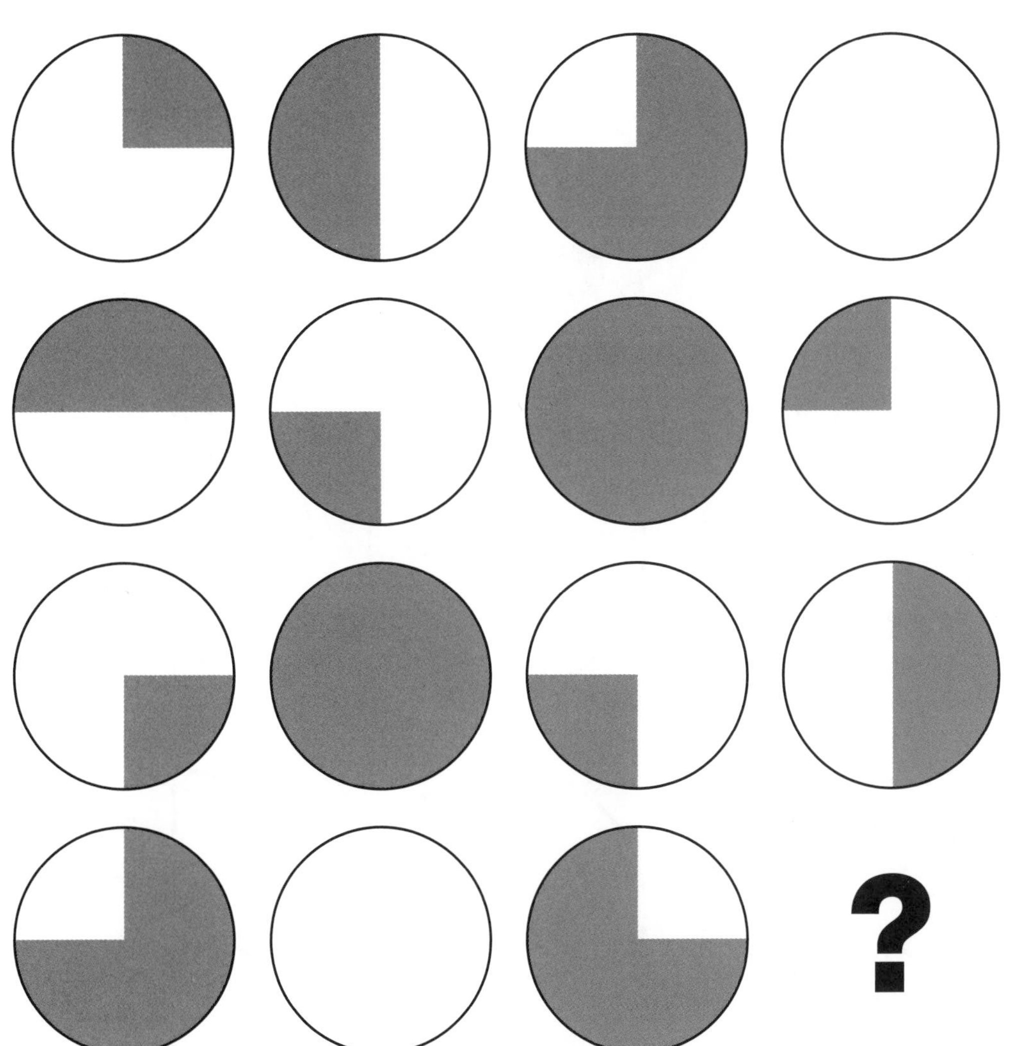

LEVEL 15

LEVEL

Which of the lower patterns completes the sequence?

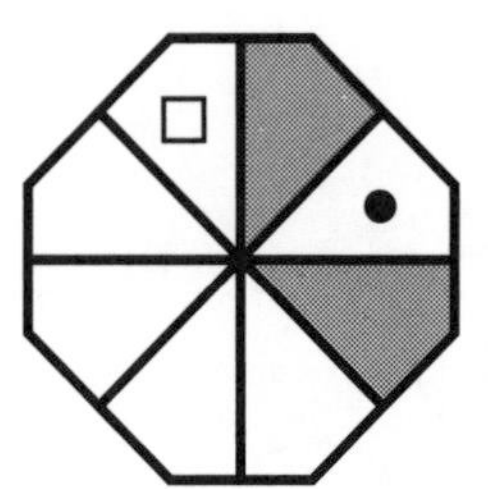
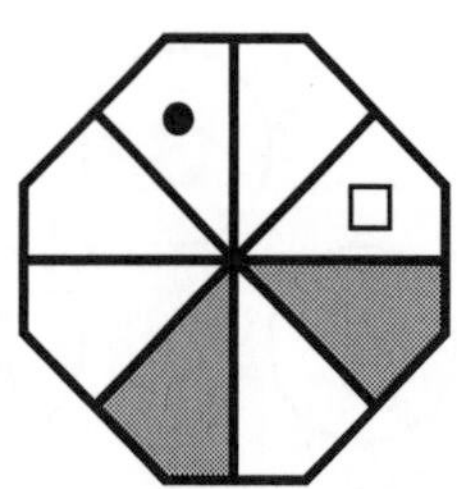
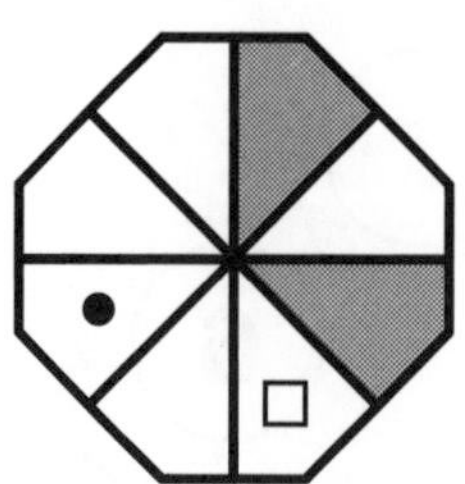
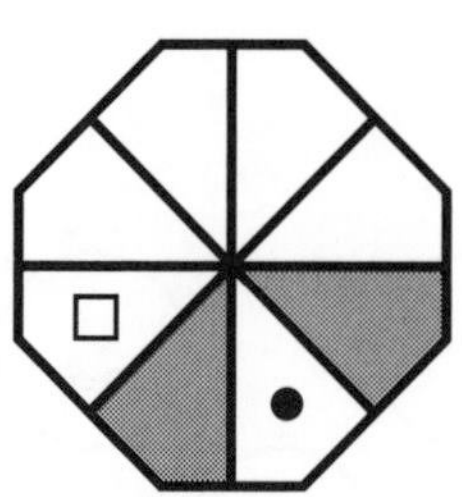

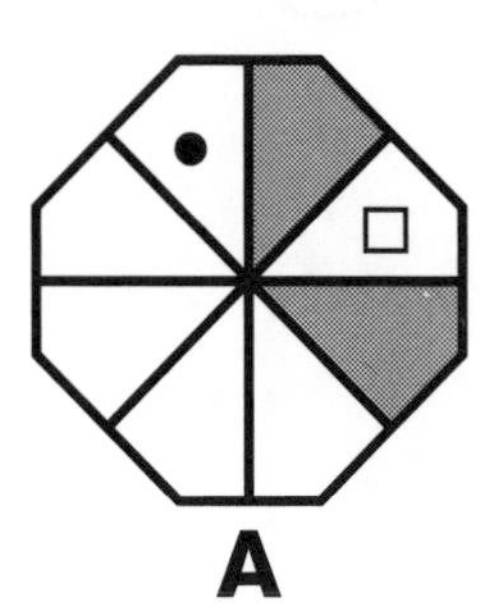

A

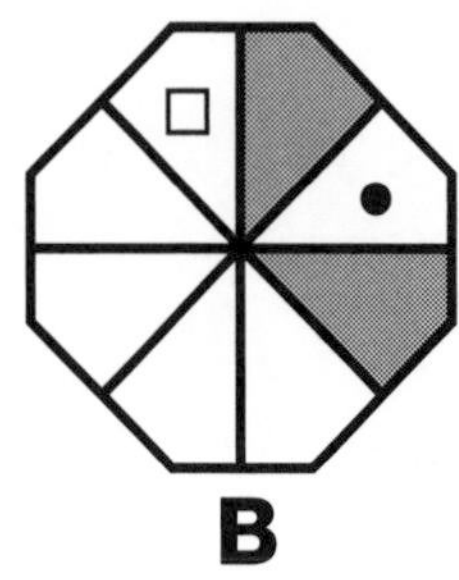

B

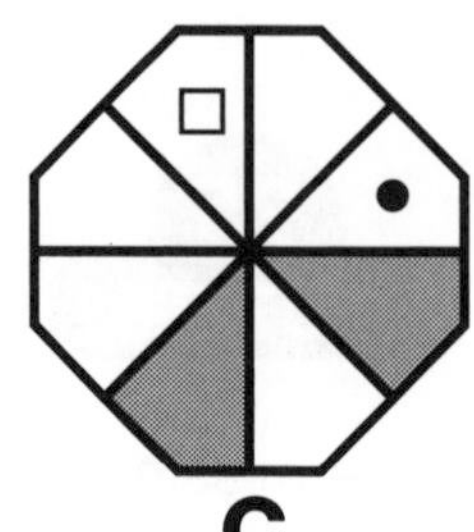

C

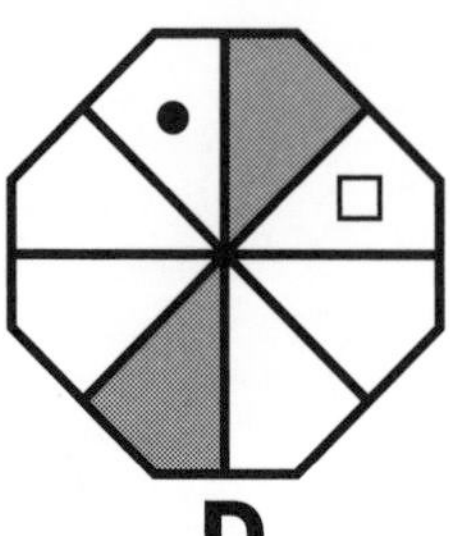

D

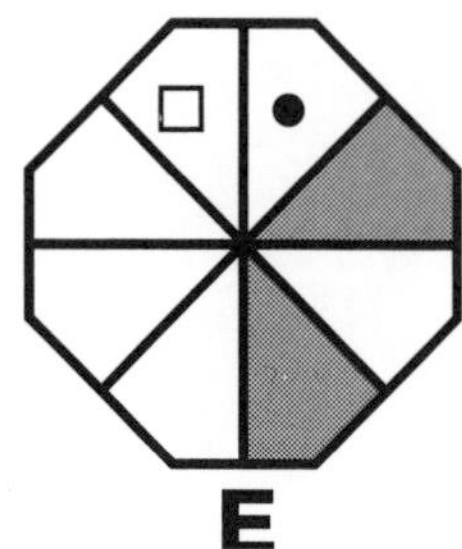

E

2 PUZZLE

Which number completes the puzzle?

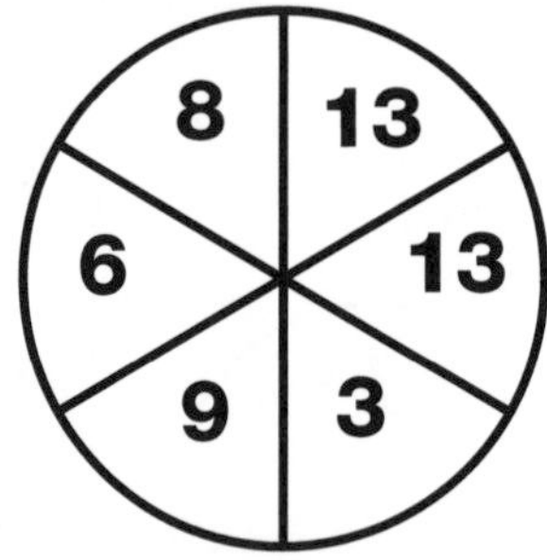

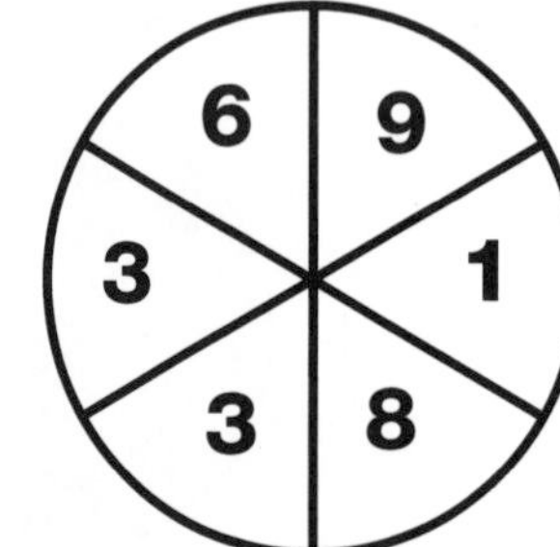

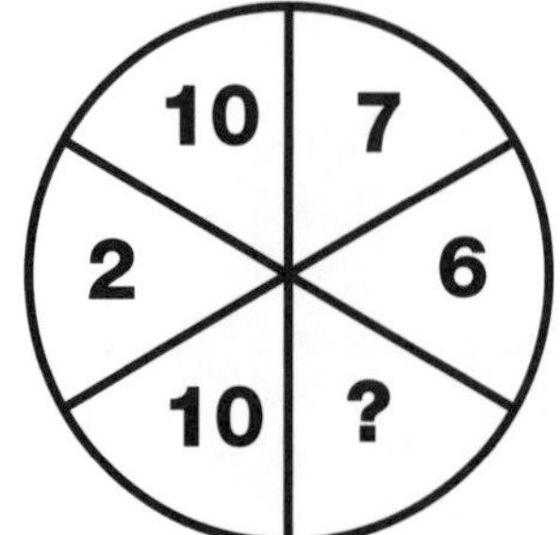

3 PUZZLE

Which of the lower watches fills the missing gap?

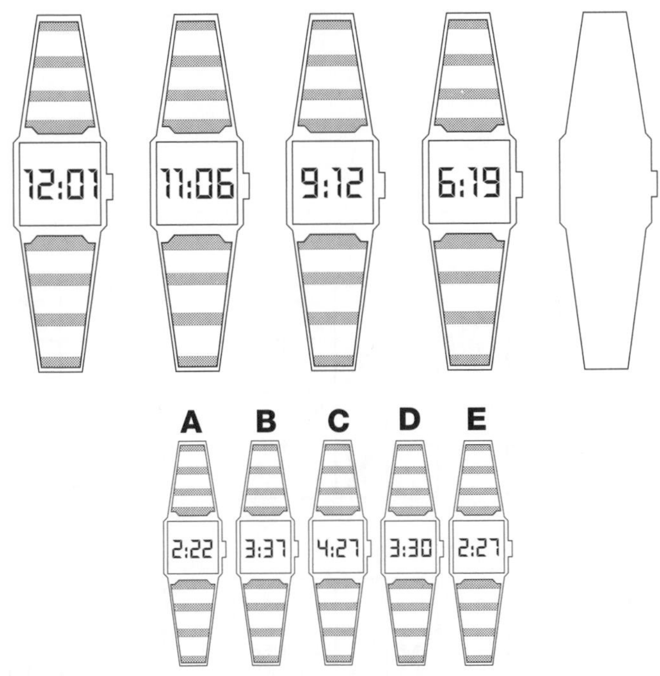

4 PUZZLE

Which letter completes the puzzle?

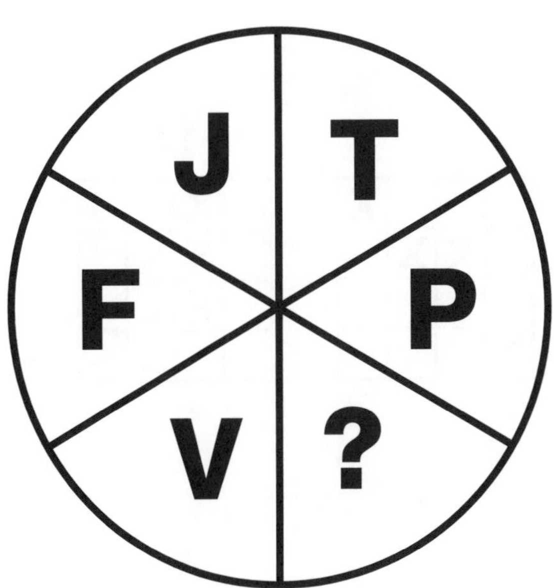

5 PUZZLE

Following a logical sequence, can you complete this puzzle?

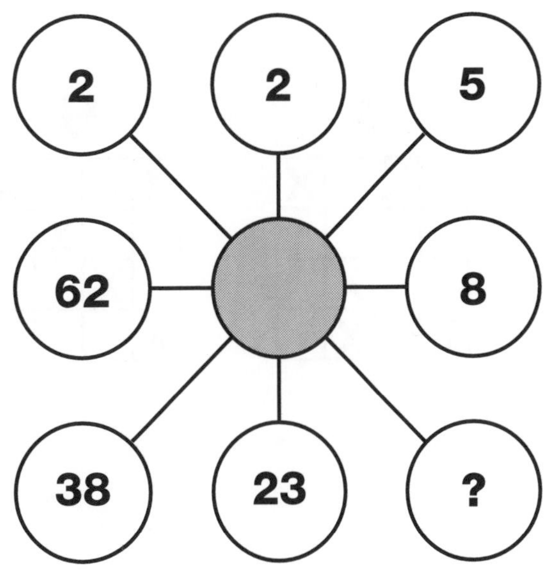

L
E
V
E
L

16

Which of the lower grids replaces the question mark?

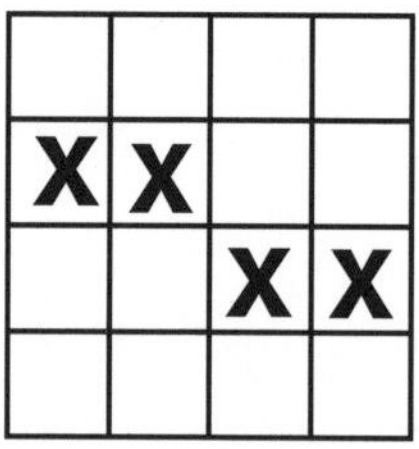 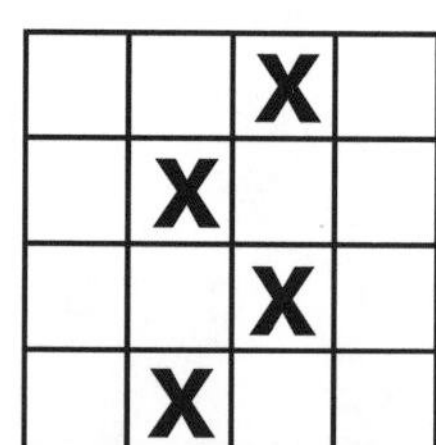 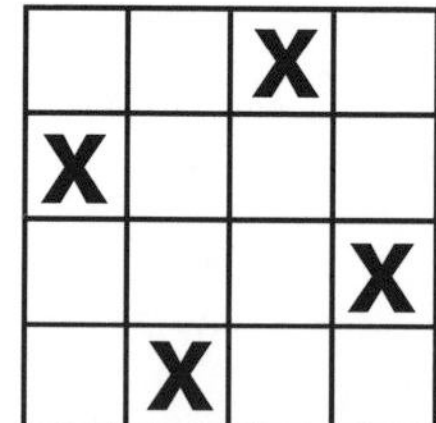

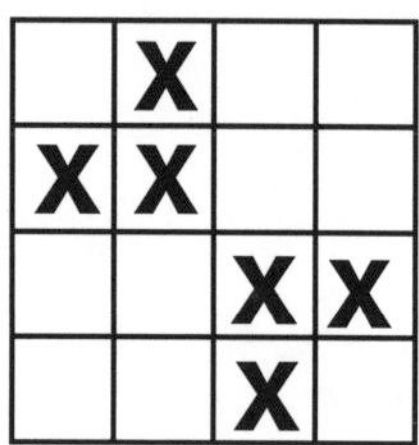 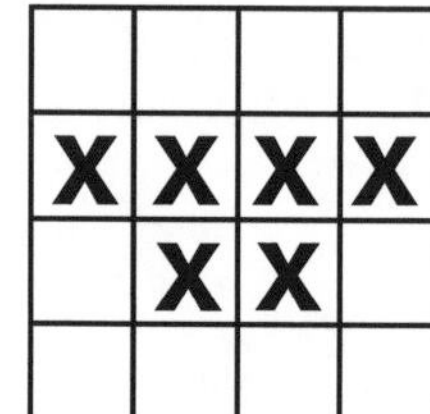 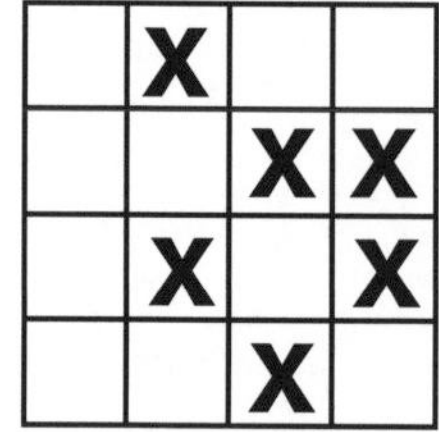

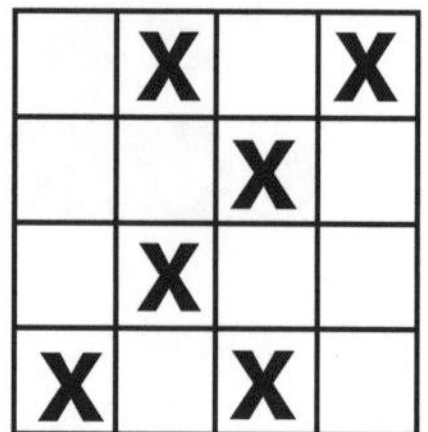 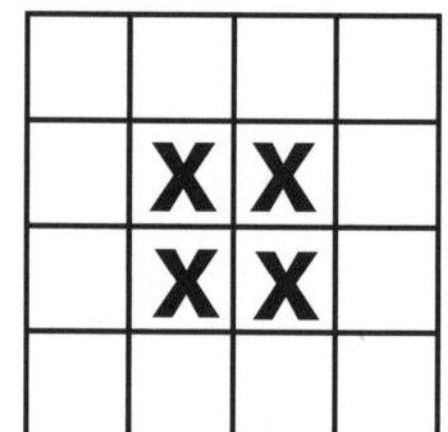 ?

A

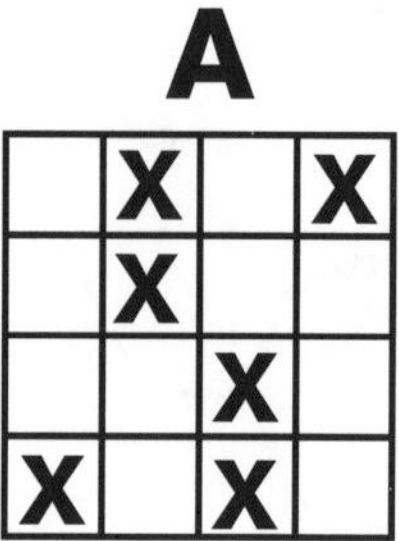

B

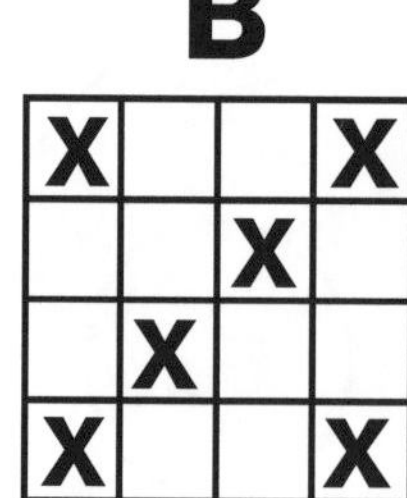

C

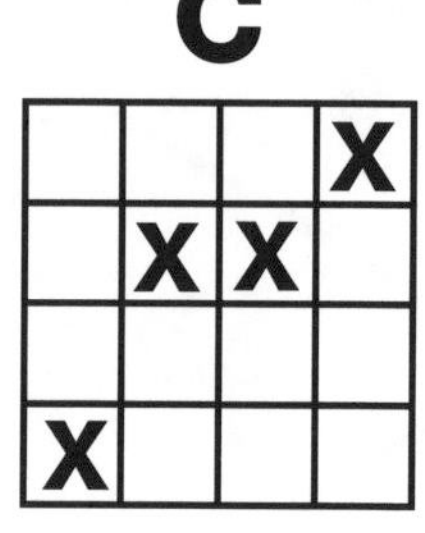

D

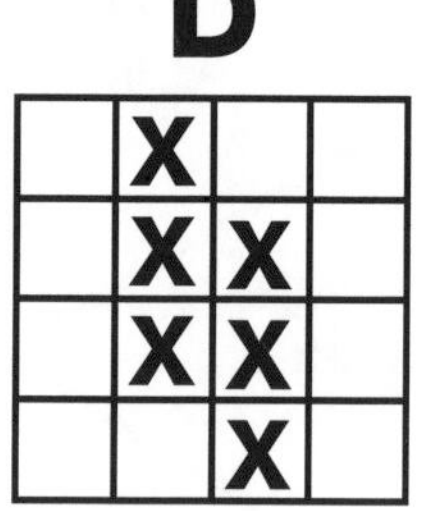

7
PUZZLE

Which letter completes the puzzle?

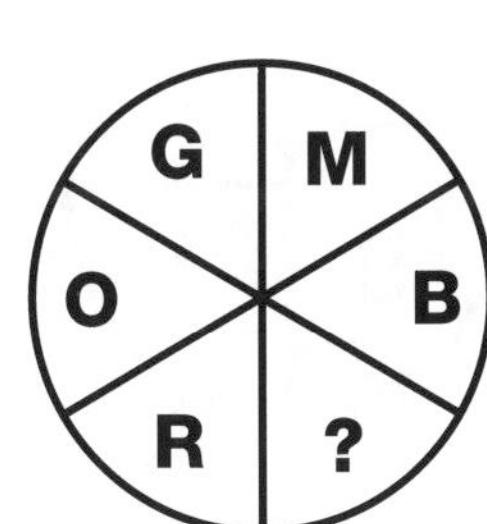

In this sequence of letters what needs to be added to make the puzzle correct?

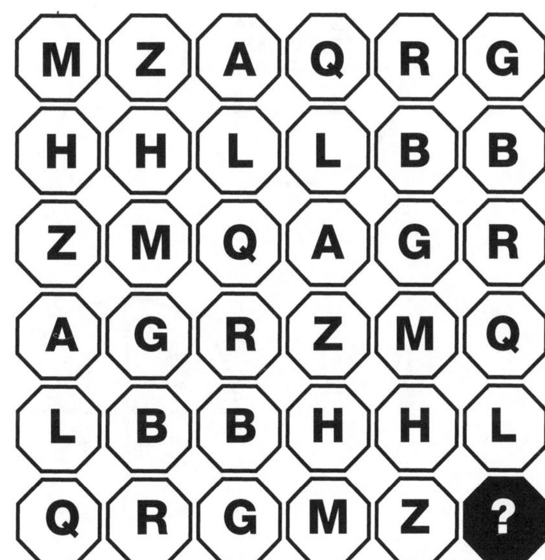

9
PUZZLE

Following a logical sequence, can you complete this puzzle?

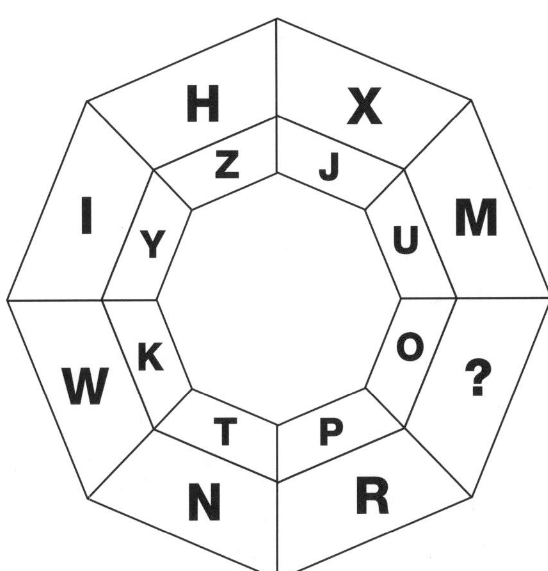

Which number is missing?

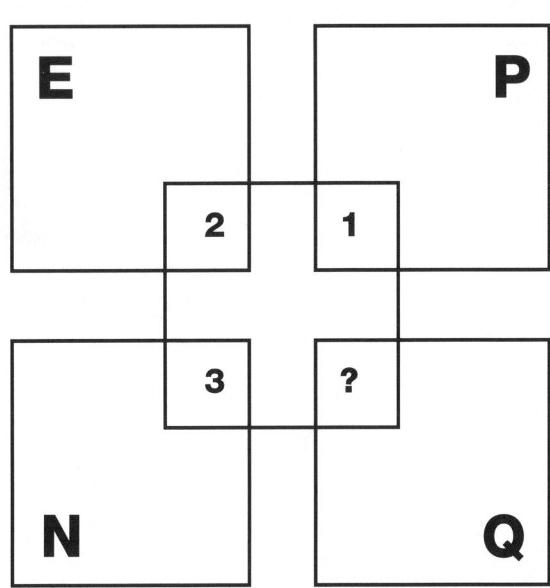

Which letter completes the puzzle?

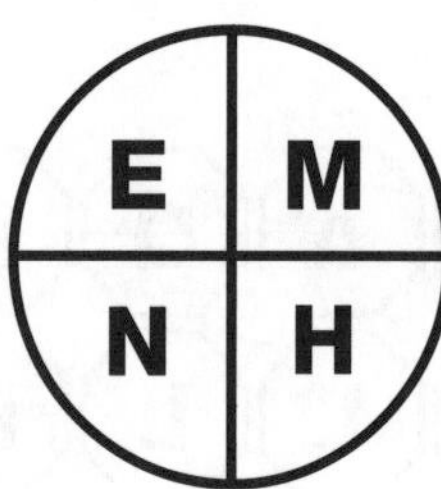

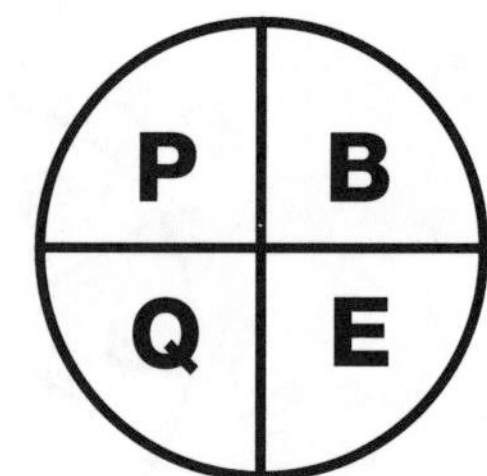

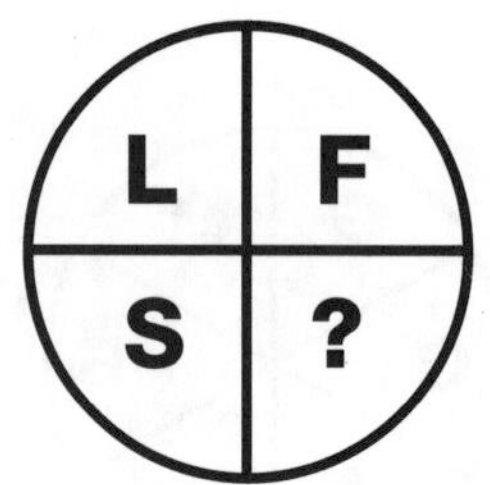

Which number completes the puzzle?

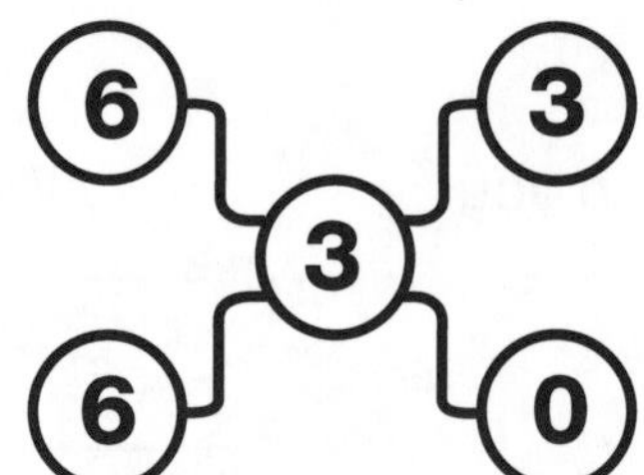

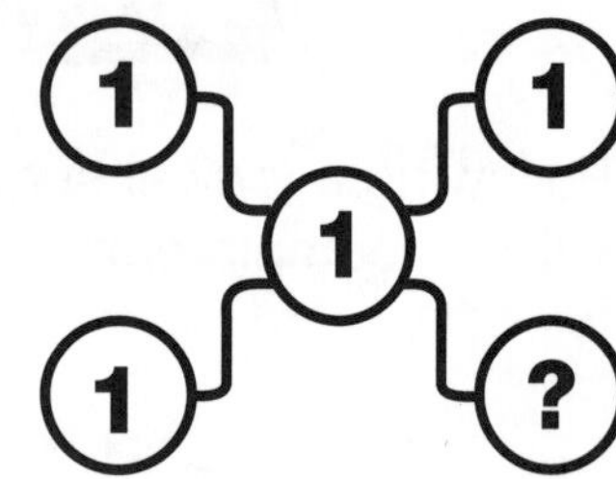

13 PUZZLE

What is missing from the last circle?

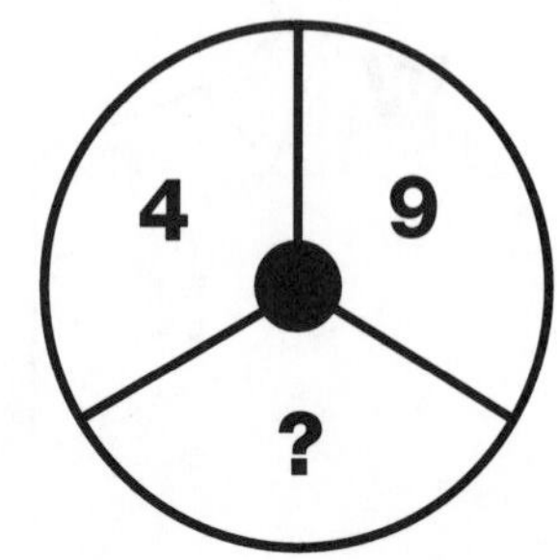

14 PUZZLE

Following a logical sequence, can you complete this puzzle?

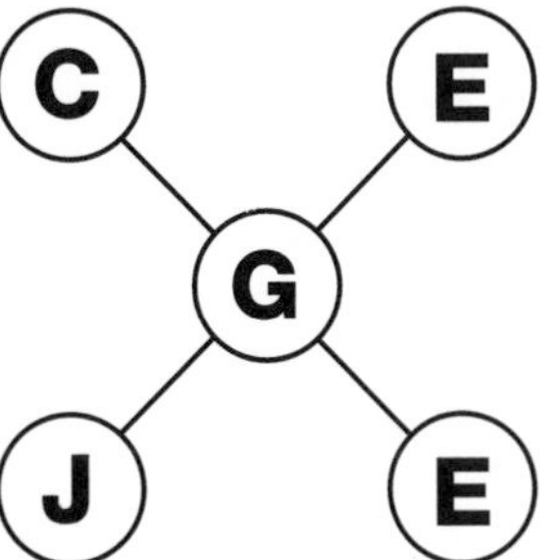

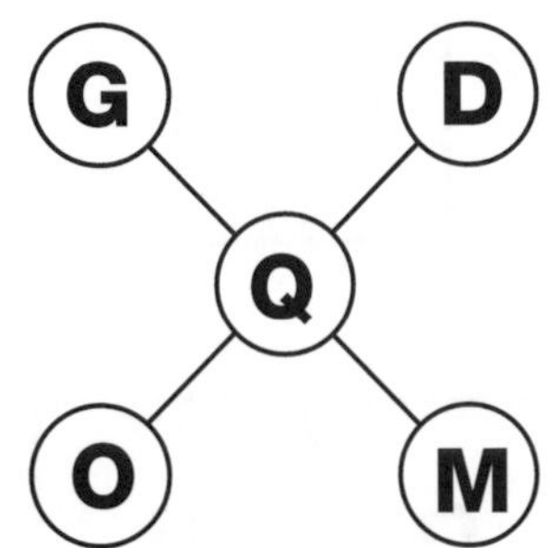

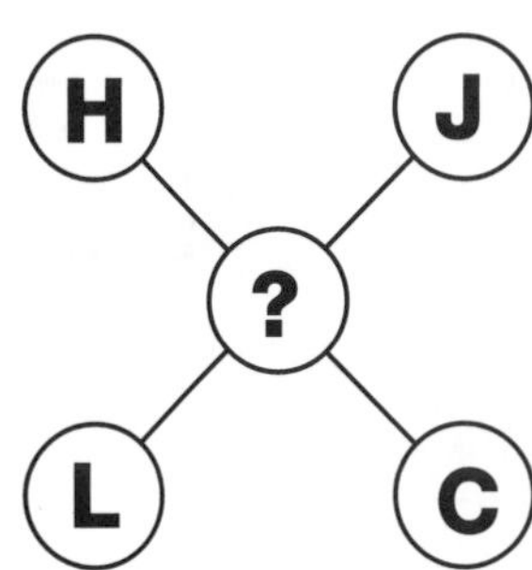

15 PUZZLE

What is missing from this arrangement of circles?

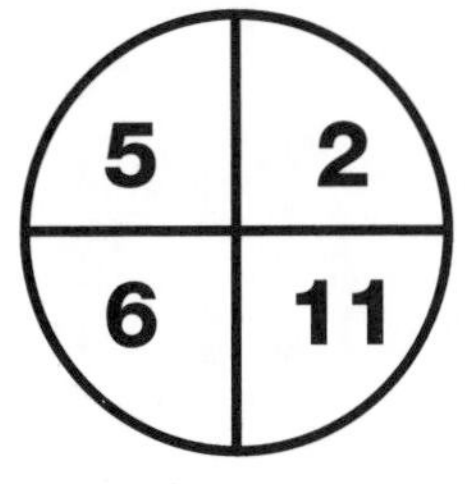

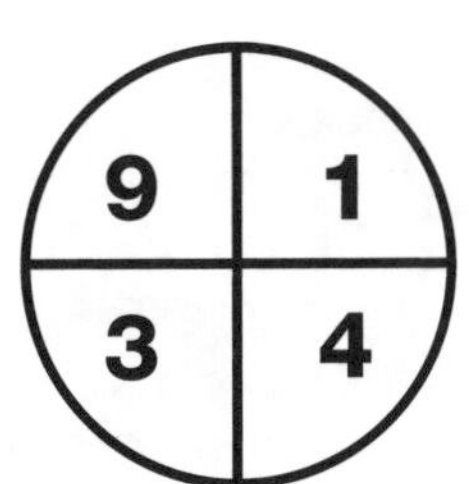

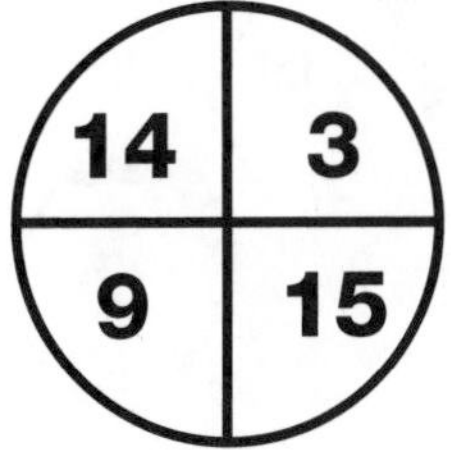

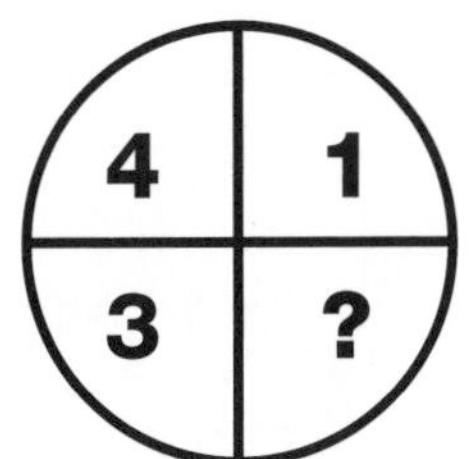

16 PUZZLE

Mr Jones' watch runs 1 second fast every hour, and Mr Brown's loses $1\frac{1}{2}$ seconds every hour. If one day, they both showed 11 am, how long would it be before they both showed the same time again? And how long would it be before both watches told exactly the right time?

LEVEL 16

Which letter completes the puzzle?

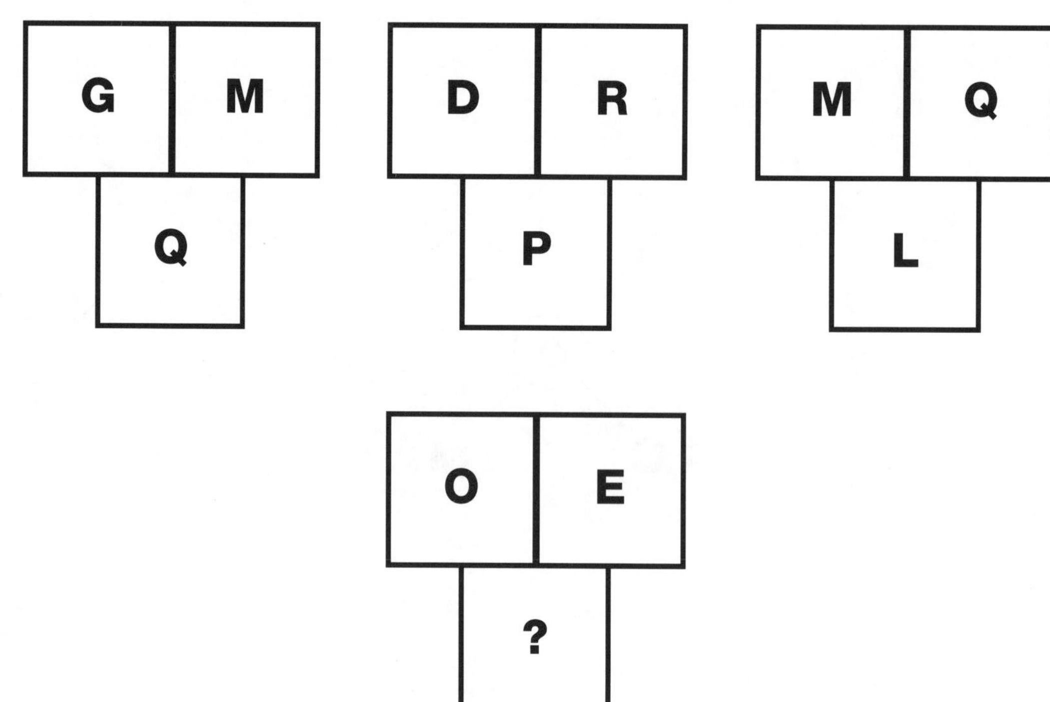

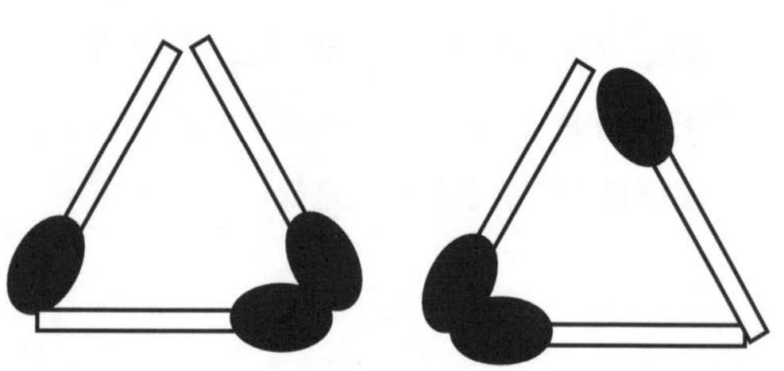

18 PUZZLE

Can you arrange these 6 matches to form 3 perfect squares, all exactly the same size? You may need to break some of them.

19 PUZZLE

What number continues this sequence?

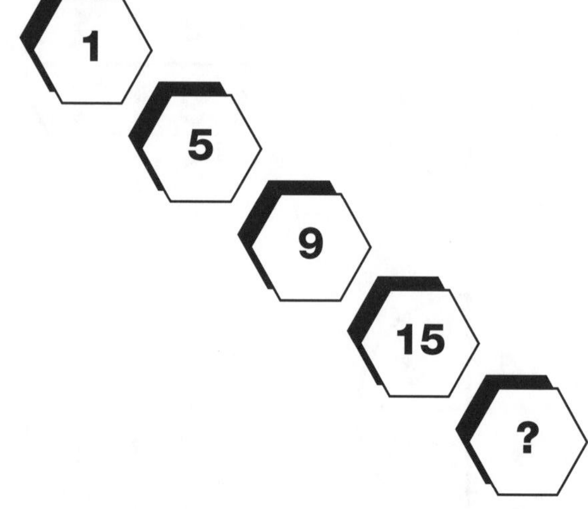

LEVEL 16

Jane is thinking of two whole numbers, and asks Freddy to work out what they are. The only clue she will give him is that their product is three times larger than their sum.

Can you work out what the two numbers are?

Following a logical sequence, can you complete this puzzle?

J 

M 

S 

Which number completes the puzzle?

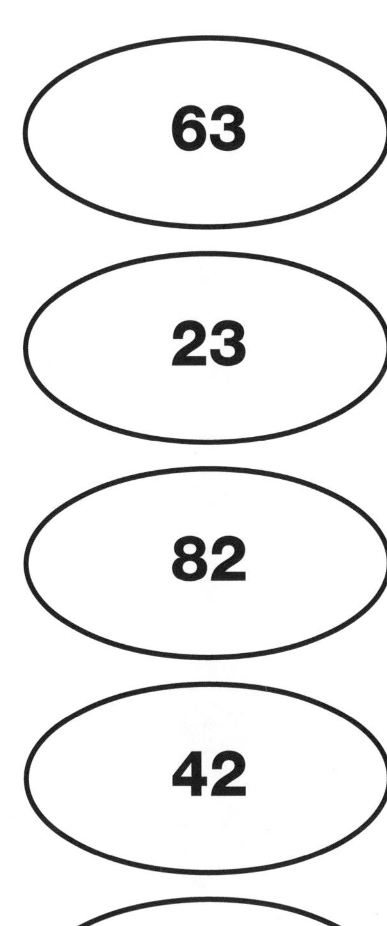

LEVEL 16

LEVEL

16

Which three numbers are missing from this grid?

2	5	13	29	12	4	21	16	15
3	11	23	8	30	19	14	11	12
7	19	6	24	15	10	9	10	11
17	4	20	13	8	7	8	9	10
3	18	9	6	6	7	8	9	10
14	7	5	32	33	34	35	36	37
5	?	26	27	28	29	30	31	28
25	22	23	24	25	26	27	26	21
20	21	22	23	24	25	22	17	13
17	18	19	20	21	20	15	?	24
16	17	18	19	?	13	33	22	40
13	14	15	14	12	29	18	34	17
12	13	12	38	27	16	30	15	23
11	11	32	23	14	28	14	19	25

1 PUZZLE

Which lower grid replaces the question mark to complete the sequence?

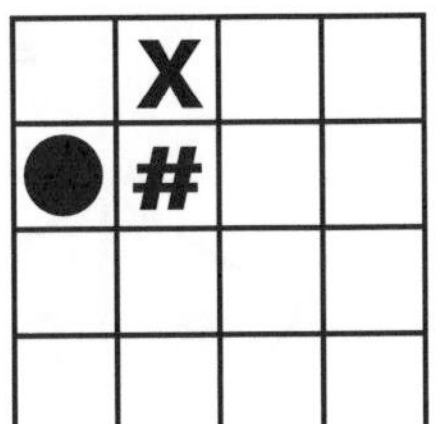
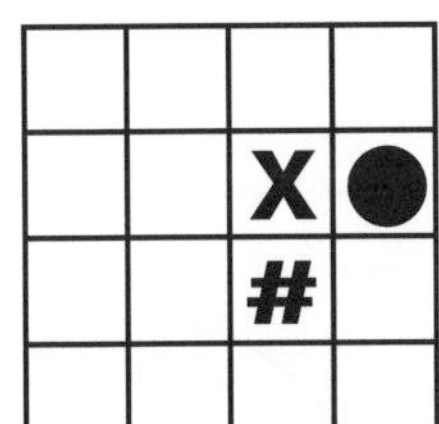
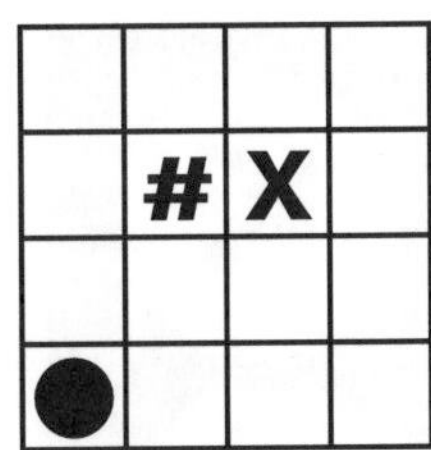
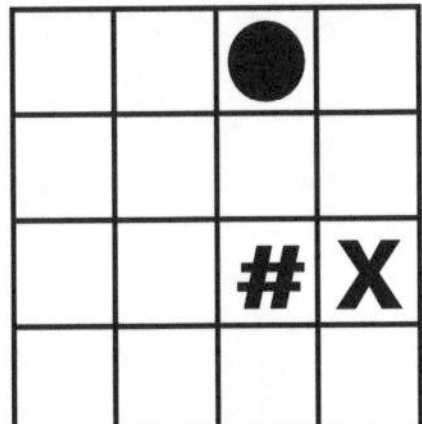
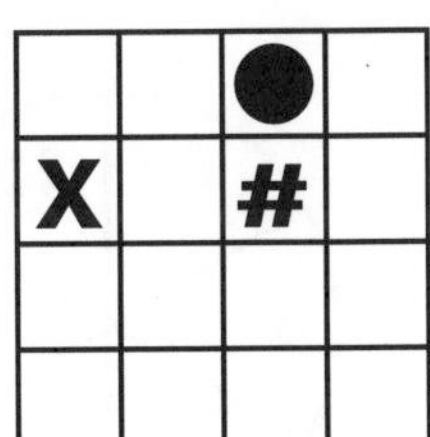
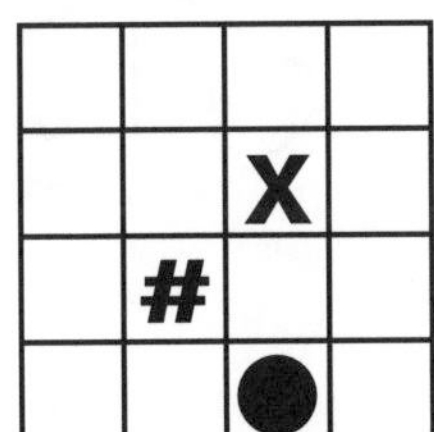
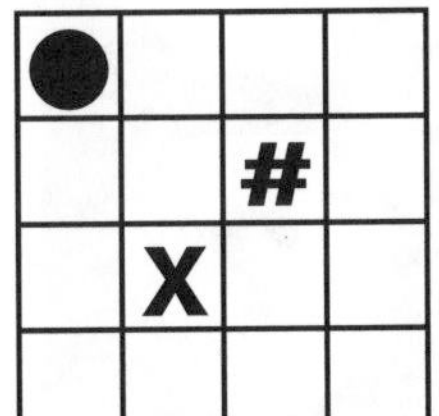
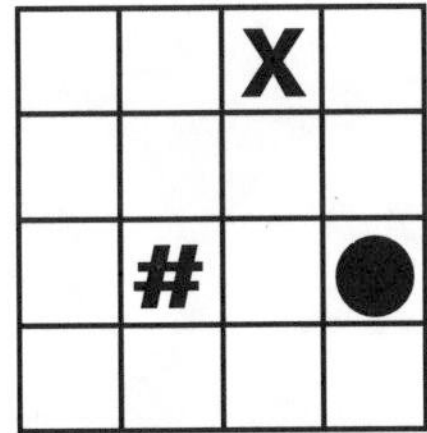
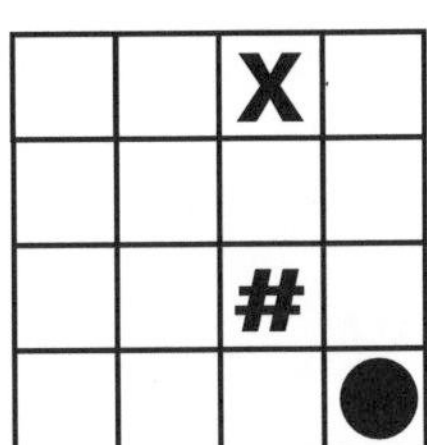
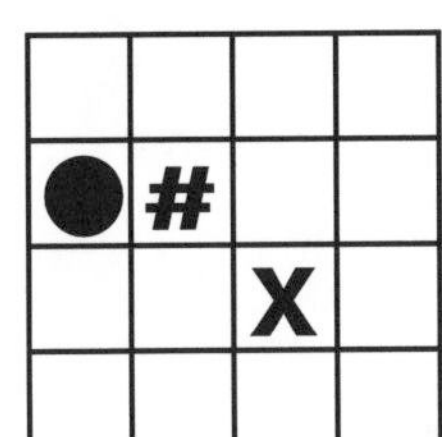
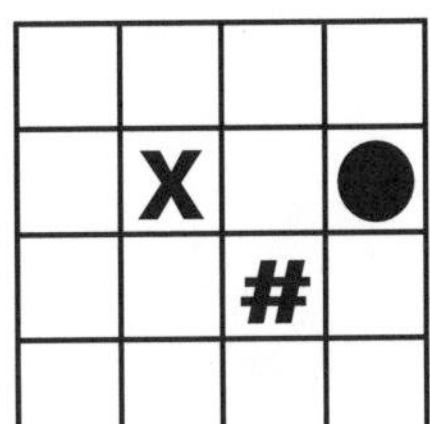
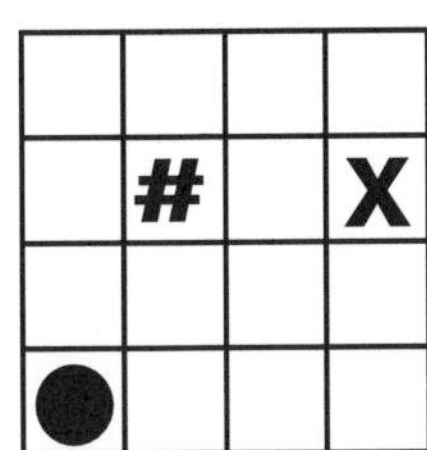
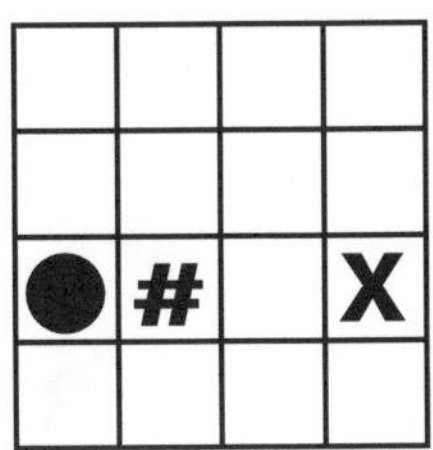
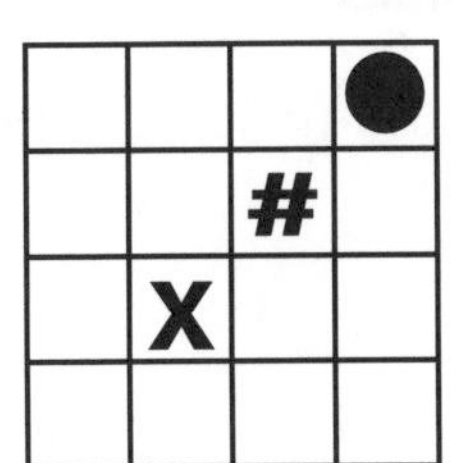
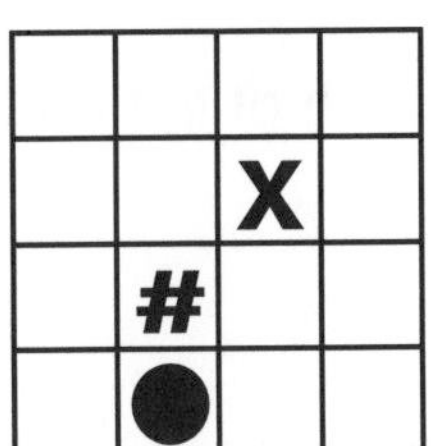

?

A

B

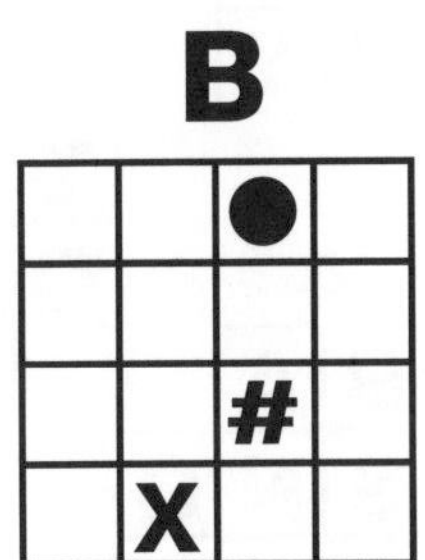

C

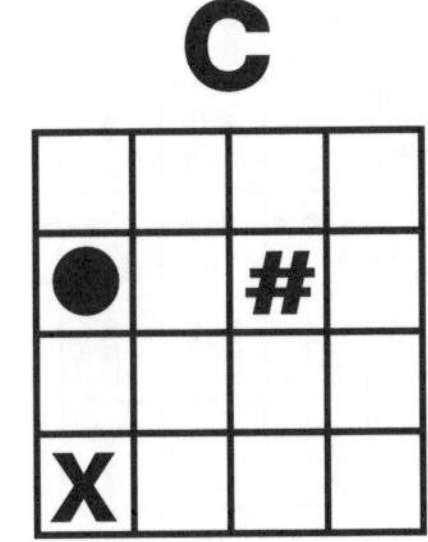

D

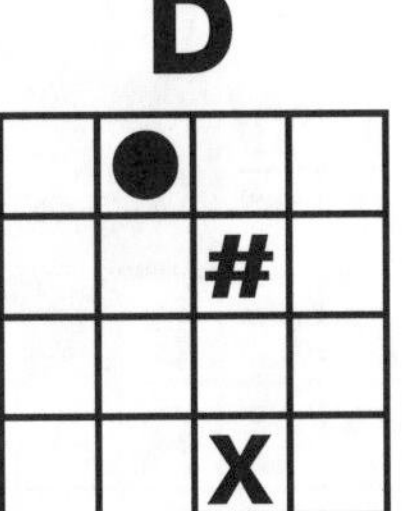

LEVEL 17

LEVEL

17

Which letter completes the puzzle?

Following a logical sequence, can you complete this puzzle?

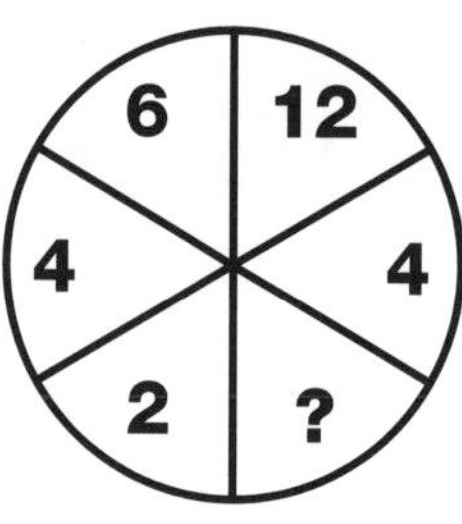

4
PUZZLE

Which of the grids fill the missing gap?

B	M	L	G	W	M	R	G	A	T
R	O	P	B	Y	H	O	M	S	F
T	C	B	O	O	A	R	J	Q	N
I	H	A	N			V	C	P	H
R	T	W					T	G	I
I	G	T					W	T	R
H	P	C	V			N	A	H	I
N	Q	J	R	A	O	O	B	C	T
F	S	M	O	H	Y	B	P	O	R
T	A	G	R	M	W	G	L	M	B

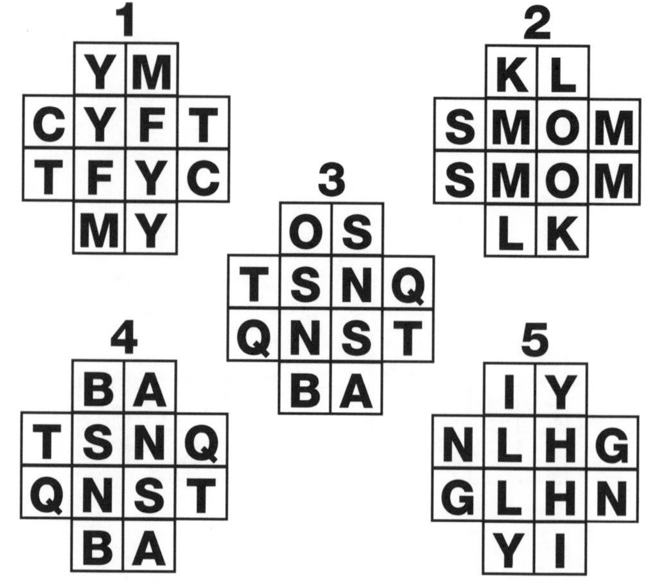

5 PUZZLE

What is missing from this arrangement of circles?

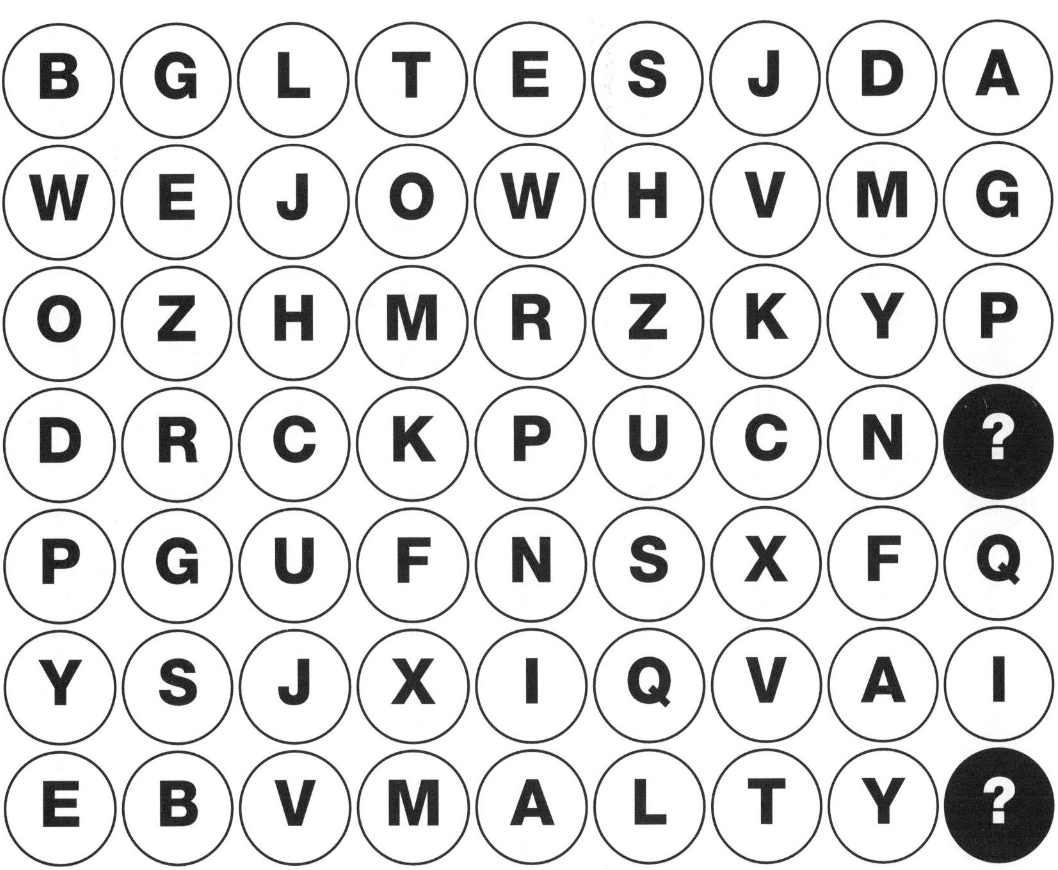

6 PUZZLE

In this sequence of letters what needs to be added to make the puzzle correct?

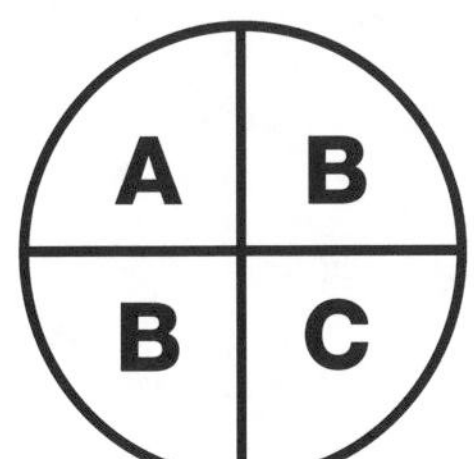

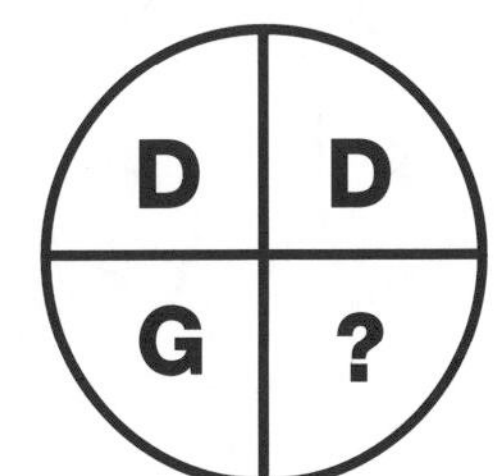

LEVEL 17

LEVEL 17

In this sequence of letters what needs to be added to make the puzzle correct?

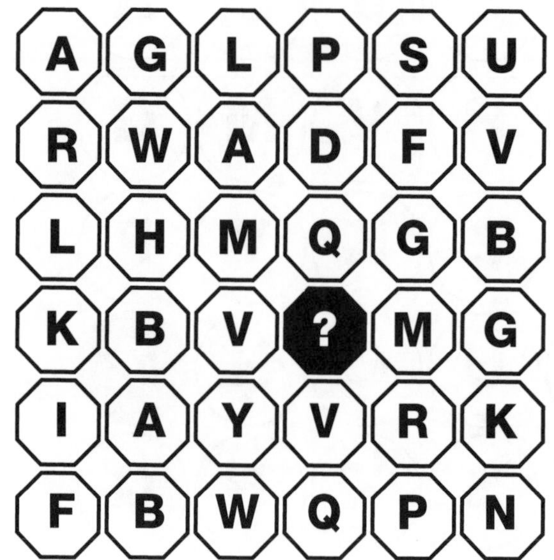

Which number completes the puzzle?

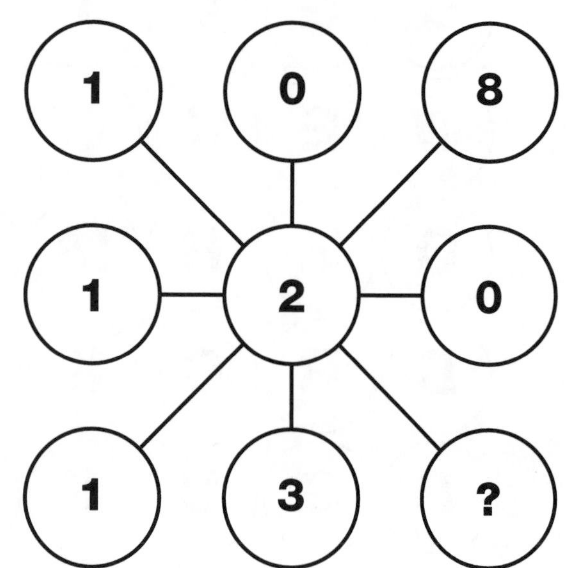

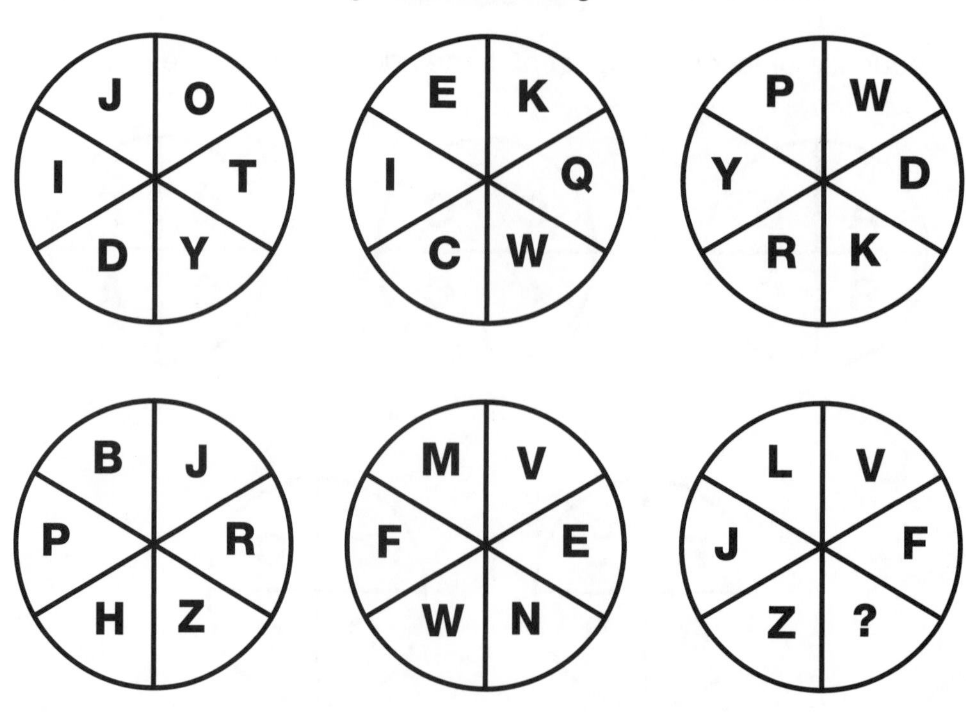

10 PUZZLE

Which letter completes the puzzle?

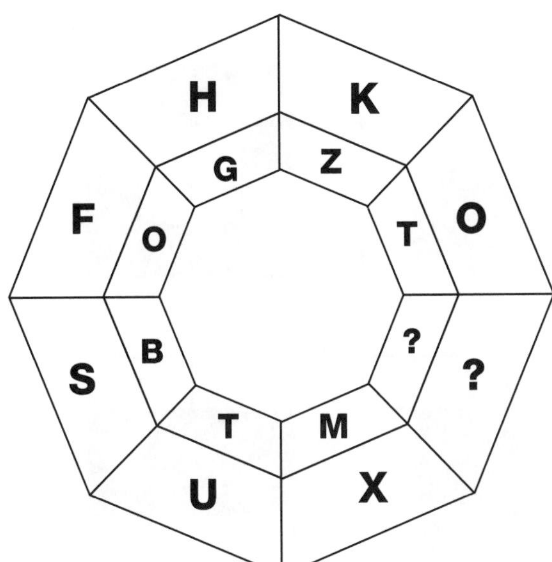

What is missing from this puzzle?

12 PUZZLE

Following a logical sequence, can you complete this puzzle?

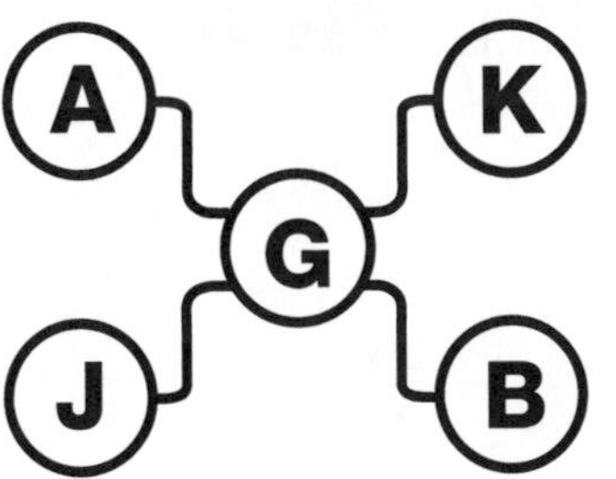

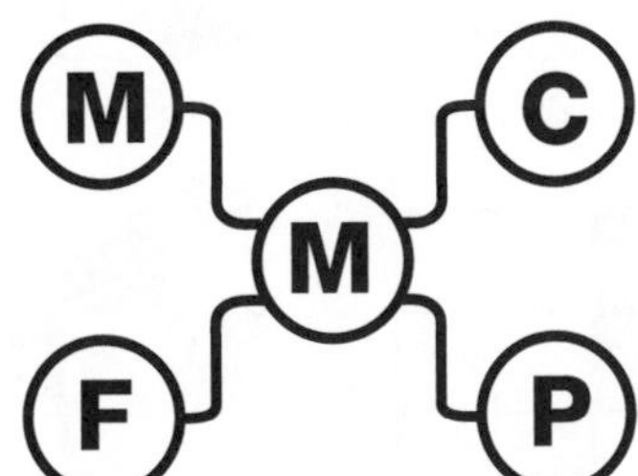

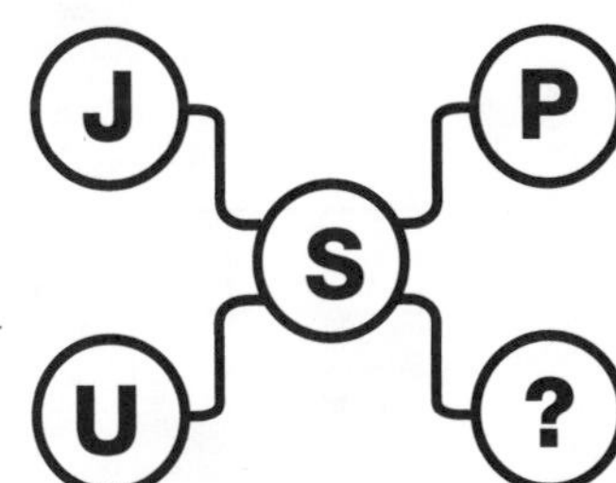

13 PUZZLE

Which letter goes in the right hand circle to complete the puzzle?

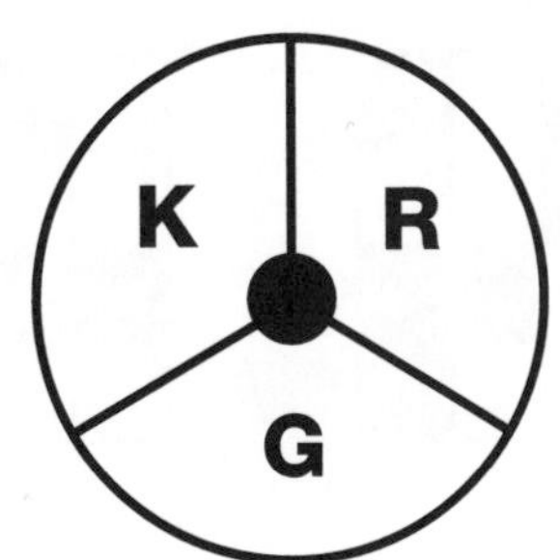

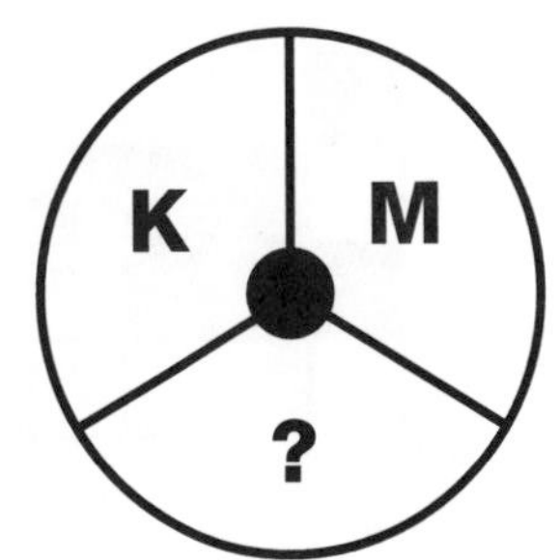

Which lower grid replaces the question mark to complete the sequence?

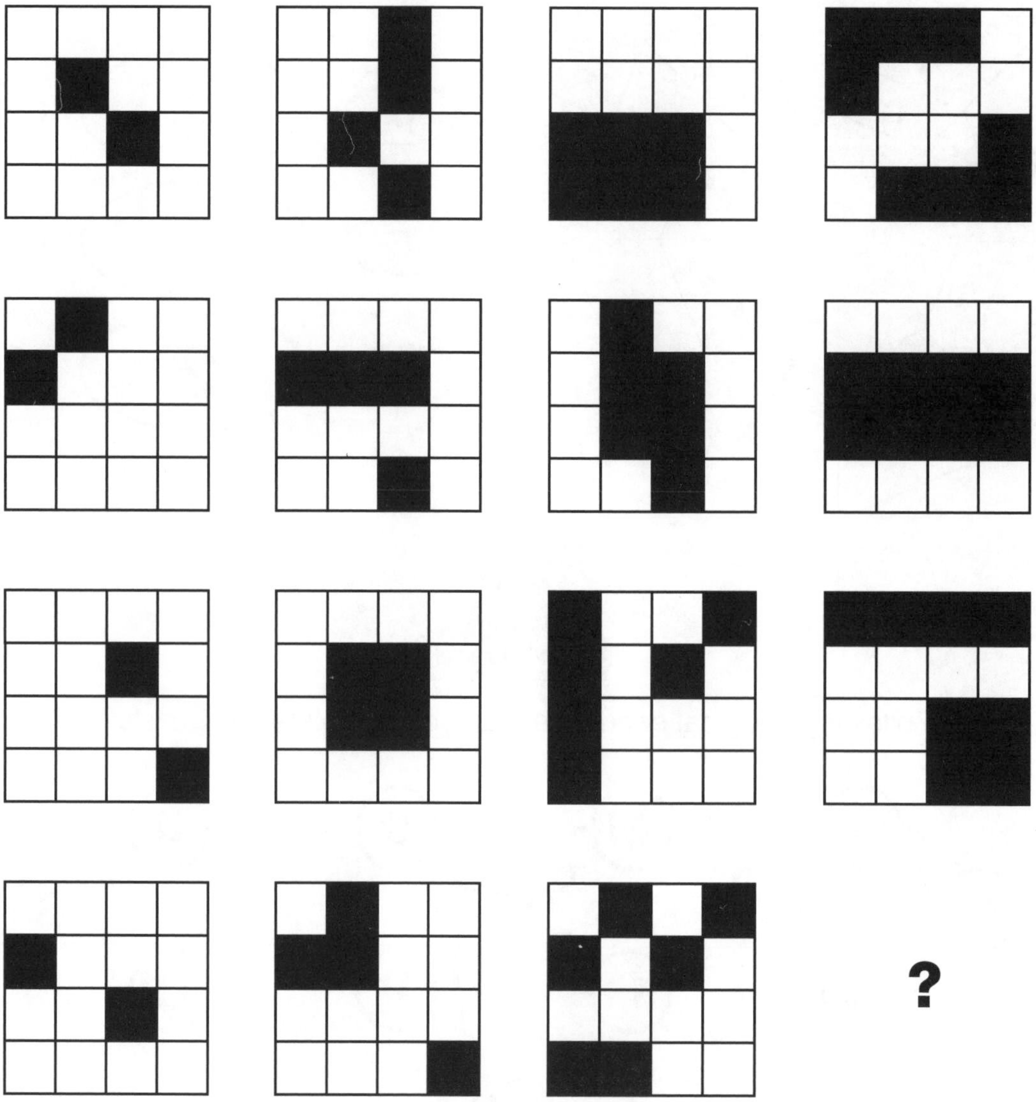

?

A

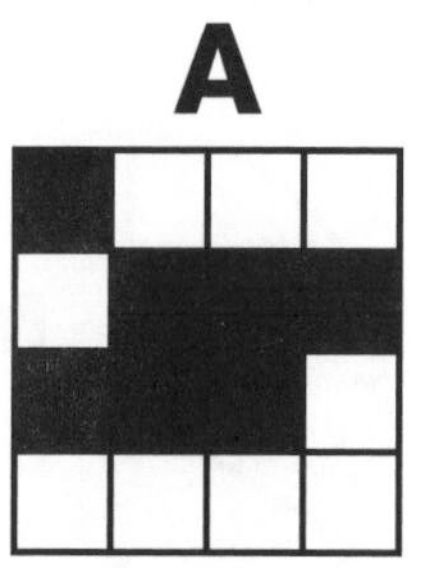

B

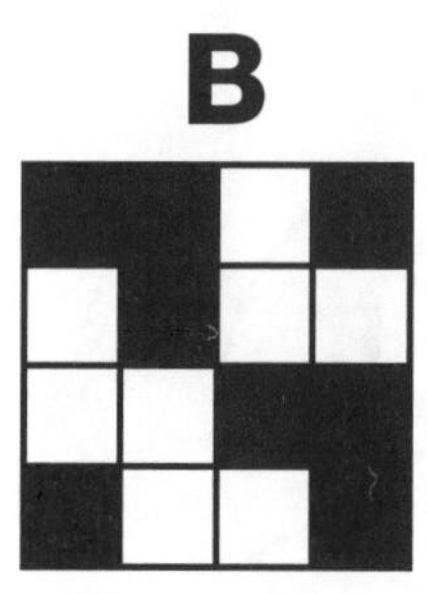

C

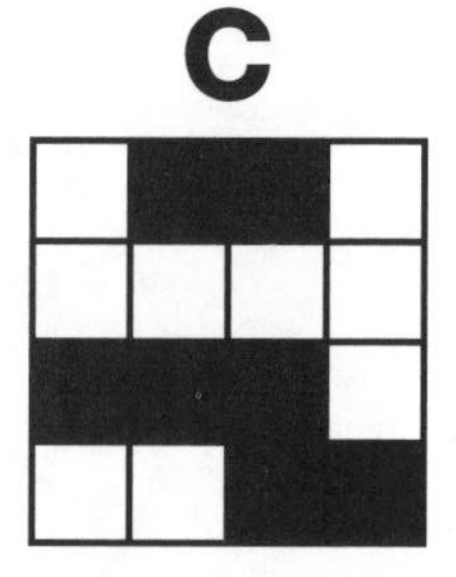

D

15 PUZZLE

Which letter completes the puzzle?

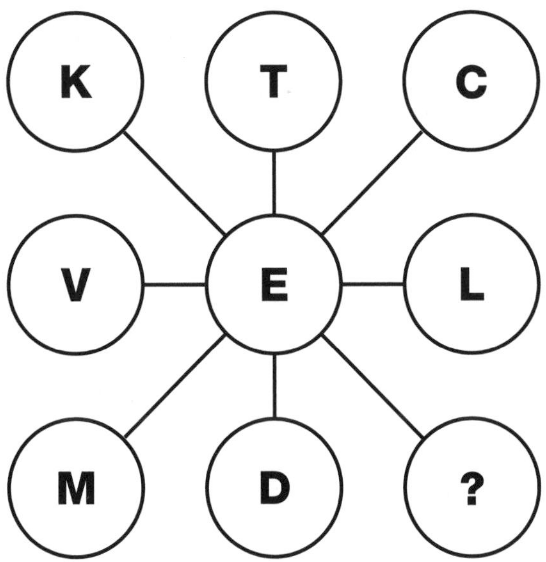

17 PUZZLE

Move just 4 matches, to create 7 squares? Can you also move the same 4 matches to create 10 squares?

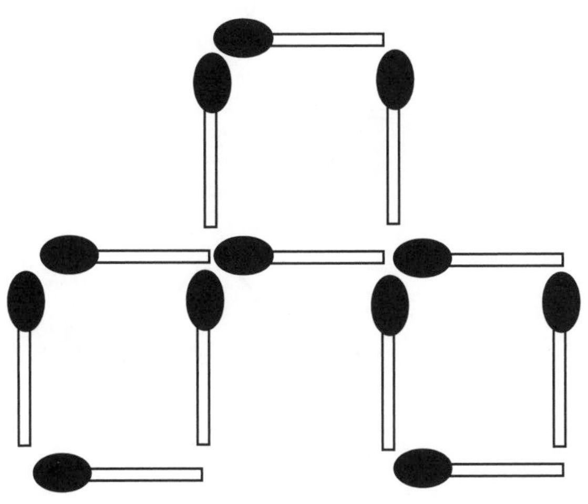

16 PUZZLE

Following a logical sequence, can you complete this puzzle?

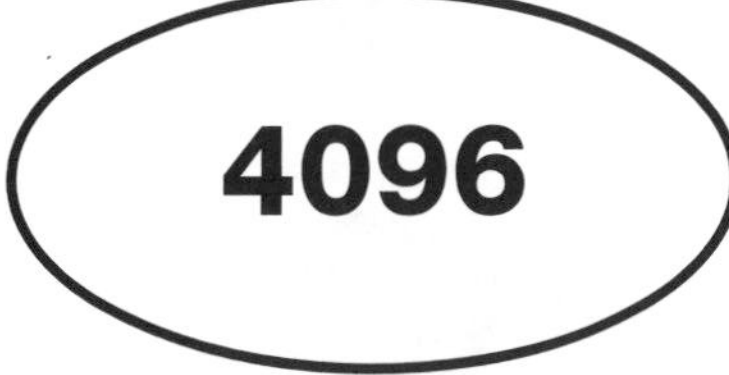

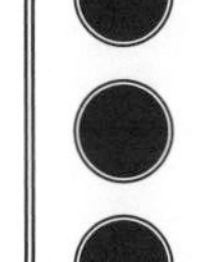

LEVEL

17

Which letter completes the puzzle?

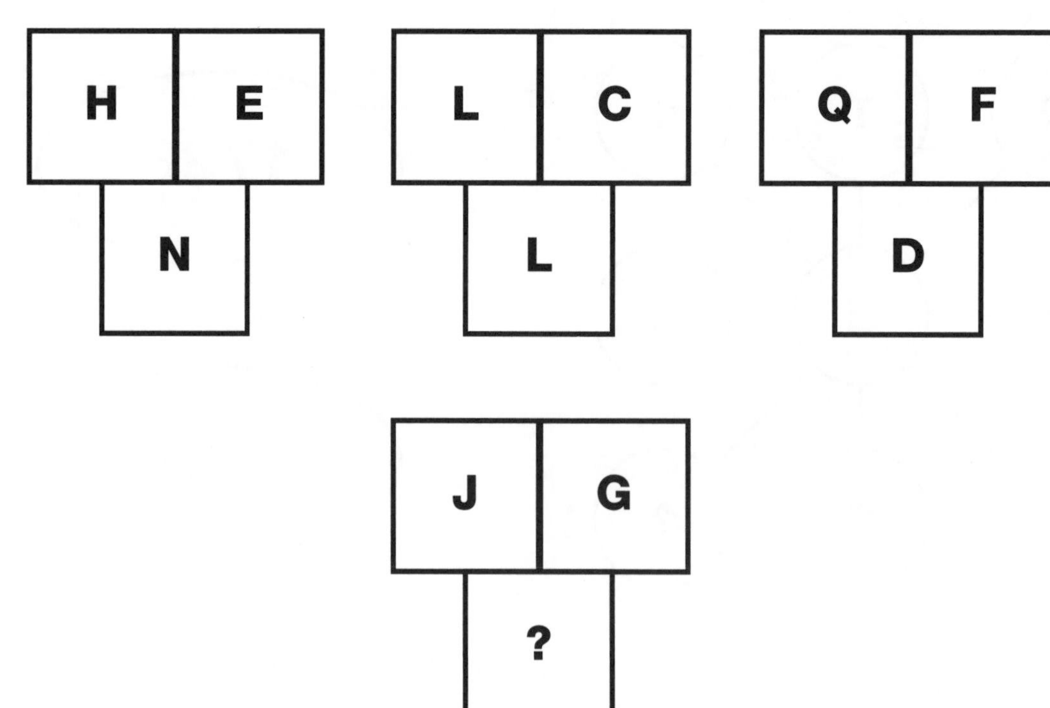

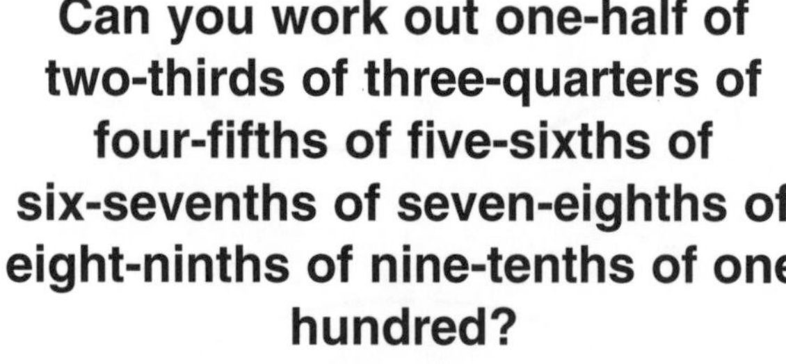

Can you work out one-half of two-thirds of three-quarters of four-fifths of five-sixths of six-sevenths of seven-eighths of eight-ninths of nine-tenths of one hundred?

20 PUZZLE

Following a logical sequence, can you complete this puzzle?

LEVEL

21 PUZZLE

What four letters need to be added to this grid?

L	P	L	H	D	Z	V	R	N
P	T	R	N	J	F	B	X	J
T	X	V	N	J	F	B	T	F
X	B	Z	R	V	Z	X	P	B
B	F	?	H	L	P	T	L	X
F	J	N	R	V	?	D	H	T
J	N	R	V	Z	D	H	L	P
Z	U	P	K	F	A	V	Q	L
E	P	K	F	A	V	Q	L	G
J	?	R	M	H	C	X	G	B
O	Z	W	F	A	V	S	B	W
T	E	B	G	L	?	N	W	R
Y	J	O	T	Y	D	I	R	M
D	I	N	S	X	C	H	M	H

Which of the lower grids replace the question mark to complete the sequence?

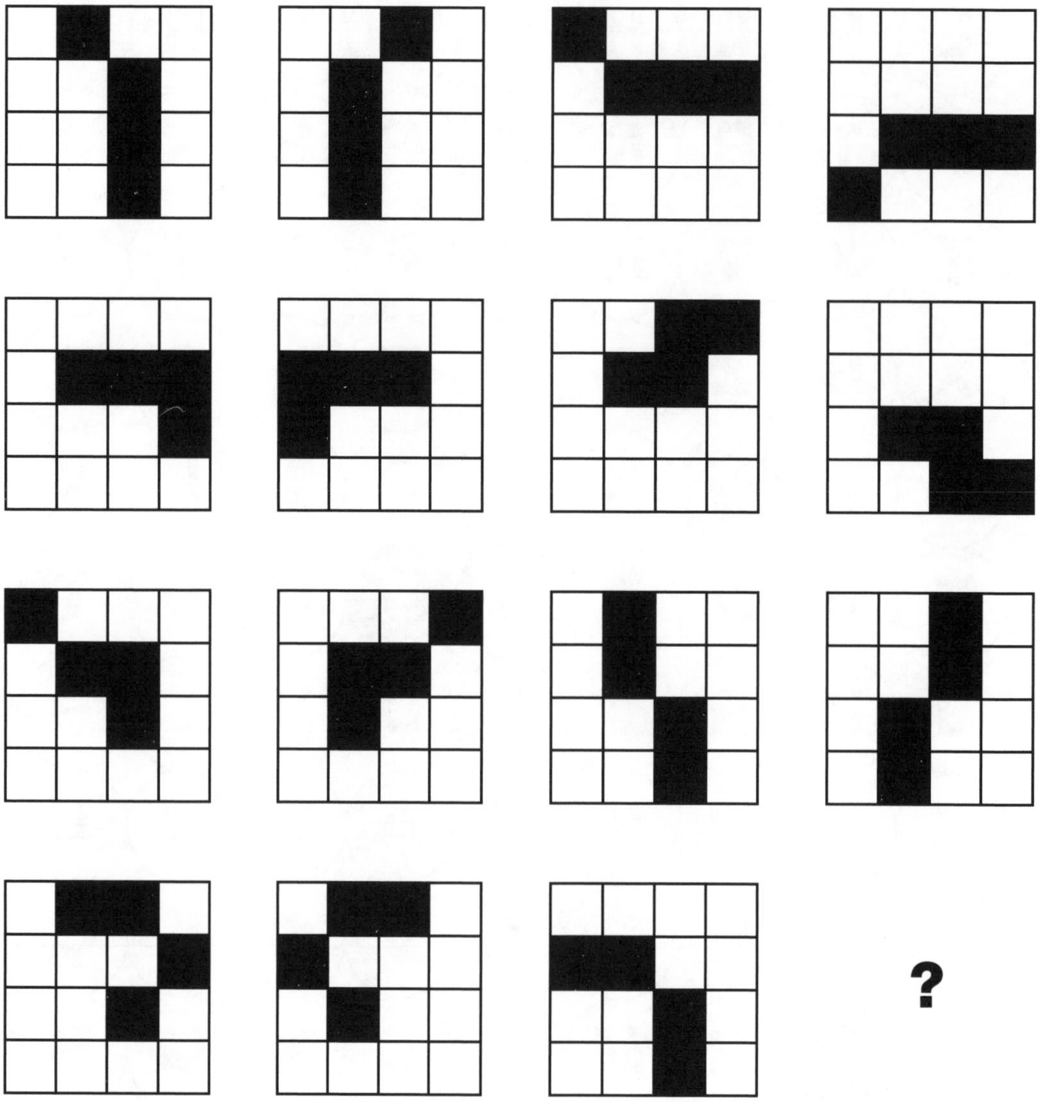

?

A  B  C  D

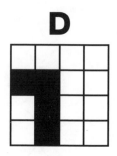

PUZZLE 2

Which grid fits in the middle?

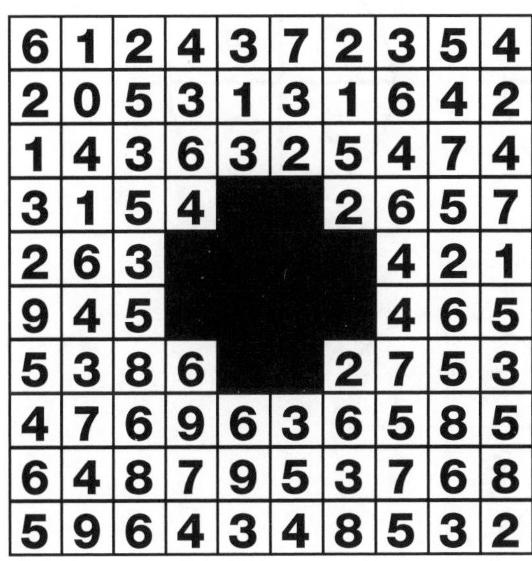

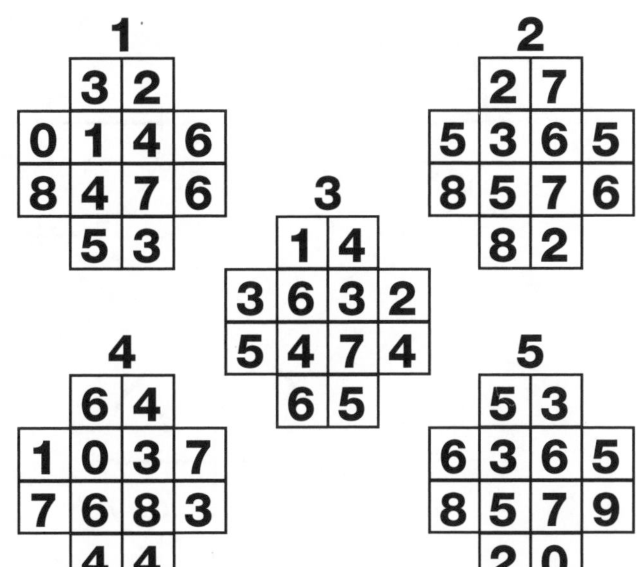

PUZZLE 3

Which letter completes the puzzle?

A	E	I	K	O	S
C	G	M	M	Q	W
Y	U	Q	I	E	A
P	T	X	U	Y	C
R	V	B	W	A	G
N	J	F	S	O	?

PUZZLE 4

Following a logical sequence, can you complete this puzzle?

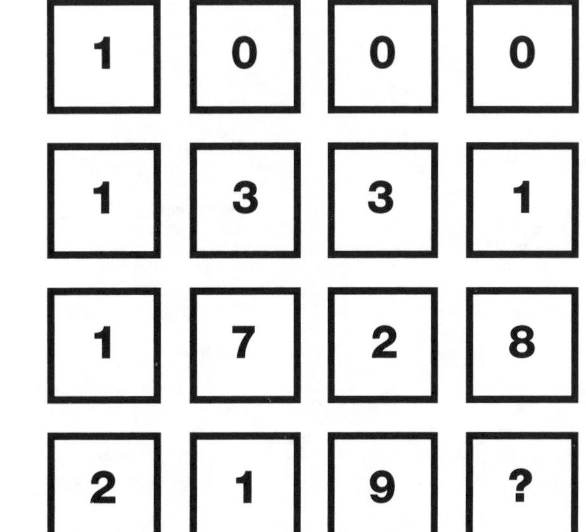

LEVEL

18

Which number completes the puzzle?

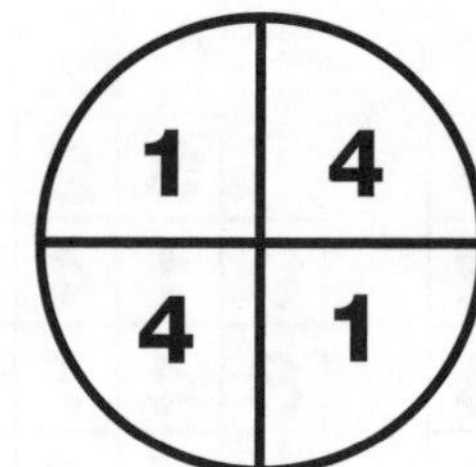

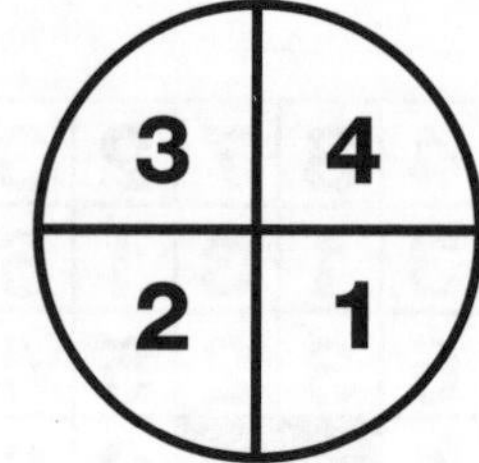

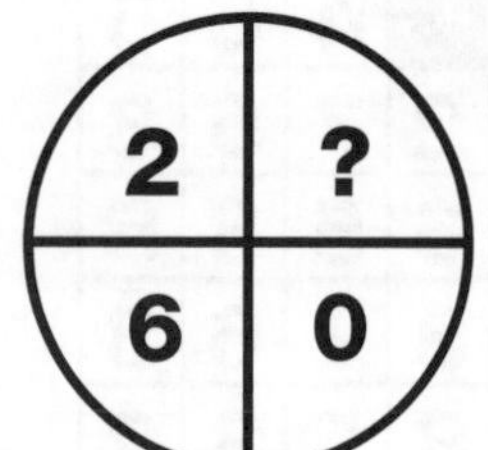

6 PUZZLE

Following a logical sequence, can you complete this puzzle?

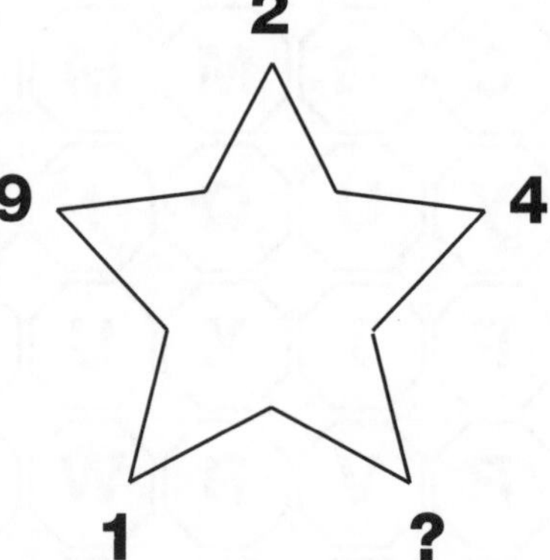

7 PUZZLE

Which three letters complete the puzzle?

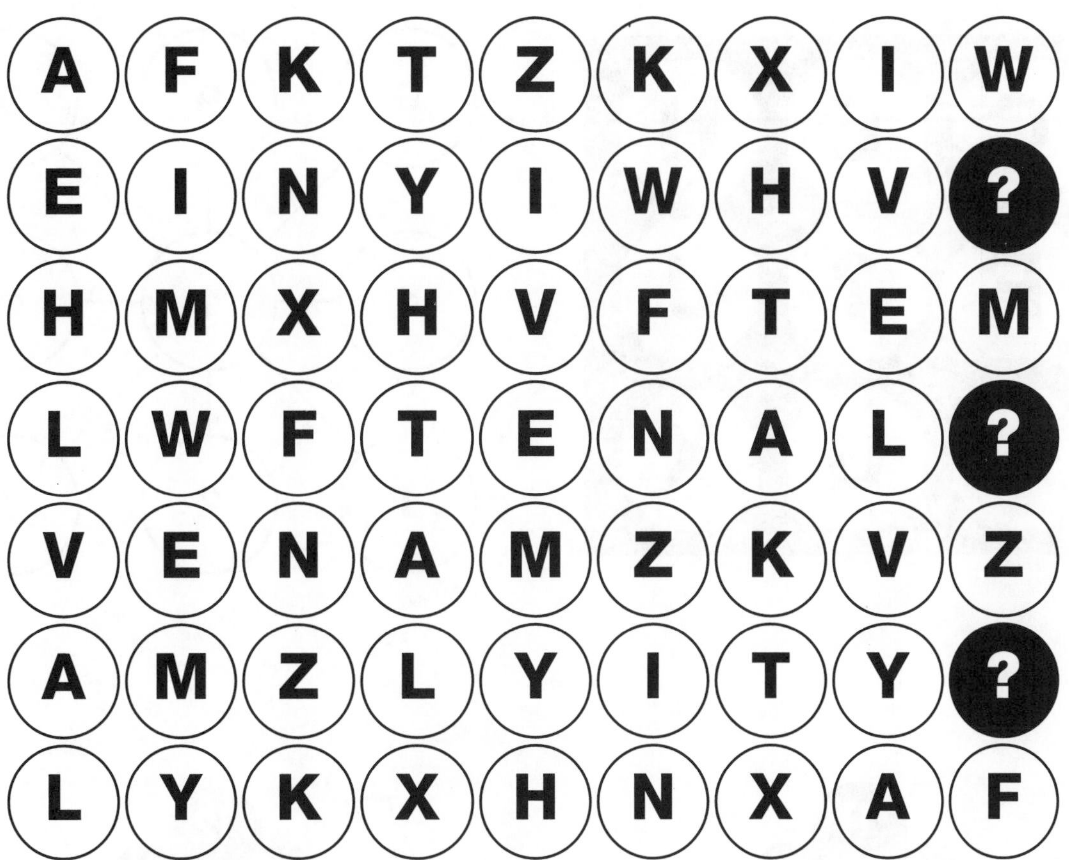

8 PUZZLE

What is missing from this puzzle?

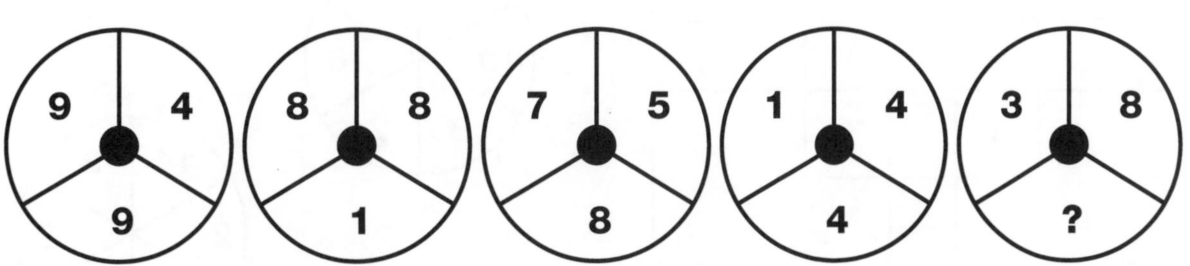

LEVEL

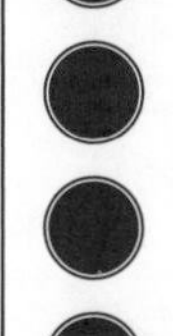

18

In this sequence of letters what needs to be added to make the puzzle correct?

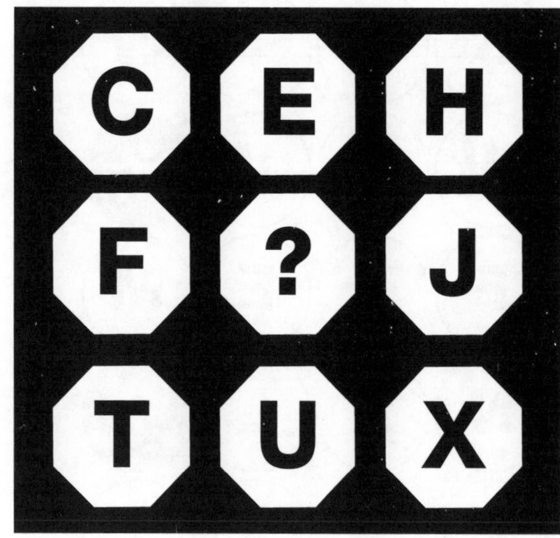

Which number completes the puzzle?

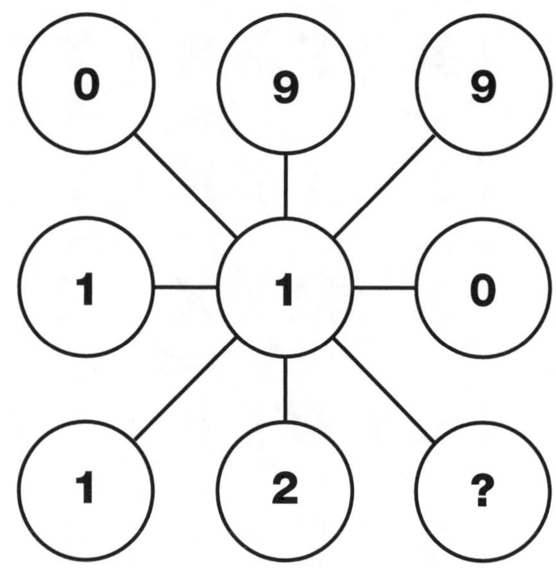

11
PUZZLE

Which letter completes the puzzle?

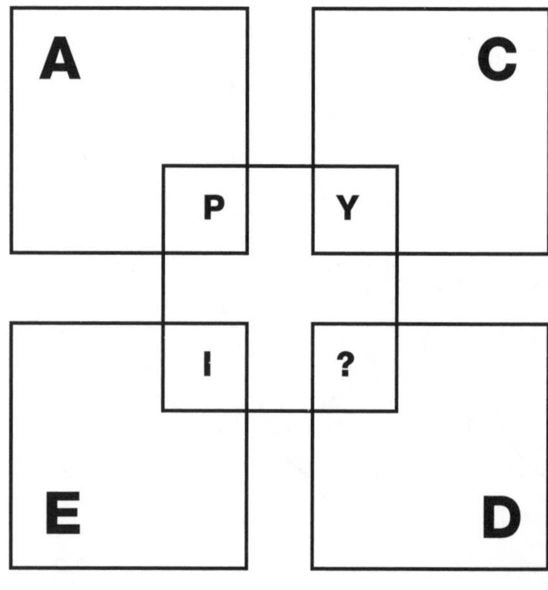

Following a logical sequence, can you complete this puzzle?

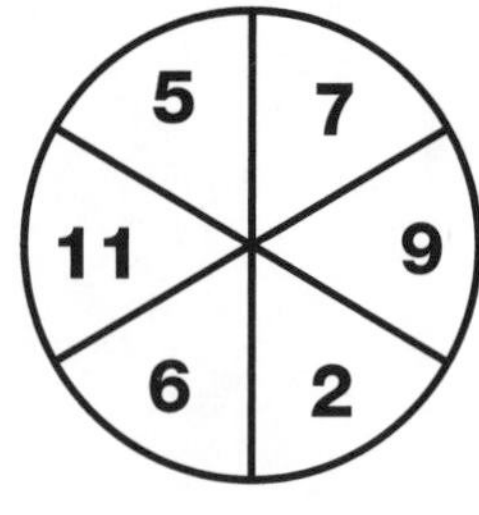

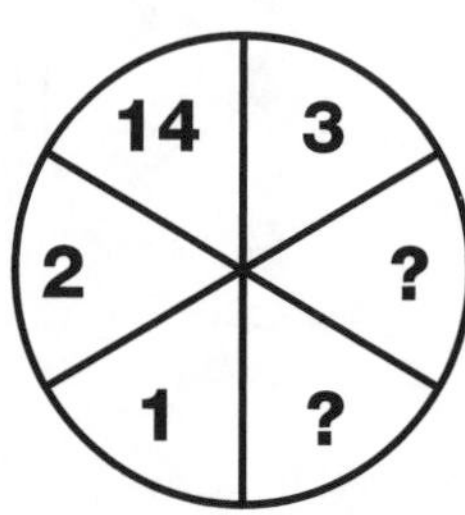

13
PUZZLE

Which of the lower grids replaces the question mark to complete the sequence?

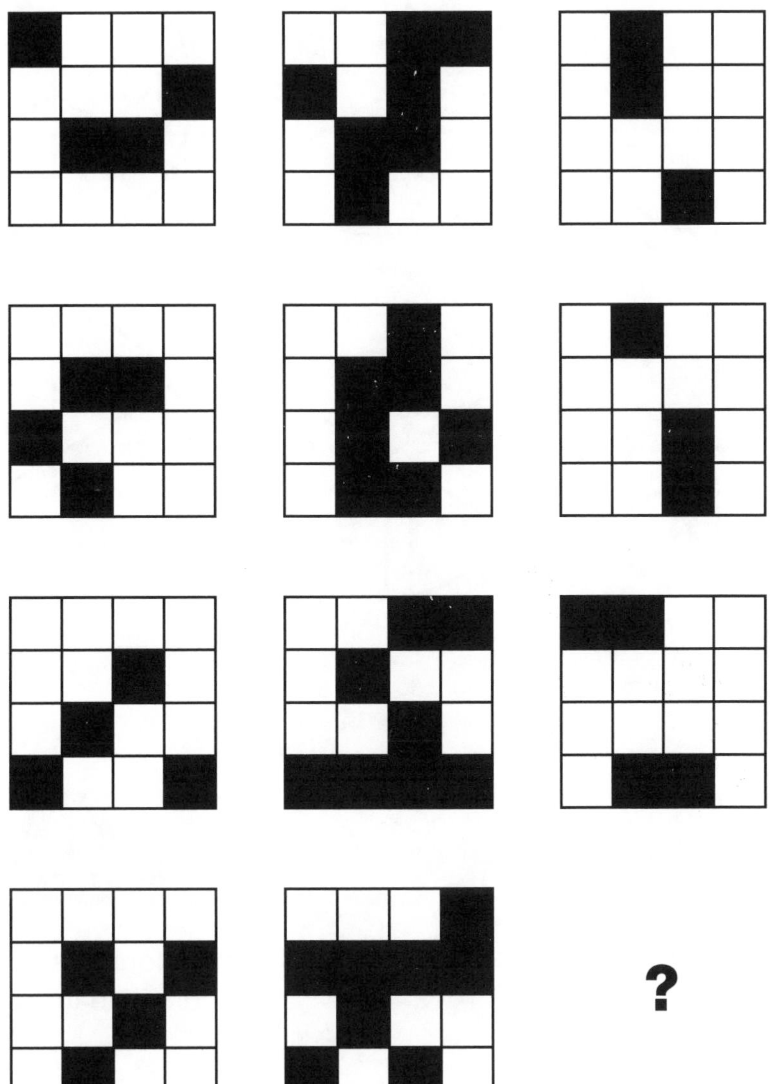

A

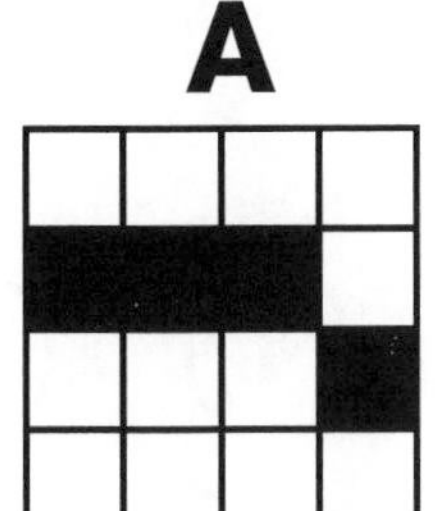

B

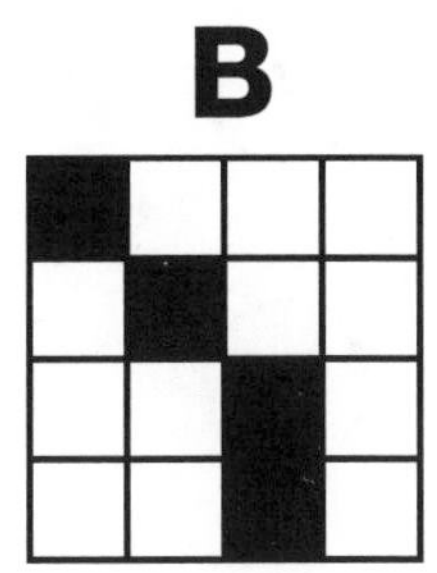

C

D

LEVEL

18

14 PUZZLE

Which number completes the puzzle?

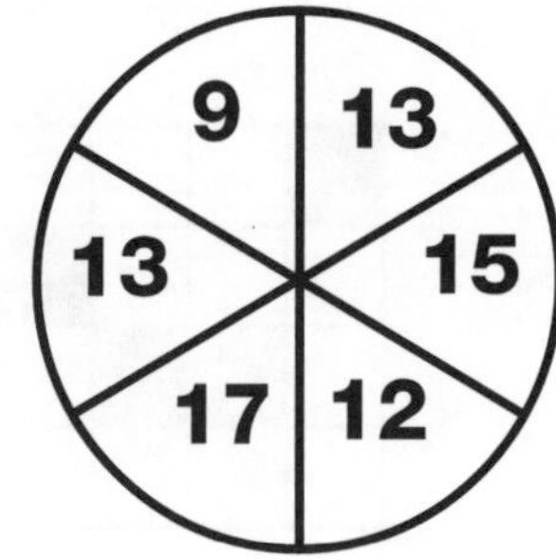

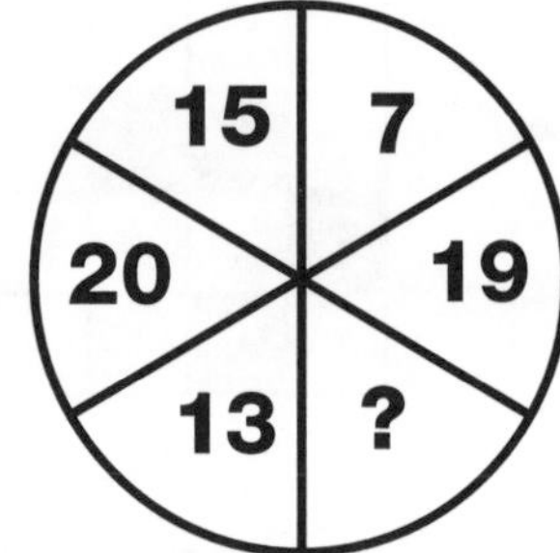

15 PUZZLE

Which letter completes the puzzle?

16 PUZZLE

Following a logical sequence, can you complete this puzzle?

Which letters replace the question marks to complete the puzzle?

J		O		T		Y		D
	K		P		U		Z	
F		R		W		B		I
	M		E		J		E	
A		Z		X		G		N
	H		S		O		J	
V		U		C		L		S
	C		N		T		O	
Q		P		H		Q		X
	X		I		Y		T	
L		?		D		V		C
	S		F		?		Y	
G		N		I		D		?
	B		W		R		M	

LEVEL

18 PUZZLE

Both of these columns of numbers add up to different totals. Can you change just one number to make the totals equal?

2	
8	6
3	4
1	5
7	9
21	24

19 PUZZLE

Here are 12 matches, arranged to form an equilateral triangle. Can you move just 4 matches to reduce the surface area of the triangle by half?
If you can do that, can you move 6 matches from the original layout to reduce the area to a quarter?

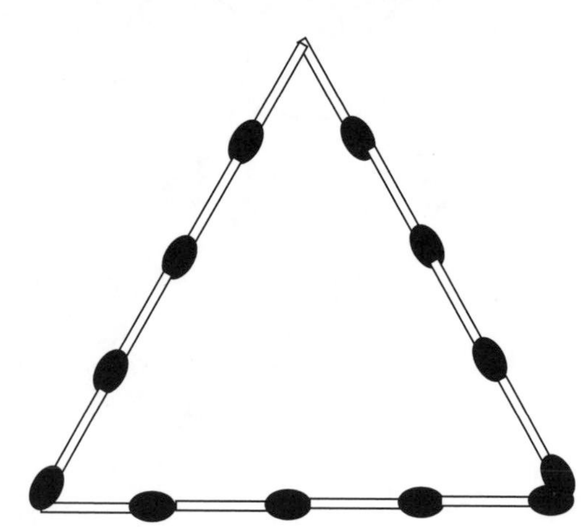

20 PUZZLE

If a group of 6 people have an average age of 21, and each person is half the age of the next person, what are the ages of the 6 people?

21 PUZZLE

Which number completes the puzzle?

1	4	4	2
2	1	4	9
2	8	5	6
3	5	6	?

18

Which grid completes the puzzle?

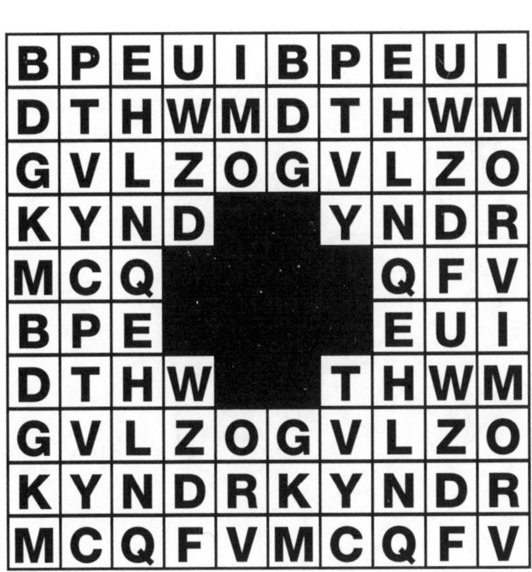

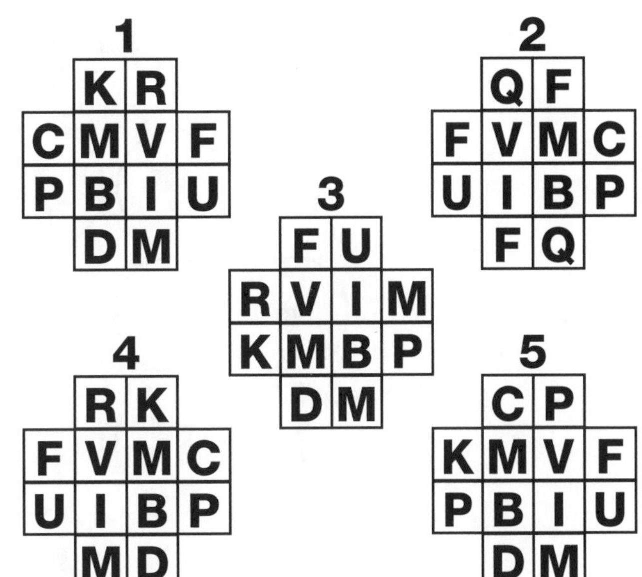

Following a logical sequence, can you complete this puzzle?

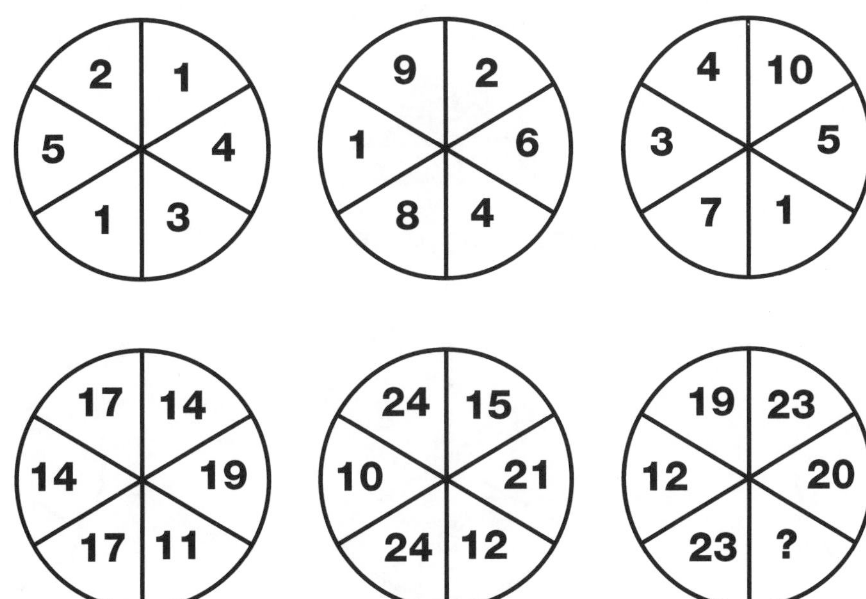

LEVEL

19

L
E
V
E
L

19

3 PUZZLE

Which letter completes the puzzle?

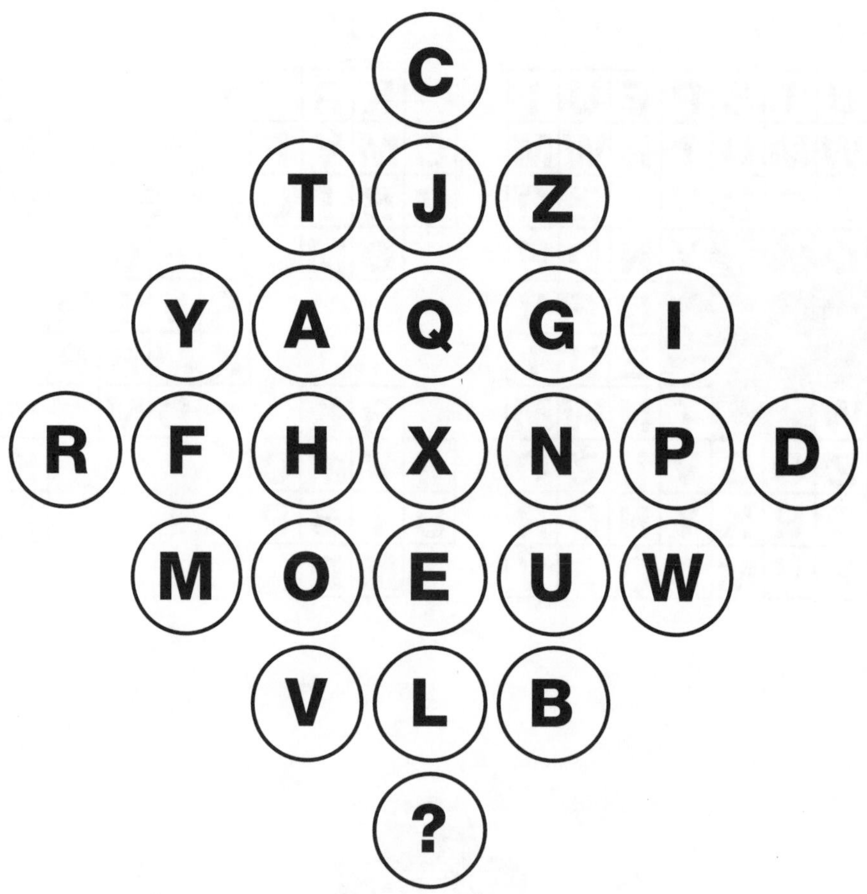

4 PUZZLE

Which number completes the puzzle?

PUZZLE 5

Fill in the empty segments.

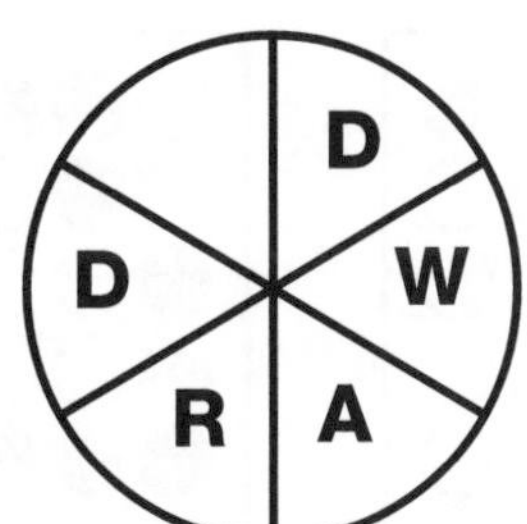

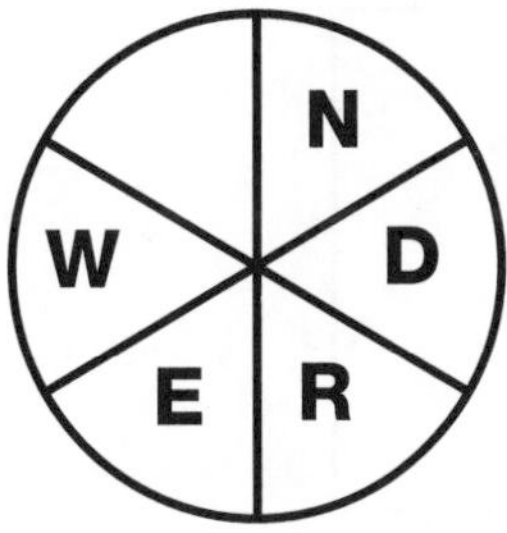

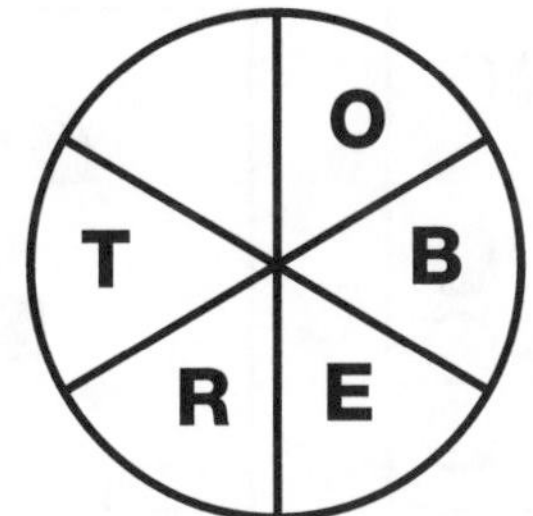

PUZZLE 6

Which number is missing?

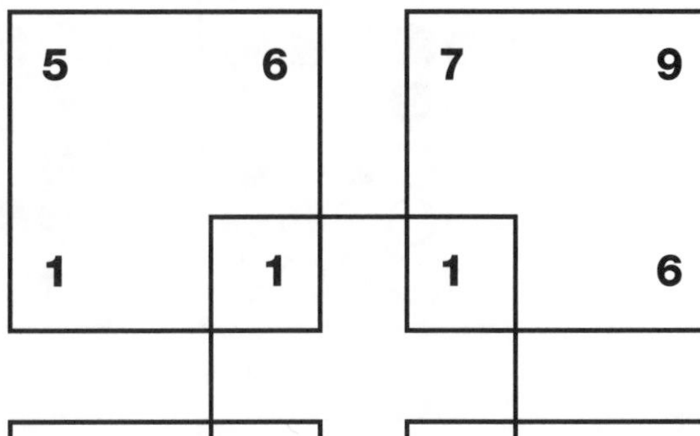

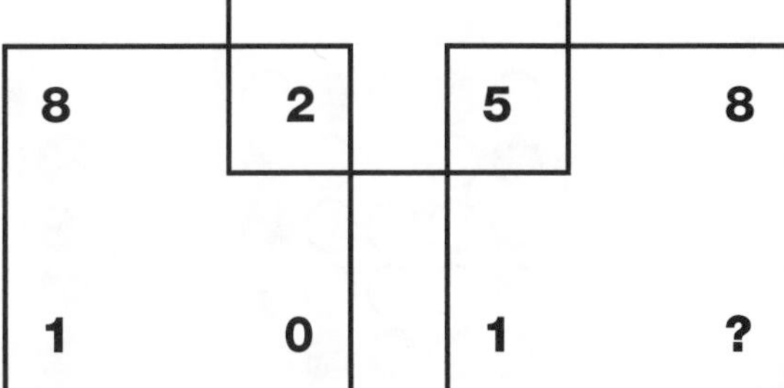

Following a logical sequence, can you complete this puzzle?

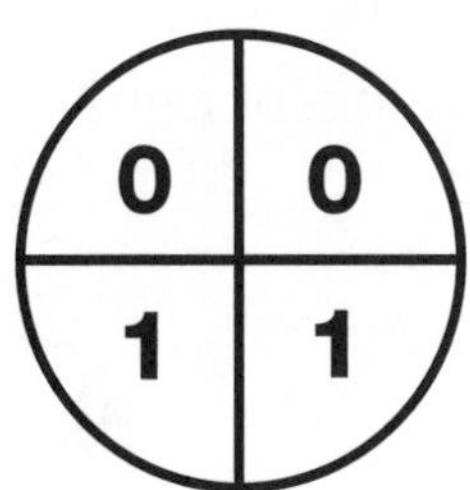

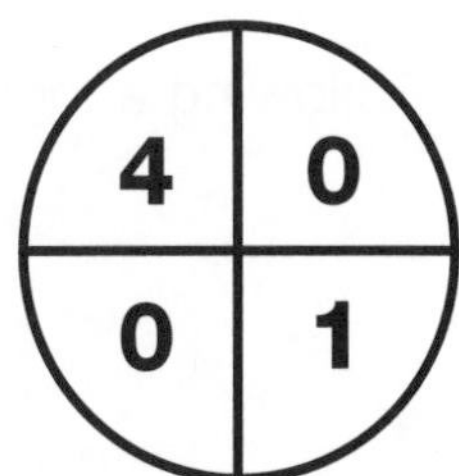

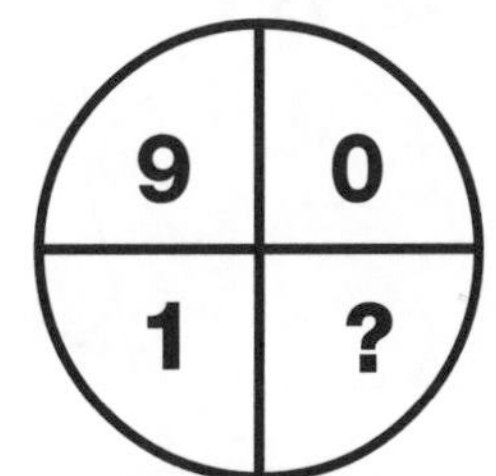

Which pattern completes the puzzle?

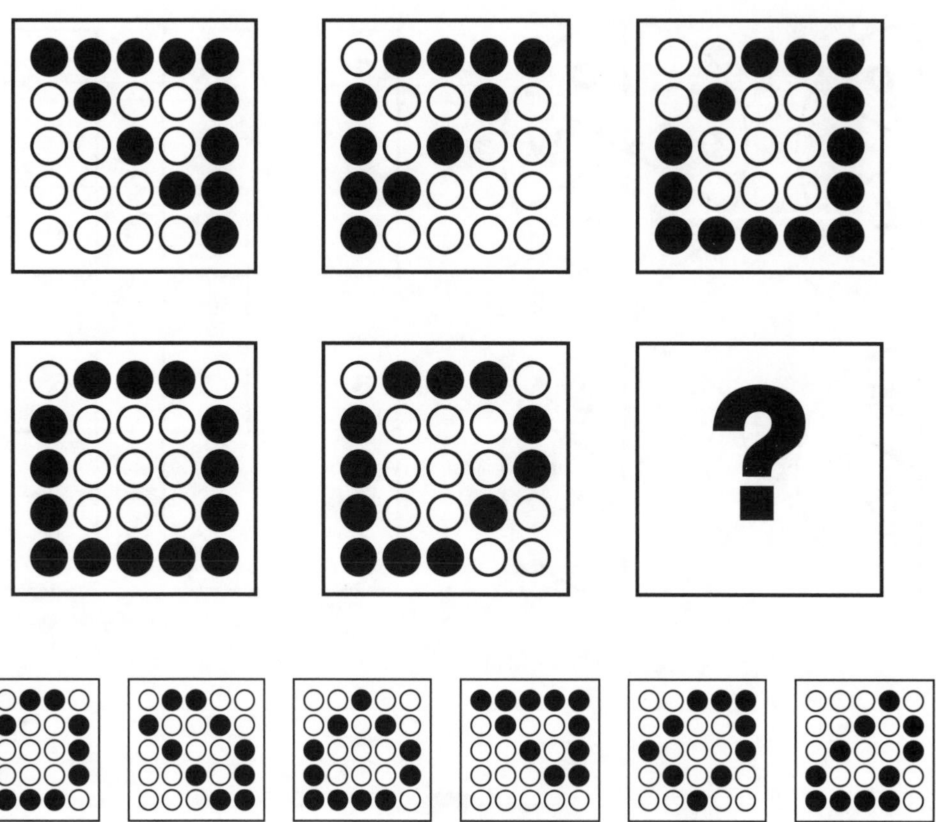

Following a logical sequence, can you complete this puzzle?

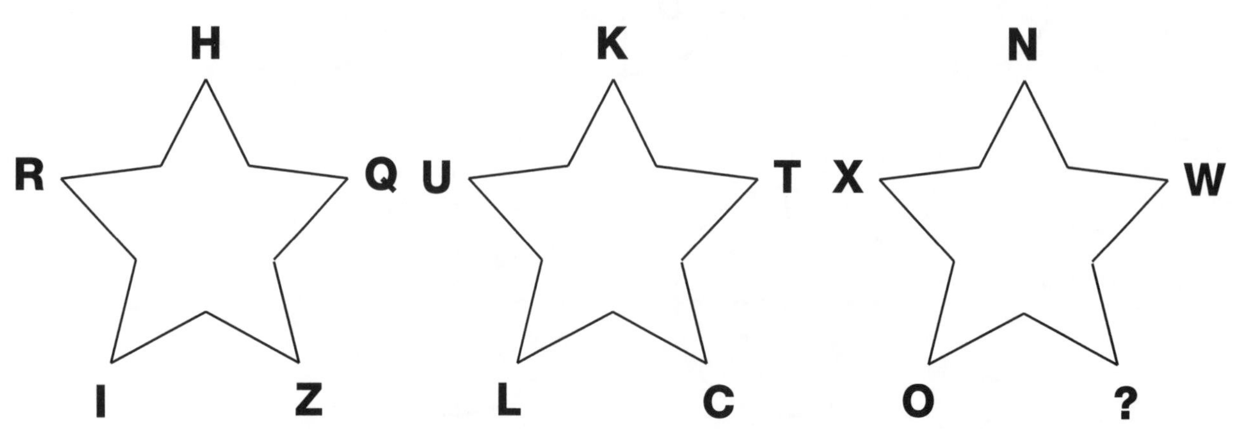

10 PUZZLE

Which of the lower grids replaces the question mark to complete the sequence?

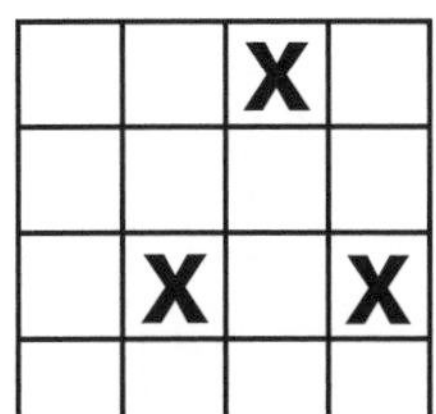
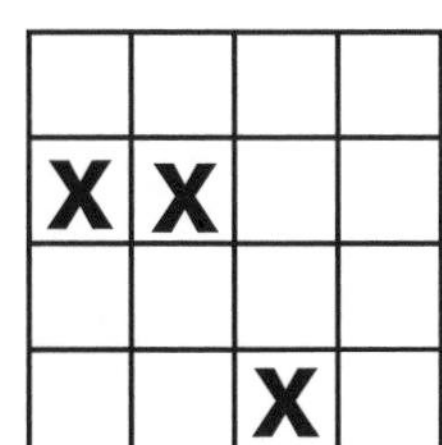
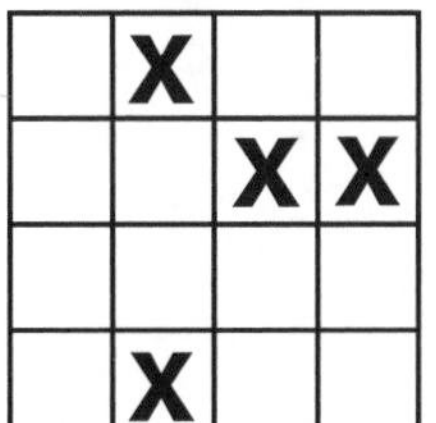
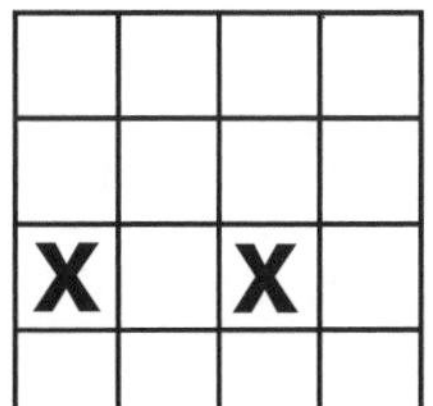
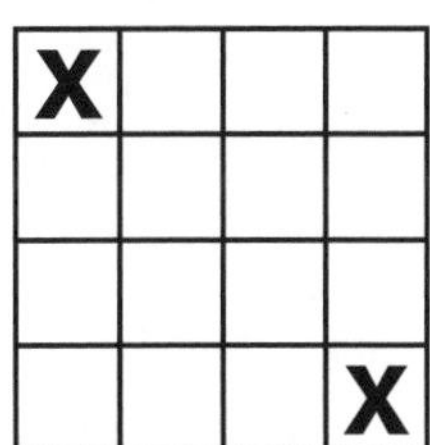
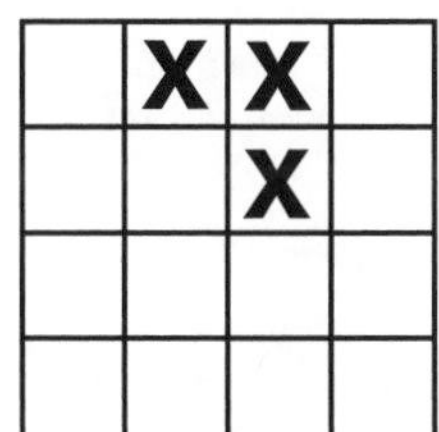
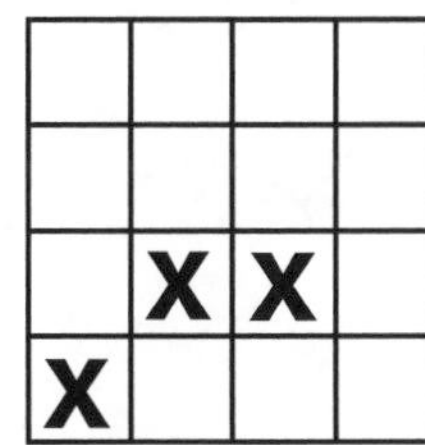
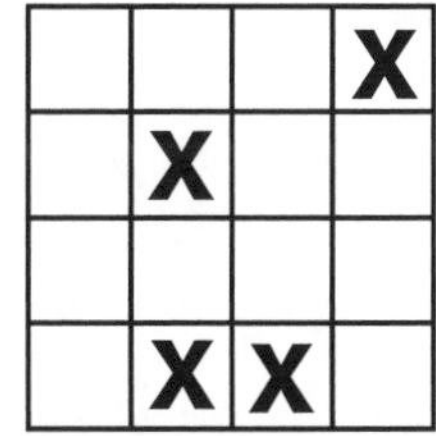
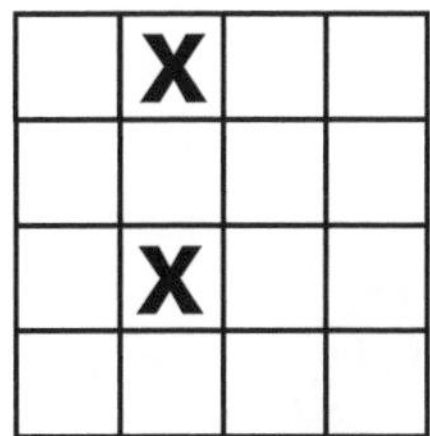
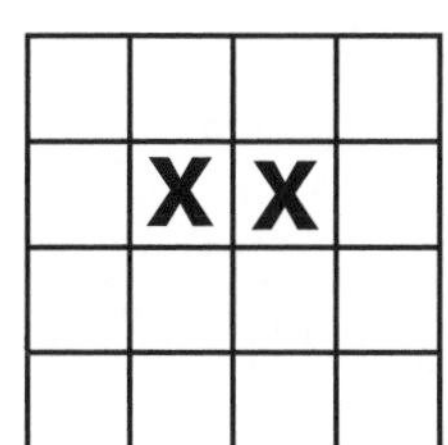
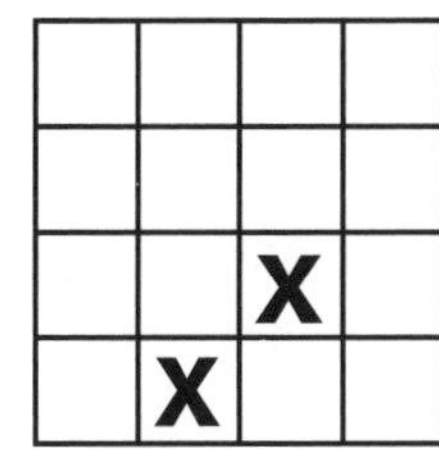
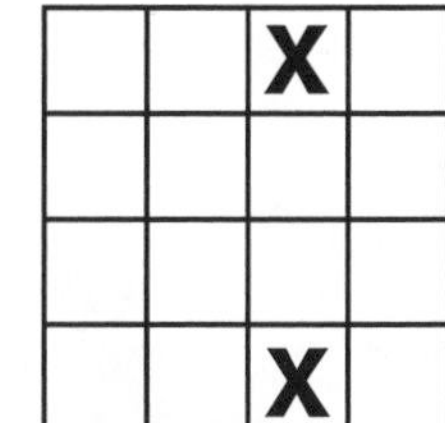
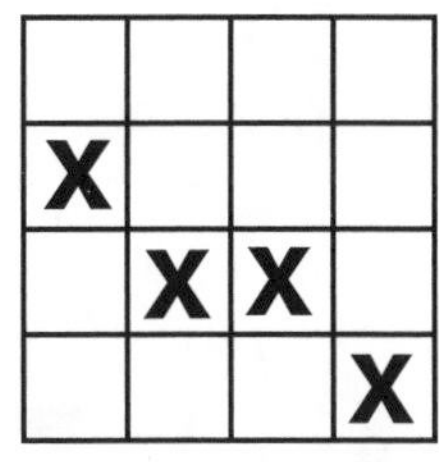
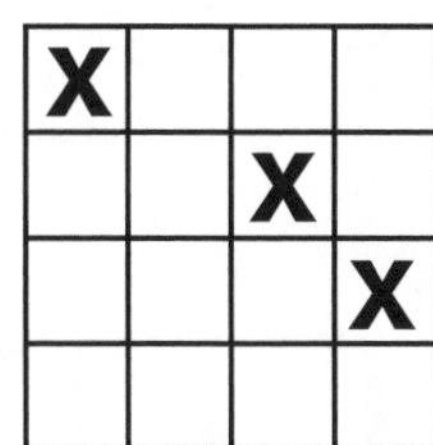
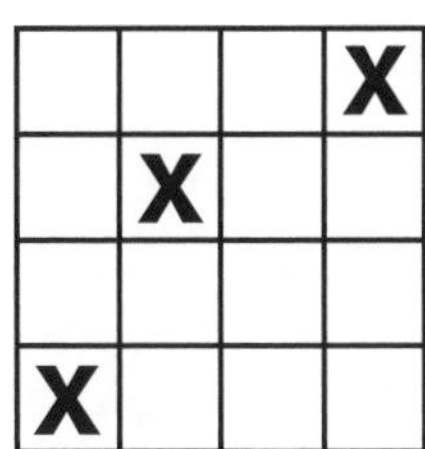

?

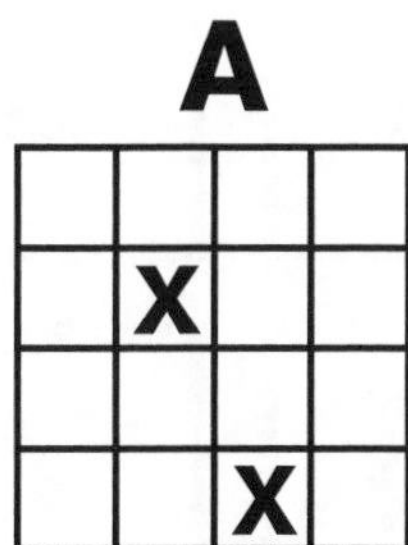
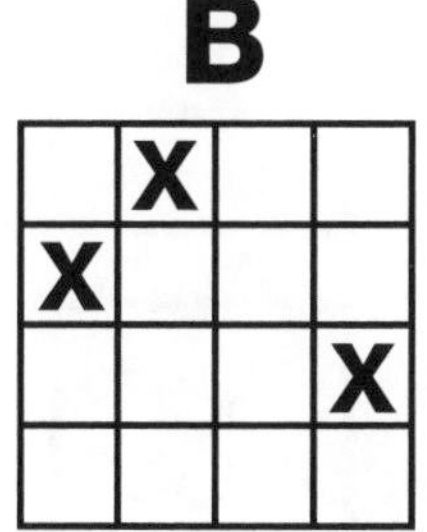
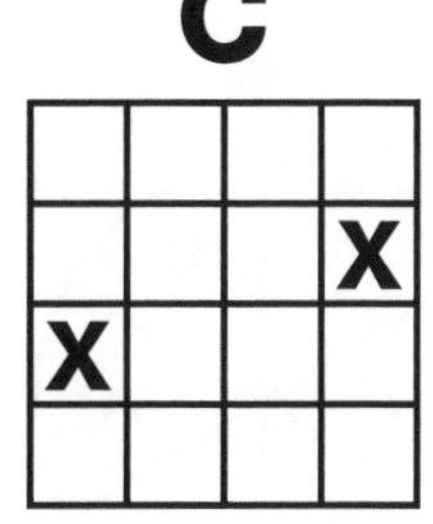
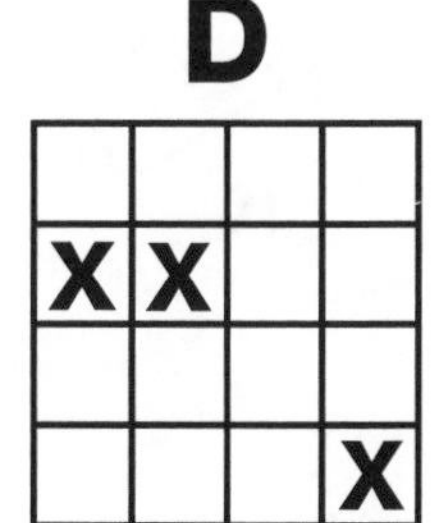

LEVEL

19

11 PUZZLE

What is missing from this arrangement of circles?

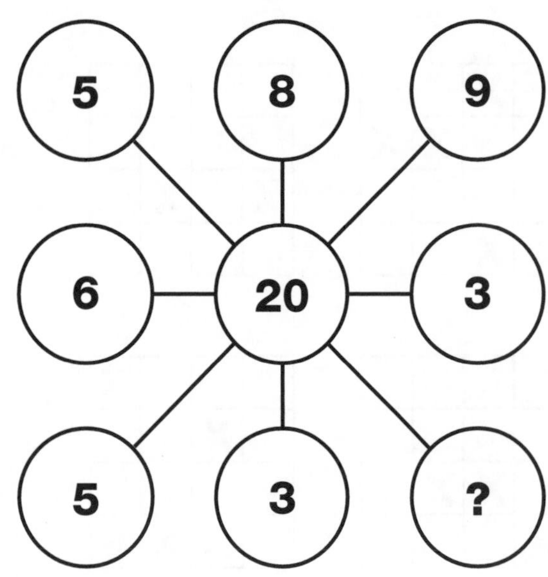

12 PUZZLE

Which number completes the puzzle?

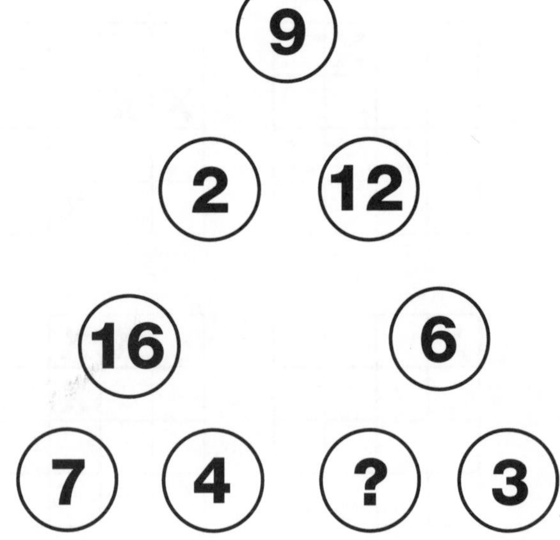

What is missing?

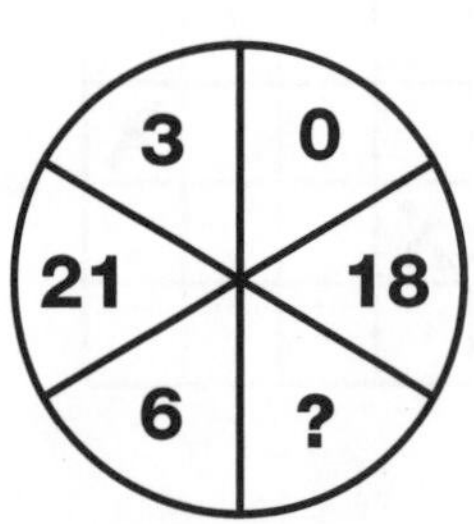

Following a logical sequence, can you complete this puzzle?

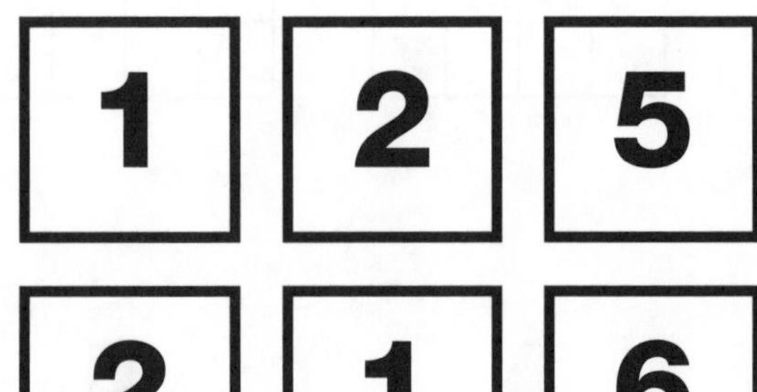

Which number completes this grid?

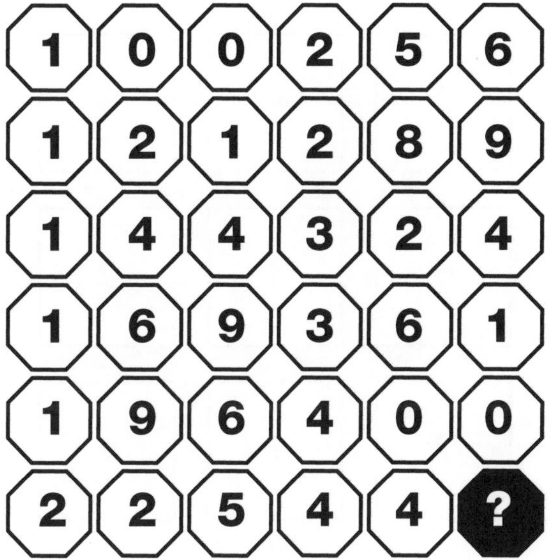

16
PUZZLE

Out of 100 members of a riding club, 60 were women, 80 were married, 70 wore black boots and 90 wore black jackets.

What is the least number of married women who wear black boots and jackets?

Which letter completes the puzzle?

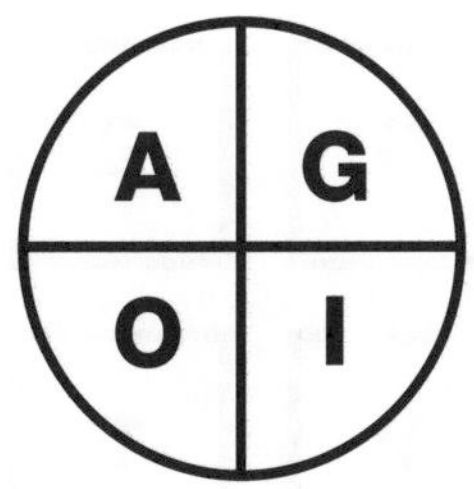

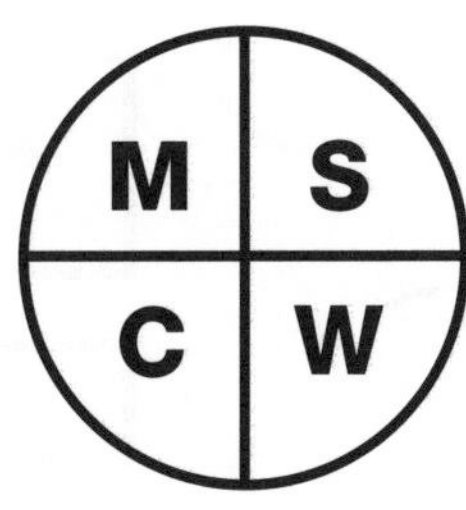

LEVEL

19

18 PUZZLE

Which letter completes the puzzle?

D	F	I	M
C	P	D	R
Q	I	?	X
F	V	M	E

19 PUZZLE

Which number completes the puzzle?

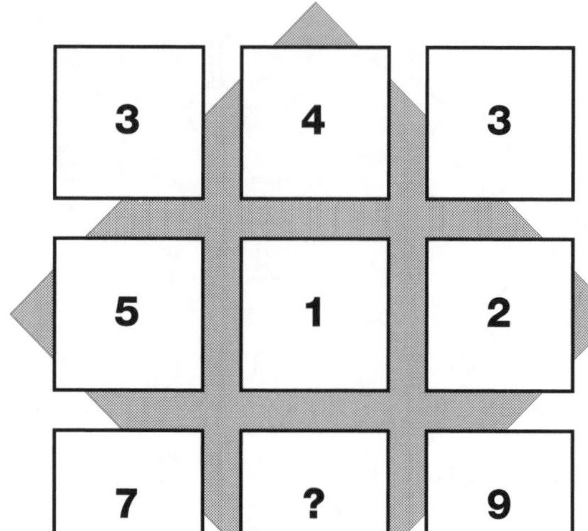

3	4	3
5	1	2
7	?	9

20 PUZZLE

In this sequence of letters what needs to be added to make the puzzle correct?

C	M	K
I	C	O
H	?	J

21 PUZZLE

Which number completes this pattern of squares?

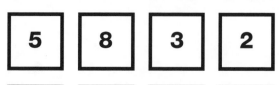

4	0	9	6
4	9	1	3
5	8	3	2
6	?	5	9

22 PUZZLE

Which one of the letters given below completes this puzzle?

A	F	I
L	N	?
X	Z	E

1	2	3	4	5
K	L	M	V	Y

23 PUZZLE

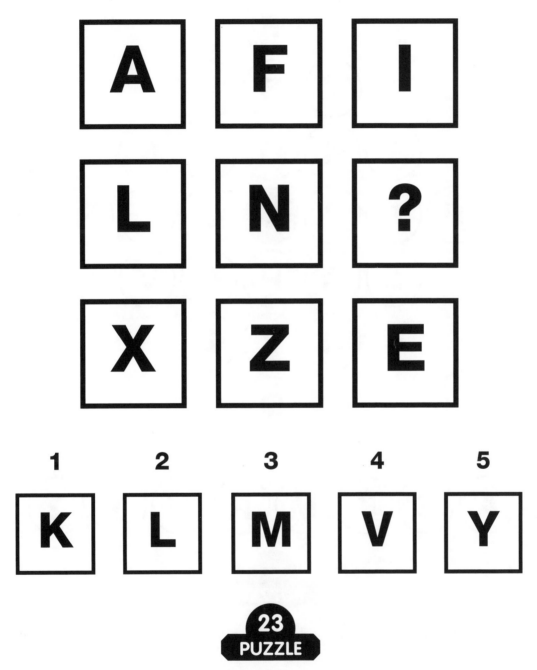

Following a logical sequence, can you complete this puzzle?

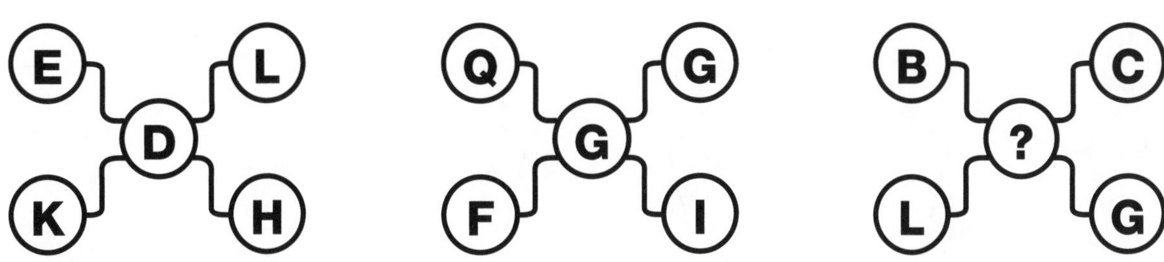

LEVEL 19

LEVEL 20

Which letter completes the puzzle?

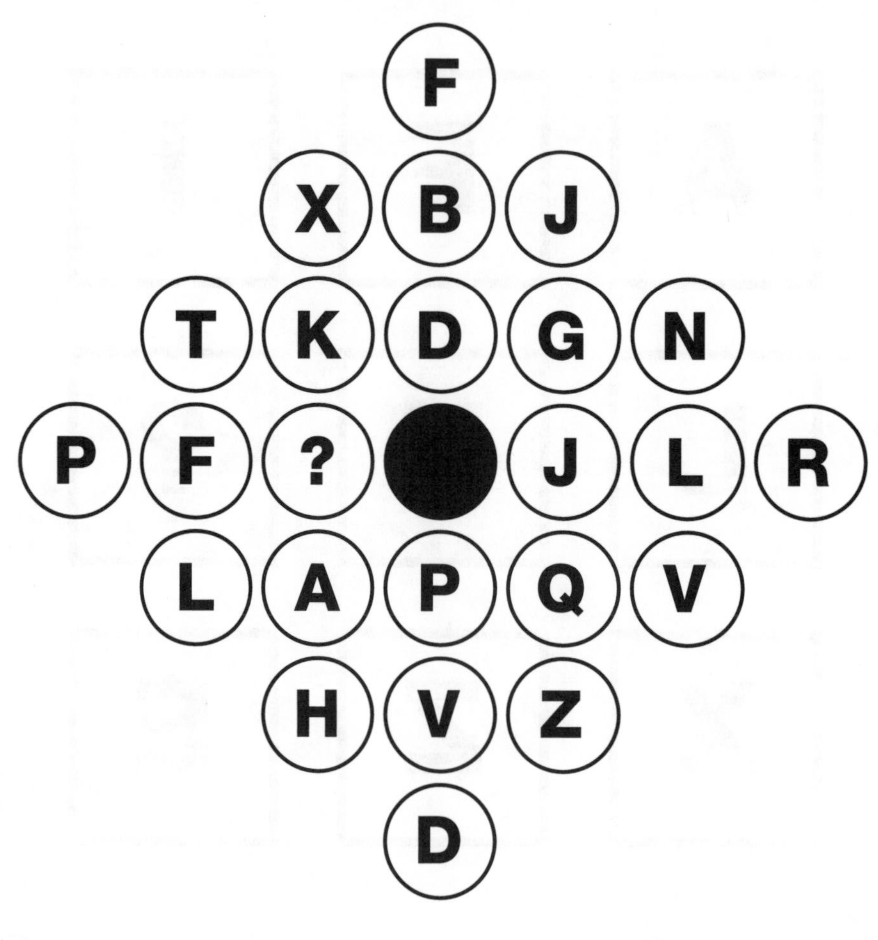

In this sequence of letters what needs to be added to make the puzzle correct?

Which of the lower grids will complete this puzzle?

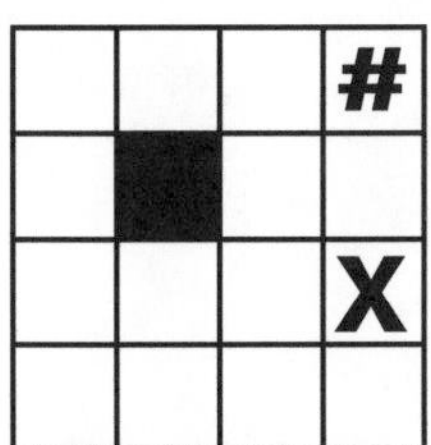   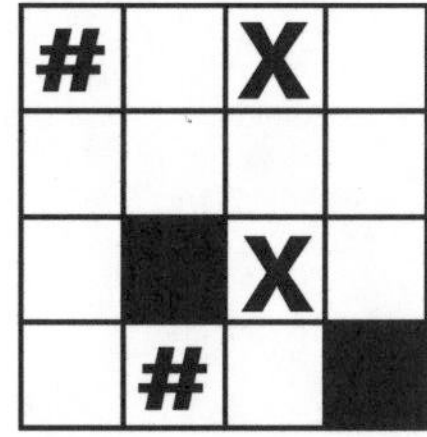

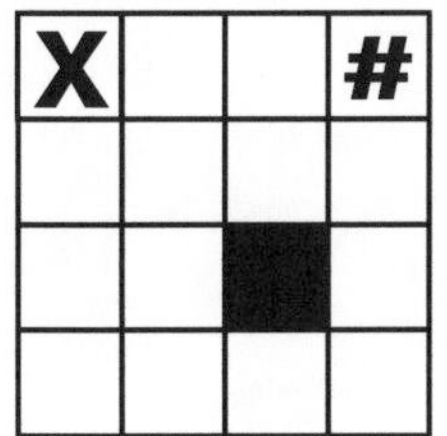   

   ?

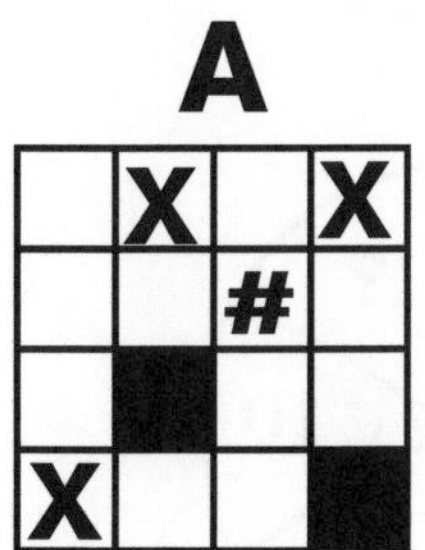

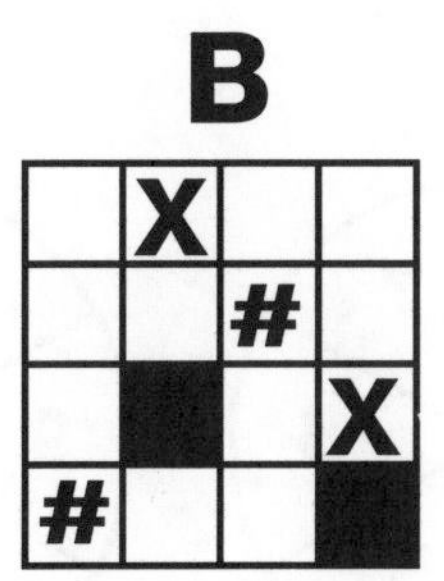

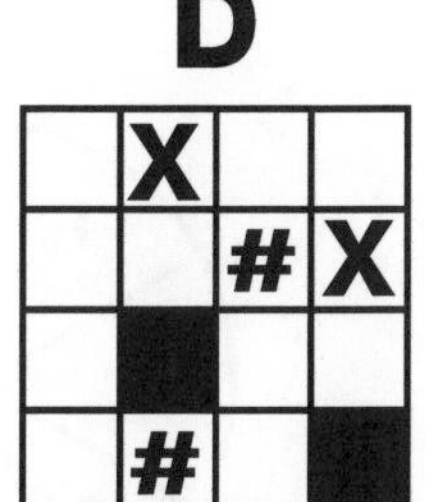

LEVEL

20

Which watch completes the puzzle?

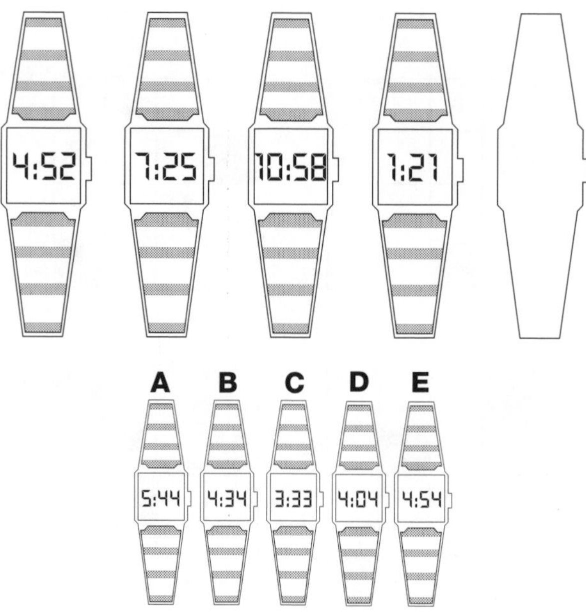

5
PUZZLE

What is missing from this puzzle?

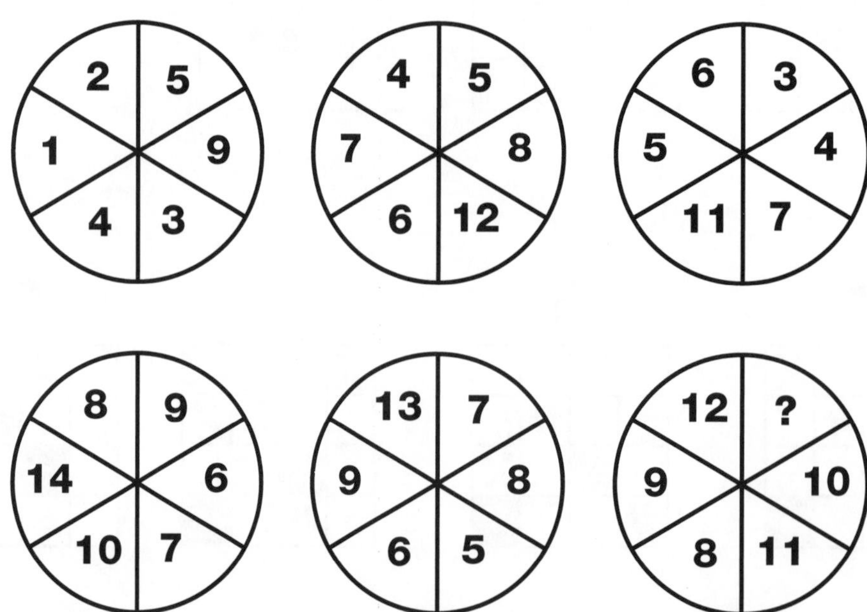

6 PUZZLE

Following a logical sequence, can you complete this puzzle?

B	C
E	A
F	D
J	B
L	H
?	?

7 PUZZLE

Which number completes the puzzle?

2		4	3		4
1		2	4		2
10		8	8		2
2		1	5		?

8 PUZZLE

Which letters complete the puzzle?

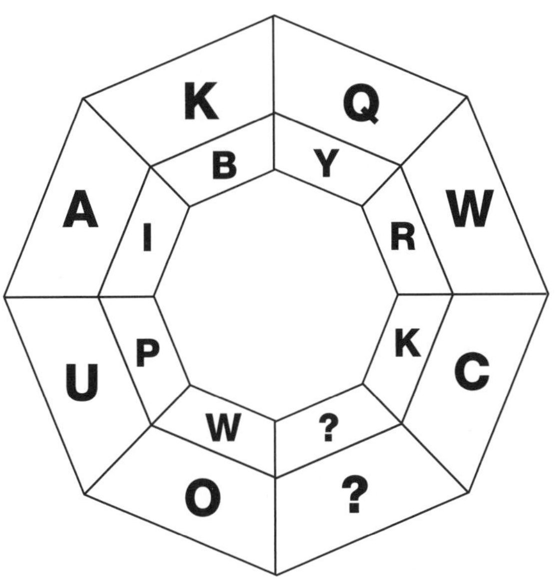

9 PUZZLE

What is missing from these circles?

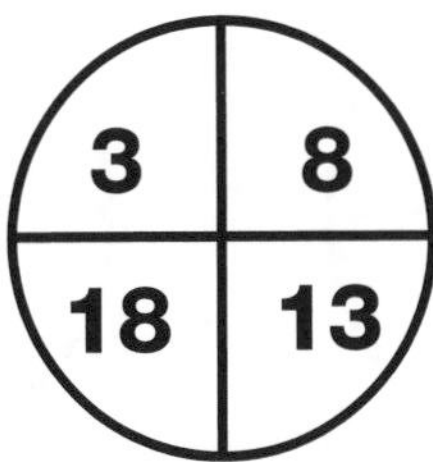

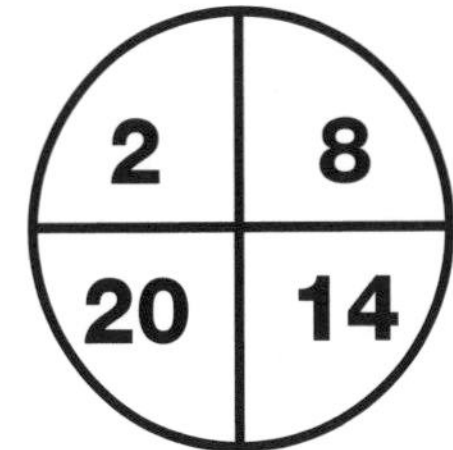

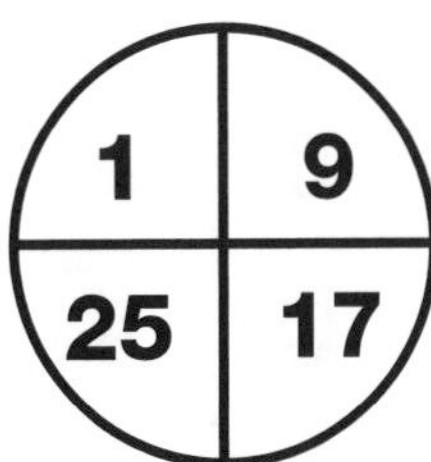

5	12
26	?

LEVEL 20

LEVEL

20

10 PUZZLE

In this sequence of letters what needs to be added to make the puzzle correct?

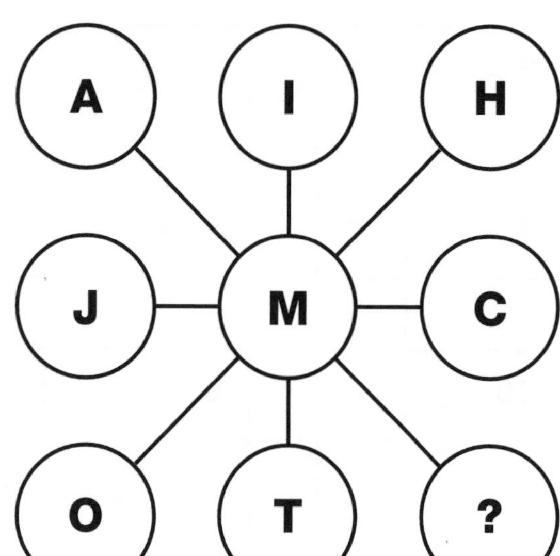

11 PUZZLE

Which letter completes the puzzle?

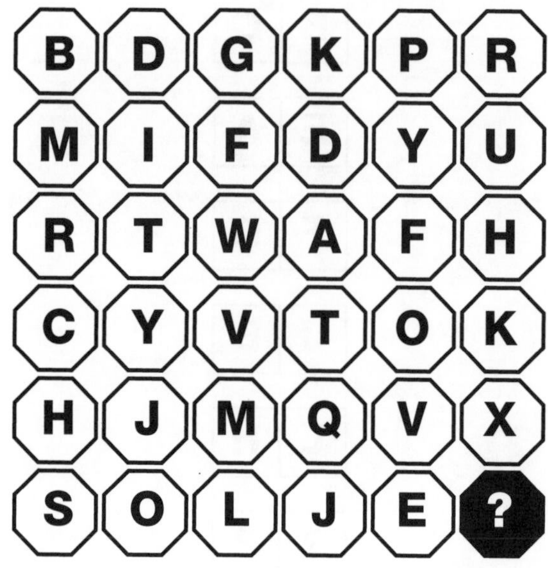

12 PUZZLE

Which number completes this puzzle?

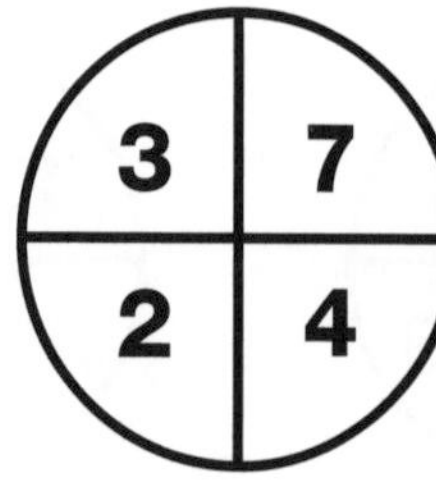

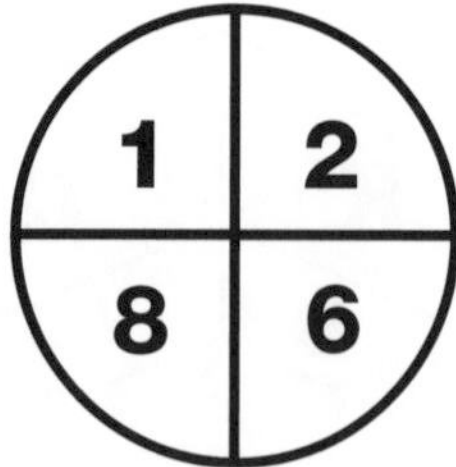

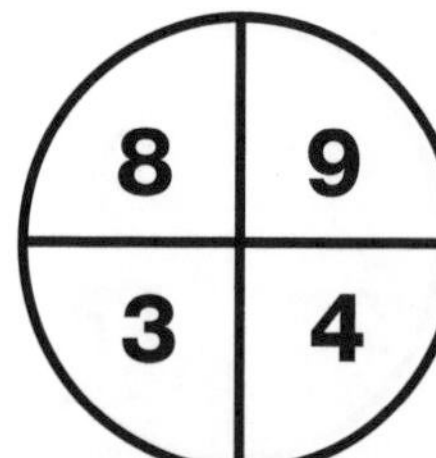

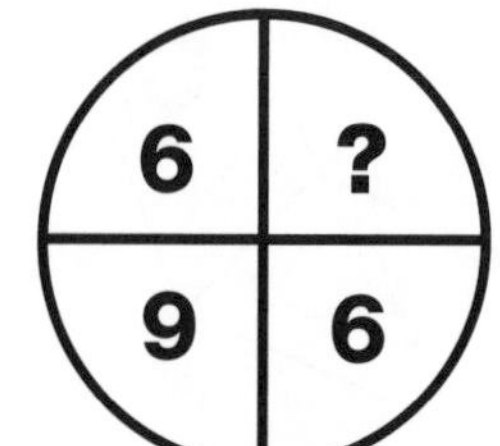

13 PUZZLE

Which number completes the puzzle?

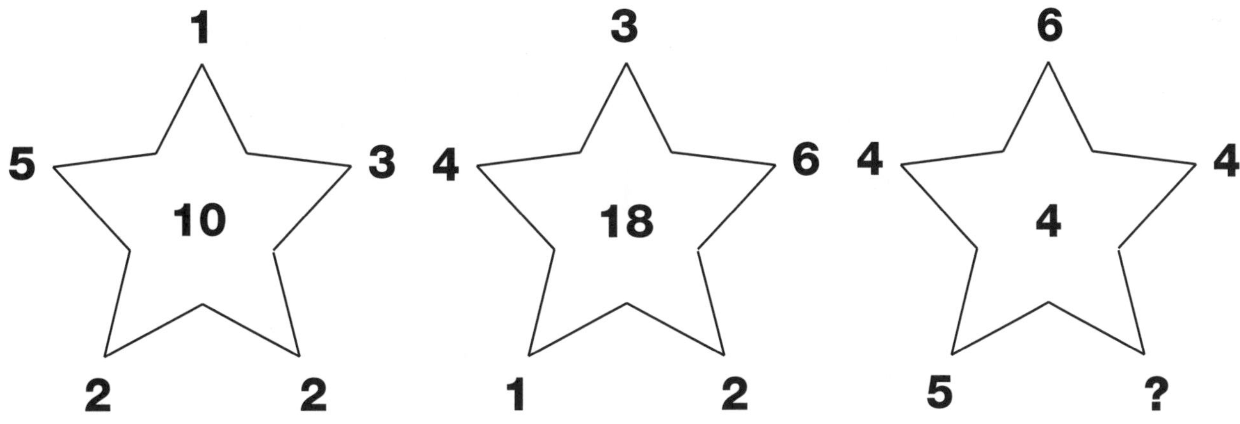

14 PUZZLE

What is missing from this arrangement of circles?

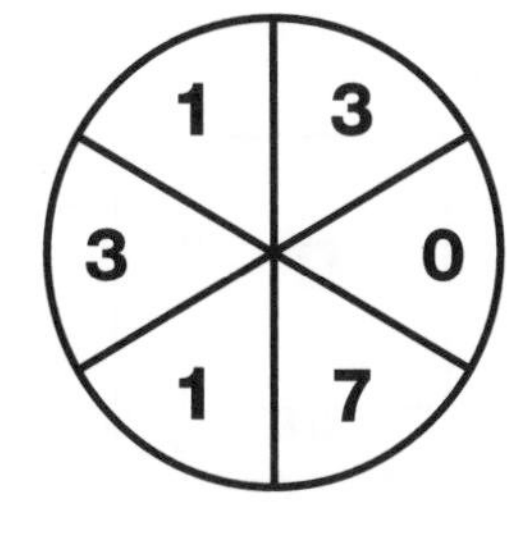

15 PUZZLE

Following a logical sequence, can you complete this puzzle?

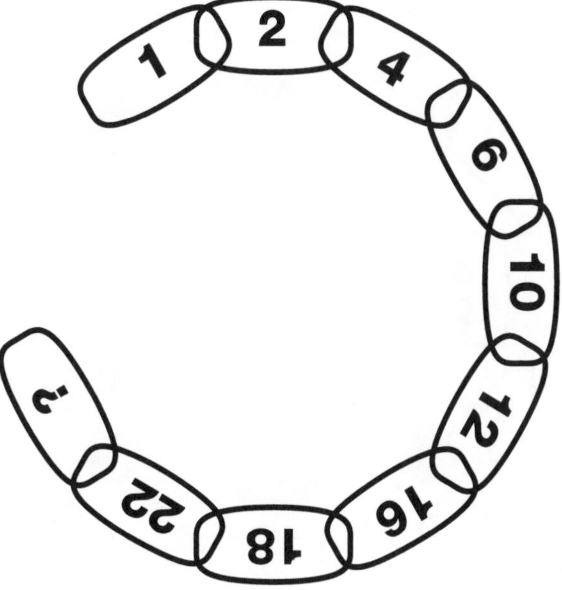

LEVEL

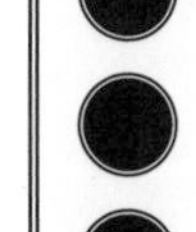

20

16 PUZZLE

Which number completes the puzzle?

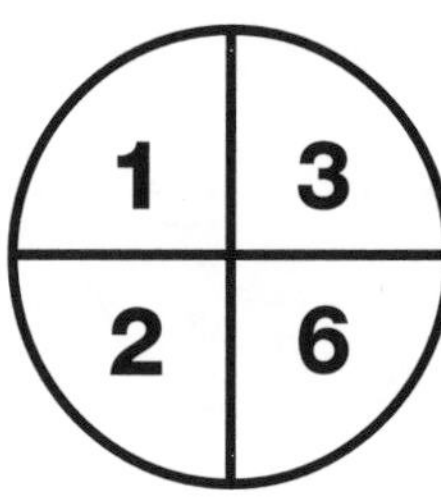

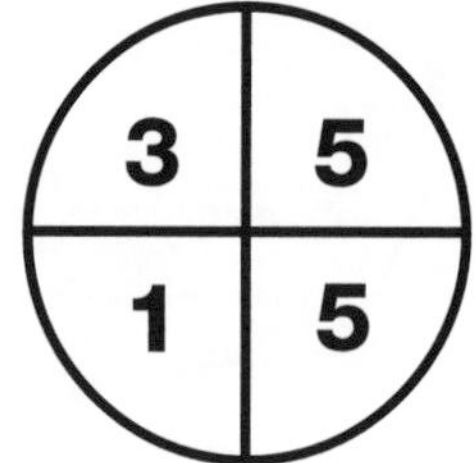

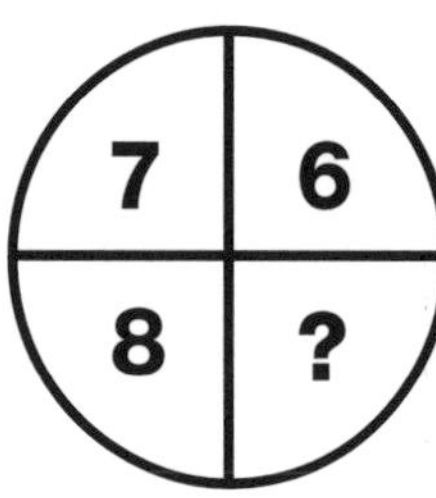

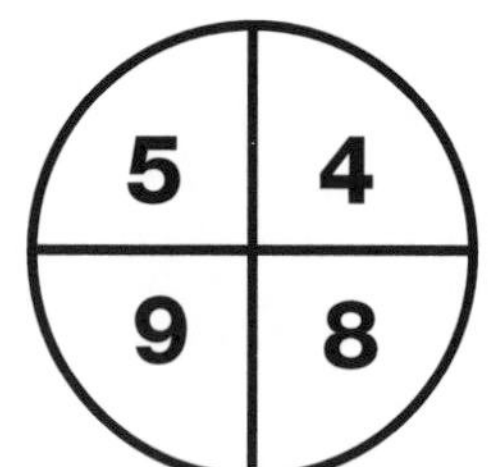

17 PUZZLE

In this sequence of letters what needs to be added to make the puzzle correct?

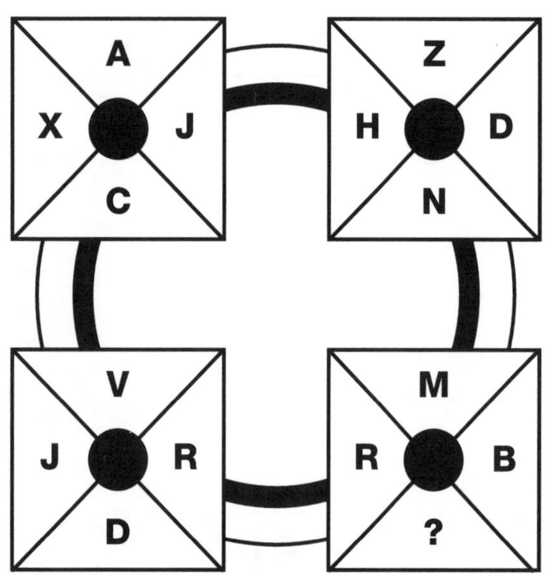

Following a logical sequence, can you complete this puzzle?

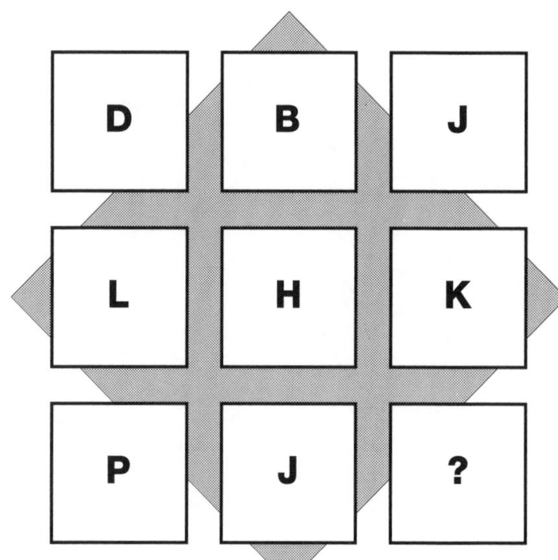

19 PUZZLE

Which letter completes the puzzle?

20 PUZZLE

Which number is missing?

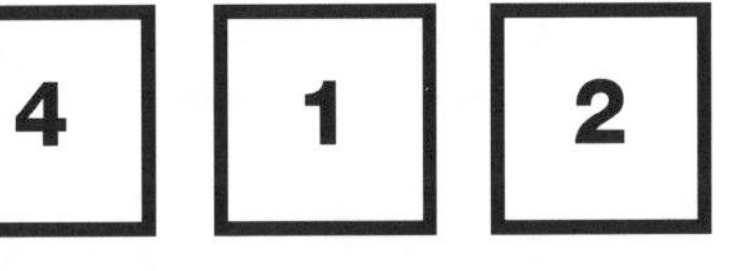

4	1	2	4
1	2	9	4
8	2	6	5
5	3	3	?

21 PUZZLE

Which of the lower patterns replaces the question mark to complete the puzzle?

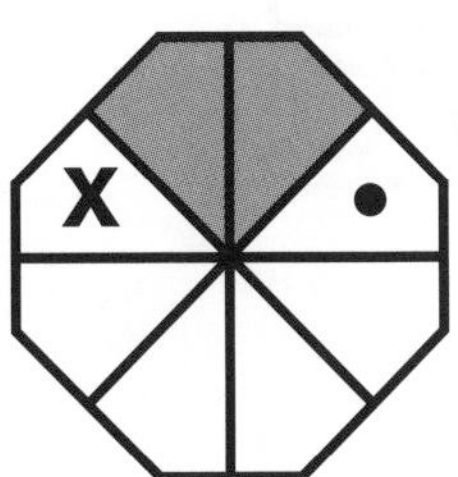
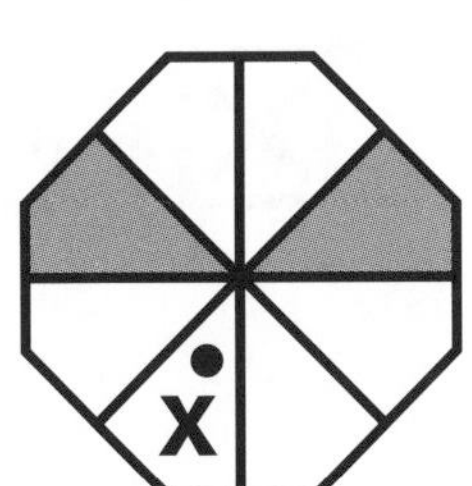
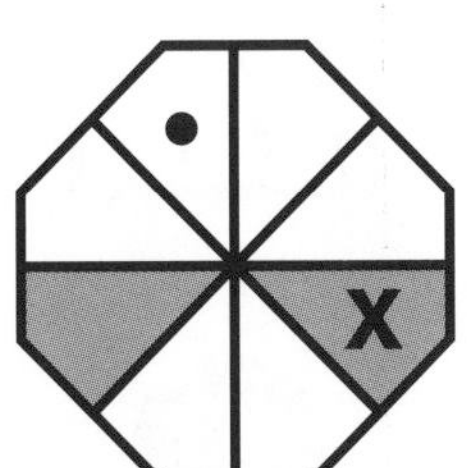
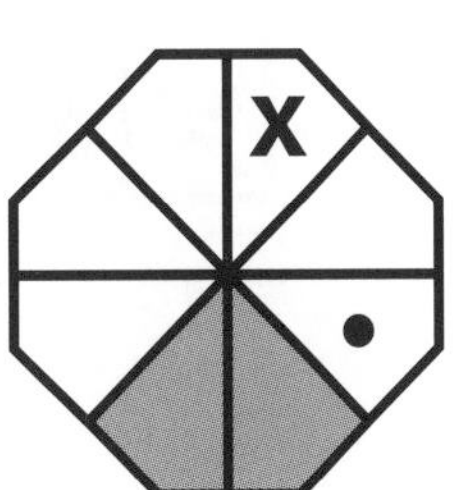

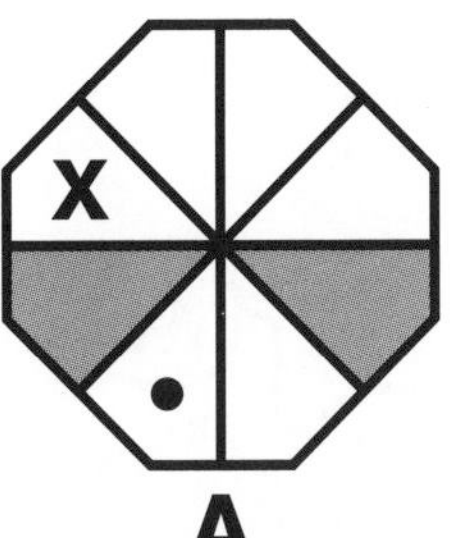
A
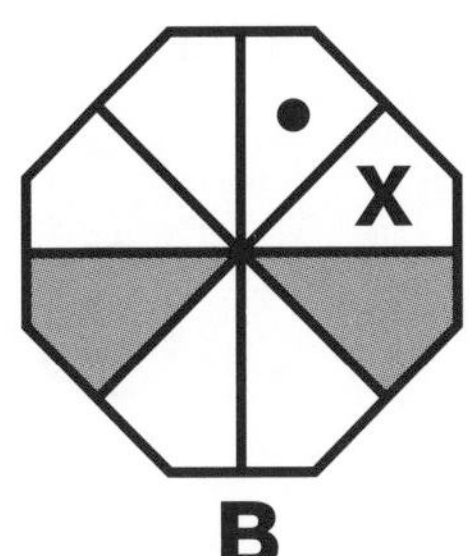
B
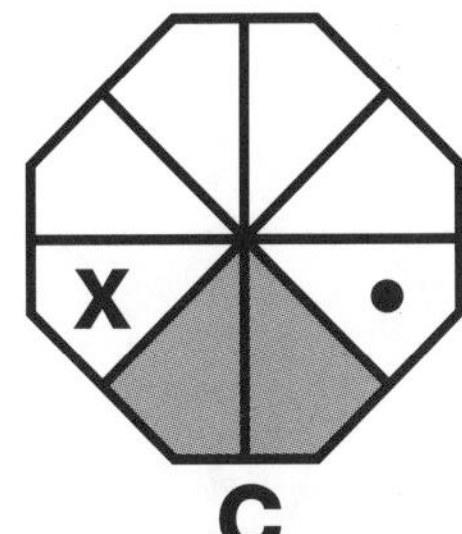
C
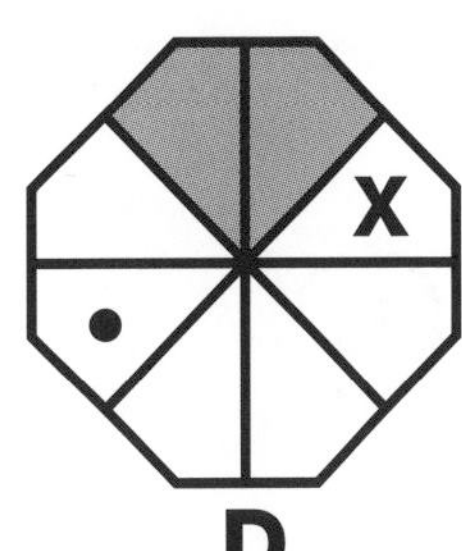
D
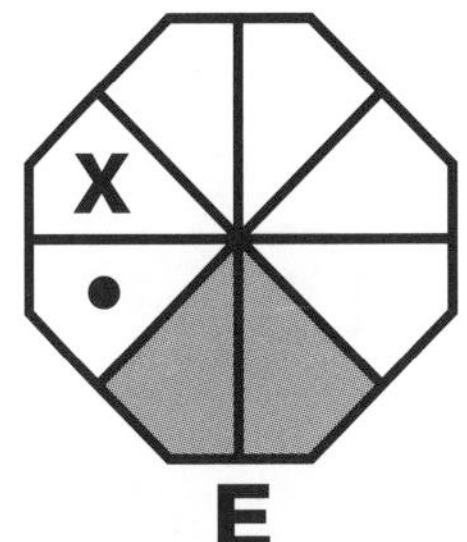
E

Which pattern completes the puzzle?

?

1 2 3 4 5

23 PUZZLE

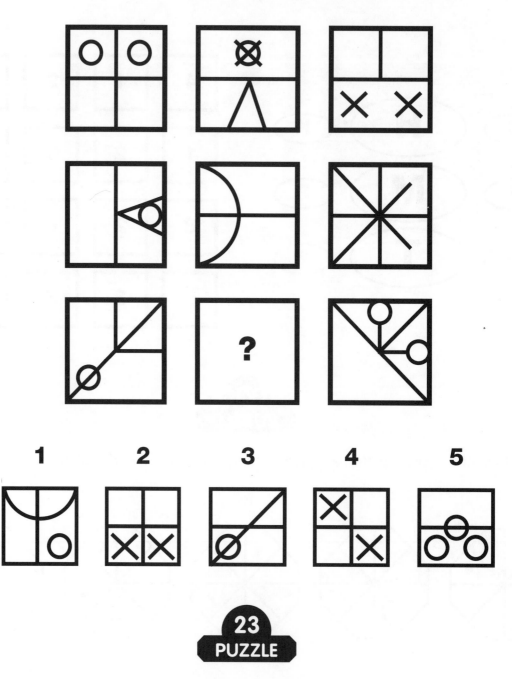

Following a logical sequence, can you complete this puzzle?

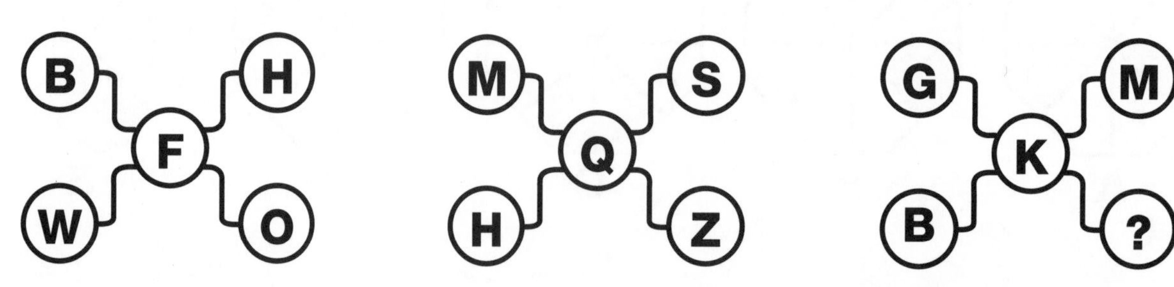

SOLUTIONS

LEVEL 

1 - 7
Starting on the top row, and taking straight lines through the centre, subtract the central number from the upper number, and put the result in the corresponding lower box.

2 - 7
Working in rows, add the left and right hand numbers to give a 2 digit result, and write this in the middle two boxes.

3 - 9
In each row, the central number equals the average of the left and right hand numbers.

4 - G
In each row, multiply the numerical values of the left and right hand letters together to give the value in the centre.

5 - 8
In each triangle, divide the top number by the lower left number and add the lower right number to give the value in the centre of the triangle.

6 - 7
In each segment, the difference between the outer and inner numbers is always 9, with the highest and lowest numbers alternating from the inner ring to the outer ring each step

7 - 5
Working in rows, the central number equals the average of the left and right hand values.

8 - C
In each figure, letters move in sequence, clockwise, in steps given by the numerical value of the central letter.

9 - 25
Starting top left and moving clockwise, numbers increase by 6 each step.

10 - N
Working in rows from left to right, letters advance through the alphabet skipping 1 letter in the top row, 2 letters in the middle, and 3 for the bottom.

11 - 7
All rows and columns add up to 15.

12 - K
Starting at the top left, and working in a Z shape around the circles, letters follow the alphabetic sequence, skipping 1,2,3... etc., letters at a time.

13 - A
As you move to the right, add 24 minutes to each time value.

14 - G
In each shape, the numbers around the outside are all multiples of the number indicated by the numerical value of the letter in the centre.

15 - 9
Working in columns, from top to bottom, double each number and subtract 1 to give the next value down.

16 - 50
As you move to the right, double each number, and subtract 2.

17 - W
Starting on the left, letters advance by 3 places, then 4, 5 and 6.

18 - 28
As you descend, add 3 to the previous number, then 4, 5, 6... etc.

19 - 81
Starting at the top, numbers follow the sequence of square numbers of 5, 6, 7, 8 and 9.

20 - A
Starting on the left, and moving right, the 2 shaded segments rotate in opposite directions, 1 space at a time, while the dot moves one segment anticlockwise.

21 - F
Taking each grid of dots in the top row, rotate the pattern by 180° to form the pattern in the bottom row.

22 - Four of Diamonds
In each row, the sum of the black cards is always 7, the sum of the red cards is always 8. One card from each suit appears in each row.

23 - 2
Taking the horizontal line of circles through the centre of the diagram, these values equal the sum of the two adjacent numbers in the pattern.

24 - 1
Starting in the top left, and moving clockwise, the sum of the digits in each circle follows the the sequence 6, 7, 8 and 9.

25 - I
Starting in the top left, and moving clockwise in a spiral, towards the centre, letters move through the alphabet, skipping 1 letter at a time.

26 -

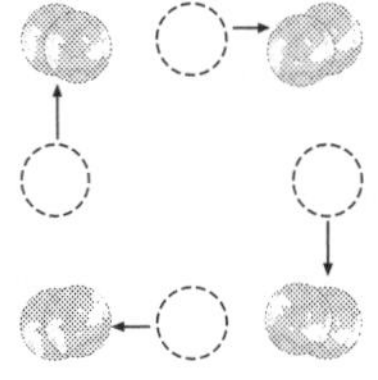

27 - 3
Add the top row of digits together, to give the result on the left hand centre space, and add the bottom row of digits together to give the result on the right hand centre space.

28 -

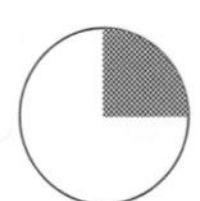

Working in columns, from top to bottom, the last circle represents the addition of the shaded segments from the top 3 circles. If a shaded segment appears in one of the top 3 circles, it appears in the same position in the bottom circle. If there are 2 shaded segments in the same position in the upper circles, then they cancel out, and become blank in the bottom circle. Shaded squares in all three remain shaded.

29 -

Reading from left to right, the sum of the dots on each domino follows the sequence 2, 4, 6, 8, 10, 12.

SOLUTIONS

LEVEL 

1 - 7
Working in rows, from top to bottom, the sum of the digits in each row follows the sequence 10, 15, 20, 25, 30.

2 - F
All patterns of dots are symmetrical around a central vertical axis.

3 - Points to the 2 (6:10)
Starting at the top, and working clockwise around the faces, the time shown increases by 1 hour and 20 minutes each step.

4 - 2
In each circle, add the numbers in the top two segments together, to get a 2 digit number, and write this number in the lower two segments.

5 - H
Starting top left, and moving down, then up the centre, and down the right hand column, to finish bottom right, the letters follow the alphabetic sequence, 6 letters at time.

6 - 4
In each row, square the central number to give a 2 digit value, and write this value in the left and right hand spaces.

7 - S
Working clockwise around each shape, letters advance by steps of 3, 4 and 5, working from left to right.

8 - J
Letters in each position on the left triangle increase by steps of 4, 5, 6 and 7 as you move to the next triangle to the right, returning to the start of the alphabet once reaching Z.

9 - J
Working in columns, add the numerical values of the top two letters, to give the numerical value of the lower letter.

10 - 9
Starting with the numbers on the top row, add the central number to each one, giving the results on the bottom row.

11 - A
Starting with the letter L and moving clockwise, letters advance through the alphabet 5 letters at a time.

12 - 3
The sum of the digits on each side of the triangle equals 15.

13 - 62
Starting at the top, add 1 to the first number, and multiply by 2 to give the next number down.

14 - 2
Working in columns, the numbers in each column add up to 17.

15 - D
The sum of the digits shown on each watch increase by 2 each step.

16 - 5
Working in rows, from left to right, take the outer shape in each box and place it in the centre of the other shapes, moving 1 place to the right each time.

17 - 5
In each diagram, the numbers around the outside increase, in sequence, by value given in the central circle

18 - H
Starting top left and working down, then top right and down again, the letters follow the alphabetic sequence, 4 letters at a time.

19 - 40
Each horizontal row of numbers follows the sequence of multiples of 3, 4 and 5.

20 - 49
As you move to the right, the numbers follow the sequence of multiples of 7.

21 - 6
Reading the top line as a 3 digit number, subtract the central number, and write the 3 digit result in the lower circles.

22 - H
Starting at the apex of each triangle, and moving around it clockwise, letters skip 3 places for the left hand triangle, 4 places for the middle, and 5 places for the right hand triangle.

23 - Minute hand points to 4.
Starting with the top clockface, and moving clockwise around the other 3, the hour hand advances 3 hours at a time, and the minute hand moves back 20 minutes each time.

24 - X
Starting top left, and moving clockwise around the 4 circles, add 2 to the value of each letter to give the values of the letters in the next circle around.

25 - 78
Starting on the left, double each number, and add 2.

26 - M
Starting on A and moving clockwise, letters advance through the alphabet 3 at a time.

27 -

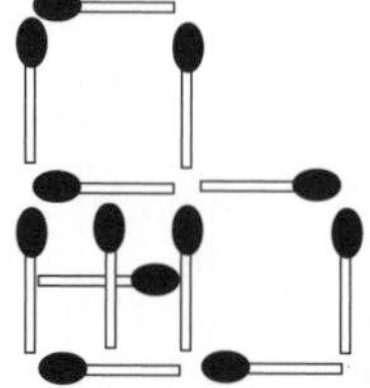

28 - 3
Add adjacent numbers on the bottom row, and put the results in the box directly above, take the difference between adjacent boxes on the next row up, putting the results in the box directly above again. Finally, take the sum of these two boxes, putting the result in the top box.

SOLUTIONS

LEVEL 

1 - 10:25
Starting at the top, and moving clockwise around the faces, the minute hand moves forward by 10 minutes in each step, and the hour hand moves back one hour.

2 - Top O, P bottom R, Q
Starting in the top left, take 2X2 squares, with letters of the alphabet written in sequence clockwise, around these groups of 4. Work from left to right, top to bottom, writing the alphabet in sequence around the block.

3 - 3
Working from left to right, top row then bottom, the sum of the numbers in each circle increases by multiples of 5.

4 - 18
Starting at the top, and working down, add the first two numbers together, to give the next number down.

5 - 19
In each row of the diagram, the sum of the numbers is 19.

6 - 8
Working in columns, the number at the bottom of each row equals the difference between the upper two numbers.

7 - 1
In each row, the central number is equal to the sum of the right and left hand numbers.

8 - E
Each shape is rotationally symmetrical by 180° around its central point.

9 - 5
In each diagram, the average of the top two numbers, and the bottom two numbers is written in the central circle.

10 - 5
In each triangle, subtract the two lower numbers from the number at the top of the triangle to give the value at the centre.

11 - 63
Working in rows from left to right, and from top to bottom, numbers follow the sequence of multiples of 7, 8 and 9.

12 - 4
Working top to bottom, reading each pair of numbers as a two digit value, the values follow the sequence of square numbers, from 3 to 8.

13 - 26
Moving clockwise from number 5, numbers increase in value by 6,7,8,9 etc.

14 - 4
Working in rows, add the centre and right hand digits together, to give the result on the left.

15 - 3
Working in columns, the sum of the 3 numbers always equals 17.

16 - 5
Taking the top three circles, add together the lower two circles, to get the value in the upper circle, repeat this formula for the three circles on the bottom left and bottom right.

17 - 5
Starting with the numbers on the top row, and moving in straight lines through the centre, multiply the top numbers by the central number, putting the results in the lower circles.

18 - 4
In each row, the centre number equals the difference between the left and right hand numbers.

19 - 31
Starting on the bottom row, add adjacent numbers together to give the value in the box above them. Repeat up to the apex of the pyramid.

20 - 343
As you move to the right, the numbers follow the cube values of the numbers 3 to 7.

21 - C
Working in rows, superimpose the pattern of dots in the left and right hand grids, to form the middle grid.

22 - 57
Starting on the left, and working to the right, add 3 to the first number, then 6 to the next, repeat this sequence, alternately adding 3 then 6.

23 - From left to right Two of Diamonds, Five of Hearts, Ace of Hearts, Ace of Spades
Working in columns, the sum of the top three cards, and the sum of the lower three cards equals the value of the central card. Also, there are two cards of each suit in each row, apart from spades of which there is only one.

24 - 13
The boxes follow the sequence of prime numbers.

25 -

26 - 1: Q, 2: R
In the first oval, all the letters have even numerical values, and in the second, they are all odd.

27 - 24
Moving clockwise around the circle, numbers follow the sequence of multiples of 6.

SOLUTIONS

LEVEL 

1 - M
In each segment, the sum of the numerical values of the outer and inner letters equals 26.

2 - 12
Working in rows, add 4 to the left hand digit to give the central value, and add 6 to this digit, to give the right hand value.

3 - E
Starting with the letter Q and moving clockwise, letters move backwards through the alphabet, in steps of 3, then 4, 5, 6 etc.

4 - 4
Working in columns, multiply the top and middle numbers together, and write the result in the lower box.

5 - D
Working from left to right, top row then bottom, the number of dots in each pattern increases by 1 each time, from 8 to 13.

6 - 4:47
Starting on the left, and moving right, add 1 to each digit and rotate their positions to the left.

7 - 1
Starting on the top row, and moving in straight lines through the central circle, values on the bottom row equal the difference between numbers on the top row and the central number.

8 - W
Starting at the top, and working down, add 5 and 3 alternating as you move down.

9 - J
Starting from B and moving clockwise, add the numerical values of the first two letters to give the value of the next letter around.

10 - K
Starting on the left, the numerical values of the letters follow the sequence of prime numbers.

11 - G
Starting with the left hand triangle, letters increase in steps of 2, 3 and 4, as you move to the right, with their positions moving 1 place clockwise around the points of the triangles.

12 - (From top to bottom) 5, 2, 3
Each row contains 4 two digit numbers, which follow the sequence of multiples of 4 for the top row, 5 for the next, then 6, 7, 8 and 9.

13 - 12
In each star, add up the digits at each point of the star, and divide by 3 to give the value at the centre.

14 - A
If you take the numerical values of each letter, all columns and rows add up to 15.

15 - T
Starting at the top, and working down through each row, left to right, letters follow the alphabetic sequence, in steps of 5.

16 - 5
In each diagram, the top left number minus the central number gives the top right number, and the bottom left added to the central number gives the bottom right.

17 - 25
In each circle, moving clockwise, double the first number and subtract 1 to give the next value.

18 - Q
In each star, letters move clockwise around the points skipping 1, 2, 3 and 4 letters each time.

19 - R
Working in columns, letters follow the alphabetic sequence, in steps of 3 for the left hand column, 4 for the middle and 5 for the right hand column.

20 -

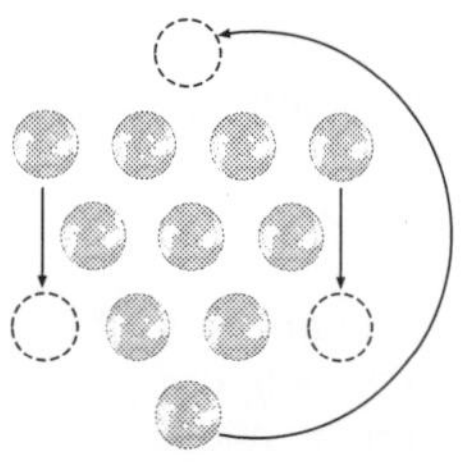

21 - 19
Starting top left, and moving in a Z shape around the circles, the numbers follow the sequence of prime numbers.

22 - A: 15, B: 4
In the first oval, all numbers are even, and in the second all numbers are odd.

23 - 16
Working clockwise, from 2, double each number to give the next one along.

24 - L
Working in rows, from left to right, letters are arranged in consecutive, alphabetical order.

25 - 5
Starting with the top left circle, and moving clockwise around the other 3, double each number and subtract 1 to give the values in the corresponding segments of the next circle around.

26 - Bananas

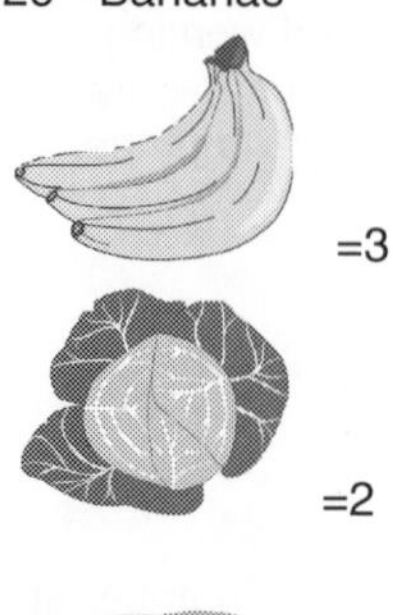

=3

=2

=4

27 -

Starting at the top, and moving clockwise, the minute hand moves back 25 minutes each time, while the hour hand moves forward 3 hours each time.

28 - A
Working in columns, the sum of the numerical values of the letters is written in the lower box.

29 - 2
Splitting the diagram vertically and horizontally, the same 5X5 pattern is displayed in each quarter.

SOLUTIONS

1 - 12
Working in columns, the sum of the top two numbers equals the value of the lower number.

2 - D
Starting in the top square, and working clockwise around it, letters advance through the alphabet, skipping 2 letters. Moving clockwise to the next square, the sequence of letters skips 3,then 4 etc.

3 - 11
Starting top left, and taking pairs of adjacent numbers, their total is always 20.

4 - O
Starting at the top left, and working in columns from left to right, letters follow the alphabetic sequence, skipping 4 letters at a time.

5 - Seven of Hearts
Working in columns, the sum of the left hand column equals 20, the next along totals 19, then 18, then 17. One card from each suit appears in each row.

6 - 6
In each diagram, multiply the top left number by the central one, to give the lower left number, and subtract the central number from the top right one to give the lower right number.

7 - 20
Starting at the top, add 7 to the first number to give the next one, then subtract 2 for the one after that, continue the same sequence for the remaining numbers.

8 - J
Starting in the top left, and moving clockwise in a spiral towards the centre, letters follow the alphabetic sequence, in steps of 8 letters.

9 - B
Working from left to right, add 1 to each digit and rotate from one place to the left.

10 - 2
In each circle, the sum of the segments always equals 13.

11 - A
Working in rows, from left to right, the number of dots in each pattern increases by 2 each time.

12 - 23
In each triangle, the value at the centre equals the sum of the square roots of the three numbers at each corner.

13 - 80
As you move right, numbers show the sequence of square numbers, from 5 to 9, subtracting 1 each time.

14 - A: Odd = 28, B: Odd = 74
In the first oval, all numbers are multiples of 3, and in the second, all numbers are a multiple of 4.

15 - 5
The value in each corner circle equals the sum of the values in the two adjacent circles.

16 - 2
Working in columns, the top number equals the sum of the lower two numbers.

17 - N
Working in rows, add the numerical values of the left hand and central letters, to give the value of the right hand letter.

18 - J
Starting with the letters on the top row, and moving in straight lines through the centre, add the numerical values of the top and central letters to give the value of the letters on the bottom row.

19 - 4
In each square, the average of the three outer numbers is written in the centre square.

20 - D
Working in columns, the sum of the numerical values of the letters in each column equals 22.

21 - 4
All columns and rows add up to 15.

22 - 43
The numbers increase by 7 each step.

23 - 3
In each circle, the sum of the 4 numbers equals 16.

24 - Pencil sharpener

25 - Jack of Spades
Starting at the top left, and working in rows, top to bottom, cards follow sequence, in steps of 1, 2, 3 etc., until 8, then 7, 6, 5 etc., There is 1 card of each suit in each line.

26 - Left to right, 28, 40, 54
In each row, numbers increase by 2, then 3, 4, 5 etc., as you go down.

27 - 1
Working in rows, starting on the left, reflect the first box around the vertical axis, to give the central box, and invert the colours of this box, to give the one on the right.

28 - M
Working from left to right, add 2 to the value of the first letter to give the next, add 4 to get the one after that, repeat this sequence, alternately adding 2 then 4.

SOLUTIONS

LEVEL 6

1 - E
If you superimpose the top row of grids onto the corresponding grids in the bottom row, the resulting pattern of dots form the letters X, Y and Z.

2 - 22
Square the two numbers at the bottom of each triangle, add them together and subtract the number at the top, to give the value in the middle of the triangle.

3 - 18
Starting at the top and moving clockwise, add the first two numbers together, and subtract 2, to give the next number in the sequence.

4 - 1
In each row, the sum of the odd numbers equals the even number.

5 - H
Taking pairs of letters from corresponding positions on the left and right hand stars, add their numerical values together, and put the result in the central star.

6 - 8
In each diagram, the difference between the sum of the odd numbers and the sum of the even numbers is written in the central circle.

7 - 9
In each diagram, the number in the centre equals the difference between the sum of the upper and lower pair of numbers.

8 - 5
In each circle, numbers in opposite segments add up to the same value 10 for top left, 11 for top right, 12 for bottom left and 13 for bottom right.

9 - S
Working in columns, add the numerical values of the top two letters together to give the value of the lower letter.

10 - 26
In each circle, multiply the lowest number by two, and add two, to give the next number.

11 - 1
In each triangle, multiply the bottom two numbers, and subtract the top number, to give the result in the centre of the triangle.

12 - 6
Reading each row as a 3 figure number, the top row minus the middle row equals the bottom row.

13 - X
Working top to bottom, left to right, letters follow the alphabetic sequence, skipping 1 letter, 2 letters, 3, 4, 5 etc.

14 - 17
Values in each box equal the sum of the two numbers in the boxes directly underneath, minus 1.

15 - D
Taking pairs of letters in opposite segments, one is the same distance from the start of the alphabet as the other is from the end.

16 - G
Starting at the apex of the triangle, and moving clockwise, letters advance through the alphabet 6 at a time.

17 - 18
Working from top to bottom, subtract 5 from the first number to give the next one down, then subtract 7, 9, 11 and 13 to give the rest.

18 - 10
Starting with the top two rows, add the numbers on the top together to give the lower left value, and multiply them together to give the lower right value. Repeat this sequence for the third and fourth row.

19 - Q
Letters on opposite sides of the central circle are the same number of letters away from the letter given in the central circle.

20 - R
Starting at the top, letters advance through the alphabet, in steps of 5, 6, 7 and 8.

21 - A, Q
In the outer circle, starting at C and moving clockwise, letters advance through the alphabet in steps of 2, 3, 4 etc. In the inner circle, starting at M and moving anti-clockwise, letters also advance through the alphabet in steps of 2, 3, 4 etc.

22 - K
Starting bottom left, and moving to alternate squares clockwise around the triangle, letters advance in steps of 3.

23 -

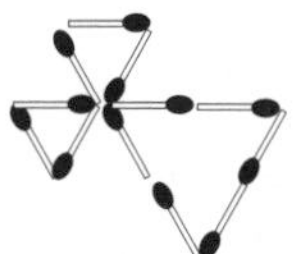

24 - 1: N, 2: O
In the first oval, the numerical values of the letters are all multiples of 3, and in the second, they are all multiples of 4.

25 -

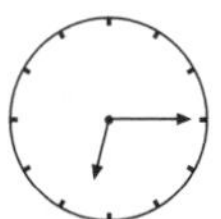

In each clockface, the hour hand points to the number which is double the minute hand's number.

26 - 109
Working from left to right, multiply each number by two, and add 3 to get the next number along.

27 - E
Divide the circle, horizontally and vertically, into quarters. The numerical values of letters in adjacent segments in each quarter of the circle add up to 20.

28 - 2
The four numbers at the corners of the diagram, and the four numbers at the centre of each side, add up to 20.

29 - 251
Starting at the top, and working down, double each number and add 5 to give the next value down.

30 - Lion

SOLUTIONS

LEVEL 

1 - N
Starting with the letters in the top row, subtract the numerical value of the central letter to give the letters on the bottom row.

2 - J
Starting at the top and moving anti-clockwise letters advance through the alphabet, 8 letters at a time.

3 - D
Starting on the left, and moving to the right, the dot moves from one segment to the one directly opposite, and back again. The # moves 1 place anticlockwise each time, as does the shaded segment.

4 - 11
The value of the numbers in the lower triangle equals the sum of the numbers, in corresponding positions on the upper two triangles.

5 - 7
Find the difference between corresponding pairs of numbers, on the left and central stars, and put the result in the same position on the right hand star.

6 - G
Starting on the left, and working down in columns, if possible, and moving to the right, letters follow alphabetic sequence, in steps of 2, 3 and 4, 2, 3 and 4 etc.

7 - N
Starting on the left, and moving to the corresponding segment on the right, letters increase in value by steps of 4, 5 and 6.

8 - 89
Starting top left and working down, then up the central column and down the right hand column, add the first two numbers together, to give the next along.

9 -

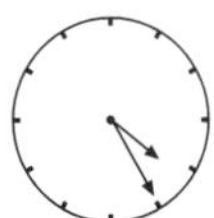

On each clockface, the numbers pointed to by the hour and minute hands add up to 9.

10 - J
Starting on the left, the letters follow the alphabetic sequence, skipping letters written with only straight lines.

11 - 100
For the left hand column, double each number, and subtract 3 to give the next number down, for the right hand column, double each number and subtract 4 to give the next number down.

12 - 6
Values on the lower triangle equal the difference between corresponding numbers on the upper two triangles.

13 - 9
In each triangle, the value in the centre equals the sum of the odd numbers around the points of the triangle, minus the sum of the even numbers.

14 - 3
Splitting the diagram into 3 smaller triangles one at the top and two at left and right, each containing 3 numbers, the sum of the number is always 15.

15 - Z
Starting top left, and moving clockwise around the outer squares, and then the inner squares, letters advance through the alphabet, skipping 3 letters at a time.

16 - 18
Starting at the top, multiply the two digits of each number together and subtract this total, to give the next value down.

17 - E
In each row the sum of the numerical values of each letter is always 20.

18 - 18
Starting top left, and moving clockwise, subtract 3 from an odd number to give the next value, and subtract 5 from an even number in the same way.

19 - M
Starting top left, and moving clockwise around the diagram. letters follow the alphabetic sequence, skipping any letters written with curved lines.

20 - 10
Working from top to bottom, add the first two numbers together, and subtract 3 to give the next value down.

21 -

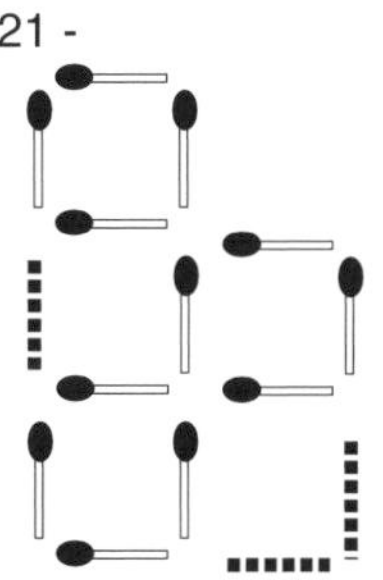

22 - 6
Add the numerical values of the letters in each row together, and put this 2 digit value in the line underneath.

23 - J
In each row, add numerical values of the left and right hand letters, and write the letter with the reverse alphabetical value in the centre square.

24 - 11
Working in rows, from left to right, multiply each number by 2 and add 1 to give the next number along.

25 - 

26 - < + +
X > >
0 0 >

Start in the top left, and move in rows to the right, then down a row and to the left etc. in a snakes and ladders pattern, using the repeated sequence of symbols:
X X > > > 0 0 < + + <.

SOLUTIONS

LEVEL 

1 - W
Follow lines of letters, from the middle left, diagonally up to the right, then diagonally down to the right etc, letters follow the alphabetic sequence, in steps of 2, 3, 4 etc.

2 - 20
In each diagram, the central number equals the sum of the four surrounding numbers.

3 - 4
In each triangle, the central number equals the average of the 3 surrounding numbers.

4 - 11
Numbers on third star are the difference between corresponding numbers on first two.

5 - O
In each set of 3 boxes, the sum of the numerical values of top two letters equals the numerical value of the lower letter.

6 - E
As you move to the right, subtract 1 from the hour value, and add 12 to the minute value. If the minutes exceeds 60, the hour value increases by 1.

7 - H
Starting top left, and moving clockwise, letters move forward by 6 places, then 7, 8, 9 etc.

8 - H
In each row, add the numerical values of the left and right hand letters, to give the reverse alphabetical value of the central letter.

9 - (top to bottom) A, H
Working in rows, from left to right, letters move through the alphabet in steps of 4 for the top row, 5 for the next, then 6, 7, 8 etc.

10 - 9
Working in columns, starting at the top, double each number and subtract 1 to give the next number down.

11 - Z
Starting top left, and working in columns, from left to right, letters move through the alphabet 5 places at a time.

12 - D
Working from left to right, one shaded section moves 1 segment clockwise at each turn, while the other moves two segments anticlockwise at each turn.

13 - 4
In each triangle, multiply the lower two numbers together, and subtract the top number, to give the result in the middle.

14 - Q
Starting on the left, letters advance 10 places in the alphabet as you move to the right, returning to the start of the alphabet after reaching Z.

15 - Q
Starting at the top, add 6 to the numerical value of the top letter to give the value of the next one down. Then 7, 8, 9 etc for the rest.

16 - 9
Working in rows, the central value equals half the sum of the other digits in each row.

17 -

18 - Y
Starting at the top and working down, the numerical value of each letter follows the sequence of square numbers, from 1 to 5.

19 - 159
Starting top left and moving clockwise, double each number and add 1 to give the next number round.

20 - 23
The reverse numerical value of each letter is written in the inner square is on the opposite side.

21 - 16
Starting from the top, add the left and right hand numbers together, to give the lower left hand number, and calculate their difference to give the lower right hand number.

22 - 35
Starting on the left, double each number, and subtract 3, to give the next number along.

23 - 13
Starting bottom left, and working clockwise, in a spiral, numbers increase by 5, then decrease by 2 alternately.

24 - 7
Starting in the top left circle and moving clockwise add 2 to each number, and rotate their positions 90° clockwise to give the values in the next circle.

25 -

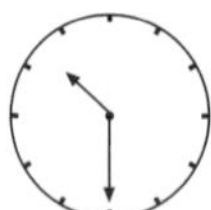

Starting with the top clockface, and moving clockwise around the others, the minute hand moves forward by 1 division, then 2, then 3, while the hour hand moves forward by 2 divisions, then 3, then 4.

SOLUTIONS

LEVEL 9

1 - 1
Starting with each odd number, multiply by 2 and add 4 to give the number in the opposite segment.

2 - V
Working from left to right, letters represent the vowels in the alphabet, displaced 1 letter forward.

3 - 2
In each row, multiply the left and right hand numbers together, and subtract 5 to give the central number.

4 - U
Starting at the top left and working in rows, left to right, the letters follow the alphabetic sequence skipping 1 letter, then 2 letters, then 3, 4 etc.

5 - 16
Using pairs of numbers in corresponding positions on the upper two triangles, calculate their difference, and put the result in the corresponding position on the lower triangle.

6 - C
In each diagram, starting with the right hand point, and working clockwise, letters advance through the alphabet in steps given by the numerical value of the top letter.

7 - 5
Split the diagram twice, along a vertical axis, to give three columns, two spaces wide. Starting at the top of each column, reading each row as 2 digit numbers, add the top two numbers together to give the next 2 digit number down. continue this pattern for each column.

8 - 51
Working from top to bottom, multiply each number by 2 and subtract 3 to give the next value down.

9 - 5
Split the diagram into quarters, of 5X5 squares. There is a random pattern of numbers in the top left square, which is rotated 90° anticlockwise around the other three quarters.

10 - C
On each watch face, the digits add up to 15.

11 - C
Working from left to right, the X moves clockwise, one segment at a time, while the • moves anticlockwise. One shaded segment moves two spaces clockwise each time, while the other moves three spaces anticlockwise.

12 - R
Working from top to bottom, double the numerical value of each letter, and subtract two, to give the next letter down.

13 - 6
The sum of each outer number and the inner number of the opposite segment is always 15.

14 - 29
In each triangle, multiply the lower two numbers and subtract the number at the top, to give the value at the centre.

15 - J
In each row, the difference between the sum of the left hand numbers and the sum of the right hand numbers equals the numerical value of the letter in the centre.

16 - 6
In each star, add the top 3 numbers together to give a 2 digit number, and write these two digits on the lower points of the star.

17 - N
The difference between the numerical values of the bottom letters is written at the top of each triangle.

18 - 9
The numbers in the segments in the central circle equal the sum of the numbers in corresponding segments of the left and right hand circles.

19 - 0
In each diagram, reading the top and bottom pair of numbers as two digit values the centre number is the difference between them.

20 - 4
Working in columns, the sum of the even numbers equals the sum of the odd numbers.

21 -

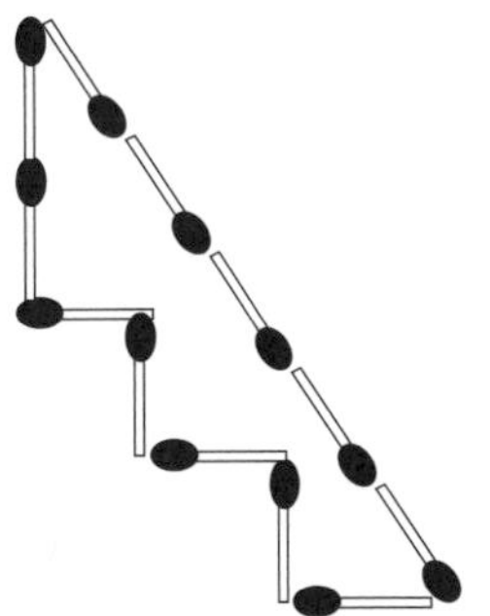

22 - 12
In each shape, starting top left and moving clockwise, numbers increase by 3, then 4.

23 - R
Moving clockwise around the circle, in alternate segments, one group of segments follows the alphabet in steps of 5, the other group in steps of 6.

24 -

8	3	4
1	5	9
6	7	2.

SOLUTIONS

LEVEL 

1 - E
In each diagram starting at the top left and moving clockwise, letters follow the alphabetic sequence, skipping the number of letters each time, as indicated by the numerical number of the central letter.

2 - 10
Take the numerical value of each letter, and add 5 to give the numerical number in the opposite segment.

3 - L
Working in rows, the sum of the numerical values of the left and centre letters equals the numerical value of the right hand letter.

4 - 39
Starting on the left, double the value in each segment; and add 1 to give the values in the circle to the right.

5 - 3
In each triangle, the number in the centre is a common denominator for the three surrounding numbers.

6 - H
In each triangle, add up the numerical values of the letters around the outside, to give the reverse numerical value of the letter at the centre.

7 -

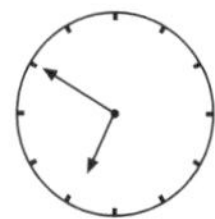

Starting at the top, and working clockwise around the faces, the minute hand moves back 5, 10 then 15 minutes, while the hour hand moves forward 2 hours then 3 then 4.

8 - Y
Starting at top left, and working in rows to the right, top to bottom, the letters follow the alphabetic sequence, skipping 1, 2 then 3 letters before repeating the sequence.

9 - 15
Working from left to right, top row then bottom, the sum of the two digits in the left hand segments of the circles follow the sequence of multiples of 6, and the sum of the right hand segments follow multiples of 4, starting at 8.

10 - F
Starting with A in the bottom left, and moving clockwise around the triangle letters follow the alphabetic sequence, jumping 12 letters, then 11, 10, 9 ..etc.

11 - 17
Starting top left, and moving clockwise in a spiral, towards the centre, add the first two numbers together, then add 1 to give the next number in the sequence.

12 - I
Working in rows, the numerical value of the central letter equals the sum of the numerical values of the left and right hand letters.

13 - 29
Working top to bottom, numbers follow the sequence of prime numbers.

14 - B
If the watch is viewed upside down, the digits appear to be the same.

15 - L
In each star, starting with the top letter and moving clockwise, letters increase in value by 4, 5, 6 and 7.

16 - B
Starting with the outer ring, add 5 to the numerical value of each letter and put the result in the inner segment, 1 place clockwise from the starting letter.

17 - 35
Working from top to bottom, double each number and subtract 3.

18 - 38
Starting top left, and working down in columns from left to right, add the first two numbers together and subtract 1 to give the next value down.

19 - 4
Working in columns, the sum of the even numbers, minus the odd number always equals 15.

20 - 10
Starting on the bottom row, the sum of the numbers in each row increases by 1 each time, from 15.

21 - Y
Starting with J, and moving clockwise, letters move through the alphabet in steps of 4, 5, 6 etc.

22 - 89
Starting with 1 and moving clockwise, double each number, and add 1, 2, 3 etc.

23 - U
Working in rows, from left to right, letters follow the alphabetic sequence, skipping 1 letter, then 2 letters.

24 - N
Starting in the top left segment of the top left circle, move clockwise around the segments, before moving onto the next circle clockwise, letters move through the alphabet in steps of 2, 3, 4, 5 etc.

25 - M, W, I
Starting at top left, move clockwise around the outer circles. letters follow the alphabetical sequence in steps of 5. Moving to the next set of circles in, the letters are in steps of 7, and the final central circles, in steps of 9.

26 -

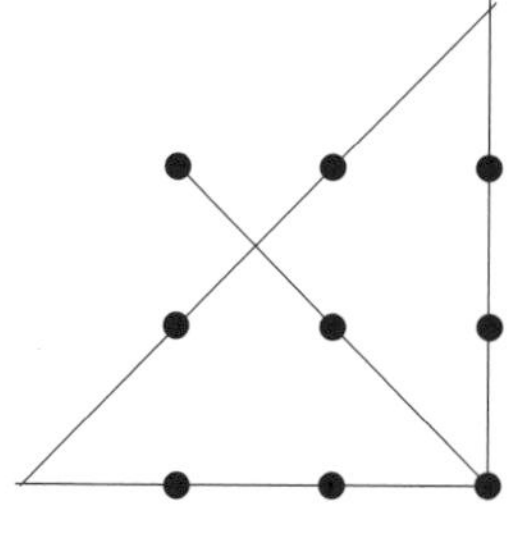

27 -

17	1	15
9	11	13
7	21	5

28 - Nine of Hearts, Seven of Spades, Nine of Diamonds
Starting top left, and moving clockwise in a spiral towards the centre, cards increase in value by 3 each time. The suits of the cards follow a repeated pattern, moving in an anti-clockwise spiral of hearts, clubs, diamonds, spades / spades, diamonds, clubs, hearts.

SOLUTIONS

LEVEL 

1 - 8
In each row and column, add the two even numbers, and subtract the odd, to always give the answer 11.

2 - L
Starting at any corner and moving clockwise, add 4 to the letter value to give the next letter, then add 5 to get the one after that. Repeat this sequence for the other two corners.

3 - 16
Working in rows, multiply the left hand column by 2, and the middle column by 3, add these together, to give the result in the right hand column.

4 - I
In each circle, starting with the top left letter, follow the alphabetic sequence, in steps of 5 letters for the top circle, 6 letters for the left hand circle, and 7 letters for the lower one.

5 - 5
In each triangle, the difference between the lower two numbers equals the difference between the top and middle numbers.

6 - 12
In each diagram, multiply the left hand pair of numbers, then subtract the central number to give the upper right hand value, and add the central number to give the lower right hand value.

7 - Outer ring, Q, inner ring, M
The letters in the outer rings are the same number of places in from the start of the alphabet as the number in the opposite inner ring are from the end of the alphabet.

8 - 15
Working in columns, the difference between the two odd numbers equals the even number.

9 - 3
In the top row, numbers in the central circle equal the sum of the corresponding segments from the left and right hand circles. On the bottom row, numbers in the central circle equal the difference between the numbers in corresponding segments from the left and right hand circles.

10 - P
Starting at the bottom of the diagram, and moving clockwise in a spiral, letters follow the alphabetical order, skipping out the vowels.

11 - 7
In each star, the value in the centre equals the average of the five surrounding values.

12 - 8
In each circle, multiply the top two numbers, and subtract the lower right number, to give the result in the lower left segment.

13 - B
Moving from left to right, the two shaded segments move 1 place around each time, in opposite directions. The circle moves between one segment, and the one directly opposite it, and the star moves 1 place anticlockwise each time.

14 - Y
Starting at the top left of the left figure, and working to the right in rows across all three diagrams, letters advance through the alphabet, five letters at a time.

15 - M
Reading down each column, letters are ten spaces apart.

16 - Create a tetrahedron (a triangle based pyramid) in 3D

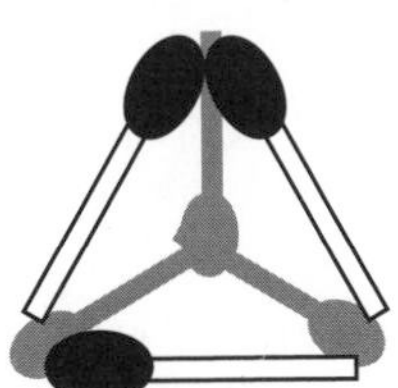

17 - 17
Starting with the bottom left number and moving along the chain, add two, then four and then subtract three. Repeat this sequence until the end.

18 -

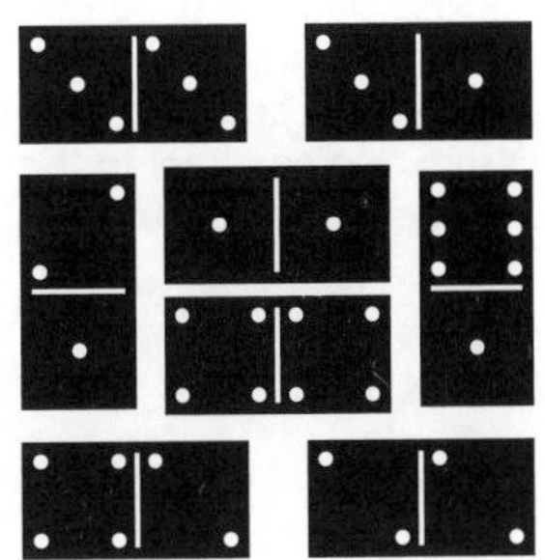

19 - A:77
B:18
In the first oval, all numbers are even multiples of 7, in the second, all numbers are odd multiples of 9.

20 - O
Starting at the top, and moving down, letters move forward 3 places, then back 7 etc.

21 - 6, 9, 8
Work in rows, from top to bottom, the sum of the digits in each row follows the sequence 45, 46, 47 etc.

22 -

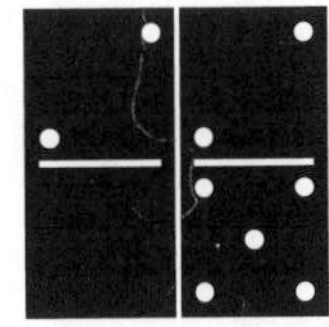

The group of dominoes is symmetrical around the centre.

SOLUTIONS

LEVEL 

1 - E
From left to right, the shaded segment moves 1 space anticlockwise each time, as does the star. The square moves two places clockwise, and the black dot moves from one segment to the segment opposite each turn.

2 -

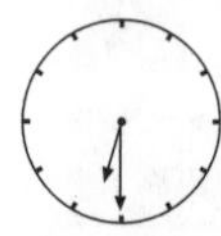

Starting with the top diagram, and moving clockwise around the others, the hour hand advances by 1, 2 and 3 segments, while the minute hand advances by 3, 2 and 1 segment.

3 - 8
Working in rows, the sum of the digits in each row follows the sequence of the square numbers, 16, 25, 36.

4 - 9
Start with the numbers in the upper left circle, and add 2 to each one to give the values in the lower left circle, add 3 to the upper middle circle values to give the values in the lower middle circle, and add 4 to the upper right circle to the lower right.

5 - 10
In each line, multiply the left and right hand numbers together, then subtract their sum from the result, to give the central number.

6 - I
Starting at the bottom left, and working clockwise, in a spiral, letters move through the alphabet in steps of 2, then 3, 4, 5 etc.

7 - N
Starting at the top of the diagram, and moving clockwise in a spiral, letters move through the alphabet 5 letters at a time.

8 - 8
in each diagram, reading the top two numbers as a two digit number, multiply this by the central number, and write the two digit result in the lower two spaces.

9 - 1000
Working from top to bottom, follow the sequence of cube numbers from 5 to 10.

10 - 10
Working in rows, the central value in each row equals the average of the left and right hand numbers.

11 - 60
In each circle, starting with the top left segment and moving clockwise, double the first number to get the next value, then add two to get the one after that. Repeat, doubling then adding two for, the rest of the circle.

12 - 26
Starting with the top two left hand numbers, add them together and subtract 1 to give the next number down. With the right hand numbers, add the first two numbers together and add 1 to give the next number down.

13 - I
In each set of boxes, working through the alphabet from the top left to the top right letter, the lower box represents the vowel you find in this sequence.

14 - 11
In each shape, subtract the sum of the even numbers from the sum of the odd numbers, putting the result in the centre.

15 - H
Starting on the top row, and working down in columns, letters follow the alphabetic sequence, in steps of 5, 4, 3, 2 and 1.

16 - 8

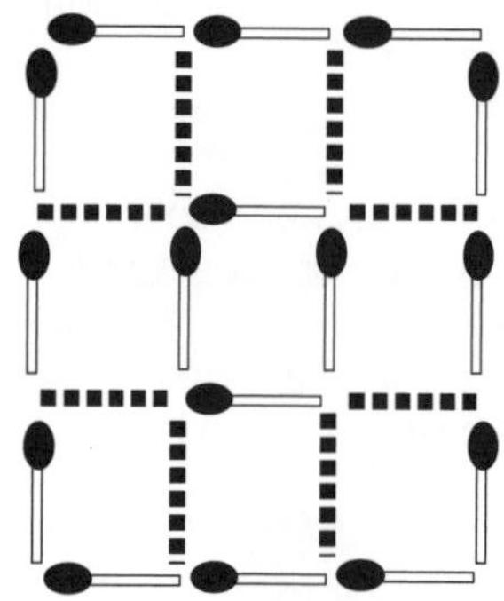

17 - 1:Z
2:K
In the first oval, the letters are those which come one place after the vowels in the alphabet, and in the second oval, the letters all come one place before the vowels.

18 - 25, 32
Starting in the top left segment and moving clockwise around the outer ring add the first two digits together and add 1 to give the next number around. Move anticlockwise around the inner ring, adding the first two digits together and subtract 1 to give the next number around.

19 -

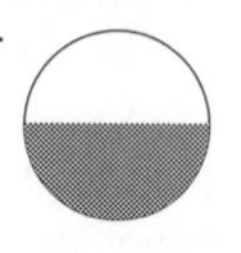

Split the diagram in to four quarters. Starting in the top left corner, repeat the pattern of circles in the other quarters, rotating the relative positions of the circles 90° anticlockwise. The colours are inverted each step.

20 - Z
Working left to right, alternately subtract 2 from the numerical value of the first letter, then add 5.

21 - Z
Starting top left and working down, then to top right, and down again, numbers follow the alphabetic sequence, skipping 6 letters each time.

22 - U
Starting at the top, and working down, letters move through the alphabet, skipping 1 letter, then 2, 3, 4 etc.

23 - E, L, W
Starting in the top left, and working down in columns, from left to right, letters move through the alphabet in steps of 2, 3, 4 etc.

24 - 124
The numbers follow the sequence of cube numbers, from 1 to 5, subtracting 1 each time.

25 - K
Starting in the top left and moving down, in columns, from left to right, the letters move forward, in steps of 4, 6, 8, 10 etc.

26 - 1
Starting in the top left, and moving clockwise in a spiral, letters are written in alternate squares in steps of 7.

SOLUTIONS

LEVEL 

1 - Z D F
F X L
L R R

Starting top left, and moving down the first column, then up the next etc, letters follow the alphabetical sequence in steps of 6.

2 - 1
The number enclosed in each square equals the sum of the small numbers in the centre of the other three squares.

3 - I
Working downwards, letters are placed in alphabetical order, skipping letters written with curved lines.

4 - 1
Working from left to right, top row then bottom, the sum total of the numbers in each circle follow the sequence 14, 15, 16, 17 etc.

5 - 6
Using the central column, square each number, to give a 2 digit result, and write these digits, using the spaces on the right and left of the central number in each row.

6 - 23
Starting top left, and moving down, alternately right and left, numbers increase by 4 each time. Following the same pattern for the top right, numbers increase by 5.

7 - B
Starting at the bottom left, and working right, then up one row, and to the left etc, letters follow the alphabetic sequence, in steps of 3 then 4, 5, 6 etc, towards the apex.

8 - Q
Taking pairs of letters in opposite segments of each circle, one letter is the same distance from the start of the alphabet, as the other is from the end.

9 - E
In each group of 3 squares, the difference between the numerical values of the top two letters equals the numerical value of the lower letter.

10 - 8 and 20
Starting at the top of the diagram, and moving down to the left, in diagonal lines, numbers increase by steps of 2 for the first diagonal line, 3 for the next, 4, 5, 6 etc.

11 - K
In each diagram, starting top left and moving clockwise to end up in the centre, letters follow the alphabetic sequence, skipping the same number of letters each time.

12 - 12
Working from left to right, starting at the top of each star, and moving clockwise, double each number and subtract 2 for the left hand star, subtract 3 for the middle, and 4 for the right hand.

13 - H
Starting top left, and working clockwise, in a spiral, letters follow the alphabetic sequence, skipping letters written with with any curved lines.

14 - M
Working from top to bottom, the numerical values of the letters follow the sequence of prime numbers.

15 - 6
In each set of boxes, the lower number equals the average of the top numbers.

16 -

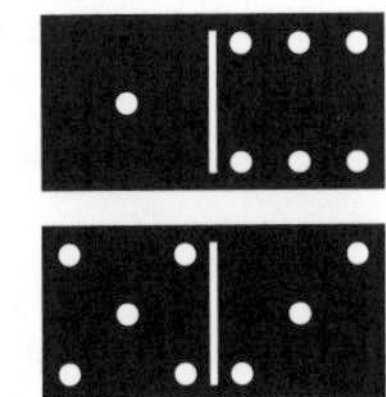

Working from left to right, the sum of the dots in each column equals 12, then 13, 14, 15 etc.

17 -

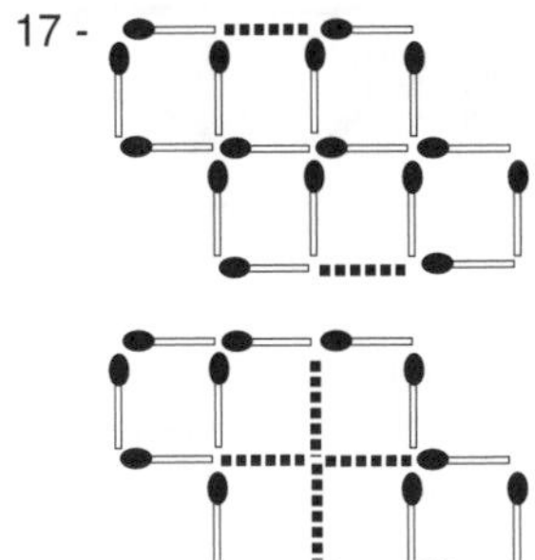

18 - 9
Starting on the top, and moving down, alternately subtract 2 and add 4 to give the next numbers in the sequence.

19 - W
Starting on E and moving clockwise, letters increase in value by 3, 5 and 7, before repeating this sequence.

20 - 4
Reading the top and bottom rows of numbers as 2 digit numbers, multiply them together to give a 3 digit number, written on the middle row.

21 - 6
All columns and rows in the diagram add up to 15.

22 - 891
Take each three digit separately. Square the centre digit and write the answer either side of it.

23 - 12 apples.

24 - From top to bottom, Five of Hearts and Ace of Spades.
In each row, the value of the right hand card equals the difference between the sum of the red cards, and the sum of the black cards on that row. The suit of the right hand card is always the same as the far left hand card.

SOLUTIONS

LEVEL 

1 - 7
In each square, the sum of the three outer numbers is written in the central square, 1 place clockwise from it.

2 - K
In each pair of boxes, the first letter is the same distance from the start of the alphabet, as the second letter is from the end of the alphabet.

3 - 40
Starting with 14 and moving clockwise, add the two digits of each number together, and add this to the original number, to give the next value around.

4 - Q
In each row, add the numerical values of the left and central letters to give the value of the letter on the right.

5 - 3
Starting at the top of the diagram, and moving down to the right, in diagonal lines, the sum of the digits in the first line equals 12. The sum of the digits in the next diagonal line equals 13 etc.

6 - 6
In each shape, multiply the top two numbers and the central number together to give a two digit result, and write these two digits in the lower two circles.

7 - A
Working in rows, from left to right, dots form straight sided shapes. The number of sides increases by 1 for each step to the right.

8 - 2
In each row of the grid, the numbers 0-9 appear once only.

9 - From left to right, U, J, Z
Starting in the top left, and working clockwise in a spiral, letters follow the alphabetic sequence, in steps of 2, 3, 4 and 5, then 2, 3, 4 and 5 etc towards the centre.

10 - N
Starting top left and moving to the right in a W shape, letters in corresponding segments in each circle follow sequences, skipping 0, 1, 2 and 3 letters at a time.

11 - 7
Starting with the numbers in the top circle, add the numbers from the corresponding segments of the left hand circle, to give the result in the lower circle.

12 - 6
Reading each line as a 3 digit number, the numbers follow the sequence of square numbers of 12, 13 and 14.

13 - 9
Starting top left and moving clockwise in a spiral, towards the centre, add the first two numbers, then subtract 1 to give the next number in the sequence.

14 - 99
Starting at the top, the first box represents 5x7, 6x8, 7x9, 8x10 and 9x11, each time the multiplications increase by 1.

15 - 4
In each star, add the top number and lower two numbers to make a two digit total, and write this two digit number in the remaining left and right hand positions.

16 - From top to bottom,

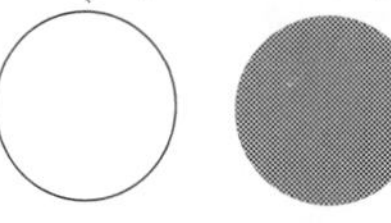

Starting top left, move towards the centre in a clockwise spiral. There are two sequences, on alternate circles, following this path. The first starts with one quarter shaded, with an extra quarter added at each turn. When the circle becomes full, a quarter segment is taken away each time. The second sequence follows the same pattern, but starts with a full circle.

17 - S
Starting with the top left segment and working to the bottom, letters move anticlockwise in steps of 4. Starting with the top right segment, letters move clockwise, in steps of 5.

18 - X
Starting top left, and moving clockwise around the diagram, in an hour glass shape, letters advance through the alphabet eight letters at a time.

19 - C
Starting top left, and working in rows, from top to bottom, letters move backwards through the alphabet, 6 letters at a time.

20 -

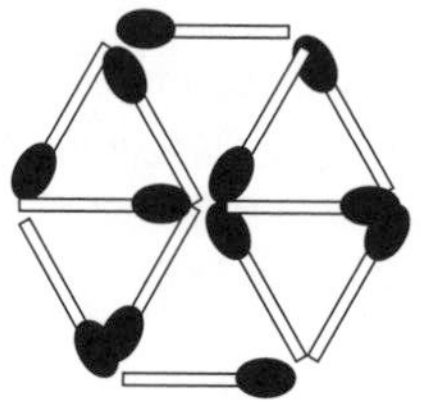

21 - U
Starting with the top left square in each figure, and moving clockwise, letters advance by 4 places at a time, then 5, 6 and 7.

22 - 4
Splitting the diagram into quarters, each quarter represents the letter M, N, O and P, written in shaded blocks.

23 - E
In each grid, there are two shapes, made up of black circles. Working in rows, from left to right, both shapes increase in size by one circle each time.

24 - 2
Starting on the left, and moving right, each pair of numbers represents multiples of 9, starting with 36, subtracting 1 each time.

SOLUTIONS

LEVEL

1 - 8
In each triangle, multiply the top and centre numbers, to give a 2 digit result, and write this result on the lower 2 points of each triangle.

2 - V
Starting with the diagram on the left, and moving 1 place to the right at each turn, letters in corresponding positions on each diagram move through the alphabet, skipping the same number of letters each time.

3 - 2
Working in rows, read the left and right hand numbers as a two digit number, and put the corresponding letter in the central square.

4 - 4
Reading each row as a 3 digit number, the rows follow the sequence of multiples of 12.

5 - E
Working from left to right, the shaded segment moves one place anticlockwise each turn, the star moves one place clockwise, while the black circles move one place, in opposite directions each turn.

6 - 1
Taking the top left and top right circles as a source, segments in the central circle equal the sum of the numbers in corresponding segments of the source circles, segments in the lower left circle equal the product of the numbers, and the lower right equals the difference.

7 - C
On each watch, the minute value equals the hour value multiplied by 3.

8 - F
Starting in the top left, and working clockwise in a spiral, to end up in the centre, letters move backwards through the alphabet, skipping 2 letters, then 3, 4, 5 etc.

9 - 11
Using the top two circles, add together numbers in corresponding segments, and put the results in the lower left hand circle. Calculate the difference between the top two circles, and put the results in the lower right hand circle.

10 - 5
In each star, the sum of the even numbers on the points, equals the sum of the odd points.

11 - 9
The sum of the numbers in the left hand column equals the sum of the numbers in the right hand column.

12 - X
Starting top left, and working in columns, from left to right, letters advance through the alphabet in steps of 2, then 3, 4, 5 etc.

13 - P
In each diagram, the midpoint between the left and right hand pairs of numbers equals the letter in the centre.

14 - 1
Reading each line as a 3 digit number, add the top two lines together, and write the result on the bottom line.

15 - 6
Working in rows, starting top left subtract 2 to give the middle value, and 3 to give the right hand value, repeat on the next line, subtracting 4, then 5, and for the bottom line, subtract 6 then 7.

16 - E
In each diagram, add together the numerical values of the letters in the top two boxes, and subtract 5, to give the value of the letter in the lower box.

17 - C
Starting top left, and working to the right along each row, letters follow the alphabetic sequence in steps of 6, 5 then 4. Repeat this sequence, top to bottom.

18 - 1212
Starting with 2 and moving clockwise, add 2 to each number, and multiply by 3 to give the next number.

19 - 25
Moving left to right, numbers increase by 7, then 6, 5 and 4.

20 - Z
Working in rows, from left to right, letters in the top row advance by 6 places at a time, letters in the middle row advance 8 places, and the bottom row advances 10 places.

21 - 5

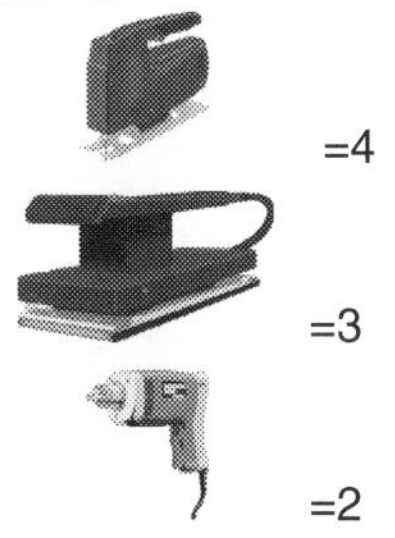

22 - 253
Working from top to bottom, numbers follow the sequence of square numbers, from 11 to 16, subtracting 3 each time.

23 - Q
Taking pairs of letters, from opposite segments of the circle, one letter is 10 places in the alphabet before the other.

24 - 4
Starting on the left, and moving right, take the first 3 numbers in a diagonal line, and add 5 to each one, to give the values in the corresponding diagonal line to the right, subtract 4 from each of these numbers to give the values in the corresponding diagonal line on the far right.

25 -

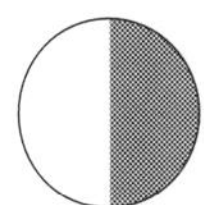

Working in rows, start with the left hand circle, and add a new segment, in a clockwise direction, to give the next circle along. also the colours of the segments in alternate circles are reversed.

SOLUTIONS

LEVEL 16

1 - B
Working from left to right, one shaded segment remains still, while the other swaps back and forth, between opposite segments. The square moves clockwise, two segment at a time, and the black circle moves anticlockwise, two segments at a time.

2 - 11
Working in rows, add numbers in corresponding segments of the left and central circles together, and put the result in the opposite segment in the right hand circle.

3 - E
As you move to the right, the hour value decreases by 1, 2, 3 and 4, while the minute value increases by 5, 6, 7 and 8.

4 - Z
Starting on J and moving clockwise, letters advance 10 places forward, then 4 places back alternately.

5 - 14
Starting at the top left, and moving around the diagram clockwise, add the first two numbers together and add 1 to give the next value.

6 - A
Working in rows, superimpose the left hand and central grids to give the pattern in the right hand grid. If crosses appear in the same position in both grids, they cancel out in the right hand grid.

7 - J
Starting with the letter in the top right segment of the top circle, and moving clockwise around the three circles, letters follow the alphabetic sequence, with the relative position of the letter revolving 1 place clockwise each turn. Follow the same sequence starting with the next segment clockwise on the top circle, but skip 1 letter each time. Repeat for the other segments, skipping an extra letter each time.

8 - A
Starting top left, work down to the bottom, then up the next column to the right etc, letters are written in a repeating sequence, M, H, Z, A, L, Q, R, B, G following this pattern.

9 - S
Starting with the top left segments, the letters move from the outer ring to the next segment in the inner ring, jumping 2 then 3 letters. The sequence that starts in the inner ring goes back 2 then 3 letters.

10 - 1
Add the numerical values of the upper two letters to give a 2 digit number, and put this in the upper central two boxes. Do the same for the lower two letters.

11 - C
In each circle, the sum of the numerical values of the letters in the top two segments equals 18. And the sum of the lower 2 segments equals 22.

12 - 0
In each diagram, read the top two numbers as a two digit number, and subtract the central value, to give a two digit result, written in the lower two places.

13 - 10
In each circle, the value in the lower segment equals double the difference between the upper left and right hand values.

14 - C
Taking the numerical values of each letter, in each diagram, the central value equals the difference between the sum of the upper pair of values and the sum of the lower pair of values.

15 - 7
Add together corresponding segments in the upper two circles, and put the results on the segments on the lower left. Calculate the difference between values in the top two circles, and put the results in the lower right circle.

16 - 720 days before both watches told the same time, and 3,600 days before they both told the right time.

17 - Q
Add together the numeric values of the top two letters and divide them by two. Write this answer in reverse numerical order, in the bottom box.

18 -

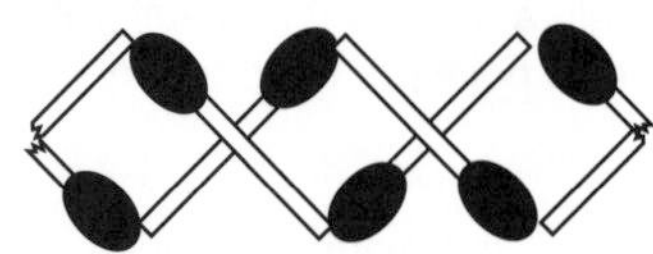

19 - 21
The numbers in each box correspond to the numerical values of the vowels in the alphabet.

20 - 4, 12

21 - 21
Starting at the top, the numbers represent multiples of 4, from 9 to 4, with the digits reversed in each case.

22 - D
Working in rows, left to right, top to bottom, letters follow the sequence of the first letter of the months of the year.

23 - From left to right, 31, 16, 39
Start at the top, following diagonal lines from the left hand edge, up to the right, numbers are arranged in the sequence of prime numbers, from 2 to 29, adding 1 after each repeat.

SOLUTIONS

LEVEL 

1 - D
Working in rows from left to right, the • moves clockwise 2 squares at a time, around the edge of the grid. The X moves in a straight line from one side of the grid to the other, and back again. The # moves 1 place clockwise around the central 4 squares in each grid. Additionally, the gird revolves a quarter turn clockwise each time you move to the right.

2 - V
Starting top left, and working anticlockwise, in a spiral towards the centre, letters move through the alphabet in steps of 3, 4, 5 etc.

3 - 48
Divide each circle in half, vertically. The top right segment equals the sum of the three segments to the left, the middle right equals the average of the three segments to the left, and the lower right equals their product.

4 - 1
The grid displays rotational symmetry, around 180° around its central point.

5 - From top to bottom, B, D
Start at top right, and work in diagonal lines from the top, down to the right. Letters follow the alphabetic sequence, in steps of 3.

6 - A
Working from left to right, top row then bottom row, the sum of the numerical values in each circle follows the sequence of even numbers, from 8 to 16.

7 - T
Starting top left, and working clockwise, in a spiral, letters move through the alphabet in steps of 6, 5, 4, 3, 2 and 1, before repeating the sequence.

8 - 2
Working in rows, from top to bottom, and reading each row as a 3 digit number, the rows follow the sequence of multiples of 12, starting with 9.

9 - P
Working in rows, left to right and top to bottom, start with the top left letter in each circle, and move clockwise around it. In the first circle, letters follow the alphabetic sequence in steps of 5, the next is in steps of 6, then 7, 8 etc.

10 - Inner, then outer, G, B
Split the diagram in half horizontally, to give upper and lower sections. Starting with the upper section, move left to right across the large segments, then right to left across the small segments. Letters move through the alphabet in steps of 2, 3, 4 etc. Repeat this sequence for the lower half, starting with the large segment on the left.

11 - 9
Reading each horizontal line as a 3 digit number, the rows represent the cubes of 7, 8 and 9.

12 - E
Working from left to right across the 3 shapes, letters in corresponding positions in each shape follow sequences, skipping 1, 2, 3, 4 and 5 letters at a time, with their relative positions rotating 90° clockwise each time.

13 - U
Starting on the left, add 2, 3 and 4 to the value of the letters, and rotate their positions 1 segment clockwise to give the letters in the next circle to the right.

14 - B
All the patterns are random, but the left hand column has 2 black squares per grid, the next has 4, then 6, and finally, the right hand column has 8 black squares per grid.

15 - U
Starting top left, and moving clockwise in a spiral towards the centre, letters follow the alphabetic sequence, skipping 8 letters each time.

16 - 4913
Starting from the top, and moving down, numbers follow the sequence of cubed numbers, from 12 to 17.

17 -

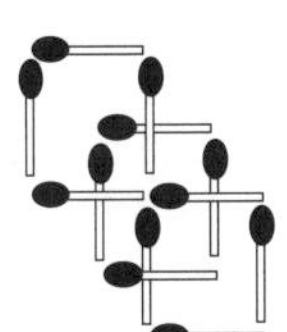

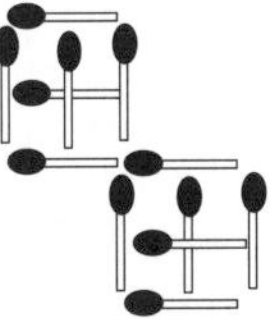

18 - J
Add the numerical values of the top two letters in each diagram, and write the letter with the corresponding reverse alphabetical value in the lower box.

19 - 10

20 - From left to right, A, G
Using the numerical values of each letter, the sum of all rows and columns equals 25.

21 - From top to bottom, D, Z, U, Q
Split the diagram, horizontally through the centre. Letters in the top half start in the top left hand corner, and move in an anticlockwise spiral towards the centre, in steps of 4 letters at a time. Letters in the bottom half start in the bottom right hand corner, and move in a anticlockwise spiral towards the centre, in steps of 5 letters at a time.

SOLUTIONS

LEVEL 

1 - B
In each row, the first two grids are reflections of each other, around a vertical axis, and the second two grids are reflections of each other around a horizontal axis.

2 - 4
Split the large square into quarters, and start with the values in the top left corner. Add 1 to each number, and write the results in the top right quarter. Add 2, to give the results in the lower right quarter, and add 3 for the lower left.

3 - K
Split the diagram into quarters, of 3x3 squares. starting in the top left of each square, and working clockwise in a spiral, towards the centre, letters follow the alphabetic sequence, 4 letters at a time.

4 - 7
Reading each row as a 4 digit number, the rows follow the sequence of the cubes of 10, 11, 12 and 13.

5 - 8
Numbers in the lower left circle equal the sum of all the odd numbers in corresponding segments of the top 3 circles. Numbers in the lower right equal the sum of the even numbers.

6 - 5
In each star, add the top three numbers to give a two digit value, and write these two digits on the lower two points of the star.

7 - From top to bottom, F, W, E
Start at top left, and work across the diagram in diagonal lines, starting on the left and moving up and to the right, letters are arranged in alphabetical order, skipping any letters written with curved lines.

8 - 6
Multiply the top two numbers of each circle together and add the digits together to get a single number.

9 - I
Working in rows, the central letter is always the vowel which appears in the alphabet, between the left and right hand letters.

10 - 1
Working in rows, top to bottom, and reading each row as a 3 digit number, they follow the sequence of multiples of 11, from 9 to 11.

11 - A
Square the numerical value of each large letter, and put the letter with the corresponding value in the smaller, central square in the opposite position.

12 - 5, 15
In each circle, numbers in alternate segments add up to 20.

13 - D
Working in rows, reflect the left and right hand grids around the vertical axis, and superimpose them to give the pattern in the central grid.

14 - 13
Starting with the top row, take the left and centre circles and add together numbers in the corresponding segments, putting the results in the segment s of the lower right circle, do the same with the lower left and centre circle, putting the results in the upper right circle.

15 - C
In each row, the sum of the numerical values of the left and right hand letters equals the numerical value of the central letter.

16 - From left to right, 2, 9
The numbers in every horizontal and vertical line add up to 25.

17 - From left to right, K, A, H
Start at the top left, and move clockwise, in a spiral, towards the centre. Letters are written in alphabetical order, in steps of 5, in alternate circles.

18 - Flip the 9 over, to read 6, making the sum of both sets of numbers 21.

19 -

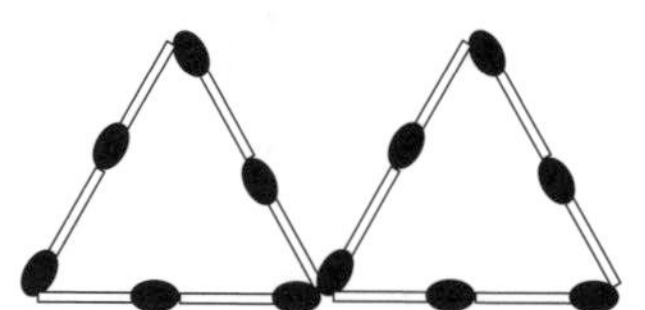

20 - 2, 4, 8, 16, 32 and 64.

21 - 3
Split the diagram in half, vertically, to give two columns of 2 digit numbers. The columns form, from top to bottom, left to right, multiples of 7, from 14 to 63.

SOLUTIONS

LEVEL 

1 - 4
Split the diagram into quarters, each one exactly the same.

2 - 9
Using the top row, double all the values in the left hand circle, and add the corresponding values in the middle and right hand circles, putting the results in the lower left hand circle, repeat the above sequence, but doubling the values in the centre circle, and putting the result in the lower centre circle, finish off by doubling the values in the upper right, and putting the results lower right.

3 - S
Starting on the left of the diagram, and working in columns from left to right, letters move through the alphabet 7 at a time.

4 - 6
Starting on the left, taking one number from corresponding segments in each circle, and reading this as a 3 digit number, the numbers follow the sequence of squares of 14, 15 and 16.

5 -
The circles spell out the names Joseph, Edward, Andrew and Robert.

6 - 3
In each square, add the top two numbers together to get a two digit number, and write this in the lower half of the square.

7 - 1
Working from left to right, along the top row and then the bottom, the sum of the numbers in each circle follows the sequence of prime numbers.

8 - A
If you draw lines through the black dots in each grid, straight sided shapes are formed. Working from left to right, top row then bottom, the number of sides in each shape increases by 1 each time, from 3 to 8.

9 - F
Letters follow the alphabetic sequence in steps of 3. The sequence starts at the top of the left hand star, and moves to the same position on the next star to the right etc. Then the next point clockwise of the star.

10 - C
Working in rows, if you superimpose the crosses in each grid, you get a perfectly symmetrical design each time.

11 - 1
Digits in the four corners of the diagram add up to 20, as do the digits in the middle of the four sides.

12 - 10
Moving clockwise around the triangle, and starting in any corner, the next number clockwise equals the sum of the two corner circles, from either side, and the number after that equals the difference of the two corner circles.

13 - 15
Starting with the numbers in the segments in the top circle, multiply by 2, and subtract two to give the values in the left hand circle, and multiply by 3 and subtract 3 to give the values in the lower circle.

14 - 3
Taking each row as a 3 digit number, rows follow the sequence of cube numbers 5, 6 and 7.

15 - 1
Split the diagram in half, vertically, to get two columns of 3 digit numbers. Starting top left, and working down, then top right, and down, the 3 digit numbers follow the sequence of square numbers from 10 to 21.

16 - It's possible for there to be none with all 4 characteristics.

17 - S
Start with the top left segment, and move to the right, across the top half of the 3 circles. Then move down to the lower half of the circles, and move left. Repeat this pattern for the lower circles. The letters follow the alphabetic sequence, 6 letters at a time.

18 - S
Starting top left, and moving clockwise in a spiral, letters follow the alphabetic sequence, in steps of 2, 3, 4 etc.

19 - 2
Reading each line as a 3 digit number, from top to bottom, each line represents the cubed values of 7, 8 and 9.

20 - I
In each horizontal line, add the numerical values of the left and right hand letters together, and put the letter with the reverse alphabetical value in the centre.

21 - 8
Reading each horizontal line as a 4 digit number, from top to bottom, each line represents the cubed values of 16, 17, 18 and 19.

22 - V
Working in rows, left to right and top to bottom, the sequence follows letters written with only straight lines, skipping every other letter in this sequence.

23 - D
In each figure, the numerical value of the central letter equals the difference between the sum of the two left hand and right hand letters.

SOLUTIONS

LEVEL 

1 - V
Starting with the top circle, letters move clockwise, around the outer circles, in steps of 4. Repeat this clockwise path, starting with the next circle down in the central column, with the letters moving in steps of 5. Move around the remaining circles in steps of 6.

2 - Q
Start at the top point on the left, moving right across the top of all 3 stars, then back to the left and across the middle points of each star, then across the lower points of each star. The letters follow the alphabetic sequence, skipping two letters at a time.

3 - D
Working in rows, from left to right, a new element is added to the grid at each step, with the grid rotating 90° clockwise each time.

4 - E
Working from left to right, add 3 to each digit separately. If the minutes exceed 60, they return to 0, and the hours return to 1 o'clock if they exceed 12.

5 - 16
Starting top left and moving right, top row then bottom row, add 3 to the numbers in each segment, and rotate their positions 1 place clockwise, to give the numbers in the next circle along. For the next circle, subtract 1 and rotate their positions 1 place clockwise, continue for the rest of the circles, adding 3 then subtracting 1 alternately.

6 - T, D
Starting with the top pair of letters, add their numerical values together to give the value of the left letter in the pair below. Calculate their difference to give the value of the right hand letter in the pair below.

7 - 6
In each square, the sum of the 3 outer numbers minus the central number is always 5.

8 - Outer ring=I,
Starting at the top left segment, the outer letters move clockwise, in steps of 6, and the inner letters move anticlockwise, in steps of 7.

9 - 19
In each circle, starting with the top left segment, and moving clockwise, numbers increase by the same amount each time, starting with 5 for the top left circle, then 6, 7 and 8 for the others.

10 - E
Working in rows, the value of the central letter equals the sum of the left and right hand letters.

11 - A
Starting top left, and working to the right, along the row , then down one row and to the left etc, letters follow the alphabet, in steps of 2, 3, 4 and 5, before repeating the sequence.

12 - 4
Starting with the top left and centre circles, add the values in corresponding segments in each circle, and put the results in the lower left circle. Do the same with the upper centre and right circles, putting the results in the lower right circle.

13 - 1
In each diagram, multiply the left and right hand digits, and subtract the top and lower digits, to give the number in the centre.

14 - 7
In each circle, read the upper and lower two segments as two digit numbers, and add them together to get a two digit result. Put this result in the middle left and right hand segments.

15 - 28
As you move clockwise, numbers follow the sequence of prime numbers, subtracting 1 each time.

16 - 7
Start with the upper left and central circles, adding values in corresponding segments of the circles, and put the results in the lower right circle. Repeat this formula, using the upper right and central circles, putting the results in the lower left circle.

17 - G
Starting with the top left square, and moving around the others in a clockwise direction, letters in each segment follow the alphabetic sequence in steps of 2, 3, 4 and 5, with their relative positions in each square moving 1 place clockwise at each turn.

18 - U
Working in columns, add the numerical values of the top two numbers together, and put the resulting letter in their bottom box.

19 - W
Working from top to bottom in columns, letters follow the alphabetic sequence, skipping 5 letters then 7 letters.

20 - 6
Working top to bottom in pairs of columns, left hand then right hand, numbers follow the sequence of multiples of 7, with the digits reversed.

21 - E
As you move to the right, the two shaded segments rotate 1 place at a time in opposite directions, the circle moves 3 segments clockwise, while the cross moves 2 segments anticlockwise.

22 - 4
In the top row, all diagrams are symmetrical around a vertical axis, in the middle row they are symmetrical around a horizontal axis, and in the bottom row, it's a diagonal axis.

23 - T
In each diagram, start on the top left and move clockwise, to end up in the centre. Letters follow the alphabetic sequence in steps of 6, 7, 8 and 9.